Edexcel *foundation*
GCSE Mathematics

Keith Pledger

Gareth Cole

Peter Jolly

Graham Newman

Joe Petran

Sue Bright

www.heinemann.co.uk
✓ Free online support
✓ Useful weblinks
✓ 24 hour online ordering

01865 888058

Inspiring generations

Heinemann is an imprint of Pearson Education Limited,
a company incorporated in England and Wales, having
its registered office at Edinburgh Gate, Harlow, Essex, CM20 2JE.
Registered company number: 872828

Heinemann is a registered trademark of
Pearson Education Limited

© Pearson Education Ltd, 2006

First published 2006

10 09 08
10 9 8 7 6 5 4 3

British Library Cataloguing in Publication Data is available from the British Library on request.

ISBN: 978 0 435534 08 0

Typeset by Tech-Set Ltd, Gateshead, Tyne and Wear
Original illustrations © Pearson Education Limited, 2006
Illustrated by Adrian Barclay and Mark Ruffle
Cover design by mccdesign
Printed and bound in China by CTPS
Cover photo: Photolibrary.com ©

Acknowledgements
Pearson Education Ltd would like to thank those schools who helped in the development and trialling of this course.

This high quality material is endorsed by Edexcel and has been through a rigorous quality assurance programme to ensure that it is a suitable companion to the specification for both learners and teachers. This does not mean that its contents will be used verbatim when setting examinations nor is it to be read as being the official specification – a copy of which is available at www.edexcel.org.uk

The publisher's and authors' thanks are due to Edexcel Limited for permission to reproduce questions from past examination papers. These are marked with an [E]. The answers have been provided by the authors and are not the responsibility of Edexcel Limited.

The authors and publisher would like to thank the following individuals and organisations for permission to reproduce photographs: NASA p1; iStockPhoto.com/Nicolas Skaanlid p2 left; Alamy Images; p2 right; iStockPhoto.com/Lidian Neeleman p6; Getty Images/PhotoDisc pp22 top, 53, 97, 145, 156, 185, 186, 242, 431; iStockPhoto.com/Matjaz Slanic p22 bottom; Action +/Neil Tingle p24; Digital Vision p28 left; iStockPhoto.com/Ryan Fuller p28 right; Photos.Com pp29, 172; Corbis pp46 left, 127, 146, 223, 238, 332, 347, 389, 410, 494; ESA p46 right; Richard Smith p72; Empics pp81, 82, 164, 206, 384, 426; Pearson Education Ltd/Debbie Rowe p96; Alamy Images/Elmtree Images p109; Getty Images/Stone p173; Alamy Images/Transtock Inc. p204; PhotoLibrary.com p211; Pearson Education Ltd/Martin Sookias p266; iStockPhoto.com/Gloria-Leigh Logan p285; iStockPhoto.com/James Goldsworthy p304; Brand X Photos p399; Digital Vision p419; Alamy Images/David Tipping p450; iStockPhoto.com/Stephen Gibson p454; Empics/AP Photo p462

Every effort has been made to contact copyright holders of material reproduced in this book. Any omissions will be rectified in subsequent printings if notice is given to the publishers.

Publishing team

Editorial	James Orr, Lindsey Besley, Evan Curnow, Nick Sample, Jim Newall, Alex Sharpe, Laurice Suess, Katherine Pate, Elizabeth Bowden, Ian Crane
Design	Phil Leafe
Production	Siobhan Snowden
Picture research	Chrissie Martin

Websites
There are links to relevant websites in this book. In order to ensure that the links are up-to-date, that the links work, and that the sites aren't inadvertently linked to sites that could be considered offensive, we have made the links available on the Heinemann website at www.heinemann.co.uk/hotlinks. When you access the site, the express code is **4084P**.

Tel: 01865 888058   www.heinemann.co.uk

Quick reference to chapters

Introduction

Introduction

This revised and updated edition has been carefully matched to the new two-tier specification for GCSE Maths. It covers everything you need to know to achieve success in your exam, up to and including Grade C. The author team is made up of Senior Examiners, a Chair of Examiners and Senior Moderators, all experienced teachers with an excellent understanding of the requirements of the Edexcel specification.

Key features

- **Chapters** are divided into **sections**, each with a simple explanation followed by clear examples or a worked exam question. These show you how to tackle questions. Each section also contains practice exercises to develop your understanding and help you consolidate your learning.

- **Key points** are highlighted throughout, like this:

  - To find the **square** of any number, multiply the number by itself.

  Each chapter ends with a summary of key points you need to remember.

- **Hint boxes** are used to make explanations clearer. They may also remind you of previously learned facts or tell you where in the book to find more information.

  > a means $1a$
  > so $1a + 1a = 2a$

- **Mixed exercises** are designed to test your understanding across each chapter. They include past exam questions which are marked with an [E]. You will find a mixed exercise at the end of every chapter.

- **Examination practice papers** are included to help you prepare for the exam at the end of your course.

- **Answers** are provided at the back of the book to use as your teacher directs.

Quick reference and detailed Contents pages

- Use the thumb spots on the edges of the **Quick reference** pages to help you turn to the right chapter quickly.

- Use the detailed **Contents** to help you find a section on a particular topic. The summary and reference codes on the right show your teacher the part(s) of the specification covered by each section in the book. (For example, NA3h refers to Number and Algebra, section 3 Calculations, subsection h.)

Use of a calculator or a computer

These symbols show you where you must, or must not, use a calculator. Sometimes you will need to use a spreadsheet package on a computer. There are also links to websites and suggested activities that require an internet search.

Coursework

A Coursework Guide is available online at www.zebramaths.co.uk

Contents

4 Patterns and sequences

5 Decimals

6 Angles and turning

7 2-D shapes

14 Units of measure

15 Percentages

22 Transformations

23 Probability

24 Presenting and analysing data 2

28 Expressions, formulae, equations and graphs

① Understanding whole numbers

1.1 Digits and place value

Onboard computers will have taken control of launch systems 30 seconds before lift–off.

Each digit has a value that depends on its position in a number. This is its **place value**.

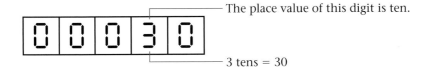

The place value of this digit is ten.

3 tens = 30

Look at this place value diagram:

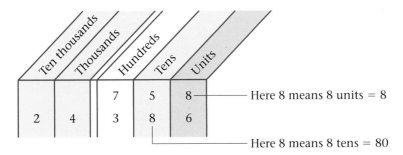

Here 8 means 8 units = 8

Here 8 means 8 tens = 80

758 has three digits. It is also called a three figure number.

Exercise 1A

1 Draw a place value diagram and write in
   (a) a four figure number with a 4 in the thousands column
   (b) a two figure number with a 3 in the tens column
   (c) a five figure number with a 1 in the hundreds column
   (d) a three figure number with a 9 in the units column
   (e) a four figure number with a 0 in the tens column
   (f) a five figure number with a 4 in the hundreds column
   (g) a three figure number with a 7 in every column
   (h) a four figure number with a 6 in the first and last columns.

2 For each teacher, write down five different numbers that they could be thinking about.

3 Write down the value of the 6 in each of these numbers:

(a) 63   (b) 3642   (c) 63 214   (d) 2546   (e) 56 345   [E]

1.2 Reading, writing and ordering numbers

Sometimes you will need to write in words a number that has been written in figures.

Ten thousands	Thousands	Hundreds	Tens	Units	
		9	8	7	Nine hundred and eighty-seven
1	6	4	1	2	Sixteen thousand four hundred and twelve

16 412

The thin space separates thousands from hundreds and makes it easier to read the number.

Sometimes you will need to write in figures a number that has been written in words.

Two thousand eight hundred and twenty-two walkers took part in Saturday's charity event.

Some of the thirty-one thousand two hundred and fifty-eight people at an outdoor rock concert

The word numbers from the newspaper examples can be written in figures, like this:

	Ten thousands	Thousands	Hundreds	Tens	Units	
Two thousand eight hundred and twenty-two		2	8	2	2	or 2822
Thirty-one thousand two hundred and fifty-eight	3	1	2	5	8	or 31 258

Zeros are used to show that a column is empty.
This shows that 5004 and 504 are different numbers:

Thousands	Hundreds	Tens	Units	
5	0	0	4	Five thousand and four
	5	0	4	Five hundred and four

Sometimes you will need to rewrite a set of numbers in order of size. Suppose you need to order this set of numbers:

15   8400   6991   2406   2410   84 000

The size of a number depends on how many digits it has. The more digits, the bigger the number.
So 84 000 is bigger than 8400 because it has more digits.

> This is only true for whole numbers.

When two numbers have an equal number of digits, the value of the digit in the highest place value column tells you which is the bigger number.
So 8400 is bigger than 6991 because 8 is bigger than 6.

> 8 400 8 is bigger than 6.
> 6 991

When two numbers have an equal number of digits and the values of the digits in the highest place value column are the same, then the value of the digit in the next place value column tells you which is the bigger, and so on.
So 2410 is bigger than 2406, because 1 is bigger than 0.

> 24 1 0 1 is bigger than 0.
> 24 0 6

Starting with the biggest number, the list above written in order of size is:

84 000   8400   6991   2410   2406   15

You will also have to deal with very big numbers such as hundreds of thousands, and millions:

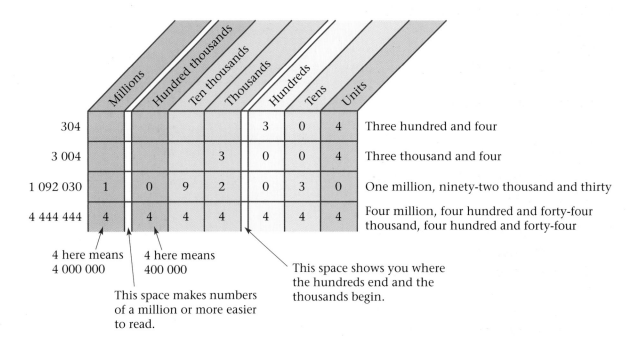

	Millions	Hundred thousands	Ten thousands	Thousands	Hundreds	Tens	Units	
304					3	0	4	Three hundred and four
3 004				3	0	0	4	Three thousand and four
1 092 030	1	0	9	2	0	3	0	One million, ninety-two thousand and thirty
4 444 444	4	4	4	4	4	4	4	Four million, four hundred and forty-four thousand, four hundred and forty-four

4 here means 4 000 000

4 here means 400 000

This space makes numbers of a million or more easier to read.

This space shows you where the hundreds end and the thousands begin.

Example 1

Write the number 1 804 603 in words.

To help you read a very large number, the digits are grouped in threes:

1 804 603 is	Millions	Thousands	Hundreds/Tens/Units
	1	804	6 0 3

One *million*, eight hundred and four *thousand*, six *hundred* and three.

Example 2

Write these numbers using digits.
(a) six thousand and twenty
(b) two million, fifty-eight thousand, three hundred and six
(c) half a million

(a) 6020
(b) 2 058 306
(c) 1 000 000 ÷ 2 = 500 000

Exercise 1B

1 Write these numbers in words.
   (a) 36   (b) 95   (c) 598
   (d) 246   (e) 5623
   (f) There are 1251 students at James Street School.

2 Write these numbers in words.
   (a) 709   (b) 890   (c) 6054
   (d) 9201   (e) 26 007   (f) 40 200
   (g) 32 000   (h) 70 090
   (i) The number of school leavers in Axeshire last year
       was 13 406.

3 Write these numbers in figures.
   (a) sixty-three
   (b) seven hundred and eight
   (c) seven thousand
   (d) eighteen thousand six hundred
   (e) seventy-five thousand
   (f) eight hundred and nine thousand
   (g) four million
   (h) one million one thousand
   (i) nine thousand and twenty
   (j) forty thousand six hundred

4 This table gives the populations of five member states of
   the European Union in 2004. Write the numbers in words.

	Country	Population
(a)	Belgium	10 348 276
(b)	Luxembourg	462 690
(c)	Spain	40 280 780
(d)	Portugal	10 524 145
(e)	France	60 424 213

5 Write the following numbers in figures.
   (a) The numbers of people employed by a local police
       force are:
   • Traffic wardens: sixty-nine
   • Civilian support staff: one thousand and ten
   • Police officers: two thousand three hundred and six.

(b) The tonnages of three cruise liners are:
  - Aurora: seventy-six thousand one hundred and fifty-two
  - QE2: seventy thousand three hundred and sixty-three
  - Queen Mary 2: one hundred and fifty-one thousand four hundred.

(c) The average daily readerships of four newspapers were:
  - *Financial Times*: two hundred and ninety-four thousand
  - *The Times*: six hundred and eighty-two thousand
  - *Daily Mirror*: two million six hundred thousand
  - *The Sun*: three million nine hundred and ninety thousand.

6 Rearrange these lists of numbers into order of size, starting with the largest number.
   (a) 86   104   79   88   114   200
   (b) 3000   3003   30 300   330 000   3033
   (c) 6 000 006   660 000   600 006   990 000   6 102 000

7 Put the numbers in the cloud in order. Start with the *smallest* number.

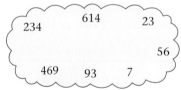

[E]

8 This table gives the prices of some secondhand cars:

Car	Price
Vauxhall Nova	£6755
Volkswagen Polo	£5423
Ford Focus	£7670
Toyota MR2	£3650
Jaguar XK8	£19 650
Land Rover Discovery	£15 560
Volvo V70	£12 375
Mercedes 500SL	£21 200

Rewrite the list in price order, starting with the least expensive.

9 This table shows the numbers of people who were seriously injured in road accidents in a part of Britain:

Year	2001	2002	2003	2004	2005
Number	37 346	33 645	31 456	29 788	26 466

In which year were:
(a) the smallest number of people seriously injured
(b) more than 35 000 seriously injured
(c) between 30 000 and 32 000 seriously injured
(d) fewer than 28 000 seriously injured?

10 The table below gives the areas, in km², of five member states of the European Union.

County	Area
Belgium	30 513
Luxembourg	2576
Spain	504 782
Portugal	92 082
France	547 026

(a) Write the area of the countries in words.
(b) List the countries in order of size, largest first.

1.3 Combining numbers

Using a number line

Here is a number line. It goes from 0 to 10.

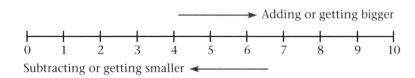

To add, move to the right.
To subtract, move to the left.

On the right is another number line. It goes up from 0 to 20.
It goes down from 20 to 0.

You can use the number line to increase or decrease numbers.

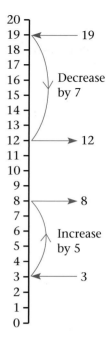

Example 3

(a) Increase 3 by 5.   (b) Decrease 19 by 7.

(a) Start at 3 on the line.
     From 3 count 5 upwards.
     The answer is 8.
(b) Start at 19 on the line.
     From 19 count 7 downwards.
     The answer is 12.

Exercise 1C

You can use a number line to help you with these questions.

1 Increase
   (a) 1 by 6   (b) 5 by 4   (c) 9 by 10
   (d) 8 by 5   (e) 12 by 3

2 Decrease
   (a) 13 by 4   (b) 7 by 6   (c) 18 by 7
   (d) 9 by 6   (e) 15 by 8

3 What increase moves
   (a) 6 to 10   (b) 3 to 11   (c) 12 to 14
   (d) 18 to 20   (e) 16 to 19?

4 What decrease moves
   (a) 7 to 4   (b) 8 to 1   (c) 12 to 3
   (d) 16 to 1   (e) 19 to 8?

5 What change moves
   (a) 6 to 11   (b) 10 to 16   (c) 19 to 14
   (d) 13 to 4   (e) 20 to 0?

> Remember to state whether the change is an increase or a decrease.

Adding

Here are some of the different ways of writing '6 add 9':
- Find the **sum** of 6 and 9.
- Work out 6 **plus** 9.
- Find the **total** of 6 and 9.
- **Add** 6 **and** 9.
- Work out 6 + 9.

Example 4

Work out 23 + 693 + 8

```
   2 3
   6 9 3
     8 +
  ———
   7 2 4
   1 1
```

Step 1 Put the digits in their correct columns.
Step 2 Add the units column: 3 + 3 + 8 = 14
Write 4 in the units column and carry the 1 ten into the tens column.
Step 3 Repeat for the tens column: 2 + 9 = 11 plus the 1 that was carried across = 12.
Write 2 in the tens column and carry the 1 into the hundreds column.
Step 4 Add the 6 and the 1 that was carried across: 7.

Exercise 1D

1 Find the total of 26 and 17.

2 Work out 58 plus 22.

3 Work out 236 + 95

4 In four maths tests, Anna scored 61 marks, 46 marks, 87 marks and 76 marks.
How many marks did she score altogether?

5 Find the sum of all the single digit numbers.

6 In a fishing competition, five competitors caught 16 fish, 31 fish, 8 fish, 19 fish and 22 fish.
Find the total number of fish caught.

7 The number of passengers on a bus was 36 downstairs and 48 upstairs.
How many passengers were on the bus altogether?

8 On her MP3 player Lena had 86 pop songs, 58 rock songs and 72 dance songs.
How many songs did she have in total?

9 Work out 38 + 96 + 127 + 92 + 48

10 On six days in June, 86, 43, 75, 104, 38 and 70 people went bungee jumping over a gorge.
How many people jumped in total?

Subtracting

Here are some different ways of writing '38 subtract 16':

- 38 **minus** 16.
- **Take** 16 **from** 38.
- 38 − 16
- Find the **difference** between 38 and 16.
- How many **less** is 16 than 38?
- 38 **take away** 16.

Example 5 _____

Take away 84 from 376.

$$\begin{array}{r} \overset{2\ \ 1}{7\ 6} \\ 8\ 4\ - \\ \hline 2\ 9\ 2 \end{array}$$

Step 1 Put the digits in their correct columns.
Step 2 In the units column take 4 away from 6, giving 2.
Step 3 In the tens column try taking 8 from 7 (not possible).
So exchange 1 hundred for 10 tens.
This gives 17 take 8, which leaves 9.
Step 4 In the hundreds column you are left with the 2 hundreds.

Example 6 _____

Work out 400 − 274

Method 1

$$\begin{array}{r} \overset{9}{} \\ 3\ 10\ 1 \\ 4\ 0\ 0 \\ 2\ 7\ 4\ - \\ \hline 1\ 2\ 6 \end{array}$$

Step 1 Put the digits in their correct columns.
Step 2 In the units column try taking 4 from 0 (not possible).
So exchange 1 hundred for 10 tens and then exchange 1 ten
for 10 units. 400 is now written as 300 + 90 + 10.
Step 3 Now, 10 − 4 = 6, 9 − 7 = 2 and 3 − 2 = 1.

Method 2

Step 1 Count on from 274 to 280 →   6
Step 2 Count on from 280 to 300 → 20
Step 3 Count on from 300 to 400 → <u>100</u> +
$$ \underline{126}$$

Exercise 1E

1 Work out 611 − 306

2 How much is 7260 minus 4094?

3 Take 1007 from 2010

4 In a car boot sale Alistair sells 17 of his 29 CDs.
How many does he have left?

5   When playing darts, James scored 111 with his first three
    darts, Sunita scored 94 with her first three darts and
    Nadine scored 75 with her first three darts.
    (a) How many more than Nadine did Sunita score?
    (b) What is the difference between James's and Sunita's scores?
    (c) How many less than James did Nadine score?

6   The winner of the darts match is the first
    one to reach 501.
    James has now scored 413, Sunita 442
    and Nadine 368.
    (a) How many is James short of 501?
    (b) How many more does Sunita need to
         score to reach 501?
    (c) How many less than 501 is Nadine's total?

7   The 'thermometer' shows the money raised each
    year in a charity appeal. At the start of 2000, the
    total raised was £27 854.
    (a) How much was raised between 2001 and 2002?
    (b) How much was raised altogether between 2000
         and 2002?
    (c) How much had to be raised in 2002 to reach the
         target of £100 000 before the end of the year?

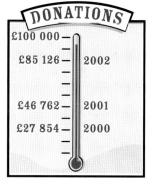

Multiplying and dividing by 10, 100 and 1000

The easiest numbers to multiply and divide by are 10, 100
and 1000. This is because they are all powers of ten and
our number system is based upon the number 10:

$$10 \times 10 = 100 \quad 100 \div 10 = 10 \quad 10 \times 100 = 1000 \quad 1000 \div 10 = 100$$

Example 7

Work out   (a) 23×10 (b) $3200 \div 100$

(a) 23×10

	H	T	U	
		2	3	
	2	3	0	= 230

The 3 moves from the units into the tens column
because $3 \times 10 = 30$

The 2 moves from the tens into the hundreds
column because $20 \times 10 = 200$

(b) $3200 \div 100$

Th	H	T	U	
3	2	0	0	
		3	2	= 32

The 3 moves from the thousands into the tens
column because $3000 \div 100 = 30$

The 2 moves from the hundreds into the units
column because $200 \div 100 = 2$

Example 8

Work out   (a) 23×400 (b) $3600 \div 30$

(a) 23×400

First multiply 23 by 4, and then multiply by 100, because 23×400 is the same as $23 \times 4 \times 100$:

$23 \times 4 = 92$ $92 \times 100 = 9200$

(b) $3600 \div 30$

First divide 3600 by 3, and then divide by 10, because $3600 \div 30$ is the same as $3600 \div 3 \div 10$:

$3600 \div 3 = 1200$ $1200 \div 10 = 120$

Exercise 1F

1 Multiply each of these numbers by
   (i) 10   (ii) 100   and   (iii) 1000.
   (a) 5   (b) 43   (c) 357   (d) 85   (e) 3000

2 Divide each of these numbers by
   (i) 10   (ii) 100   and   (iii) 1000.
   (a) 5000   (b) 74 000   (c) 865 000   (d) 4 000 000

3 Work out
   (a) 35×20 (b) 26×200 (c) 122×30
   (d) 213×300 (e) 47×40 (f) 36×4000
   (g) 215×500 (h) 365×6000

4 Work out
   (a) $600 \div 20$ (b) $8000 \div 200$ (c) $9000 \div 30$
   (d) $27\,000 \div 900$ (e) $800 \div 400$ (f) $12\,000 \div 60$
   (g) $30\,000 \div 150$ (h) $400\,000 \div 800$

Multiplying

Here are some different ways of writing '80 multiplied by 16':
- Find the **product** of 80 and 16.
- 16 **times** 80.
- **Multiply** 80 by 16.
- **Work out** 80×16.

There are many methods for multiplying two numbers together.

Example 9

Work out 43×6

Traditional method

```
    4 3
      6×        3 × 6 = 18
  ───────
  2 5 8        4 × 6 = 24 plus the 1 carried = 25
    1
```

Doubling method

$43 \times 2 = 86$
$43 \times 2 = 86$
$43 \times 2 = 86 +$
───────────
$43 \times 6 = 258$

3 lots of 43×2 are needed.

Napier's Bones

Step 1 Make a grid:

Step 2 Put in the values of 6×3 and 6×4:

Step 3 Working from right to left, add along the diagonals:

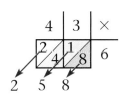

One topic which is almost always tested on the non-calculator paper is long multiplication, or multiplying numbers by a 2 digit number. You should practise doing calculations like these **without** a calculator.

Example 10

Work out 256×37

Traditional method

```
      2 5 6
        3 7×
    ─────────
      1 7 9 2
      7 6 8 0+
    ─────────
      9 4 7 2
```

Step 1 Multiply 256 by 7.
Step 2 Multiply 256 by 30 (don't forget the 0).
Step 3 Add.

Grid method

200	50	6	×
6000	1500	180	30
1400	350	42	7

$7400 + 1850 + 222 = 9472$

Step 1 Write each digit with its place value.
Step 2 Multiply out and put the answers in the boxes.
Step 3 Add all the numbers in the boxes together.

Napier's Bones

Step 1 Make a grid:

2	5	6	×
			3
			7

Step 2 Put in the values of 3×2, 3×5, 3×6, 7×2, 7×5 and 7×6:

2	5	6	×
0/6	1/5	1/8	3
1/4	3/5	4/2	7

Step 3 Working from right to left, add along the diagonals:

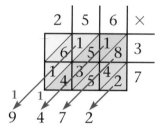

1 1
9 4 7 2

Exercise 1G

1 Work out
   (a) 34×20 (b) 65×7 (c) 53×3
   (d) 314×6 (e) 523×7 (f) 221×4
   (g) 146×5 (h) 132×2

2 Work out
   (a) 34×12 (b) 65×15 (c) 53×33
   (d) 314×16 (e) 523×47 (f) 221×64
   (g) 146×53 (h) 132×25

3 Find the product of 36 and 30.

4 How many is 321 multiplied by 14?

5 In a climbing competition 19 competitors scale a 24 metre high cliff. What is the total distance climbed?

6 What is the product of 63 and 36?

7 Wasim and Jan are training for a charity run.
During each session Wasim runs 50 metres 30 times and Jan runs 7 times round the 400 metre track.
   (a) How far does Wasim run each session?
   (b) How far does Jan run each session?

By the day of the run, Wasim has trained for 12 sessions and Jan for 20 sessions.
   (c) How far has each run in training by run day?

8 Packets of Cheese Flips come in three sizes.
There are 36 Cheese Flips in the economy size, 3 times as many in the large size and 6 times as many in the family size.
How many Cheese Flips are in each size packet?

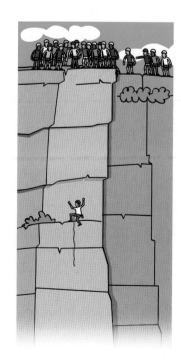

9   The distance from Mr Singh's home to work is 17 miles.
    He makes the journey 12 times a week.
    How far does he travel
    (a) in one week
    (b) in ten weeks
    (c) in a year?

> Remember: 52 weeks make 1 year.

10 Do questions **1–9** again using a different method.

Dividing

Here are some of the different ways of writing '140 divided by 20':

- **Divide** 140 by 20.
- **Share** 140 **between** 20.
- How many times does 20 **go into** 140?
- Work out $140 \div 20$
- Work out $\frac{140}{20}$
- **How many** 20s are there **in** 140?

> Remember to write $140 \div 20$, **not** $20 \div 140$

Here are some different methods for carrying out a division:

Example 11

Work out $256 \div 8$

Traditional short division

Step 1   8 into 2 does not go so try

Step 2   8 into 25 goes 3 times remainder 1

Step 3   8 into 16 goes 2 times.

Chunking method

```
 1 2 1 5 6
   8 0 −    10
 0 1 1 7 6
   8 0 −    10
   9 6
   8 0 −    10
   1 6
     8 −     1
     8
     8 −     1
     0
```

Step 1   Subtract 10 lots of 8 (that is $10 \times 8 = 80$).

Step 2   Keep subtracting 80 until you cannot do it any more.

Step 3   Now keep subtracting 8 until you cannot do it any more.

Step 4   Add up the parts of your answer:

$10 + 10 + 10 + 1 + 1 = 32$

Example 12

Work out $8704 \div 17$

Traditional long division

Follow these steps:

	Step 1	**Step 2**	**Step 3**	
	17 divides into 87 5 times remainder 2	17 divides into 20 1 time remainder 3	17 divides into 34 2 times exactly	So 17 divides into 8704 512 times.

$$17\overline{)8704}$$

Step 1:
$$\begin{array}{r} 5 \\ 17\overline{)8704} \\ -\,85 \\ \hline 2 \end{array}$$

Step 2:
$$\begin{array}{r} 51 \\ 17\overline{)8704} \\ -\,85\!\downarrow \\ \hline 20 \\ -\,17 \\ \hline 3 \end{array}$$

Step 3:
$$\begin{array}{r} 512 \\ 17\overline{)8704} \\ -\,85\;| \\ \hline 20\;| \\ -\,17\!\downarrow \\ \hline 34 \\ 34 \\ \hline 0 \end{array}$$

Short division method

$$17\overline{)87^20^34} \quad \begin{array}{l}5\;1\;2\end{array}$$

This is a shorter way of setting out the steps than in the long division method.

Chunking method

$$
\begin{array}{r}
8\;7\;0\;4 \\
1\;7\;0\;0\,- \\ \hline
^6\not{7}^10\;0\;4 \\
1\;7\;0\;0\,- \\ \hline
^4\not{5}^13\;0\;4 \\
1\;7\;0\;0\,- \\ \hline
^2\not{3}^16\;0\;4 \\
1\;7\;0\;0\,- \\ \hline
1\;9\;0\;4 \\
1\;7\;0\;0\,- \\ \hline
^1\not{2}^10\;4 \\
1\;7\;0\,- \\ \hline
^2\not{3}^14 \\
1\;7\,- \\ \hline
1\;7 \\
1\;7\,- \\ \hline
0
\end{array}
\qquad
\begin{array}{l}
100 \\[1.2em]
100 \\[1.2em]
100 \\[1.2em]
100 \\[1.2em]
100 \\[0.6em]
10 \\[0.4em]
1 \\[0.4em]
1
\end{array}
$$

Step 1
You could take 17 away.
A better way is to take 17×10 or 170 away.
But even better is to take 17×100 or 1700 away.

Step 2
When you can't take 1700 away any more you try 170.

Step 3
When you can't take 170 away any more you try 17.

Step 4
Add up the parts of your answer:
$100 + 100 + 100 + 100 + 100 + 10 + 1 + 1 = 512$

Exercise 1H

1 Work out
   (a) 48 ÷ 2   (b) 69 ÷ 3   (c) 56 ÷ 4   (d) 96 ÷ 6
   (e) 640 ÷ 4   (f) 565 ÷ 5   (g) 72 ÷ 4   (h) 712 ÷ 8
   (i) 828 ÷ 9   (j) 637 ÷ 7   (k) 408 ÷ 2   (l) 1020 ÷ 3

2 Work out
   (a) 256 ÷ 16   (b) 660 ÷ 15
   (c) 512 ÷ 32   (d) 861 ÷ 21
   (e) 756 ÷ 36   (f) 1020 ÷ 30
   (g) 1440 ÷ 36   (h) 7500 ÷ 25

3 (a) Work out 315 ÷ 15
   (b) How many 50s make 750?
   (c) Work out $\dfrac{680}{17}$
   (d) Work out 600 divided by 30.
   (e) Divide 8 into 112.

4 Five people shared a prize draw win of £2400 equally.
   How much did each person receive?

5 In an online computer game tournament players are put
   into groups of 24, with the group winners going through
   to the final.
   How many finalists will there be if there are
   (a) 240 players   (b) 720 players   (c) 864 players?

6 An aeroplane can hold 18 parachute jumpers at a time.
   How many trips does the plane have to make for
   (a) 126 jumps   (b) 234 jumps   (c) 648 jumps?

7 A packing case will hold 72 economy size boxes,
   24 large size boxes or 12 family size boxes.
   How many packing cases would be needed to pack
   (a) 864 economy size boxes
   (b) 984 large size boxes
   (c) 960 family size boxes?

Exercise 1I

Work out these multiplications and divisions.

1 194 × 15	2 3178 ÷ 14	3 306 × 32
4 186 × 36	5 7421 ÷ 41	6 612 × 81
7 12 285 ÷ 91	8 547 × 51	9 32 630 ÷ 65
10 785 × 89	11 20 608 ÷ 28	12 35 342 ÷ 82

You can check your
answers using a
calculator.

13 A lorry delivers 226 boxes of crisps. There are 48 packets in each box.
How many packets are there altogether?

14 A recycling box can hold 24 mobile phones.
How many complete boxes can be filled with 8000 mobiles?

Hint: there will be some mobile phones left over.

15 There are 12 items in one dozen.
How many items are there in 888 dozen?

1.4 Solving number problems

When you are solving number problems, you need to choose whether to add, subtract, divide or multiply.

Example 13

Find the cost of 7 bath pearls at 50p each.

You could find the cost by adding:

  50p + 50p + 50p + 50p + 50p + 50p + 50p = £3.50

or by multiplying:

  50p × 7 = £3.50

Here multiplying is quicker than adding.

Example 14

The key words here are **equal shares**. They tell you to **divide**:

  £2000 ÷ 5 = £400

Exercise 1J

In this exercise you will need to choose whether to add, subtract, multiply or divide.

> Look at the size of each answer when you have worked it out. This may help you check whether you have chosen + − × or ÷ correctly.

1   Between them, Owen and his friends keep
    12 pet hamsters and 21 pet rabbits.
    How many pets do they have altogether?

2   Ranjit and Jane both collect stamps.
    Ranjit has 1310 stamps and Jane has 942 stamps.
    How many more stamps has Ranjit than Jane?

3   42 packing cases of tins of beans are delivered to Simpson's
    Superstore. The packing cases each hold 48 tins of beans.
    How many tins of beans are delivered altogether?

4   A librarian has 343 DVDs to display in the music library.
    They fill exactly 7 shelves.
    How many DVDs are on each shelf?

5   Robina was given 20 face paints for her birthday.
    4 of the paints were blue, 6 were green and 7 were red.
    The others were brown.
    (a)   How many of Robina's paints were brown?
    (b)   How many more green paints than blue
          paints did she have?

    Robina gave 2 paints of each colour to her sister
    Amanda.
    (c)   How many paints did Robina give to Amanda
          altogether?
    (d)   How many paints did Robina have left?

6   Jason bought three boxes of toffees. There were 30 toffees
    in each box. Jason ate 14 toffees himself then shared all the
    rest equally between himself and his three sisters.
    (a)   How many toffees did Jason have to start with?
    (b)   When they were shared out, how many toffees did
          each person get?

7   This table shows the numbers of students in each year group
at Gordon School:

Year 7	Year 8	Year 9	Year 10	Year 11
112	121	104	98	126

(a) How many students are at the school altogether?

(b) How many fewer students are in Year 10 than in Year 8?

(c) Each class in Year 11 has 21 students.
How many classes are there in Year 11?

(d) There are 3 times as many students in Bennett School
as in Gordon School.
How many students are in Bennett School?

8   A bus company owns twelve 48-seater coaches.
Every Saturday all the coaches are used for trips.

(a) How many people can be carried at the same time in
the twelve coaches?

One Saturday, seven of the coaches each carried 39 people.
The other coaches each had 11 empty seats.

(b) How many people went on trips altogether that
Saturday?

1.5 Rounding numbers

Sometimes an exact answer is not needed because:

- an approximate answer
is good enough

- *or* an approximate answer
is easier to understand
than an exact answer

- *or* there is no exact
answer.

To give an approximate answer you can **round** to the nearest
ten, hundred, thousand and so on.

To round to the nearest ten,
look at the digit in the units column.
- If it is less than 5 round down.
- If it is 5 or more round up.

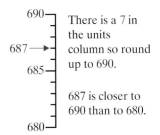

There is a 7 in the units column so round up to 690.

687 is closer to 690 than to 680.

Example 15

Round 687 to the nearest ten.

687 to the nearest ten is 690.

To round to the nearest hundred,
look at the digit in the tens column.
- If it is less than 5 round down.
- If it is 5 or more round up.

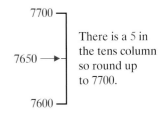

There is a 5 in the tens column so round up to 7700.

Example 16

Round 7650 to the nearest hundred.

7650 to the nearest hundred is 7700.

To round to the nearest thousand,
look at the digit in the hundreds column.
- If it is less than 5 round down.
- If it is 5 or more round up.

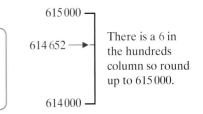

There is a 6 in the hundreds column so round up to 615 000.

Example 17

Round 614 652 to the nearest thousand.

614 652 to the nearest thousand is 615 000.

Exercise 1K

1 Round to the nearest ten
   (a) 57   (b) 63   (c) 185
   (d) 194   (e) 991   (f) 2407

2 Round to the nearest hundred
   (a) 314   (b) 691
   (c) 2406   (d) 3094
   (e) 8777   (f) 29 456

3 Round to the nearest thousand
   (a) 2116   (b) 36 161
   (c) 28 505   (d) 321 604
   (e) 717 171   (f) 2 246 810

4

	Length (ft)	Cruising speed (mph)	Takeoff weight (lbs)
Airbus A310	153	557	36 095
Boeing 737	94	577	130 000
Saab 2000	89	403	50 265
Dornier 228	54	266	12 566
Lockheed L1011	177	615	496 000

For each of these aircraft, round
   (a) the length to the nearest ten feet
   (b) the takeoff weight to the nearest hundred pounds
   (c) the cruising speed to the nearest ten mph.

5 The table gives the areas of five European Union states and
   their populations in 2004.

Country	Area (km²)	Population
Greece	131 944	10 645 343
Italy	301 225	57 436 280
Netherlands	33 812	16 318 199
Germany	356 733	83 251 851
Ireland	70 283	3 883 159

Round
   (a) the areas to the nearest thousand km²
   (b) the populations to the nearest hundred thousand.

6 Round each number to the nearest 100, 1000, 10 000,
   100 000 or million, as appropriate. Explain your rounding.
   (a) James has a flock of 142 chickens.
   (b) Mrs Wilson sold 306 portions of fish and chips.
   (c) Asif needed 6318 bricks to build his new bungalow.
   (d) A crowd of 40 157 spectators watched Chelsea last night.
   (e) A pop group earned £45 376 290 in a year.
   (f) Newhouse General Hospital treated 13 296 patients
       last year.

Rounding to 1 significant figure

Sometimes you will be asked to round a number to
1 significant figure (1 s.f.).

> To write a number to 1 significant figure, look at the place value
> of the first digit and round the number to this place value.

Example 18

Write these numbers to 1 significant figure.
(a) 32   (b) 452   (c) 8780

(a) 32

The first digit is in the tens column. So you need to round to
the nearest ten.

32 to the nearest ten is 30.
32 to 1 significant figure is 30.

(b) 452

The first digit is in the hundreds column, so round to the
nearest hundred.

452 to 1 significant figure is 500.

(c) 8780

The first digit is in the thousands column, so round to the
nearest thousand.

8780 to 1 significant figure is 9000.

Is your answer reasonable?

When you do a calculation it helps to have a rough estimate
of what answer to expect.

> Rounding is used to help you estimate an answer.
> To estimate an answer round each number in the calculation
> to 1 significant figure.

Example 19

Estimate the answer to $\dfrac{289 \times 96}{184}$

Rounding each of the numbers to 1 significant figure gives

$$\frac{300 \times 100}{200}$$

Working out the simplified calculation gives 150.

Example 20

Work out the exact value of $\dfrac{18 \times 104}{48}$ by calculator.

Check your answer by estimating.

By calculator: $\dfrac{18 \times 104}{48} = \dfrac{1872}{48} = 39$

By estimating: $\dfrac{18 \times 104}{48}$ is about $\dfrac{20 \times 100}{50} = 40$

Exercise 1L

1 Write down these numbers to 1 significant figure.
   (a) 12   (b) 49   (c) 4
   (d) 203   (e) 4960   (f) 501
   (g) 3497   (h) 65   (i) 6034
   (j) 8921   (k) 78 321   (l) 81 476

2 England won 165 medals at the 2002 Commonwealth
   Games. Write this number to 1 s.f.

3 The population of Clifton is 2437. What is the
   population of Clifton to 1 s.f.?

4 Showing all your rounding, make an estimate of the
   answer to

   (a) $\dfrac{63 \times 57}{31}$ (b) $\dfrac{206 \times 311}{154}$

   (c) $\dfrac{9 \times 31 \times 97}{304}$ (d) $\dfrac{2006}{12 \times 99}$

   (e) $\dfrac{498}{11 \times 51}$ (f) $\dfrac{103 \times 87}{21 \times 32}$

> Check your answers with
> a calculator.

5 For each of the following calculations
   (i) work out the exact value by calculator
   (ii) check your answer by estimating.

   (a) $\dfrac{201 \times 96}{51}$ (b) $\dfrac{11 \times 999}{496}$

   (c) $\dfrac{146 \times 51}{69}$ (d) $\dfrac{1000}{9 \times 12}$

   (e) $\dfrac{5206}{131 \times 7}$ (f) $\dfrac{913 \times 81}{39 \times 298}$

> If you use your calculator
> to find an answer, you can
> check it by estimating.

6 A football grandstand has 49 rows of seats. Each row seats 98 people.
(a) Estimate the capacity of the grandstand.
(b) Is your estimate bigger or smaller than the actual number?
Explain your answer.

7 1335 rugby fans went to an away match by coach. Each coach carried 47 people.
Estimate the number of coaches needed.

8 Thelma worked out the answer to $916 \times 402 \div 1010$ on her calculator. Her answer was 36.458
By estimating, show whether her answer could be correct.

9 The headteacher lives 16 miles from Inglefield School.
He went to school on 195 days last year.
Estimate how many miles he travelled to and from school.

10 A machine operator produces 121 microchips every hour.
He works 39 hours each week for 47 weeks in the year.
Estimate the operator's annual chip production.

Mixed exercise 1

1
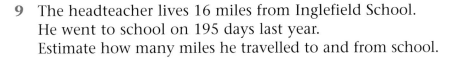

(a) Write down the number marked with an arrow.

(b) Write down the number marked with an arrow.   [E]

2 Write these numbers in order of size.

    75   56   37   9   59

Start with the smallest number.   [E]

3 Fatima sold 24 teddy bears for a total of £696.
She sold each teddy bear for the same price.
Work out the price at which Fatima sold each teddy bear. [E]

4 54 327 people watched a concert.
(a) Write 54 327 to the nearest thousand.
(b) Write down the value of the 5 in the number 54 327.   [E]

5 Every day a quarter of a million babies are born in the world.
   (a) Write a quarter of a million using figures.
   (b) Work out the number of babies born in 28 days. Give your answer in millions. [E]

6 Nick fills his van with large wooden crates.
   The weight of each crate is 69 kg.
   The greatest weight the van can hold is 990 kg.
   Work out the greatest number of crates that the van can hold. [E]

7 800 people took part in a wilderness trek, with 144 failing to finish.
   Work out how many people completed the trek.

8 Sammy does 24 sit-ups every day.
   How many sit-ups will he complete in a year of 365 days?

9 For each of these calculations round each number to 1 significant figure and give an estimate for your answer.
   (a) $\dfrac{205 \times 49}{499}$ (b) $\dfrac{689 + 304}{290 - 98}$ (c) $\dfrac{590}{187 + 103}$

10 Round the following numbers to the nearest ten.
   (a) 77   (b) 643   (c) 18
   (d) 4555   (e) 109   (f) 7001

11 Fiona has four cards.
   Each card has a number written on it.

   | 4 | 9 | 1 | 5 |

   Fiona puts all four cards on the table to make a number.
   (a) Write the smallest number Fiona can make using all four cards.
   (b) Write the largest number Fiona can make using all four cards.

   Fiona uses the cards to make a true statement.

   (c) Write this calculation.
       Use each of the numbers on Fiona's cards **once**.

   Fiona needs a fifth card to show the result of the multiplication 4915×10.

   (d) Write down the number for the fifth card she needs. [E]

12 Karen needs to check her electricity bill.
    (a) Subtract the 1st reading from the 2nd reading
         to find the units used.
    (b) Multiply the units used by 25 to find the
         cost in pence of all the units used.
    (c) Divide the number of pence by 100 to
         find the cost in pounds.
    (d) Add the standing charge to find the total
         amount Karen owes.

1st reading	3707
2nd reading	3939
Cost of each unit	25p
Standing charge	£12

Summary of key points

1 Each digit has a value that depends on its position in a number. This is its **place value**.
   For example:

       325

   The place value of this digit is hundred. 3 hundreds = 300

2 **To round to the nearest ten,**
   look at the digit in the units column.
   ● If it is less than 5 round down.
   ● If it is 5 or more round up.

3 **To round to the nearest hundred,**
   look at the digit in the tens column.
   ● If it is less than 5 round down.
   ● If it is 5 or more round up.

4 **To round to the nearest thousand,**
   look at the digit in the hundreds column.
   ● If it is less than 5 round down.
   ● If it is 5 or more round up.

5 To write a number to 1 significant figure (1 s.f.), look at the place value of the first
   digit and round the number to this place value.

6 Rounding is used to help you estimate an answer. To estimate an answer round
   each number in the calculation to 1 significant figure.

7 There is often more than one method for a calculation.
   Make sure you can:
   ● add
   ● subtract
   ● multiply (see pages 12–14 for different methods)
   ● divide (see pages 15–16 for different methods).

2 Number facts

2.1 Negative numbers

The temperature here is 31 degrees below zero Celsius.

The Dead Sea is the lowest place on the surface of the Earth. It is 396 m below sea level.

You use negative numbers to represent quantities that are less than zero.

$-31\,°C$ is 31 degrees below zero.

$-396\,m$ is 396 m below sea level.

Exercise 2A

1 Write down the highest and the lowest number in each list.
   (a) 5, −10, −3, 0, 4
   (b) −7, −2, −9, −13, 0
   (c) −3, 6, 13, −15, −6
   (d) −13, −2, −20, −21, −5

2 Write the two missing numbers in each sequence.
   (a) 4, 3, 2, 1, —, —, −2
   (b) 10, 7, 4, 1, —, —, −8
   (c) −13, −9, −5, −1, —, —, 11
   (d) 13, 8, 3, −2, —, —, −17
   (e) 21, 12, 3, −6, —, —, −33
   (f) −13, −10, −7, −4, —, —, 5

3 Use the number line to find the number that is
   (a) 5 more than 2   (b) 4 more than −7
   (c) 7 less than 6   (d) 2 less than −3
   (e) 6 less than 0   (f) 10 more than −7
   (g) 6 more than −6   (h) 4 less than −3
   (i) 10 less than 5   (j) 1 more than −1

9
8
7
6
5
4
3
2
1
0
−1
−2
−3
−4
−5
−6
−7

4 What number is
   (a) 30 more than −70   (b) 50 less than −20
   (c) 80 greater than −50   (d) 90 smaller than 60
   (e) 130 smaller than −30   (f) 70 bigger than 200
   (g) 170 bigger than −200   (h) 100 bigger than −100
   (i) 140 more than −20   (j) 200 less than −200?

5 The table gives the highest and lowest temperatures
   recorded in several cities during one year.

	New York	Brussels	Tripoli	Minsk	Canberra
Highest temperature	27 °C	32 °C	34 °C	28 °C	34 °C
Lowest temperature	−9 °C	−6 °C	8 °C	−21 °C	7 °C

   (a) Which city recorded the lowest temperature?
   (b) Which city recorded the biggest difference between
        its highest and lowest temperatures?
   (c) Which city recorded the smallest difference between
        its highest and lowest temperatures?

6 The temperature of the fridge compartment of a
   fridge–freezer is set at 4 °C. The freezer compartment is
   set at −18 °C.
   What is the difference between these temperature settings?

7 The temperature of a shop freezer should be set at −18 °C.
   It is set to −12 °C by mistake.
   What is the difference between these temperature
   settings?

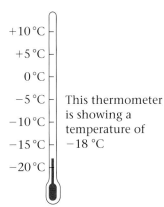

This thermometer is showing a temperature of −18 °C

2.2 Using negative numbers

You can use **negative numbers** to describe quantities such as
temperatures less than 0 °C.

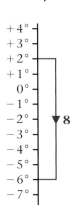

You can use a number line to help you answer
questions.

For example:

The temperature at the top of a mountain was
2 °C at 12 noon. By 6 pm it had fallen by 8 °C.
So the new temperature at 6 pm was −6 °C.

Temperatures below 0 °C (the
freezing point of water) are
negative.

Example 1

(a) The temperature was 5 °C. It fell by 8 degrees. What is the new temperature?
(b) What is the difference in temperature between 4 °C and −4 °C?

(a) From 5 °C count 8 degrees down to −3 °C.
(b) From 4 °C count to −4 °C. There is a difference of 8 degrees between the two temperatures.

Temperature falls by 8°

Worked examination question

The temperature during an autumn morning went up from −3 °C to 6 °C.
(a) By how many degrees did the temperature rise?

During the afternoon the temperature then fell by 8 degrees from 6 °C.
(b) What was the temperature at the end of the afternoon?

(a) Counting from −3 °C to 6 °C gives 9 degrees.
(b) Counting down 8 degrees from 6 °C gives −2 °C.   [E]

Exercise 2B

Use this number line going from −10 °C to +10 °C to help you with these questions.

1 Rearrange each list of temperatures in numerical order, lowest temperature first
   (a) 4 °C, −5 °C, 2 °C, −12 °C, 7 °C, 0 °C, −7 °C, −1 °C, 9 °C
   (b) 5 °C, −3 °C, 2 °C, 10 °C, −8 °C, −2 °C, 8 °C, 0 °C, −9 °C
   (c) 7 °C, 3 °C, −7 °C, −4 °C, −1 °C, 8 °C, −6 °C, 5 °C, −3 °C
   (d) −4 °C, 9 °C, 4 °C, −2 °C, 7 °C, −8 °C, 1 °C, −3 °C, 6 °C
   (e) 5 °C, −5 °C, 7 °C, −7 °C, 4 °C, −9 °C, −3 °C, −1 °C, 8 °C, 0 °C

2 Find the number of degrees between each pair of temperatures.
   (a) −3 °C, 2 °C   (b) −4 °C, −1 °C   (c) 2 °C, 8 °C
   (d) −6 °C, 4 °C   (e) 7 °C, −3 °C   (f) 1 °C, 9 °C
   (g) −3 °C, −8 °C   (h) −7 °C, 6 °C

3 Find the new temperature after
   (a) a 2° rises from −4 °C   (b) a 7° fall from 4 °C
   (c) 8 °C falls by 15°   (d) −4 °C rises by 7°
   (e) −5 °C rises by 8°   (f) 4 °C falls by 10°
   (g) −3 °C falls by 6°

+10°
+9°
+8°
+7°
+6°
+5°
+4°
+3°
+2°
+1°
0°
−1°
−2°
−3°
−4°
−5°
−6°
−7°
−8°
−9°
−10°

Adding and subtracting negative numbers

You can also use negative numbers in calculations.

You need to be able to add and subtract negative numbers. To help you get used to working with subtraction signs and negative numbers they are written like this when they appear together in this section:

Sometimes 3 is written $^+3$.

$^-5$ means negative 5, or 5 below zero
$7 - 4$ means 7 subtract 4
$7 - {}^-5$ means 7 subtract negative 5

This table shows lunchtime and evening temperatures in different parts of the world:

Place	Temperature at lunchtime in °C	Temperature in the evening in °C
Bahrain	20	15
London	5	−2
Alaska	−8	−14

- The difference between the lunchtime temperature and the evening temperature in Bahrain can be written:

  lunchtime temperature − evening temperature
  $= {}^+20 - {}^+15 = {}^+5$ or $20 - 15 = 5$
  (Note that $\qquad {}^+20 + {}^-15 = {}^+5$)

- The difference in London is $\quad 5 - {}^-2 \ = {}^+7$
  (Note that $\qquad\qquad 5 + {}^+2 \ = \ 7$)

- The difference in Alaska is $\quad {}^-8 - {}^-14 = \ 6$
  (Note that $\qquad\qquad {}^-8 + {}^+14 = \ 6$)

Subtracting a positive number has the same effect as adding the negative number: $- {}^+4 = + {}^-4$

Subtracting a negative number has the same effect as adding the positive number: $- {}^-3 = + {}^+3$

A good way of remembering how to deal with adding and subtracting positive and negative numbers is:

- When you have **two signs that are the same** next to each other, you replace them with a **+**
- When you have **two signs that are different** next to each other, you replace them with a **−**

This means that:

$+ + = +$	so $\ 2 + {}^+5 = 7$ and	${}^-2 + {}^+5 = 3$
$- - = +$	$2 - {}^-5 = 7$	${}^-2 - {}^-5 = 3$
$+ - = -$	$2 + {}^-5 = {}^-3$	${}^-2 + {}^-5 = {}^-7$
$- + = -$	$2 - {}^+5 = {}^-3$	${}^-2 - {}^+5 = {}^-7$

Exercise 2C

Work out these additions and subtractions.

1 (a) $^+3 + {}^-3$ (b) $^-4 + 0$
(c) $^-9 - {}^+5$ (d) $^-9 + {}^+5$

2 (a) $^-5 - {}^-6$ (b) $^+12 - {}^-5$
(c) $^-10 + {}^+8$ (d) $^+6 - {}^-4$

3 (a) $^+8 + {}^-13$ (b) $^+5 - 0$
(c) $^+13 - {}^+15$ (d) $^-2 + {}^-4$

4 (a) $^-3 - {}^+8$ (b) $^-3 + {}^+6$
(c) $^+11 - {}^-6$ (d) $^-12 + {}^+7$

5 (a) $^-7 + {}^-7$ (b) $^+4 - {}^+1$
(c) $^+3 + {}^-8$ (d) $^-3 - {}^+6$

> **Remember:**
> $+ \ + = +$
> $- \ - = +$
> $+ \ - = -$
> $- \ + = -$

Multiplying and dividing negative numbers

The next exercise uses patterns to investigate how to multiply and divide with negative numbers.

Exercise 2D

First number

-5	-4	-3	-2	-1	0	1	2	3	4	5	$\times$
										25	5
											4
						6					3
											2
							4				1
											0
											-1
											-2
											-3
											-4
											-5

Second number

> First number $\times$ second number
> $= 2 \times 3 = 6$

1 Copy the multiplication grid above.

2 Complete the yellow square for numbers 1 to 5 on your grid.

3 Look at the patterns in the yellow square. Continue these patterns to complete all the horizontal and vertical rows in the table.

4 From your grid write down the values of

(a) $+5 \times +2$ (b) $+4 \times -3$
(c) $-2 \times +4$ (d) -3×-5
(e) $+3 \times +1$ (f) $+2 \times -3$
(g) $-5 \times +4$ (h) -4×-1

This table shows the signs you get when you multiply two numbers together:

+	×	+	=	+
+	×	−	=	−
−	×	+	=	−
−	×	−	=	+

This table shows the signs you get when you divide one number by another:

+	÷	+	=	+
+	÷	−	=	−
−	÷	+	=	−
−	÷	−	=	+

If you know that $-3 \times +4 = -12$ then you also know that $-12 \div +4 = -3$ and $-12 \div -3 = +4$.

> Remember: when multiplying or dividing, two like signs give a +, two unlike signs give a −

Exercise 2E

1 Copy and complete this multiplication grid for first number × second number.

First number

×	+5	+3	−6	−2
+2				
+8				
−3				
−4				

Second number (rows +2, +8, −3, −4)

2 Copy and complete this division grid for first number ÷ second number.

First number

÷	+6	−12	−18	+24
+3				
−2				
−6				
+1				

Second number (rows +3, −2, −6, +1)

Example 2

Work out   (a) $+5 \times -2$ (b) $+16 \div +2$
               (c) $-1 \times +3$ (d) $-20 \div -5$

(a) $+5 \times -2 = -10$ (b) $+16 \div +2 = +8$
(c) $-1 \times +3 = -3$ (d) $-20 \div -5 = +4$

Exercise 2F

Work out these multiplications and divisions.

1 (a) $+3 \times -1$ (b) $+24 \div -8$ (c) $+4 \div +1$
   (d) $+2 \times +6$ (e) $-12 \div +3$ (f) $-3 \times +4$

2 (a) $-9 \times +10$ (b) $-32 \div -8$ (c) $-20 \div -4$
   (d) $-2 \times +7$ (e) $+10 \div -5$ (f) -3×-4

3 (a) $-5 \times +4$ (b) $-16 \div -8$ (c) $-4 \times +5$
   (d) $-18 \div -3$ (e) $+18 \div +2$ (f) $-6 \times +7$

4 (a) -8×-3 (b) $-30 \div +2$ (c) $-16 \div +4$
   (d) -3×-9 (e) $+5 \times -8$ (f) $+24 \div +8$

5 (a) $-50 \div -5$ (b) $-7 \times +8$ (c) $+6 \times +6$
   (d) -3×-7 (e) $-9 \div +3$ (f) $-7 \times +6$

2.3 Factors, multiples and primes

You need to be able to recognise the following types of numbers by knowing some of their properties.

- **Even** numbers are whole numbers which divide exactly by 2.
  2, 4, 6, 18, 24 are even numbers.

- Odd numbers are whole numbers which do not divide exactly by 2.
  1, 9, 15, 23, 27 are odd numbers.

- The **factors** of a number are whole numbers that divide exactly into the number.
  The factors include 1 and the number itself.
  For example, the factors of 12 are 1, 2, 3, 4, 6 and 12.

- **Multiples** of a number are the results of multiplying the number by a positive whole number. For example, some multiples of 3 are 3, 6, 9, 12, 15, 18, 21, 24.

- A **prime** number is a whole number greater than 1 which has only two factors: itself and 1. The first ten prime numbers are 2, 3, 5, 7, 11, 13, 17, 19, 23, 29.
  1 is not a prime number as it can only be divided by **one** number (itself).

- A **prime factor** is a factor that is a prime number.
  For example, the prime factors of 18 are 2 and 3.

Exercise 2G

1 Write down all the even numbers in this list:
   2, 18, 37, 955, 1110, 73 536, 500 000

2 Write down all the odd numbers in this list:
   108, 537, 9216, 811, 36 225, 300 000

3 The first six prime numbers are 2, 3, 5, 7, 11 and 13.
Write down the next seven prime numbers.

4 Here is a list of numbers:
15, 20, 25, 30, 37, 39, 49, 69, 70, 71, 400, 450
Write down
(a) the largest even number
(b) the largest odd number
(c) the largest prime number.

5 Find one factor, other than 1 and the number itself, of
(a) 9   (b) 24   (c) 32
(d) 55   (e) 108   (f) 625

6 Find all six factors of 12.

7 Find all the factors of
(a) 32   (b) 200
(c) 340   (d) 1000

8 Find all the common factors of
(a) 4 and 6   (b) 9 and 12   (c) 15 and 25
(d) 6 and 14   (e) 14 and 35

> A common factor of 4 and 6 is a number that is a factor of *both* 4 *and* 6, e.g. 2.

9 Find all the common factors of
(a) 20 and 30   (b) 90 and 100   (c) 12 and 28
(d) 6 and 18   (e) 18 and 45

10 Find two common factors of
(a) 20 and 50   (b) 12 and 40   (c) 70 and 105
(d) 30 and 42   (e) 18 and 42

11 Find three multiples of 9.

12 Find the nearest number to 100 that is a multiple of 9.

13 Find
(a) three multiples of 6 that are bigger than 50
(b) three multiples of 20 that are between 1000 and 2000
(c) three multiples of 15 that are bigger than 100.

14 Write down
(a) three numbers that have a factor of 8
(b) three numbers that have a factor of 150
(c) three numbers that only have odd-number factors.

15 (a) Copy this set of numbers:
    (b) Draw a line — through numbers with
         factor 3.
    (c) Draw a line | through numbers with
         factor 20.
    (d) Draw a line \ through any multiples
         of 30.
    (e) Draw a line / through any multiples
         of 90.
    (f) Which number has all four lines through it?

10	20	30	40	50
60	70	80	90	100
110	120	130	140	150
160	170	180	190	200
210	220	230	240	250

2.4 Square numbers and cube numbers

These numbers sometimes occur in number patterns in
investigations.

A **square number** is the result of multiplying a whole number
by itself.

Square numbers:

$1 \times 1 = 1$ 1st square number
$2 \times 2 = 4$ 2nd square number
$3 \times 3 = 9$ 3rd square number
$4 \times 4 = 16$ 4th square number

4×4 can also be written as:
• the square of 4
• 4 squared
• 4^2

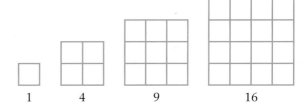

A square number can be shown as a
pattern of squares.

A **cube number** is the result of multiplying a whole number by
itself, then multiplying by the number again.

Cube numbers:

$1 \times 1 \times 1 = 1$ 1st cube number
$2 \times 2 \times 2 = 8$ 2nd cube number
$3 \times 3 \times 3 = 27$ 3rd cube number
$4 \times 4 \times 4 = 64$ 4th cube number

$4 \times 4 \times 4$ can also be written as:
• the cube of 4
• 4 cubed
• 4^3

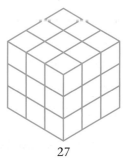

A cube number can be shown as a
pattern of cubes.

Example 3

1, 3, 4, 6, 8, 13, 16, 18, 24, 27, 30

From the list write down
(a) the square numbers   (b) the cube numbers.

(a) 1, 4, 16   (b) 1, 8, 27

Exercise 2H

1 Find
   (a) the 8th square number   (b) the 7th cube number
   (c) the 12th square number   (d) the 10th cube number
   (e) the first 12 square numbers (f) the first 8 cube numbers.

2 From each list write down all the numbers which are
   (i) square numbers   (ii) cube numbers.

   (a) 50, 20, 64, 30, 1, 80, 8, 49, 9
   (b) 10, 21, 57, 4, 60, 125, 7, 27, 48, 16, 90, 35
   (c) 137, 150, 75, 110, 50, 125, 64, 81, 144
   (d) 90, 180, 216, 100, 81, 75, 140, 169, 125

2.5 Finding squares and square roots of numbers

You will need to find squares of numbers and square roots of numbers when you use Pythagoras' theorem (Chapter 25).

Squares

To find the **square** of any number, multiply the number by itself.
The square of 3.7 = 3.7^2 = 3.7 × 3.7 = 13.69
The square of −6.2 = -6.2^2 = −6.2 × −6.2 = 38.44

Square roots

4 × 4 = 16 so we say that 4 is a **square root** of 16; it is a number which multiplied by itself gives 16.

You can write the square root of 16 as $\sqrt{16}$.

1.5 × 1.5 = 2.25

So 1.5 is a square root of 2.25, written $\sqrt{2.25}$.

Finding a **square root** of a number is the opposite (inverse) of squaring. A square root of 64 (written $\sqrt{64}$) is 8, since $8^2 = 64$.

Notice that
−4 × −4 = 16
so −4 is also a square root of 16.
You can write $\sqrt{16} = \pm 4$

Square roots are often not whole numbers. You can find the square root of any positive number. Most calculators have a function key that finds the square root of a number. You often need to round the answer on the calculator display.

Your calculator may have a key with this symbol:

$\sqrt{}$ square root

___ **Example 4** ___

Use a calculator to find $\sqrt{18}$.

$\sqrt{18} = 4.242\,640\,6\,\ldots = 4.24$ (to 2 d.p.)

Using the square root key on your calculator:

Remember:
$\sqrt{18}$ can also be -4.24, if it is a sensible answer to the problem you are solving.

2.6 Finding cubes and cube roots of numbers

Cubes

To find the **cube** of any number, multiply the number by itself then multiply by the number again.

The cube of $5.3 = 5.3^3 = 5.3 \times 5.3 \times 5.3 = 148.877$

The cube of $-2.1 = (-2.1)^3 = -2.1 \times -2.1 \times -2.1 = -9.261$

Cube roots

$2 \times 2 \times 2 = 8$ so we say that 2 is the **cube root** of 8: it is a number which multiplied by itself, then multiplied by itself again, gives 8.

You can write the cube root of 8 as $\sqrt[3]{8}$.

$3.4 \times 3.4 \times 3.4 = 39.304$

So 3.4 is the cube root of 39.304, written $\sqrt[3]{39.304}$.

Finding the **cube root** is the opposite (or inverse) of finding the cube.

Cube roots are often not whole numbers. You can find the cube root of any positive or negative number. Some calculators have a cube root function key to find the cube root of numbers. As with square roots, you often have to round the answer.

Your calculator may have a key with this symbol:

 cube root

___ **Example 5** ___

Use a calculator to find $\sqrt[3]{18}$.

Using the cube root key on your calculator:

$\sqrt[3]{18} = 2.620\,741\,3\,\ldots = 2.62$ (to 2 d.p.)

Notice that $\sqrt[3]{-64} = -4$ because
$-4 \times -4 \times -4 = -64$

Exercise 2I

Use your calculator to work out:

1. (a) 13^2 (b) 3.5^2 (c) 40^2
   (d) 8.7^2 (e) $(-19.6)^2$ (f) $(-57.4)^2$

2. (a) 6^3 (b) 2.4^3 (c) 20^3
   (d) $(-1.3)^3$ (e) $(-13.4)^3$ (f) 36.2^3

> Sometimes you are asked to leave your answer as a square root or cube root.
> e.g. $x^2 = 5$
> $x = \sqrt{5}$
> This is called writing your answer in **surd form**.

3. (a) $\sqrt{121}$ (b) $\sqrt{225}$ (c) $\sqrt{16\,900}$
   (d) $\sqrt{2.89}$ (e) $\sqrt{0.49}$ (f) $\sqrt{33.64}$

4. In this question give your answers correct to 2 d.p.
   (a) $\sqrt{253}$ (b) $\sqrt{18.4}$ (c) $\sqrt{29.44}$

5. In this question give your answers correct to 3 s.f.
   (a) $\sqrt[3]{68}$ (b) $\sqrt[3]{26.5}$ (c) $\sqrt[3]{882.5}$

> To round to 3 s.f. look at the place value of the 3rd digit from the left, and round the number to this place value.

2.7 Finding square roots and cube roots by trial and improvement

You can also find square roots and cube roots by **trial and improvement**.

Example 6

Use a trial and improvement method to find $\sqrt[3]{20}$ (the cube root of 20), correct to 2 decimal places.

Start by trying whole numbers of about the right size.

Next try a value between 2 and 3: try 2.5.

Next try 2.8, bigger than 2.5.

Next try 2.7, smaller than 2.8.

Next try a value between 2.7 and 2.8: try 2.75.

The solution is between 2.71 and 2.72, so try the value halfway between 2.71 and 2.72: try 2.715.

Try this number	Cube of the number		Bigger or smaller than 20?
2	$2 \times 2 \times 2$	$= 8$	smaller
3	$3 \times 3 \times 3$	$= 27$	bigger
2.5	$2.5 \times 2.5 \times 2.5$	$= 15.625$	smaller
2.8	$2.8 \times 2.8 \times 2.8$	$= 21.952$	bigger
2.7	$2.7 \times 2.7 \times 2.7$	$= 19.683$	smaller
2.75	2.75^3	$= 20.797$	bigger
2.71	2.71^3	$= 19.903$	smaller
2.72	2.72^3	$= 20.124$	bigger
2.715	2.715^3	$= 20.012\,876$	bigger

The solution is between 2.71 and 2.715. Any number in this range rounds to 2.71 (to 2 d.p.), so an approximate value for $\sqrt[3]{20}$ is 2.71 (correct to 2 d.p.).

Exercise 2J

Use a trial and improvement method to find these roots correct to 2 decimal places. Use a calculator to check your answers.

1 $\sqrt{7}$	**2** $\sqrt[3]{15}$	**3** $\sqrt[3]{12}$	**4** $\sqrt{10}$
5 $\sqrt{20}$	**6** $\sqrt{32}$	**7** $\sqrt[3]{30}$	**8** $\sqrt[3]{42}$
9 $\sqrt{13}$	**10** $\sqrt[3]{50}$	**11** $\sqrt{28}$	**12** $\sqrt[3]{33}$

> Remember: show all your attempts and working when you have used a trial and improvement method; it gives evidence of the methods you have used.

2.8 Writing numbers as a product of their prime factors

Sometimes you will be asked to write a number as a **product of its prime factors**. This involves splitting the number into all its prime factors. When you multiply the prime factors together you get the number again. Here are two ways of doing this.

> A product results from multiplying two or more numbers together. A number which is itself prime cannot be written as a product of primes.

Method 1: Dividing by prime numbers in order

Example 7

Write 60 as a product of its prime factors.

Step 1 Divide by 2:
$$\frac{30}{2)\overline{60}}$$

Step 2 Divide the answer 30 by 2:
$$\begin{array}{r} 15 \\ 2)\overline{30} \\ 2)\overline{60} \end{array}$$

Step 3 15 is not divisible by 2, so try the next prime, 3:
$$\begin{array}{r} 5 \\ 3)\overline{15} \\ 2)\overline{30} \\ 2)\overline{60} \end{array}$$

5 is prime.

Answer $60 = 2 \times 2 \times 3 \times 5$ — as a product of prime factors
$= 2^2 \times 3 \times 5$ — as a product of powers of its prime factors

Start with the first prime (2)

Choose next prime

Will your prime divide into the number exactly? No

Yes Divide the number by the prime

Is the answer prime? No

Yes Stop

Method 2: Factor trees

Start with the number and keep splitting into pairs of factors until all the factors are prime numbers.

Example 8

Write 48 as a product of its prime factors.

$48 = 6 \times 8$

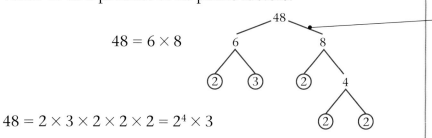

There is often more than one way of splitting a number in a factor tree (e.g. 48 could have been split into 2×24), but all ways give the same answer.

$48 = 2 \times 3 \times 2 \times 2 \times 2 = 2^4 \times 3$

Writing a number as the product of its prime factors is called writing it in **prime factor form**.

Exercise 2K

1   Write these numbers as products of their prime factors.
    (a)   45   (b)   36   (c)   29   (d)   100

2   Write these numbers in prime factor form.
    (a)   24   (b)   32   (c)   18   (d)   13

A number which is itself prime cannot be written as a product of primes.

Finding the highest common factor (HCF)

The **highest common factor** or HCF is exactly what it says.

The **HCF** of two numbers is the highest factor that is common to both of them (or the highest number that divides into both exactly).

Example 9

Find the highest common factor of 60 and 48.

Write each number in prime factor form and pick out the common factors:

$60 = 2 \times 2 \times 3 \times 5$
$48 = 2 \times 2 \times 2 \times 2 \times 3$

The common factors are 2, 2 and 3. To find the HCF we multiply these together: $2 \times 2 \times 3 = 12$.

The HCF of 48 and 60 is 12.

12 is the highest number that divides into 48 and 60 exactly.

Finding the lowest common multiple (LCM)

The **lowest common multiple** or LCM is also exactly what it says.

> The **LCM** of two numbers is the lowest multiple that is common to both of them (or the lowest number that is a multiple of them both).

Example 10

Find the lowest common multiple of 4 and 5.

The multiples of 4 are: 4 8 12 16 20 24 28 ...
The multiples of 5 are: 5 10 15 20 25 30 ...

The lowest number that is in both lists is 20.
The LCM of 4 and 5 is 20.
20 is the lowest number that 4 and 5 both divide into.

Exercise 2L

1 Find the highest common factor of
(a) 4 and 8   (b) 9 and 12   (c) 18 and 24
(d) 18 and 30   (e) 21 and 35

2 Find the lowest common multiple of
(a) 3 and 4   (b) 4 and 6
(c) 7 and 14   (d) 6 and 15

3 Find the lowest common multiple of
(a) 12 and 15   (b) 36 and 16   (c) 50 and 85

4 Find the HCF and LCM of
(a) 12 and 18   (b) 120 and 180   (c) 24 and 84
(d) 91 and 130   (e) 72 and 96   (f) 40 and 60

Mixed exercise 2

1 Write these numbers in order of size.

   5 −6 −10 2 −4

Start with the smallest number.   [E]

2 Using only the numbers in the cloud, write down
(a) all the multiples of 6
(b) all the square numbers
(c) all the factors of 12
(d) all the cube numbers.   [E]

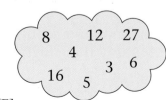

3   Here is a map of the British Isles.
    The temperatures in some places,
    one night last winter are shown
    on the map.

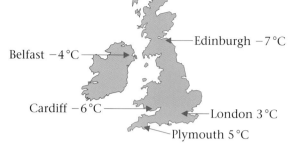

Belfast −4 °C

Edinburgh −7 °C

Cardiff −6 °C

London 3 °C

Plymouth 5 °C

    (a) Write down the names of the
         two places that had the biggest
         difference in temperature.
    (b) Two pairs of places have a
         difference in temperature of 2 °C
         Write down the names of these places.   [E]

4   Sally wrote down the temperature at different
    times on 1st January 2003.

Time	Temperature
Midnight	−6 °C
4 am	−10 °C
8 am	−4 °C
Noon	7 °C
3 pm	6 °C
7 pm	−2 °C

    (a) Write down
         (i)   the **highest** temperature
         (ii) the **lowest** temperature.
    (b) Work out the difference in the temperature
         between
         (i)   4 am and 8 am   (ii) 3 pm and 7 pm
    At 11 pm that day the temperature had fallen
    5 °C from its value at 7 pm.
    (c) Work out the temperature at 11 pm.   [E]

5   (a) Express 108 as the product of powers of its prime
         factors.
    (b) Find the highest common factor (HCF) of 108 and
         24.   [E]

6   (a) Express the following numbers as products of their
         prime factors.
         (i)   60   (ii) 96
    (b) Find the highest common factor of 60 and 96.
    (c) Work out the lowest common multiple of 60
         and 96.   [E]

7   4, 5, 8, 9, 12, 14, 16, 20, 27, 35, 36, 37
    From the numbers in the list write down
    (a) the odd numbers   (b) the multiples of 3
    (c) the factors of 48   (d) the prime numbers
    (e) the square numbers   (f) the cube numbers.

8   Work out
    (a) $4 + {}^-2$ (b) $3 + {}^-5$ (c) $3 + {}^-3$ (d) ${}^-2 + 3$
    (e) ${}^-2 + {}^-3$ (f) ${}^-6 + 4$ (g) ${}^-6 + {}^-4$ (h) ${}^-5 + 5$
    (i) $3 - 4$ (j) $3 - {}^-4$ (k) $5 - 2$ (l) $5 - {}^-2$
    (m) ${}^-4 - 5$ (n) ${}^-3 - {}^-5$ (o) ${}^-7 - 6$ (p) ${}^-8 - {}^-4$

9 Calculate
- (a) 4×-2
- (b) -3×-2
- (c) -5×6
- (d) -6×-2
- (e) $12 \div -3$
- (f) $-18 \div -3$
- (g) $-24 \div 6$
- (h) $-45 \div -9$
- (i) $\dfrac{6}{-2}$
- (j) $\dfrac{-6}{-2}$
- (k) $\dfrac{-16}{2}$
- (l) $\dfrac{-14}{-2}$

Summary of key points

1 You can use **negative numbers** to describe quantities such as temperatures less than 0 °C. You can also use negative numbers in calculations: $^-2 + {}^-4 = {}^-6$

2 Rules for negative numbers.

Adding/Subtracting	Multiplying/dividing
$+ \ + = +$	$+ \ + = +$
$- \ - = +$	$- \ - = +$
$+ \ - = -$	$+ \ - = -$
$- \ + = -$	$- \ + = -$

3 **Even** numbers are whole numbers which divide exactly by 2. 2, 4, 6, 18, 24 are even numbers.

4 Odd numbers are whole numbers which do not divide exactly by 2. 1, 9, 15, 23, 27 are odd numbers.

5 The **factors** of a number are whole numbers that divide exactly into the number. The factors include 1 and the number itself. For example, the factors of 12 are 1, 2, 3, 4, 6 and 12.

6 **Multiples** of a number are the results of multiplying the number by a positive whole number. For example, some multiples of 3 are 3, 6, 9, 12, 15, 18, 21, 24.

7 A **prime** number is a whole number greater than 1 which has only two factors: itself and 1. The first ten prime numbers are 2, 3, 5, 7, 11, 13, 17, 19, 23, 29. 1 is not a prime number as it can only be divided by **one** number (itself).

8 A **prime factor** is a factor that is a prime number. For example, the prime factors of 18 are 2 and 3.

9 A **square number** is the result of multiplying a whole number by itself. The first six square numbers are 1, 4, 9, 16, 25, 36.

10 A **cube number** is the result of multiplying a whole number by itself then multiplying by the number again. The first six cube numbers are 1, 8, 27, 64, 125, 216.

11 To find the **square** of any number, multiply the number by itself.

12 Finding a **square root** of a number is the opposite (inverse) of squaring:
$$\sqrt{64} = \pm 8$$

13   To find the **cube** of any number, multiply the number by itself then multiply by the number again.

14   Finding the **cube root** is the opposite (inverse) of finding the cube:

$$\sqrt[3]{125} = 5$$

15   Writing a number as the product of its prime factors is called writing it in **prime factor form**. For example, $60 = 2^2 \times 3 \times 5$

16   The **highest common factor** (HCF) of two numbers is the highest factor that is common to both of them.

17   The **lowest common multiple** (LCM) of two numbers is the lowest multiple that is common to both of them (or the lowest number that is a multiple of them both).

③ Essential algebra

3.1 Using letters to represent numbers

Algebra is the branch of mathematics in which letters are used to represent numbers.

This can help solve some mathematical problems.

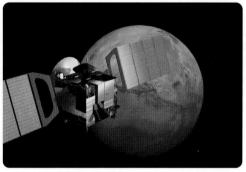

If you know how fast a cyclist is travelling you can use algebra to work out how far he will get in a given time:

$$d = v \times t$$

(distance = velocity × time)

Very complicated algebra is used to calculate the right orbit for spacecraft.

You can use letters even when you do not know the number itself.

Example 1

Jas has some CDs. If he buys 3 more CDs, how many will he have altogether?

You do not know how many CDs Jas starts with, but you can use algebra to say:

> Jas starts with x CDs
> x CDs and 3 CDs is $x + 3$ CDs

Example 2

Ann wins some cinema tickets. She gives 6 to friends. How many tickets has she got left?

You do not know how many tickets she had to start with, but you can say she had y. After giving away 6 tickets she has $y - 6$ tickets left.

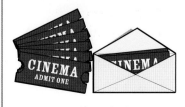

Example 3

Yasmin has some sweets. So has Ali.
How many sweets do they have altogether?

Use two different letters: x for Yasmin's sweets and y for Ali's.

Altogether they have $x + y$ sweets.

y sweets

x sweets

Exercise 3A

Use algebra to write:

1 3 more than a **2** x with 4 added

3 x more than 7   **4** 2 less than b

5 c with 3 taken away   **6** p less than q

7 x more than y **8** 4 together with a

9 $3b$ with 6 subtracted

10 Paul has d DVDs. He buys 3 more.
How many DVDs has Paul got now?

11 Rob has a apples. He eats 2 apples.
How many apples has Rob got now?

12 Tom has £x. He spends £5.
How much money has Tom got now?

3.2 Adding with letters

In algebra you can add letters that are the same. For example:

$a + a$ can be written as $2a$
$a + a + a$ can be written as $3a$

> a means $1a$
> so $1a + 1a = 2a$

Exercise 3B

Write these in a shorter form. The first one is done for you.

1 $a + a + a + a + a + a = 6a$

2 $p + p + p + p$

3 $b + b + b + b + b$

4 $q + q + q + q + q + q$

5 $c + c$

6 $n + n + n$

7 $w + w + w + w + w$

8 $y + y + y + y + y$

9 $z + z + z + z + z + z + z$

10 $a + a + a + a + a + a + a$

11 $b + b + b + b + b$

12 $p + p + p + p + p + p + p + p$

Write these out in a longer form. The first one is done for you.

13 $4a = a + a + a + a$ **14** $2p$

15 $5p$ **16** $7a$ **17** $2y$ **18** $4q$ **19** $3c$

20 $5d$ **21** $10a$ **22** $5h$ **23** $6g$ **24** $4z$

3.3 Expressions and terms

An **algebraic expression** is a collection of letters, symbols and numbers:

$a + 3b - 2c$ is an algebraic expression

These are each called **terms**.

Terms which use the same letter or arrangement of letters are called **like terms**:

a and $3a$ are like terms

$2g$ and $8g$ are like terms

Sometimes you can make algebraic expressions simpler by adding or subtracting like terms:

You can combine **like terms** by adding them:

$2a + 3a = 5a$

$3b + 4b + b = 8b$

You can combine **like terms** by subtracting them:

$5a - 3a = 2a$

$7a - a = 6a$ ←

Remember:
this is $7a - 1a$

Exercise 3C

Make these expressions simpler by adding or subtracting like terms.

1 $2a + 4a$ **2** $3b + 4b$ **3** $5c + 2c$

4 $5d - 3d$ **5** $7e - 3e$ **6** $5f - f$

7 $3a + 2a + 2a$ **8** $2a + 5a + a$ **9** $5c + 3c + 4c$

10 $6g + 7g + g$ **11** $7g - 3g$ **12** $9s - 6s$

13 $15q - q$ **14** $3p + 7p + 8p$ **15** $12p - 6p$

3.4 Collecting like terms

Sometimes algebraic expressions have more than one term and you can simplify them by collecting like terms together.

___ Example 4 _____

Simplify $2a - 4b + 3a + 5b$

Collect the a terms and the b terms:

$2a - 4b + 3a + 5b$ •

$2a + 3a - 4b + 5b$

Combine the a terms and the b terms:

$5a + b$

> Remember:
> The $+$ or $-$ sign is part of each term.
> The minus sign is part of the term $-4b$.

___ Example 5 _____

Simplify the following expressions completely.

(a) $3a + 5b + 3b + a$ (b) $5p + 3q - 2p + q$

(c) $5a + 7 - 3a - 4$

(a) $3a + 5b + 3b + a = 4a + 8b$

(b) $5p + 3q - 2p + q = 3p + 4q$

(c) $5a + 7 - 3a - 4 = 2a + 3$

You can simplify algebraic expressions by **collecting like terms** together.

Exercise 3D

Simplify these expressions completely by collecting like terms.

1   $3a + 4b + 4a + 2b$ 2 $6m + 5n + 3m + 2n$

3   $2p + 3q - p + 2q$ 4 $8e + 6c + 8e$

5   $5y + 7p - 3y + 5p$ 6 $2a + 8g + 3a + 5g - a$

7   $4k + 3q + 5k - 2q$ 8 $9d + 7f - 8d + 3f$

9   $5h + 8 - 2h + 2$ 10 $3f + 2f + 4e - 2e$

11 $7g + 8n - 3g - n$ 12 $5 + g + 2 + 3g - 3 - 2g$

13 $2a + 3a + 4a + 5a$ 14 $3b + b + 5b - 4b$

15 $7c + 8c - 5c - 6c$ 16 $5d + 4d - 3d + 6d - 7d$

17 $2a + 7b + 5a - 6b$ 18 $2c + 4b + 6c - 3b + 7b - 2c$

19 $3p + 2p - 4p + 3 - 2$ 20 $7y + 4z + 2y - 3z + 5y + 3z$

21 $12a - 7a + 9a - 2a + 5a$ 22 $3p + 4p + 5p - 8p - 4p$

23 $6s + 4s - 3s + 5s - 5s$ 24 $3a + 2 + 5a - 1 - 7a - 1$

3.5 Multiplying with letters and numbers

Remember: $2a$ is $a + a$ and $3a$ is $a + a + a$. But:

> $2a$ also means   2 lots of a or 2 multiplied by a or $2 \times a$
> $3a$ means   3 lots of a or 3 multiplied by a or $3 \times a$

In algebra, when you want to multiply two items you just write them next to each other, like this:

> $2 \times a$ is written $2a$ $c \times d$ is written cd
> $a \times b$ is written ab $3 \times e \times f$ is written $3ef$

> Don't forget that $12ab$ is $12 \times a \times b$ not $1 \times 2 \times a \times b$!

Exercise 3E

Use multiplication signs to write these expressions out in a longer form. The first one is done for you.

1   $pq = p \times q$ 2 rst 3 $2ef$

4   $5abc$ 5 $7klm$ 6 $9ab$

7   $15abc$ 8 $3pqrs$ 9 $16st$

10 $6yz$ 11 $8defg$ 12 $20abcd$

Write these expressions in a simpler form. The first one is done for you.

13 $p \times q = pq$ **14** $e \times f \times g$ **15** $r \times s \times t$

16 $2 \times e \times f$ **17** $2 \times c \times d$ **18** $h \times d \times s$

19 $2 \times s \times f$ **20** $3 \times d \times e \times f$ **21** $4 \times p \times q$

22 $3 \times h \times j$ **23** $5 \times k \times v$ **24** $12 \times r \times s \times t$

3.6 Multiplying algebraic expressions

Sometimes you can simplify an algebraic expression, such as $2a \times 3b$, by multiplying the terms by each other:

Multiply the numbers.

$$2a \times 3b = 2 \times a \times 3 \times b$$

Multiply the letters.

$$= 6 \times ab$$
$$= 6ab$$

___ **Example 6** _____

Simplify (a) $5a \times 4b$ (b) $3p \times 4q$

(a) $5a \times 4b$ so $5 \times 4 = 20$
         $a \times b = ab$ and $20 \times ab = 20ab$

(b) $3p \times 4q$ so $3 \times 4 = 12$
         $p \times q = pq$ and $12 \times pq = 12pq$

Exercise 3F

Simplify these expressions by multiplying the terms by each other. The first one is done for you.

1 $2a \times 4b = 8ab$ **2** $3c \times 5d$

3 $3p \times 4q$ **4** $5s \times 4t$

5 $6f \times 5g$ **6** $7p \times 4q$

7 $9m \times 4n$ **8** $3a \times 4b \times 2c$

9 $3r \times 4s \times 2t$ **10** $5p \times 4q$

11 $2a \times 6b$ **12** $5p \times 4q \times 2r$

13 $3t \times 4s$ **14** $4p \times 7t$

15 $9e \times 5c$ **16** $8g \times 4q \times 2r$

17 $4d \times 12r$ **18** $12s \times 5t$

19 $5y \times 6t$ **20** $2s \times 4t \times 5r$

3.7 Dividing algebraic expressions

You will sometimes need to divide algebraic expressions. To do this you will need to divide the numbers, and cancel the letters if possible.

Example 7

Simplify (a) $12a \div 4$ (b) $\dfrac{20ab}{5b}$

(a) $12a \div 4$ or $\dfrac{12a}{4}$ so $12 \div 4 = 3$ and $3 \times a = 3a$

(b) $\dfrac{20ab}{5b}$ or $20ab \div 5b$ so $20 \div 5 = 4$

$ab \div b = a$ and $4 \times a = 4a$

$\dfrac{{}^{4}\cancel{20}a\cancel{b}}{\cancel{5}\cancel{b}}$

Exercise 3G

Simplify these expressions by dividing them by each other. The first one is done for you.

1 $12pq \div 3q = 4p$ 2 $3p \div 3$

3 $5a \div a$ 4 $12n \div 3$

5 $4e \div 2$ 6 $15s \div s$

7 $24b \div 6$ 8 $14ab \div 2b$

9 $18st \div 3t$ 10 $\dfrac{30xy}{5x}$

11 $\dfrac{30pq}{pq}$ 12 $\dfrac{12abc}{3c}$

13 $\dfrac{18ac}{6a}$ 14 $\dfrac{30xy}{2y}$

15 $\dfrac{36pq}{6}$

3.8 Calculating powers

There is a short way of writing repeated multiplication by the same number.

	How you write it:	How you say it:	
3×3	3^2	3 to the power 2	usually called 3 squared
$3 \times 3 \times 3$	3^3	3 to the power 3	usually called 3 cubed
$3 \times 3 \times 3 \times 3$	3^4	3 to the power 4	often called 3 to the fourth

Example 8

Work out (a) 3^2 (b) 5^3 (c) 2^6

(a) $3^2 = 3 \times 3 = 9$

(b) $5^3 = 5 \times 5 \times 5 = 125$

(c) $2^6 = 2 \times 2 \times 2 \times 2 \times 2 \times 2 = 64$

Use the power button on your calculator to work out numbers raised to a power.

Example 9

Work out (a) $3^3 \times 4^2$ (b) $\dfrac{8^3}{2^3}$ (c) $5^2 + 3^3$

(a) $3^3 \times 4^2 = 27 \times 16 = 432$

(b) $\dfrac{8^3}{2^3} = \dfrac{512}{8} = 64$

(c) $5^2 + 3^3 = 25 + 27 = 52$

A power is also known as an index. The plural of index is indices.

Example 10

Find the value of x.

(a) $8^x = 64$ (b) $3^x = 81$

(a) $8 \times 8 = 64$ so $8^2 = 64$ and $x = 2$

(b) $3 \times 3 \times 3 \times 3 = 81$ so $3^4 = 81$ and $x = 4$

Exercise 3H

1 Find the values of these powers:

(a) 3^2 (b) 2^3 (c) 1^4 (d) 5^4

(e) 2^5 (f) 4^3 (g) 2^4 (h) 2^7

(i) 6^3 (j) 5^3 (k) 5^2 (l) 10^5

For example:
$6^2 = 6 \times 6 = 36$

Work out the values of the powers in questions **2–4**.

2 (a) 3^6 (b) 5^5 (c) 0^2 (d) 9^4

3 (a) 4^2 (b) 10^3 (c) 9^5 (d) $4^3 + 3^2$

4 (a) 12^3 (b) 3^4 (c) 14^2 (d) $8^4 \div 2^3$

Find the value of x in questions **5–8**.

5 (a) $3^x = 27$ (b) $2^x = 8$ (c) $10^x = 100\,000$

6 (a) $6^x = 1296$ (b) $5^x = 125$ (c) $4^x = 256$

7 (a) $13^x = 169$ (b) $4^x = 4096$ (c) $11^x = 1331$

8 (a) $2^x = 1024$ (b) $9^x = 729$ (c) $15^x = 225$

There are 2^6 small squares on a chessboard.

3.9 Multiplying and dividing powers of the same number

Sometimes you need to write the product of two or more powers of a number as a single power of the same number.

$$2^2 \times 2^3 = (2 \times 2) \times (2 \times 2 \times 2) = 2^5$$
$$3^3 \times 3^4 = (3 \times 3 \times 3) \times (3 \times 3 \times 3 \times 3) = 3^7$$

> Notice that:
> $2^2 \times 2^3 = 2^{2+3} = 2^5$
> $3^3 \times 3^4 = 3^{3+4} = 3^7$

To **multiply** powers of the same number, add the indices:
$$3^3 \times 3^4 = 3^{3+4} = 3^7$$

You can use a similar method when you divide one power of a number by another power of the same number.

$$5^6 \div 5^2 = \frac{5 \times 5 \times 5 \times 5 \times 5 \times 5}{5 \times 5} = 5 \times 5 \times 5 \times 5 = 5^4$$

$$4^5 \div 4^2 = \frac{4 \times 4 \times 4 \times 4 \times 4}{4} = 4 \times 4 \times 4 = 4^3$$

> Notice that:
> $5^6 \div 5^2 = 5^{6-2} = 5^4$
> $4^5 \div 4^2 = 4^{5-2} = 4^3$

To **divide** powers of the same number, subtract the indices:
$$4^5 \div 4^2 = 4^{5-2} = 4^3$$

Example 11

Write these expressions as a single power of the number.
(a) $3^2 \times 3^3$ (b) $5^3 \times 5$
(c) $3^4 \times 3^2 \times 3^6$ (d) $7^5 \div 7^4$

(a) $3^2 \times 3^3 = 3^{2+3} = 3^5$
(b) $5^3 \times 5 = 5^{3+1} = 5^4$
(c) $3^4 \times 3^2 \times 3^6 = 3^{4+2+6} = 3^{12}$
(d) $7^5 \div 7^4 = 7^{5-4} = 7^1$

Raising a number to the power 1

Notice that $\frac{3^3}{3^2} = \frac{3 \times 3 \times 3}{3 \times 3} = 3$ and $\frac{3^3}{3^2} = 3^{3-2} = 3^1$

So $3^1 = 3$.

Any number raised to the **power 1** is equal to the number itself:
$$3^1 = 3$$

Raising a number to the power 0

Notice too that $\dfrac{3^2}{3^2} = 1$　and　$\dfrac{3^2}{3^2} = 3^{2-2} = 3^0$　So $3^0 = 1$.

Any non-zero number, raised to the **power 0** is equal to 1:
$3^0 = 1$

Raising the power of a number to a further power

$(10^2)^3 = 10^2 \times 10^2 \times 10^2$
$= (10 \times 10) \times (10 \times 10) \times (10 \times 10) = 10^6$

To raise a power of a number to a **further power**, multiply the indices: $(10^2)^3 = 10^{2 \times 3} = 10^6$

Exercise 3I

Simplify these expressions by writing as a single power of the number.

1　(a)　$6^8 \times 6^3$　　　(b)　$8^3 \times 8^5$　　　(c)　$2^4 \times 2^2$

2　(a)　$4^3 \div 4^2$　　　(b)　$6^6 \div 6^3$　　　(c)　$7^5 \div 7$

3　(a)　$4^2 \times 4^3$　　　(b)　$5^3 \div 5$　　　(c)　$3^9 \div 3^8$

4　(a)　$5^6 \times 5^4 \times 5^3$　　　(b)　$2^3 \times 2^7 \times 2$

5　(a)　$10^2 \times 10^2 \times 10$　　　(b)　$9^4 \div 9^4$

6　(a)　$6^3 \times 6^7 \times 6$　　　(b)　$5^2 \times 5^2 \times 5^2$

7　(a)　$3^5 \times 3 \times 3^2$　　　(b)　$\dfrac{4^7 \times 4^5}{4^6}$

8　(a)　$\dfrac{6^8}{6^2 \times 6^3}$　　　(b)　$\dfrac{5^8 \times 5^4}{5^7}$　　　(c)　$\dfrac{4^9}{4^2 \times 4^5}$

9　(a)　$(5^2)^3$　　　(b)　$(7^4)^2$

10　Write in standard form
　(a)　8963　　　(b)　493　　　(c)　30298

Standard form on a calculator

When the answer to a calculation is very large or very small, the calculator may display the answer in standard form.

2.1⁰⁶	2.1E06

These both mean
2.1×10^6
$= 2.1 \times 1\,000\,000$
$= 2\,100\,000$

Make sure you know how to enter numbers in standard form into a calculator.

Writing in standard form

Make sure you know how to write a number in standard form.

$5278 = 5.278 \times 10^3$

3.10　Using powers to multiply letters

When you want to multiply together two letters that are the same, you can write them as powers:

	How you write it:	How you say it:	
$a \times a$	a^2	a to the power 2	usually called a squared
$a \times a \times a$	a^3	a to the power 3	usually called a cubed
$a \times a \times a \times a$	a^4	a to the power 4	often called a to the fourth
$a \times a \times a \times a \times a$	a^5	a to the power 5	often called a to the fifth

Exercise 3J

1 Write these expressions in a simpler way using powers.

(a) $b \times b \times b$

(b) $p \times p$

(c) $r \times r \times r \times r \times r \times r \times r$

(d) $s \times s \times s \times s \times s$

(e) $q \times q \times q \times q$

(f) $c \times c \times c \times c \times c$

> For example: $d \times d = d^2$

2 Simplify these expressions using powers.

(a) $a \times a \times a \times a$

(b) $s \times s \times s$

(c) $t \times t \times t \times t \times t \times t$

(d) $v \times v \times v$

(e) $f \times f \times f \times f \times f$

(f) $y \times y \times y \times y \times y$

3 Write out these expressions in full.

(a) a^3 (b) a^4 (c) d^2 (d) e^5

(e) f^4 (f) p^5 (g) a^7 (h) s^2

(i) k^6 (j) n^3 (k) n^7 (l) a^{12}

> For example: $c^2 = c \times c$

4 Write these in a simpler form.

(a) a to the power 5

(b) b to the power 6

(c) c squared

(d) d cubed

(e) e to the power 7

3.11 Using powers to simplify

Section 3.9 showed how to multiply and divide with powers of numbers. You can use similar ideas in algebra.

$$x^4 \times x^3 = (x \times x \times x \times x) \times (x \times x \times x) = x^7$$

> Notice that:
> $x^4 \times x^3 = x^{4+3} = x^7$

To **multiply** powers of the same letter add the indices:
$$x^a \times x^b = x^{a+b}$$

$$x^6 \div x^2 = \frac{x \times x \times x \times x \times x \times x}{x \times x} = x \times x \times x \times x = x^4$$

> Notice that:
> $x^6 \div x^2 = x^{6-2} = x^4$

To **divide** powers of the same letter subtract the indices.
$$x^a \div x^b = x^{a-b}$$

Sometimes you will be asked to simplify an expression containing different powers of the same letter multiplied or divided.

> To **simplify** an expression containing different powers of the same letter multiplied or divided, write the expression as a single power of the letter.

Example 12

Simplify (a) $x^8 \times x^3$ (b) $x^{16} \div x^2$ (c) $x^4 \times x^3 \times x^5$

(a) $x^8 \times x^3 = x^{8+3} = x^{11}$

(b) $x^{16} \div x^2 = x^{16-2} = x^{14}$

(c) $x^4 \times x^3 \times x^5 = x^{4+3+5} = x^{12}$

Example 13

Simplify (a) $3y^2 \times 4y^3$ (b) $12y^8 \div 4y^3$

(a) $3y^2 \times 4y^3 = 3 \times 4 \times y^2 \times y^3 = 12 \times y^{2+3} = 12y^5$

(b) $12y^8 \div 4y^3 = \dfrac{12y^8}{4y^3} = \dfrac{12}{4} \times \dfrac{y^8}{y^3} = 3 \times y^{8-3} = 3y^5$

Exercise 3K

Simplify these expressions.

1 (a) $x^8 \times x^2$ (b) $y^3 \times y^8$ (c) $w^9 \times w^5$

2 (a) $a^5 \times a^3$ (b) $b^3 \times b^3$ (c) $d^7 \times d^4$

3 (a) $p^5 \div p^2$ (b) $q^{12} \div q^2$ (c) $t^8 \div t^4$

4 (a) $j^9 \div j^3$ (b) $k^5 \div k^4$ (c) $n^{25} \div n^{23}$

5 (a) $x^5 \times x^2 \times x^2$ (b) $y^2 \times y^4 \times y^3$ (c) $z^3 \times z^5 \times z^2$

6 (a) $3x^2 \times 2x^3$ (b) $5y^9 \times 3y^{20}$ (c) $6z^8 \times 4z^2$

7 (a) $12p^8 \div 4p^3$ (b) $15q^5 \div 3q^3$ (c) $6r^5 \div 3r^2$

Raising a letter to the power 1 or 0

Notice that $\dfrac{x^3}{x^2} = \dfrac{x \times x \times x}{x \times x} = x$ and $\dfrac{x^3}{x^2} = x^{3-2} = x^1$

Any letter raised to the **power 1** is equal to the letter itself:
$x^1 = x$

Notice too that $\dfrac{y^2}{y^2} = 1$ and $\dfrac{y^2}{y^2} = y^{2-2} = y^0$

Any letter raised to the **power 0** is equal to 1:
$y^0 = 1$

Raising a power to a further power

$$(x^2)^3 = x^2 \times x^2 \times x^2$$
$$= (x \times x) \times (x \times x) \times (x \times x) = x^6$$

To raise a power of a letter to a **further power**, multiply the indices:

$$(x^a)^b = x^{ab}$$

___ **Example 14** ___

Simplify: (a) $(x^4)^5$ (b) $(3y^5)^3$

(a) $(x^4)^5 = x^{4\times5} = x^{20}$

(b) $(3y^5)^3 = 3^3 \times (y^5)^3 = 27 \times y^{5\times3} = 27y^{15}$

Exercise 3L

Simplify these expressions.

1 (a) $(d^3)^4$ (b) $(e^5)^2$ (c) $(f^3)^3$ (d) $(g^7)^9$

2 (a) $(g^6)^4$ (b) $(h^2)^2$ (c) $(k^4)^0$ (d) $(m^0)^{56}$

3 (a) $(3d^2)^7$ (b) $(4e)^3$ (c) $(3f^{129})^0$

4 (a) $\dfrac{a^4 \times a^5}{a^9}$ (b) $\dfrac{b^7 \times b}{b^4}$ (c) $\dfrac{c^3 \times c^4}{c^2 \times c^5}$

5 (a) $4d^9 \times 2d$ (b) $8e^8 \div 4e^4$ (c) $(4f^2)^2$

3.12 Putting in the punctuation

In maths, brackets help show the order in which you should carry out the operations $\div$, $\times$, $+$ and $-$. For example:

$$2 + (3 \times 4) = 2 + 12 = 14 \quad \text{and} \quad (2 + 3) \times 4 = 5 \times 4 = 20$$

So $2 + (3 \times 4)$ is different from $(2 + 3) \times 4$ even though they both use the same numbers and the $+$ and $\times$ symbols in the same order.

Always deal with the operations in brackets first.
Then $\div$ and $\times$. Then $+$ and $-$.

BIDMAS is a made-up word to help you remember the order of operations:

BIDMAS

| Brackets | Indices | Divide | Multiply | Add | Subtract |

When the operations are the same, you do them in the order they appear.

Example 15

Work out (a) $(3 \times 2) - 1$ (b) $3 \times (2 - 1)$

(a) $(3 \times 2) - 1 = 6 - 1 = 5$
(b) $3 \times (2 - 1) = 3 \times 1 = 3$

> Work out the Brackets first.

Example 16

Work out (a) $3 + 2 \times 5 - 1$ (b) $24 \div 4 \div 2$

(a) $3 + 2 \times 5 - 1$

$= 3 + 10 - 1$

$= 13 - 1$
$= 12$

(b) $24 \div 4 \div 2$
$= 6 \div 2$
$= 3$

> There is no Bracket or Divide, so start with Multiply, then Add, then Subtract.

> Operations are the same so do them in the order they appear.

Example 17

Work out (a) $(2 + 3)^2$ (b) $2^2 + 3^2$

(a) $(2 + 3)^2 = 5^2 = 25$
(b) $2^2 + 3^2 = 4 + 9 = 13$

Notice that the answers are different: $(2 + 3)^2$ is not the same as $2^2 + 3^2$.

> Brackets first, then Indices.

> Indices first, then Add.

Exercise 3M

1   Use BIDMAS to help you find the value of these expressions:

(a) $5 + (3 + 1)$
(b) $5 - (3 + 1)$
(c) $5 \times (2 + 3)$
(d) $5 \times 2 + 3$
(e) $3 \times (4 + 3)$
(f) $3 \times 4 + 3$
(g) $20 \div 4 + 1$
(h) $20 \div (4 + 1)$
(i) $6 + 4 \div 2$
(j) $(6 + 4) \div 2$
(k) $24 \div (6 - 2)$
(l) $24 \div 6 - 2$
(m) $7 - (4 + 2)$
(n) $7 - 4 + 2$
(o) $((15 - 5) \times 4) \div ((2 + 3) \times 2)$

> $9 + 2 \times 5 = 19$, not 55. Can you explain why?

2   Make these expressions correct by replacing the • with
+ or − or × or ÷ and using brackets if you need to.
The first one is done for you.

(a)   4 • 5 = 9 becomes 4 + 5 = 9   (b)   4 • 5 = 20
(c)   2 • 3 • 4 = 20   (d)   3 • 2 • 5 = 5
(e)   5 • 2 • 3 = 9   (f)   4 • 2 • 8 = 10
(g)   5 • 4 • 5 • 2 = 27   (h)   5 • 4 • 5 • 2 = 23

3   Work out

(a) $(3 + 4)^2$ (b) $3^2 + 4^2$ (c) $3 \times (4 + 5)^2$
(d) $3 \times 4^2 + 3 \times 5^2$ (e) $2 \times (4 + 2)^2$ (f) $2^3 + 3^2$
(g) $2 \times (3^2 + 2)$ (h) $\dfrac{(2 + 5)^2}{3^2 - 2}$ (i) $\dfrac{5^2 - 2^2}{3}$
(j) $4^2 - 2^4$ (k) $2^5 - 5^2$ (l) $4^3 - 8^2$

3.13   Using brackets in algebra

Brackets are often used in algebra. For example:

$2 \times (a + b)$ means   add a to b *before* multiplying by 2

Usually this is written: $2(a + b)$, without the × . This avoids
confusion with the letter x which is used a lot in algebra.

$2(a + b)$ means $2 \times a + 2 \times b = 2a + 2b$

Working this out is called **expanding the brackets**. Actually
the brackets disappear!

Example 18

Expand the brackets in these expressions:

(a) $3(b + c)$ (b) $3(2a - b)$

(a) $3(b + c) = 3 \times b + 3 \times c = 3b + 3c$
(b) $3(2a - b) = 3 \times 2a + 3 \times -b = 6a - 3b$

Expanding the brackets means multiplying to remove the
brackets.

Exercise 3N

Expand the brackets in these expressions.

1 $2(p + q)$ **2** $3(c + d)$ **3** $5(y - n)$
4 $3(t + u)$ **5** $7(2p + q)$ **6** $2(3a - 2b)$
7 $4(2a + b)$ **8** $3(a - 2b)$ **9** $3(4r - 5s)$
10 $10(a - 7b)$ **11** $4(6s + 4t)$ **12** $5(6p + 4q - 2r)$
13 $12(3a + 4b)$ **14** $7(4s - 5t)$ **15** $3(5a - 4b + 2c)$

Adding expressions with brackets

You can simplify an expression by first expanding the brackets and then collecting like terms.

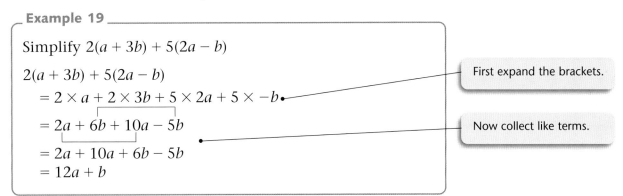

Example 19

Simplify $2(a + 3b) + 5(2a - b)$

$2(a + 3b) + 5(2a - b)$

$= 2 \times a + 2 \times 3b + 5 \times 2a + 5 \times -b$

$= 2a + 6b + 10a - 5b$

$= 2a + 10a + 6b - 5b$

$= 12a + b$

First expand the brackets.

Now collect like terms.

Exercise 30

Expand the brackets in these expressions and then collect like terms.

Remember:
$4a$ means $a + a + a + a$
and $4 \times a$
$3ab$ means $3 \times a \times b$
$3(c + d)$ means $3c + 3d$

1   $2(a + b) + 3(a + b)$

2   $3(a - 2b) + 4(2a + 3b)$

3   $5(2a - b) + 4(2a + b)$

4   $3(p + q) + 4(p + q)$

5   $4(5a + c) + 2(3a - c)$

6   $3(p + 2q) + 3(5p - 2q)$

7   $5(4t - 3s) + 8(3t + 2s)$

8   $7(2d + 3e) + 6(2e - 2d)$

9   $5(3z + b) + 4(b - 2z)$

10   $2(a + b + 2c) + 3(2a + 3b - c)$

11   $3(4a - 2b) + 5(a + b)$

12   $6(p + 2q + 3r) + 2(3p - 4q - 9r)$

13   $4(3a + 5b) + 5(2a - 4b)$

14   $5(5g + 4h) + 4(h - 5g)$

15   $2(a + 2b - 3c) + 3(5a - b + 4c) + 4(a + b + c)$

Subtracting expressions with brackets

Example 20

Expand the brackets in the expression $15 - (6 + 2)$

The minus sign belongs with the term in brackets.

$15 - (6 + 2)$ means $15 + -1 \times (6 + 2)$

$= 15 \quad - 6 \quad\quad - 2$

$= 7$

Remember:
When you multiply:
like signs give $+$
$2 \times 3 = 6$
$-2 \times -3 = 6$
unlike signs give $-$
$2 \times -3 = -6$
$-2 \times 3 = -6$

Example 21

Expand   (a) $-(a + b)$ (b) $-(a - b)$

(a) $-(a + b)$ means $-1 \times (a + b) = -a - b$

(b) $-(a - b)$ means $-1 \times (a - b) = -a + b$

> $-1 \times +b = -b$

> $-1 \times -b = +b$

Exercise 3P

1 Work out
  (a) $10 - (3 + 2)$ (b) $20 - (5 - 2)$ (c) $12 - (6 - 4)$
  (d) $10 - (3 + 4)$ (e) $12 - (5 + 3)$ (f) $6 - (7 - 5)$
  (g) $14 - (8 + 6)$ (h) $15 - (3 - 2)$

2 Expand the bracket in these expressions.
  (a) $-(p + q)$ (b) $-(p - q)$ (c) $-(a + b + c)$
  (d) $-(a + b - c)$ (e) $-(r + s)$ (f) $-(r - s)$
  (g) $-(p + q - r)$ (h) $-(p - q + r)$

Example 22

Write $3a + 2b - (a + b)$ as simply as possible.

$3a + 2b - (a + b) = 3a + 2b - a - b$
$ = 2a + b$

Exercise 3Q

Write these expressions as simply as possible.

1 $4a + 3b - (a + b)$ **2** $5p + 2q - (p + q)$

3 $3(2a + 4) - (3a + 5)$ **4** $2y - 3z - (y + z)$

5 $3(3r + 4s) - 2(r + s)$ **6** $3(2a + 5) - 2(3a + 4)$

7 $5(2s + 3t) - 4(s + 2t)$ **8** $4(3a + b) - 3(2a + 5b)$

9 $2(m + 3n) - (2m + n)$ **10** $5(8h - 3k) - 4(7h + 2k)$

11 $3(c + 2d) - 2(c + 3d)$ **12** $4a - (3a + 5b)$

Example 23

> Watch out for the $-$ sign inside the bracket.

Write $3a + 2b - 2(a - b)$ as simply as possible.

Multiplying gives $-2 \times -b = +2b$

$3a + 2b - 2(a - b) = 3a + 2b - 2a + 2b$
$ = a + 4b$

Exercise 3R

Simplify these expressions. They *all* have − signs inside brackets.

1 $4a + 3b − (a − b)$ 2 $5p + 2q − (p − q)$

3 $3(2a + 4) − (3a − 5)$ 4 $2y − 3z − (y − z)$

5 $3(3r + 4s) − 2(r − s)$ 6 $3(2a + 5) − 2(3a − 4)$

7 $5(2s + 3t) − 4(s − 2t)$ 8 $4(3a + b) − 3(2a − 5b)$

9 $2(m + 3n) − (2m − n)$ 10 $5(8h − 3k) − 4(7h − 2k)$

11 $3(c + 2d) − 2(c − 3d)$ 12 $4a − (3a − 5b)$

More about expanding brackets

You can expand an expression such as $a(x + y)$ in the same way as $2(a + b)$ on page 60.

__ Example 24 _____

Expand $a(x + 2y)$

$$a(x + 2y) = a \times (x + 2y)$$
$$= a \times x + a \times 2y$$
$$= ax + 2ay$$

> In algebra letters are usually put in alphabetical order.

__ Example 25 _____

Expand $b^2(3a + b)$

$$b^2(3a + b) = b^2 \times 3a + b^2 \times b$$
$$= 3ab^2 + b^3$$

Exercise 3S

1 Expand
   (a) $x(a + 2)$ (b) $y(3 − x)$
   (c) $ax(b + 2c)$ (d) $a(2a^2 + 1)$
   (e) $ab(a + b)$ (f) $a^2(x + y)$
   (g) $2p(3p − 4q)$ (h) $3a(2a + 3b)$
   (i) $abc(3 − a − bc)$ (j) $q(p + pr)$

2 Expand and simplify
   (a) $a(b + c) + c(a + b)$ (b) $b(3 − b) + 2(b^2 − b)$
   (c) $2x(x + 3) − 5(x^2 + x)$ (d) $r^2(3s − r) − 2s(rs − r^2)$
   (e) $2p(q + 1) + 3q(2 − p)$ (f) $p(x − y) − y(x − p)$

3.14 Factorising algebraic expressions

The opposite process to multiplying out brackets is called **factorising**. Factorising means splitting an expression into parts.

You can factorise numbers:

$12 = 4 \times 3$ 4 and 3 are both factors of 12.

$12 = 2 \times 6$ 2 and 6 are factors of 12 as well.

You can also factorise algebraic expressions:

$ab = a \times b$ a and b are factors of ab

$2pq = 2 \times p \times q$ 2, p and q are factors of $2pq$

$x^2 = x \times x$ x and x are factors of x^2

To factorise a more complex expression you need to find factors common to all the terms.

Example 26

Factorise $12a + 4b$

$12a + 4b = \textcircled{4} \times 3 \times a + \textcircled{4} \times b$ ——— 4 is common to both terms.

$= 4(\qquad)$ ————————— Place 4 outside a bracket.

$= 4(3a + b)$ ——————— Work out what is missing from inside the bracket.

This process is called factorising.

$4(3a + b) = 12a + 4b$ ——————— Check that the factorised expression is equivalent to the original.

Example 27

Factorise $2x^2 + 5x$

This can be written as:

$2 \times \textcircled{x} \times x + 5 \times \textcircled{x}$ ——— x is common to both terms.

$= x(\qquad)$ ———————— Place x outside a bracket.

$= x(2x + 5)$ —————— Now make the expression equivalent to the original.

Example 28

Factorise $12a^2 - 4ab$

This can be written as:

$\textcircled{4} \times 3 \times \textcircled{a} \times a - \textcircled{4} \times \textcircled{a} \times b$ — 4 and a are common to both terms.

$= 4a(\qquad)$ ——————— Place $4a$ outside a bracket.

$= 4a(3a - b)$ —————— Now make the expression equivalent to the original.

You won't be splitting us up...

Factorising means splitting up an expression using brackets.

Exercise 3T

1 Factorise
(a) $x^2 + 3x$ (b) $a^2 - ab$ (c) $p^2 + pq$
(d) $3a + 12b$ (e) $5a + 10$ (f) $2b - 4c$
(g) $4 + 8a$ (h) $2a - 2$ (i) $3a + 9$
(j) $5p + 25$ (k) $4a + 16$ (l) $4p - 8$
(m) $7x - 14$ (n) $7y + 7$ (o) $7y^2 + y$
(p) $5q - 15$ (q) $x^2 + 2x$ (r) $y^2 + 3y$
(s) $3a - 3$ (t) $2a^4 + 3a$ (u) $3xy - 4xz$
(v) $4a^2 - 5a$ (w) $5a^5 - 4a$ (x) $5x^2 + 4x$

Factorise each of the expressions in questions **2–7**.

2 (a) $2x + 6$ (b) $6y + 2$ (c) $15b - 5$
(d) $4r - 2$ (e) $3x + 5xy$ (f) $12x + 8y$
(g) $12x - 16$ (h) $9 - 3x$ (i) $9 + 15g$

3 (a) $3x^2 + 4x$ (b) $5y^2 - 3y$ (c) $2a^2 + a$
(d) $5b^2 - 2b$ (e) $7c - 3c^2$ (f) $d^2 + 3d$
(g) $6m^2 - m$ (h) $4xy + 3x$ (i) $n^3 - 8n^2$

4 (a) $8x^2 + 4x$ (b) $6p^2 + 3p$ (c) $6x^2 - 3x$
(d) $3b^2 - 9b$ (e) $12a + 3a^2$ (f) $15c - 10c^2$
(g) $21x^4 + 14x^3$ (h) $16y^3 - 12y^2$ (i) $6d^4 - 4d^2$

5 (a) $ax^2 + ax$ (b) $pr^2 - pr$ (c) $ab^2 - ab$
(d) $qr^2 - q^2$ (e) $a^2x + ax^2$ (f) $b^2y - by^2$
(g) $6a^3 - 9a^2$ (h) $8x^3 - 4x^4$ (i) $18x^3 + 12x^5$

6 (a) $12a^2b + 18ab^2$ (b) $4x^2y - 2xy^2$
(c) $4a^2b + 8ab^2 + 12ab$ (d) $4x^2y + 6xy^2 - 2xy$
(e) $12ax^2 + 6a^2x - 3ax$ (f) $a^2bc + ab^2c + abc^2$

7 (a) $5x + 20$ (b) $12y - 10$ (c) $3x^2 + 5x$
(d) $4y - 3y^2$ (e) $8a + 6a^2$ (f) $12b^2 - 8b$
(g) $cy^2 + cy$ (h) $3dx^2 - 6dx$ (i) $9c^2d + 15cd^2$

Mixed exercise 3

1 (a) Simplify
(i) $c + c + c + c$ (ii) $p \times p \times p \times p$
(iii) $3g + 5g$ (iv) $2r \times 5p$
(b) Expand $5(2y - 3)$
(c) Factorise $15a + 10$ [E]

2 Audrey sells packets of sweets.
There are three sizes of packets.

There are n sweets in the small packet.
There are twice as many sweets in the medium packet as there are in the small packet.

(a) Write down an expression, in terms of n, for the number of sweets in the medium packet.

There are 15 more sweets in the large packet than in the medium packet.

(b) Write down an expression, in terms of n, for the number of sweets in the large packet.

A small packet of sweets costs 20p.
Sebastian buys q small packets of sweets.

(c) Write down an expression, in terms of q, for the cost in pence of the sweets.   [E]

3 Eggs are sold in boxes.
A small box holds 6 eggs.

Hina buys x small boxes of eggs.

(a) Write down in terms of x, the total number of eggs in these small boxes.

A large box holds 12 eggs.
Hina buys 4 less of the large boxes of eggs than the small boxes.

(b) Write down, in terms of x, the number of large boxes she buys.

(c) Find, in terms of x, the total number of eggs in the large boxes that Hina buys.

(d) Find, in terms of x, the total number of eggs that Hina buys.
Give your answer in its simplest form.   [E]

4 (a) Simplify $y + y$
(b) Simplify $p^2 + p^2 + p^2$
(c) Factorise $x^2 - 3x$
(d) Expand the bracket $5(2q + 7)$ [E]

5 Factorise each of these expressions.
(a) $5x + 10$ (b) $6y - 9$ (c) $4a + 9ab$
(d) $10xy - 11y$ (e) $2xy + 4x$ (f) $6a - 9ab$
(g) $4x^2 - 8x$ (h) $12xy^2 + 4x^2y - 2xy$

6 Simplify fully

    (a) $x^5 \times x^3$ (b) $4y^3 \times 5y^5$ (c) $12p^5 \div 3p^2$

7 Work out

    (a) $5^6 \div 5^4$ (b) $64 \div 2^4$ (c) $\dfrac{9^2 \times 3^3}{27}$

8 Find the value of x when $2^x \times 2^2 = 2^8$

9 Write in standard form the numbers shown on these calculator displays.

    (a) $\boxed{7.8^{05}}$ (b) $\boxed{9.8E\ 10}$

10 Write these numbers in standard form.

    (a) 270   (b) 7605   (c) 94 155

11 Use your calculator to work out

    (a) $2.3 \times 10^4 \times 5$ (b) $5.1 \times 10^6 \times 3$

Summary of key points

1 An **algebraic expression** is a collection of letters, symbols and numbers:

    $a + 3b - 2c$ is an algebraic expression

    These are each called **terms**.

    Terms which use the same letter or arrangement of letters are called **like terms**.
    a and $3a$ are like terms $2g$ and $8g$ are like terms

2 You can combine **like terms** by adding or subtracting them:

    $2a + 3a = 5a$ and $3b + 4b - b = 6b$

3 You can simplify algebraic expressions by **collecting like terms** together:

    $2a - 4b + 3a + 5b$ simplifies to $5a + b$

4 The ^{2} in 7^2 is called an **index** or **power**. It tells you how many times the given number must be multiplied by itself.

5 To **multiply** powers of the same number or letter, add the indices:

    $3^3 \times 3^4 = 3^{3+4} = 3^7$ $x^a \times x^b = x^{a+b}$

6 To **divide** powers of the same number or letter, subtract the indices:

    $4^5 \div 4^2 = 4^{5-2} = 4^3$ $x^a \div x^b = x^{a-b}$

7 Any number or letter raised to the **power 1** is equal to the number or letter itself:

$$3^1 = 3 \qquad x^1 = x$$

Any non-zero number or letter, raised to the **power 0** is equal to 1:

$$3^0 = 1 \qquad y^0 = 1$$

8 To raise a power of a number or letter to a **further power**, multiply the indices:

$$(10^2)^3 = 10^{2\times3} = 10^6 \qquad (x^a)^b = x^{ab}$$

9 To **simplify** an expression containing different powers of the same letter multiplied or divided, write the expression as a single power of the letter.

10 **BIDMAS** is a made-up word to help you remember the order of operations:

BIDMAS

Brackets   Indices   Divide   Multiply   Add   Subtract

11 When the operations are the same you do them in the order they appear.

$$10 \div 2 \div 5 = 5 \div 5 = 1$$

12 **Expanding** the brackets means multiplying to remove the brackets:

$$4(3a + b) = 12a + 4b$$

13 **Factorising** means splitting up an expression using brackets:

$$12a + 4b = 4(3a + b)$$

4 Patterns and sequences

4.1 Number patterns

Sometimes you will need to find the missing numbers in a number pattern like this one:

2, 4, 6, 8, 10, —, —, 16, 18

Algebra can help you do this. But first let's explore some number patterns.

2, 4, 6, 8, 10, —, —, 16, 18

The two missing numbers are 12 and 14.

The rule for this pattern is: **add 2 each time.** •

> This pattern is also the two times table, and all the numbers are multiples of 2.

0, 4, 8, 12, 16, —, —, 28, 32

The two missing numbers are 20 and 24.

The rule for this pattern is: **add 4 each time.** •

> This pattern is also the four times table, and all the numbers are multiples of 4.

In a number pattern or **sequence** there is a **rule** to get from one number to the next.

Exercise 4A

Find the two missing numbers in these number patterns.
Write down the rule for each pattern too.

1. 3, 6, 9, —, —, 18, 21
2. 5, 10, 15, 20, —, —, 35, 40
3. 1, 2, 3, 4, —, —, 7, 8
4. 7, 14, 21, 28, —, —, 49, 56
5. 0, 6, 12, —, —, 30, 36
6. 10, 20, 30, —, —, 60, 70
7. 5, 7, 9, 11, —, —, 17, 19
8. 4, 7, 10, 13, —, —, 22, 25
9. 3, 8, 13, 18, —, —, 33, 38
10. 1, 5, 9, 13, —, —, 25, 29

Smaller and smaller

Sometimes the numbers in a pattern get smaller each time.

The rule for my pattern is that I eat six small fish each time!

Example 1

Find the missing numbers in this number pattern:

18, 16, 14, 12, —, —, 6, 4, 2, 0

The missing numbers are 10 and 8.

The rule for this pattern is: **take away 2 each time**.

Exercise 4B

Find the two missing numbers in these number patterns.
Write down the rule for each pattern too.

1   21, 18, 15, 12, —, —, 3   2   24, 20, 16, —, —, 4, 0
3   30, 25, 20, —, —, 5, 0   4   49, 42, 35, 28, —, —, 7
5   28, 25, 22, 19, 16, —, —, 7   6   37, 32, 27, 22, —, —, 7
7   19, 17, 15, —, —, 9, 7   8   25, 21, 17, —, —, 5, 1
9   33, 28, 23, —, —, 8, 3   10   45, 38, 31, 24, —, —, 3

Larger and larger

Example 2

Find the missing numbers in this number pattern:

1, 2, 4, 8, —, —, 64, 128

The missing numbers are 16 and 32.

The rule for this pattern is: **multiply by 2 each time**.

The numbers in the pattern are also all powers of 2:

$1 = 1$ $= 2^0$
$2 = 2$ $= 2^1$
$4 = 2 \times 2$ $= 2^2$
$8 = 2 \times 2 \times 2$ $= 2^3$
$16 = 2 \times 2 \times 2 \times 2 = 2^4$
etc.

Exercise 4C

Find the missing numbers in these number patterns.
Write down the rule for each pattern too.

1   1, 3, 9, —, —, 243   2   1, 4, 16, —, 256
3   1, —, 25, 125, —, 3125   4   1, 10, 100, —, —, 100 000
5   3, 6, 12, —, —, 96   6   2, 6, 18, —, —, 486
7   2, 8, 32, —, —, 2048   8   2, 20, 200, —, —, 200 000
9   2, 10, 50, —, 1250   10   3, 15, 75, —, 1875

Example 3

Find the missing number in this number pattern:

　　243, 81, 27, —, 3, 1

The rule for this pattern is: **divide by 3 each time.**

The missing number is 9.

The numbers in the pattern are also all powers of 3:

$$243 = 3 \times 3 \times 3 \times 3 \times 3 = 3^5$$
$$81 = 3 \times 3 \times 3 \times 3 \quad\quad = 3^4$$
$$27 = 3 \times 3 \times 3 \quad\quad\quad = 3^3$$
$$9 = 3 \times 3 \quad\quad\quad\quad = 3^2$$
$$3 = 3 \quad\quad\quad\quad\quad = 3^1$$
$$1 = 3 \div 3 \quad\quad\quad\quad = 3^0$$

Exercise 4D

Find the missing numbers in these number patterns.
Write down the rule for each pattern too.

1　128, 64, 32, —, 8, 4, —, 1

2　256, 64, —, 4, 1

3　100 000, 10 000, —, —, 10

4　625, 125, —, 5, 1

5　96, 48, 24, —, —, 3

6　486, 162, 54, —, —, 2

7　2048, 512, 128, —, —, 2

8　200 000, 20 000, 2000, —, —, 2

9　1250, 250, 50, —, 2

10　1875, 375, 75, —, 3

4.2 Finding the rule for a number pattern

Examples 4, 5 and 6 have some more difficult number patterns, with some hints on how to find their rules.

Example 4

Pattern ——————— 1,　4,　7,　10,　13,　…

Differences between —— +3　+3　+3　+3
pairs of numbers

The dots mean the pattern continues.

The rule is: **add 3 each time.**
So the next number is 16.

Example 5

Pattern ————1,   4,   9,   16,   25,   ...
Differences ———— +3   +5   +7   +9

The rule is: **add the next odd number each time.**
The *difference* goes up by 2 each time.

Example 6

Pattern ————1,   1,   2,   3,   5,   8,   13,   ...
Differences ———— +0   +1   +1   +2   +3   +5

The rule is: **add the previous two numbers each time.**
The *differences have the same pattern* as the pattern itself.

This is called the Fibonacci sequence. It is named after a
famous Italian mathematician.

Fibonacci numbers
(1, 1, 2, 3, 5, 8, 13, 21, 34, ...)
often appear in nature.
Ordinary field daisies have
34 petals.

Exercise 4E

Write out each pattern in the same way as in Examples 4, 5
and 6. Find the differences and rule for each one, and the
next number.

1 1, 3, 5, 7, 9, ...   **2** 1, 5, 9, 13, 17, ...

3 1, 8, 27, 64, 125, ...   **4** 2, 4, 6, 8, 10, ...

5 2, 5, 8, 11, 14, ...   **6** 3, 7, 11, 15, 19, ...

7 2, 2, 4, 6, 10, 16, ...   **8** 3, 3, 6, 9, 15, 24, ...

9 3, 5, 7, 9, 11, 13, ...   **10** 4, 7, 10, 13, 16, ...

11 2, 7, 12, 17, 22, ...   **12** 3, 8, 13, 18, 23, ...

4.3 Using algebra to write the rule for a number pattern

You can use algebra to write a rule to find any number in a
pattern or sequence.

Each number in a pattern is called a **term**.

Here is a pattern made with crosses.

A sequence is a set of
numbers in order.

```
 ×       ××      ×××     ××××    ×××××
 ×       ××      ×××     ××××    ×××××
```
Pattern number 1 | Pattern number 3 | Pattern number 5
        Pattern number 2   Pattern number 4

To find the number of crosses in pattern number 20 you need a rule to find the **20th term**.

> The number of crosses in pattern number 20 is the 20th term.

Step 1 Make a table. Fill in the pattern numbers and numbers of crosses.

Step 2 Find the differences between the numbers of crosses.

Pattern number	Number of crosses
1	2
2	4
3	6
4	8
5	10
⋮	

Pattern number	Number of crosses	Difference
1	2	
2	4	+2
3	6	+2
4	8	+2
5	10	+2
⋮		

It is easy to use the rule **+2** to find the next term, but not so easy to find the 20th term.

You can use the difference (2) to help you find another rule:

> 1st term $= 1 \times 2 = 2$
> 2nd term $= 2 \times 2 = 4$
> 3rd term $= 3 \times 2 = 6$

The new rule is: **multiply the term number by 2**.

This is the **general rule** for this pattern: the nth term is $2n$.

You can use the general rule to find any term:

> 20th term $= 20 \times 2 = 40$

When you know the nth term of a pattern, you can calculate any term in the pattern by replacing 'n' with the pattern number.

Example 7

(a) Find the general rule for the nth term in this pattern:

   1, 4, 7, 10, 13, ...

(b) Use the general rule to find the 20th term.

(a) Make a table:

Term number	Term	Difference
1	1	
2	4	+3
3	7	+3
4	10	+3
5	13	+3

> The rule is add 3. So the number in front of the n is 3.

$$\text{1st term } = 1 \times 3 - 2 = 1$$
$$\text{2nd term} = 2 \times 3 - 2 = 4$$
$$\text{3rd term } = 3 \times 3 - 2 = 7$$

The nth term is $n \times 3 - 2$

The general rule is $3n - 2$

(b) The 20th term is $(3 \times 20) - 2 = 58$

> When you have multiplied the term number by 3, you then need to subtract 2 in order to get the number in the sequence.

Exercise 4F

1

4 matches   7 matches   10 matches

(a) Draw the next two patterns.

(b) Complete this table.

Term number	1	2	3	4	5
Matches used	4	7	10		

(c) Write down the rule to find the 6th term.

(d) Find the general rule for the nth term.

2 For these patterns:

(a) Draw the next two patterns.

(b) Write down the rule to find the next pattern.

(c) Find the nth term in the pattern.

(d) Use your rule to find the 10th term.

    (i) $\begin{array}{l} \times \\ \times \end{array}$ $\begin{array}{l} \times\times \\ \times\times \end{array}$ $\begin{array}{l} \times\times\times \\ \times\times\times \end{array}$ $\begin{array}{l} \times\times\times\times \\ \times\times\times\times \end{array}$

    (ii) $\begin{array}{l} \times \\ \times\times \end{array}$ $\begin{array}{l} \times\ \times\times \\ \times\times\ \times \end{array}$ $\begin{array}{l} \times\ \times\times\ \times \\ \times\times\ \times\ \times\times \end{array}$

    (iii)

    (iv)   [E]

    (v) $\begin{array}{l} \ \ \ \times \\ \times\ \ \times\times \end{array}$ $\begin{array}{l} \ \ \times\times \\ \times\times\ \ \times\times\times \end{array}$ $\begin{array}{l} \ \ \times\times\times \\ \times\times\times\ \ \times\times\times\times \end{array}$ $\begin{array}{l} \ \ \times\times\times\times \\ \times\times\times\times\ \ \times\times\times\times\times \end{array}$

    (vi) $\begin{array}{l} \times \\ \times\times \end{array}$ $\begin{array}{l} \times\times \\ \times\times\times \end{array}$ $\begin{array}{l} \times\times\times \\ \times\times\times\times \end{array}$ $\begin{array}{l} \times\times\times\times \\ \times\times\times\times\times \end{array}$

3 Find the general rule for the number of matches needed to make the *n*th pattern in this sequence:

4 Write each pattern in a table in the same way as in Example 7. Find the general rule for the *n*th term. Then use your rule to find the 20th term.

(a) 3, 6, 9, 12, 15, 18, 21, …

(b) 5, 10, 15, 20, 25, 30, 35, 40, …

(c) 1, 2, 3, 4, 5, 6, 7, 8, …

(d) 7, 14, 21, 28, 35, 42, 49, 56, …

(e) 0, 6, 12, 18, 24, 30, 36, …

(f) 10, 20, 30, 40, 50, 60, 70, …

(g) 5, 7, 9, 11, 13, 15, 17, 19, …

(h) 4, 7, 10, 13, 16, 19, 22, 25, …

(i) 3, 8, 13, 18, 23, 28, 33, 38, …

(j) 1, 5, 9, 13, 17, 21, 25, 29, …

(k) 1, 3, 5, 7, 9, 11, …

(l) 3, 5, 7, 9, 11, 13, …

(m) 2, 5, 8, 11, 14, 17, …

(n) 5, 8, 11, 14, 17, 20, …

(o) 1, 5, 9, 13, 17, 21, …

(p) 2, 6, 10, 14, 18, 22, …

(q) 2, 7, 12, 17, 22, 27, …

(r) 4, 9, 14, 19, 24, 29, …

(s) 40, 35, 30, 25, 20, …

(t) 38, 36, 34, 32, 30, …

> To find the general term of a sequence that gets smaller, you subtract a multiple of *n* from a fixed number. For example, $15 - 2n$ is the general term for 13, 11, 9, 7, 5, …

4.4 Is a number part of a sequence?

Sometimes you will be asked: *How do you know if a number is part of a pattern or sequence?*

You have to find out if the number is in the sequence or not, and then explain how you know this.

Example 8

Here is a number pattern:

2, 7, 12, 17, 22, ...

(a) Explain why 422 is in the pattern.

(b) Explain why 325 is not in the pattern.

There are different ways of answering questions like these. Here are some possibilities:

(a) (i) Every even term ends in 2 and they go up 2, 12, 22, ..., so 422 will be in the pattern as it ends in a 2.

(ii) The nth term is $5n - 3$, so if 422 is in the pattern

$$5n - 3 = 422$$
$$5n = 425$$
$$n = 85, \text{ so } 422 \text{ is the 85th term in the pattern.}$$

(b) (i) 325 ends in a 5 and every member of the pattern ends in either a 2 or a 7, so 325 cannot be in the pattern.

(ii) The nth term is $5n - 3$ so if 325 is in the pattern

$$5n - 3 = 325$$
$$5n = 328$$
$$n = 65.6$$

If 325 is in the pattern n must be a whole number. But 65.6 is not a whole number so 325 is not in the pattern.

Exercise 4G

For each of these number patterns, explain whether the numbers in brackets are members of the number pattern.

1   1, 3, 5, 7, 9, 11, ...   (21, 34)

2   3, 5, 7, 9, 11, 13, ...   (63, 86)

3   2, 5, 8, 11, 14, 17, ...   (50, 66)

4   5, 8, 11, 14, 17, 20, ...   (101, 98)

5   1, 5, 9, 13, 17, 21, ...   (101, 150)

6   2, 6, 10, 14, 18, 22, ...   (101, 98)

7   2, 7, 12, 17, 22, 27, ...   (97, 120)

8   4, 9, 14, 19, 24, 29, ...   (168, 169)

9   40, 35, 30, 25, 20, ...   (85, 4)

10 38, 36, 34, 32, 30, ...   (71, 82)

4.5 Using a graphical calculator to produce number sequences

You can use the [Ans] and [EXE] keys together to generate number sequences. For example:

Press [1] [EXE]

Press [Ans] [+] [1] [EXE] [EXE] [EXE] ... Keep pressing [EXE]
The calculator appears to be 'counting'.

Each time [EXE] is pressed, 'Ans + 1' is calculated, where Ans is the *last answer displayed*.

> [Ans] recalls the most recent answer.

> [EXE] performs (or repeats) the most recent calculation(s).

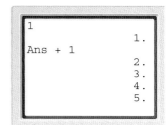

___ Example 9 _____

(a) Use the [Ans] and [EXE] keys to produce the even numbers, starting with 2.

(b) Show how the [Ans] and [EXE] keys can be used to produce the sequence 2, 6, 18, 54, ...

(a) [2] [EXE] [Ans] [+] [2] [EXE] [EXE] [EXE] ...

(b) [2] [EXE] [Ans] [×] [3] [EXE] [EXE] [EXE] ...

Exercise 4H

Write down the key presses, including [Ans] and [EXE], which will generate the following sequences.

1 1, 3, 5, 7, 9, ...
2 5, 10, 15, 20, 25, ...
3 2, 4, 8, 16, 32, ...
4 3, 9, 27, 81, 243, ...
5 10, 9, 8, 7, 6, ...
6 16, 8, 4, 2, 1, ...
7 200, 20, 2, 0.2, 0.02, ...
8 $-5, -7, -9, -11, -13,$ ...

4.6 Investigating number sequences with a spreadsheet

You can generate many number sequences on the same spreadsheet and compare them.

Before you start Exercise 4I, you need to find out, for your spreadsheet package:

- how to enter numbers and formulae in the cells of your spreadsheet
- how to copy a formula from one cell to other cells.

Now work through the exercise to practise these skills.

Exercise 4I

1 Generate the whole numbers from
1 to 10 in column A:
   Put the number 1 in cell A1.
   Put the formula = A1 + 1 in cell A2.
   Copy the formula in A2 down
   column A as far as A10.

2 Generate the even numbers in
column B:
   Put the number 2 in cell B1.
   Put the formula = B1 + 2 in cell B2.
   Copy the formula in B2 down
   column B as far as B10.

3 Generate the odd numbers in
column C:
   Put the number 1 in cell C1.
   Put the formula = C1 + 2 in cell C2.
   Copy the formula in C2 down
   column C as far as C10.

4 Generate the triangular numbers in
column D:
   Put the number 1 in cell D1.
   Put the formula = D1 + A2 in cell
   D2.
   Copy the formula in D2 down
   column D as far as D10.

5 Add consecutive odd numbers and
put the answers in column E:
   Put the formula = C1 + C2 in cell E2.
   Copy the formula in E2 down
   column E as far as E10.
   What do you notice about the
   numbers in column E?

6 Add consecutive triangular
numbers and put the answers in
column F:
   Put the formula = D1 + D2 in cell F2.
   Copy the formula in F2 down
   column F as far as F10.
   What is the name of the sequence of numbers in
   column F?

Formula: = A1 + 1	Formula: = B1 + 2	Formula: = C1 + 2	
	A	**B**	**C**	**D**
1	1	2	1	
2	2	4	3	
3	3	6	5	
4	4	8	7	
5	5	10	9	
6	6	12	11	
7	7	14	13	
8	8	16	15	
9	9	18	17	
10	10	20	19	

Formula: = D1 + A2	Formula: = C1 + C2	Formula: = D1 + D2	
C	**D**	**E**	**F**	**G**
1	1			
3	3	4	4	
5	6	8	9	
7	10	12	16	
9	15	16	25	
11	21	20	36	
13	28	24	49	
15	36	28	64	
17	45	32	81	
19	55	36	100	

Mixed exercise 4

1 The table shows some rows in a number pattern.

Row 1	1	$= \dfrac{1 \times 2}{2}$
Row 2	1 + 2	$= \dfrac{2 \times 3}{2}$
Row 3	1 + 2 + 3	$= \dfrac{3 \times 4}{2}$
Row 4	1 + 2 + 3 + 4	
Row 8		

(a) Copy the table and complete row 4 and row 8.
(b) Work out the sum of the first 100 whole numbers.   [E]

2 Here are the first five terms of a number sequence:
      3   8   13   18   23
(a) Write down the next **two** terms of the sequence.
(b) Explain how you found your answer.
(c) Explain why 387 is **not** a term of the sequence.   [E]

3 Here are some patterns made up of dots:

Pattern number 1   Pattern number 2   Pattern number 3

(a) Draw Pattern number 4.
(b) Copy and complete the table.

Pattern number	1	2	3	4	5
Number of dots	10	14	18		

(c) How many dots are used in Pattern number 10?   [E]

4 Here are some patterns made with crosses:

Pattern   Pattern   Pattern   Pattern
number 1   number 2   number 3   number 4

(a) Draw pattern number 5.

(b) Copy and complete the table for pattern number 5 and pattern number 6.

Pattern number (n)	1	2	3	4	5	6
Number of crosses (C)	5	8	11	14		

(c) Work out the pattern number that has 26 crosses.

(d) Work out the number of crosses in pattern number 10.

(e) Write down a formula for the number of crosses, C, in terms of the pattern number, n.   [E]

Summary of key points

1 In a number pattern or **sequence** there is always a **rule** to get from one number to the next.
For example:

  4, 7, 10, 13, ...   The rule is: add 3
  50, 46, 42, 38, ...   The rule is: take away 4
  2, 4, 8, 16, ...   The rule is: multiply by 2
  100 000, 10 000, 1000, ...   The rule is: divide by 10

2 When you know the nth term of a pattern, you can calculate any term in the pattern by replacing 'n' with the pattern number

3 To find the nth term of a number pattern, use a table of values.
For example

Pattern number	Term	Difference
1	1	The rule is add 3 so the number in front of the n is 3.
2	4	
3	7	Check for the plus or minus number by putting the value of the term number into the nth term
4	10	
n	$3n - 2$	

⑤ Decimals

5.1 Understanding place value

Some things in life can only have whole number values. For example, the number of people in a party is always a whole number.

Here there are *whole* numbers of people and animals.

Other items can also have other values. For example, the weight of a packet of sugar is 2.2 lbs and the height of a person may be 1.76 metres.

> 2.2 is read as two point two.
> 1.76 is read as one point seven six.

These are *decimal* numbers. Values that are not whole numbers can be recorded using decimals (with differing degrees of accuracy).

> In a decimal number, the **decimal point** separates the whole number from the part that is smaller than 1.

Example 1

A Formula One Grand Prix driver has his lap time recorded as 53.398 seconds.

You can better understand what 53.398 seconds really means by drawing a decimal place value diagram.

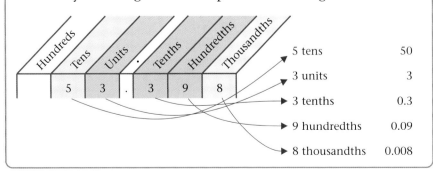

5 tens	50
3 units	3
3 tenths	0.3
9 hundredths	0.09
8 thousandths	0.008

> Read the whole number and then read the digits in order:
> fifty-three point three nine eight.

Example 2

A woman 400 m hurdler's time is 54.08 seconds.
Draw up a place value table.

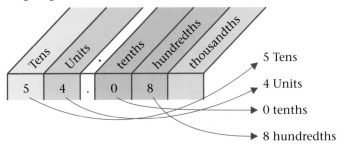

5 Tens
4 Units
0 tenths
8 hundredths

Even though there are no *tenths* the 0 has to be recorded
to keep the 8 in its correct place value position.

Example 3

Write down the place value of the underlined digit in each
number.

(a) 3<u>2</u>.8   (b) 0.38<u>5</u>   (c) 10.<u>0</u>3   (d) 4.2<u>9</u>0

(a) 2 units   (b) 5 thousandths
(c) 0 tenths   (d) 9 hundredths

Exercise 5A

1 Draw a place value diagram like the ones in Examples 1
and 2 and write in these numbers:
    (a) 41.6   (b) 4.16   (c) 34.6   (d) 1.463
    (e) 0.643   (f) 1.005   (g) 5.01   (h) 0.086

2 What is the place value of the underlined digit in each
number?
    (a) 2<u>5</u>.4   (b) 2.<u>5</u>4   (c) 25.4<u>6</u>   (d) 3.5<u>4</u>6
    (e) <u>1</u>8.07   (f) 9.66<u>9</u>   (g) 216.0<u>3</u>1   (h) 2.135<u>7</u>
    (i) 9.1<u>0</u>2   (j) 3.<u>3</u>36   (k) 2.59<u>1</u>   (l) 0.0<u>2</u>7

5.2 Writing decimal numbers in order of size

To arrange decimal numbers in order of size you need to have
a good understanding of place value.

Sort decimal numbers in order of size by first comparing the
whole number parts, then the digits in the tenths place, then
the digits in the hundredths place, and so on.

Example 4

Write these decimal numbers in order of size, starting with the largest: 3.069, 5.2, 3.4, 3.08, 7.0

Step 1 Look at the whole number parts:
7 is bigger than 5; 5 is bigger than 3
Ordered: 7.0, 5.2   Unordered: 3.069, 3.4, 3.08

Step 2 Look at the tenths place:
4 is bigger than 0
Ordered: 7.0, 5.2, 3.4   Unordered: 3.069, 3.08

Step 3 Look at the hundredths place:
8 is bigger than 6
So the order is: 7.0, 5.2, 3.4, 3.08, 3.069

Exercise 5B

1 Rearrange these decimal numbers in order of size, starting with the largest.
(a) 0.62, 0.71, 0.68, 0.76, 0.9
(b) 3.4, 3.12, 3.75, 2.13, 2.09
(c) 0.42, 0.065, 0.407, 0.3, 0.09
(d) 3.0, 6.52, 6.08, 3.58, 3.7
(e) 0.06, 0.13, 0.009, 0.105, 0.024
(f) 2.09, 1.08, 2.2, 1.3, 1.16

2 Put these decimal numbers in order of size, smallest first.
(a) 4.85, 5.9, 5.16, 4.09, 5.23
(b) 0.34, 0.09, 0.37, 0.021, 0.4
(c) 5, 7.23, 5.01, 7.07, 5.009
(d) 1.001, 0.23, 1.08, 1.14, 0.07

3 The table gives the price of a pack of Sudso soap powder in different shops.

Shop	Stall	Corner	Market	Main	Store	Super
Price	£1.29	£1.18	£1.09	£1.31	£1.20	£1.13

Remember:
£1.80 means 1 pound and 80 pence.
£1.08 means 1 pound and 8 pence.
The position of the zero is important!

Write the list of prices in order, starting with the lowest price.

4   The table gives the heights in metres of six girls.

Rachel	Ira	Sheila	Naomi	Latif	Jean
1.56	1.74	1.78	1.65	1.87	1.7

Write the list of names in descending order of height, starting with the tallest.

5   The fastest lap times (in seconds) of six drivers were:

Ascarina	53.072	Bertolini	53.207
Rascini	52.037	Alloway	57.320
Silverman	53.027	Killim	53.702

Write down the drivers' times in order, starting with the fastest.

6   A new cereal gives these weights per 100 g of vitamins and minerals:

Fibre	1.5 g	Iron	0.014 g
Vitamin B6	0.002 g	Thiamin B1	0.0014 g
Riboflavin B2	0.0015 g	Sodium	0.02 g

Write down the weights in order, starting with the lowest.

5.3 Rounding decimal numbers

As with ordinary numbers, it is sometimes helpful to round a decimal number and give the result correct to the nearest whole number, or correct to so many decimal places (d.p.).

To round a decimal to the nearest whole number, look at the digit in the tenths column (or first decimal place). If it is 5 or more, round the whole number up. If it is less than 5, do not change the whole number.

Example 5

Round £5.11 to the nearest pound.

In this example the first decimal place is **less** than 5 so you do not change the whole number.

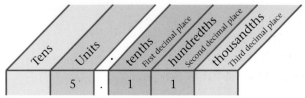

£5.11 to the nearest pound is £5.

Example 6

Round 7.815 to the nearest whole number.

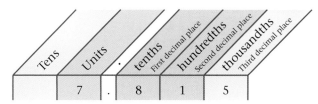

7 is in the units column
8 is in the first decimal place
1 is in the second decimal place
5 is in the third decimal place

8 in the first decimal place is more than 5 so you round up.

7.815 rounded to the nearest whole number is 8.

Example 7

Terry spent £37.52 on a new computer game.
Round the cost to the nearest pound.

Because the digit in the first decimal place is 5, the whole number is rounded up to £38.

To round a decimal to one decimal place (1 d.p.), look at the second decimal place. If it is 5 or more round up. If it is less than 5, leave it and any remaining digits in the decimal part out.

Example 8

Round the following numbers to *one* decimal place.

(a) 25.27   (b) 25.72   (c) 25.55   (d) 25.528

(a) The second decimal place is 7 which is 5 or more so round the 2 up to 3. The answer is 25.3.
(b) The second decimal place is 2 which is less than 5 so leave this digit out. The answer is 25.7.
(c) The second decimal place is 5 so round the 5 in the first decimal place up to 6. The answer is 25.6.
(d) The second decimal place is 2 which is less than 5 so leave this and any other digits in the decimal part out. The answer is 25.5.

Exercise 5C

1 Round these numbers to the nearest whole number.
   (a) 7.8   (b) 13.29   (c) 14.361   (d) 5.802
   (e) 10.59   (f) 19.62   (g) 0.771   (h) 20.499
   (i) 0.89   (j) 100.09   (k) 19.55   (l) 1.99

2 Round these numbers to one decimal place.
   (a) 3.6061   (b) 5.3391   (c) 0.0901   (d) 9.347
   (e) 10.6515   (f) 7.989   (g) 2.0616   (h) 0.4999
   (i) 2.45   (j) 125.67   (k) 0.05   (l) 9.890

3 Round
   (a) 13.6 mm to the nearest mm
   (b) 80.09 m to the nearest m
   (c) 0.907 kg to the nearest kg
   (d) £204.49 to the nearest £
   (e) 3.601 lb to the nearest lb
   (f) 2.299 tonne to the nearest tonne
   (g) 10.5001 g to the nearest g
   (h) 8.066 min to the nearest min

5.4 Rounding to a number of decimal places

There are times when you work something out on your
calculator and the number fills the whole display. The answer
is far more accurate than you need. Instead of using all the
digits you can round the number to a given number of
decimal places.

Reminder: $14.576 = 14 + 0.5 + 0.07 + 0.006$

Each of the digits 5,
7 and 6 in the number
14.576 represents a
quantity which is
less than 1. They
are decimal values.

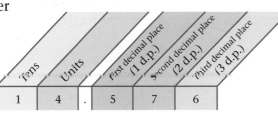

14.57|6 = 14.58
(correct to 2 d.p.).

Does 6.25 round to 6.2 or 6.3?

6.3, as a 5 is normally rounded up.

You can round (or correct) numbers to a given number of
decimal places (d.p.). Count the number of places from the
decimal point. Look at the next digit after the one you want.
If it is 5 or more, you need to round up.

Example 9

Round these numbers (i) to 3 d.p. (ii) to 2 d.p.
(a) 4.4315   (b) 7.3962

(a) (i) In the number 4.4315 the next digit after the
        3rd d.p. is 5. So round up and the 1 becomes 2.
        So 4.4315 rounded to 3 d.p. is 4.432 •
    (ii) In the number 4.4315 the next digit after the
        2nd d.p. is 1, so you round down and the 3 remains
        the same.
        So 4.4315 rounded to 2 d.p. is 4.43
(b) (i) 7.3962 to 3 d.p. is 7.396
    (ii) 7.3962 to 2 d.p. is 7.40 •
        The 6 makes the 9 round up to 10 and this changes
        the 3 to a 4.

> You can write either
> 4.4315 = 4.432
> (correct to 3 decimal
> places) or
> 4.4315 = 4.432 (to 3 d.p.)

> Note: the final zero is
> important because 2 d.p.
> means that two decimal
> digits need to be shown.
> In this case the 4 and the
> 0 must both be included.

Exercise 5D

In questions **1** to **4** round the numbers
(i) to 3 d.p.   (ii) to 2 d.p.

1 (a) 4.2264   (b) 9.7868
   (c) 0.4157   (d) 0.058 38

2 (a) 10.5167   (b) 7.5034
   (c) 21.7295   (d) 9.088 95

3 (a) 15.5978   (b) 0.4081
   (c) 7.2466   (d) 6.050 77

4 (a) 29.1582 cm   (b) 0.054 86 kg
   (c) 13.3785 km   (d) £5.9976

5 Round each number to the number of decimal places
   given in brackets.
   (a) 5.6166 (3 d.p.)   (b) 0.0112 (1 d.p.)
   (c) 0.923 98 (4 d.p.) (d) 0.8639 (2 d.p.)
   (e) 9.6619 (1 d.p.)

5.5 Rounding to a number of significant figures

In Chapter 1 you looked at rounding numbers to '1 significant
figure'. You will also often be asked to round answers to
'2 significant figures' or '3 significant figures'. 'Significant'
means 'important'.

When you are estimating the number of people at a hockey match you don't need to say that there were exactly 8742 people there. You can give your answer to 2 significant figures:

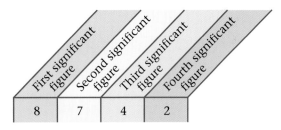

There were about 8700 people (to 2 s.f.).
This is called 'rounding to 2 significant figures'.

You can round (or correct) numbers to a given number of **significant figures (s.f.)**. The first significant figure is the first non-zero digit in the number, counting from the left.

Rounding to a significant figure which is on the right of the decimal point is like the process you used in rounding to decimal places. You look at the next digit after that significant figure.

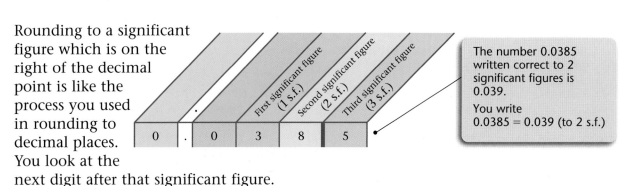

The number 0.0385 written correct to 2 significant figures is 0.039.

You write
0.0385 = 0.039 (to 2 s.f.)

___ **Example 10** ___

Round 642.803
(a) to 1 s.f.   (b) to 2 s.f.   (c) to 3 s.f.   (d) to 4 s.f.   (e) to 5 s.f.

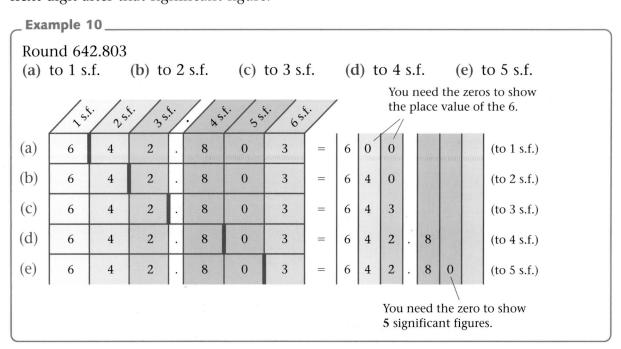

You need the zeros to show the place value of the 6.

You need the zero to show 5 significant figures.

Exercise 5E

In questions **1** to **5** round the numbers
(i) to 1 s.f.   (ii) to 3 s.f.

1 (a) 0.061 75   (b) 0.1649   (c) 96.303   (d) 41.475

2 (a) 734.56   (b) 0.079 47   (c) 5.6853   (d) 586.47

3 (a) 0.014 48   (b) 2222.8   (c) 76.249   (d) 0.3798

4 (a) 8.3846   (b) 35.959   (c) 187.418   (d) 0.066 63

5 (a) 94.746 cm   (b) 851.126 m*l*
     (c) 6.2534 g   (d) 0.062 62 mg

6 Round each number to the number of significant figures
    given in brackets.
     (a) 0.098 12 (2 s.f.)   (b) 54.875 (4 s.f.)
     (c) 7.6542 (1 s.f.)   (d) 3125.4 (2 s.f.)
     (e) 5942.7 (1 s.f.)   (f) 52.973 (3 s.f.)

5.6 Adding and subtracting decimals

Example 11

Two children weigh 24.5 kg and 35.75 kg. What is their
combined weight?

Combined weight is 24.5 kg + 35.75 kg

Put the decimal points
under each other.

Keep digits in their
columns as in a place
value diagram.

$$\begin{array}{r} 2\,4\,.\,5 \\ 3\,5\,.\,7\,5 \\ \hline . \\ \hline \end{array}$$

Decimal point in the
answer should be in
line.

Then add:

$$\begin{array}{r} 2\,4\,.\,5 \\ +\,3\,5\,.\,7\,5 \\ \hline 6\,0\,.\,2\,5 \\ \hline {\scriptstyle 1\;\;1} \end{array}$$

Example 12

Add 13.6 and 125.403

$$\begin{array}{r} 1\,3\,.\,6 \\ +\,1\,2\,5\,.\,4\,0\,3 \\ \hline 1\,3\,9\,.\,0\,0\,3 \\ \hline {\scriptstyle 1} \end{array}$$

When working out a decimal addition or subtraction, always
put the decimal points under each other.

Exercise 5F

Work these out, showing all your working.

1	1.5 + 4.6	**2**	3 + 0.25
3	26.7 + 42.2	**4**	125.7 + 0.32
5	0.1 + 0.9	**6**	16.1 + 2.625
7	9.9 + 9.9	**8**	10 + 1.001
9	0.005 + 1.909	**10**	117 + 1.17
11	6.3 + 17.2 + 8.47	**12**	13.08 + 9.3 + 6.33
13	0.612 + 3.81 + 14.7	**14**	8.6 + 3.66 + 6.066
15	7 + 3.842 + 0.222	**16**	23.43 + 5.36 + 2.216
17	3.07 + 12 + 0.0276	**18**	5.02 + 31.5 + 142.065

Example 13

Fiona buys a kettle costing £12.55. She pays with a £20 note. How much change should she receive?

£20 − £12.55

$$\begin{array}{r} 2\overset{1}{0}.\overset{9}{0}\overset{9}{0}\overset{1}{0} \\ - \ 12.55 \\ \hline 7.45 \end{array}$$

You need to write 20 as 20.00

She receives £7.45 change.

Shopkeepers often give change by counting on:
£12.55 + 5p = £12.60
£12.60 + 40p = £13.00
£13.00 + £7 = £20.00
Change is
£7 + 40p + 5p = £7.45

Example 14

Bill earns £124.65 per week but needs to pay £33.40 in tax and national insurance. What does he take home?

£124.65 − £33.40

$$\begin{array}{r} \overset{1}{1}24.65 \\ - \ 33.40 \\ \hline 91.25 \end{array}$$

Remember to put the decimal points under each other.

Bill takes home £91.25

 Exercise 5G

1 Work out these money calculations, showing all your working. (Amounts are given in £s.)

Use the shopkeepers' 'counting on' method for some of these questions.

(a)	19.90 − 13.70	(b)	5.84 − 1.70	(c)	23.50 − 9.40
(d)	100.70 − 3.40	(e)	0.59 − 0.48	(f)	1 − 0.65
(g)	16.90 − 10.71	(h)	21.64 − 10.50	(i)	2.50 − 1.60
(j)	5.84 − 1.77	(k)	23.50 − 9.47	(l)	14 − 0.75

2 Work out these calculations, showing all your working.

(a)	6.125 − 4.9	(b)	14.01 − 2.361
(c)	3.29 − 1.036	(d)	204.06 − 35.48

5.7 Multiplying decimals

When multiplying decimals, the answer must have the same number of decimal places as the total number of decimal places in the numbers being multiplied.

Example 15

Find the cost of 5 books at £4.64 each.

$$
\begin{array}{r}
464 \\
\times \quad 5 \\
\hline
2320 \\
\hline
{\scriptstyle 3\ 2}
\end{array}
$$

Multiply the numbers together ignoring the decimals.

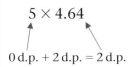

$0\,\text{d.p.} + 2\,\text{d.p.} = 2\,\text{d.p.}$

Count the total number of decimal places (d.p.) in the numbers you are multiplying.

The answer must have 2 d.p.
So the cost is £23.20

The answer must have the same number of decimal places.

Example 16

Work out 0.52×0.4

$$
\begin{array}{r}
52 \\
\times \quad 4 \\
\hline
208 \\
\hline
\end{array}
$$

0.52×0.4

$2\,\text{d.p.} + 1\,\text{d.p.} = 3\,\text{d.p.}$

The answer must have 3 d.p. so it is 0.208

Example 17

Find the cost of 25 books at £5.75 each.

Long multiplication

$$
\begin{array}{r}
575 \\
\times \quad 25 \\
\hline
2875 \\
+11500 \\
\hline
14375 \\
\end{array}
$$

575×5
575×20

£143.75

Decimal point is placed to give 2 decimal places.

Napier's Bones

5	.7	5	×

1   1 0 / 1 4 / 1 0   2

1 1 2 / 3 / 2 5
   / 5 / 5 / 5
4

3 . 7   5

£143.75

Adding method

£	5.75	
+£	5.75	
£	11.50	2 lots
£	11.50	2 lots
£	5.75	1 lot
£	28.75	5 lots
£	115.00	20 lots
£143.75		

Remember the different ways of multiplying shown in Chapter 1.

Exercise 5H

Work these out, showing all your working.

1 Find the cost of
  (a) 6 books at £2.25 each
  (b) 4 tins of biscuits at £1.37 each
  (c) 8 ice creams at £0.65 each
  (d) 1.5 kilos of pears at £0.80 per kilo.

2 (a) 7.6×4 (b) 0.76×4 (c) 0.76×0.4
  (d) 2.25×5 (e) 2.25×0.5 (f) 0.225×0.5
  (g) 22.5×0.05 (h) 2.25×0.005 (i) 0.225×0.005

3 (a) 24.6×7 kg   (b) 3.15×0.03 seconds
  (c) 0.12×0.12 m   (d) 0.2×0.2 miles
  (e) $1.5 \times 0.6\,l$ (f) 0.03×0.04 hours

4 (a) 6.42×10 (b) 64.2×10 (c) 0.642×10
  (d) 56.23×10 (e) 5.623×10 (f) $0.056\,23 \times 10$

  Look carefully at your answers to question **4**.
  What do you notice?

5 (a) 0.045×100 (b) 0.45×100 (c) 4.5×100
  (d) 0.0203×100 (e) 0.203×100 (f) 2.03×100

  What do you notice about your answers to question **5**?

6 A book costs £4.65. Work out the cost of buying
  (a) 25 copies   (b) 36 copies   (c) 55 copies.

7 It costs £7.85 for one person to enter the Fun Beach.
  How much does it cost
  (a) 15 people   (b) 25 people   (c) 43 people?

8 A bucket holds 4.55 litres of water. How much water is
  contained in
  (a) 15 buckets   (b) 25 buckets   (c) 65 buckets?

5.8 Division with decimals

Example 18

Five friends win £216.35 in a charity lottery. They share
the money equally. How much do they each get?

$216.35 \div 5$

Put the decimal points in line.

$$\begin{array}{r} 4\,3.2\,7 \\ 5\overline{)2\,1^{1}6.^{1}3^{3}5} \end{array}$$

Because 5 is a whole number, divide straight away.

Example 19

Work out (a) $5.215 \div 7$ (b) $4.5 \div 6$

(a) $\quad 0.745$
$\quad 7\overline{)5.^52^31^35}$

(b) $\quad 0.75$
$\quad 6\overline{)4.^45^30}$

> 6 divides into 45, 7 times remainder 3.

> Add a zero in the next decimal place. Place the 3 remainder next to the zero.

> 6 into 30 goes 5 times.

Exercise 5I

Work these out, showing all your working.

1 (a) $64.48 \div 4$ (b) $3.165 \div 5$ (c) $133.56 \div 9$
   (d) $205.326 \div 6$ (e) $35.189 \div 7$ (f) $0.0368 \div 8$

2 (a) $34.5 \div 10$ (b) $3.45 \div 10$ (c) $0.345 \div 10$
   (d) $78 \div 10$ (e) $7.8 \div 10$ (f) $0.78 \div 10$
   (g) $65 \div 10$ (h) $65 \div 100$ (i) $65 \div 1000$

Write down anything you notice about your answers to question **2**.

3 (a) $5 \div 2$ (b) $6 \div 5$ (c) $3.5 \div 4$
   (d) $0.72 \div 3$ (e) $1.56 \div 3$ (f) $1.24 \div 8$
   (g) $14.4 \div 12$ (h) $1.3 \div 8$

4 Seven people share £107.80 equally. How much will each receive?

5 How many 3 litre jugs would be needed to hold 43.5 litres of lemonade?

Example 20

Work out $70 \div 8$

$\quad 8.75$
$8\overline{)7^70.^60^40}$

Example 21

1.2 metres of fabric costs £1.56. What is the cost per metre?

$\quad 1.56 \div 1.2$ ———— not a whole number

To change 1.2 to a whole number multiply by 10:

$\quad 1.2 \times 10 = 12$

Do the same to 1.56: $1.56 \times 10 = 15.6$
The division becomes $15.6 \div 12$

$\quad 1.3$
$12\overline{)15.^36}$ The answer is 1.3 or £1.30

> If the number you are dividing by is **not** a whole number, change it to a whole number. Remember to do the same to the number that is to be divided.

Exercise 5J

Work these out, showing all your working.

1 $7.75 \div 2.5$ **2** $7.92 \div 2.2$ **3** $9.86 \div 5.8$

4 $18.9 \div 12.6$ **5** $0.129 \div 0.03$ **6** $0.27 \div 0.1$

7 $6.634 \div 0.62$ **8** $0.2121 \div 0.21$ **9** $3.5 \div 1.4$

10 (a) $12 \div 20$ (b) $9 \div 12$ (c) $4 \div 16$ (d) $10 \div 50$
     (e) $6 \div 30$ (f) $5 \div 25$ (g) $25 \div 8$ (h) $16 \div 40$

11 Benni wins £5050. He splits the £5050 equally between 12 charities.
How much does each charity receive?

12 Rodney cuts a 3 m long plank of wood into 12 equal parts. How long is each of the 12 pieces of wood?

13 How many books each costing £3.50 can be bought for £20?

Mixed exercise 5

1 Write these numbers to 3 significant figures.
     (a) 345 750   (b) 3478
     (c) 3.5784   (d) 0.004 503

2 Write these numbers to 2 decimal places.
     (a) 3.476   (b) 0.0576
     (c) 23.875   (d) 456.7523

3 Find the value of
     (a) $2.6 + 34.56 + 5$ (b) $3.75 + 20 + 36.2$
     (c) $7.54 - 3.22$ (d) $5.67 - 0.84$
     (e) $5 - 3.55$ (f) 3.24×6
     (g) 4.56×0.8 (h) 5.75×2.5
     (i) $12.5 \div 5$ (j) $18 \div 50$
     (k) $24.6 \div 0.4$ (l) $12.5 \div 50$

4 Write the following numbers in order of size, starting with the largest:
     0.606, 9.253, 0.727, 3.510, 0.660

5 Work out the following, and then round your answers to 2 significant figures.
     (a) Jean has a 5.3 mile round trip to work. If she travels to work on 21 days in a month, how far does she travel?

> 'Round trip' means Jean travels to and from work a total of 5.3 miles each day.

(b) In the four weeks in May, Michael manages to save £3.92, £6.51, £9.12 and £1.77. How much does he save altogether in May?

(c) Manik starts the day with £50. After buying a shirt for £11.99, he splits the change equally between his three children.
How much does each receive?

6 Natasha has one pound sixty pence. Her friend Kelly has two pounds five pence. Write down, in figures, how much money each girl has.

Summary of key points

1 In a decimal number, the **decimal point** separates the whole number from the part that is smaller than 1.

2 Sort decimal numbers in order of size by first comparing the whole number parts, then the digits in the tenths place, then the digits in the hundredths place, and so on.

3 To round a decimal to the nearest whole number, look at the digit in the tenths column (or first decimal place). If it is 5 or more, round the whole number up. If it is less than 5, do not change the whole number.

4 To round a decimal to one decimal place (1 d.p.), look at the second decimal place. If it is 5 or more, round up. If it is less than 5, leave it and any remaining digits in the decimal part out.

5 You can round (or correct) numbers to a given number of **decimal places (d.p.)**. Count the number of places from the decimal point. Look at the next digit after the one you want. If it is 5 or more, you need to round up.

6 You can round (or correct) numbers to a given number of **significant figures (s.f.)**. The first significant figure is the first non-zero digit in the number, counting from the left. For example, 5.245 is 5.2 to 2 s.f.

7 When working out a decimal addition or subtraction, always put the decimal points under each other.

8 When multiplying decimals, the answer must have the same number of decimal places as the total number of decimal places in the numbers being multiplied.

9 When dividing decimals by decimals make sure you always divide by a whole number. You do this by multiplying both numbers by 10 or 100 or 1000 etc.

6 Angles and turning

6.1 Turning

The London Eye is turning ...

You can show clockwise ↻ and anticlockwise ↺ turns like this:

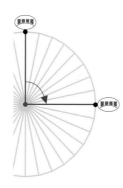

$\frac{1}{4}$ turn clockwise

$\frac{1}{2}$ turn clockwise

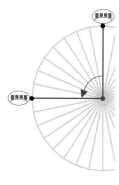

$\frac{1}{4}$ turn anticlockwise

Example 1

An aeroplane is flying North. In which direction will it be flying after:

(a) a $\frac{1}{4}$ turn clockwise   (b) a $\frac{1}{2}$ turn clockwise   (c) a $\frac{1}{4}$ turn anticlockwise?

(a)

It will be flying East.

(b)

It will be flying South.

(c)

It will be flying West.

Example 2

Sam is standing in a market square facing North.
What building will he be facing after

(a) a $\frac{1}{4}$ turn clockwise   (b) a $\frac{1}{2}$ turn anticlockwise

(c) a $\frac{3}{4}$ turn clockwise   (d) a $\frac{1}{4}$ turn anticlockwise

(e) a $\frac{3}{4}$ turn anticlockwise

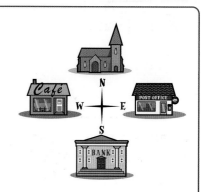

(a) Post Office   (b) Bank

(c) Café   (d) Café

(e) Post Office

Exercise 6A

1   Write down which of these are turning movements:
    (a) a car door opening
    (b) a ship changing direction
    (c) opening a book
    (d) a person crossing the road
    (e) a skier skiing straight down a mountain
    (f) a weather vane as the wind changes.

2   Lisa is facing East. Which way will she be facing after
    (a) a $\frac{1}{4}$ turn clockwise   **(b)** a $\frac{1}{4}$ turn anticlockwise
    (c) a $\frac{1}{2}$ turn clockwise   **(d)** a $\frac{1}{2}$ turn anticlockwise?
    What do you notice about your answers to (c) and (d)?

3   Ajay is walking South-West. Which direction is he
    walking in after
    (a) a $\frac{1}{4}$ turn clockwise   **(b)** a $\frac{1}{2}$ turn
    (c) a $\frac{1}{4}$ turn anticlockwise?

4   How much does the hour hand of a clock turn between
    (a) 3pm and 6pm   **(b)** 1pm and 7pm
    (c) 11am and 2pm?

6.2 Measuring angles

An **angle** is a measure of *turn*. It is a change of direction.
There is no change of position.

An angle can be measured as a turn or using degrees.

There are 360 degrees or 360° in a full turn.
The sign for a degree is °.

That makes 90° in a $\frac{1}{4}$ turn, 180° in a $\frac{1}{2}$ turn and
270° in a $\frac{3}{4}$ turn.

           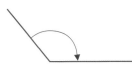

An angle that is a $\frac{1}{4}$ turn is called a **right angle**. A right angle has 90°.

An angle that is less than a $\frac{1}{4}$ turn or 90° is called an **acute angle**.

An angle that is more than a $\frac{1}{4}$ turn or 90° and less than a $\frac{1}{2}$ turn or 180° is called an **obtuse angle**.

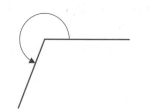 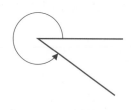

An angle that is a
$\frac{1}{2}$ turn or 180° is called a
straight line or **straight
angle**.

An angle that is more than a $\frac{1}{2}$ turn or 180° and
less than a full turn or 360° is called a **reflex angle**.

Example 3

Name the different types of angles in this diagram:

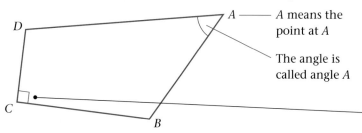

A —— A means the
point at A

The angle is
called angle A

⌐ is the symbol for a
right angle.

Angle A is less than a $\frac{1}{4}$ turn. It is an acute angle.

Angle B is more than a $\frac{1}{4}$ turn and less than a $\frac{1}{2}$ turn. It is
an obtuse angle.

Angle C is a $\frac{1}{4}$ turn. It is a right angle. Lines BC and CD are
perpendicular.

Angle D is more than a $\frac{1}{4}$ turn and less than a $\frac{1}{2}$ turn. It is
an obtuse angle.

Exercise 6B

In questions **1–8** write down whether the marked angles are
acute, obtuse, right or reflex.

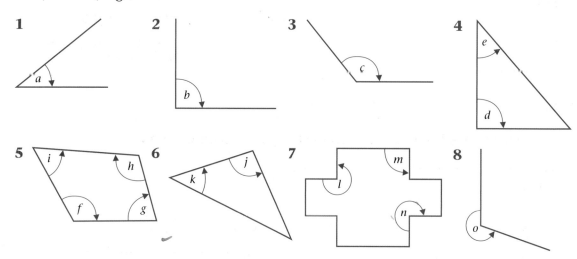

In questions **9–16** estimate the size of the marked angles in degrees.

9

10

q

11

r

12

s

13

t

14

u

15

v

w

16

x

6.3 Naming angles

You can use letters to name the sides and angles of shapes. This shape is named *ABCD* using the letters for the corners and going round clockwise:

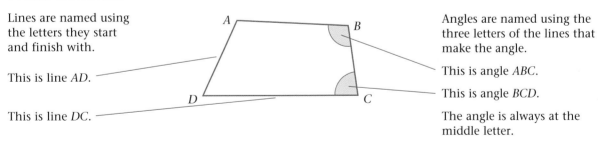

Lines are named using the letters they start and finish with.

This is line *AD*.

This is line *DC*.

Angles are named using the three letters of the lines that make the angle.

This is angle *ABC*.

This is angle *BCD*.

The angle is always at the middle letter.

Exercise 6C

Use letters to identify all the lines and shaded angles in each diagram.

1

2

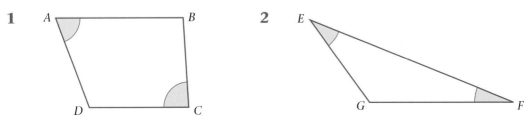

3

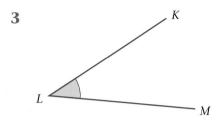

4

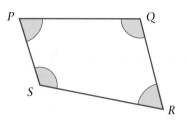

5

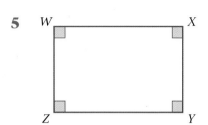

6

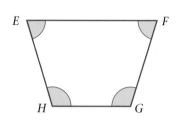

6.4 Measuring angles with a protractor

You can use a **protractor** to measure angles accurately.

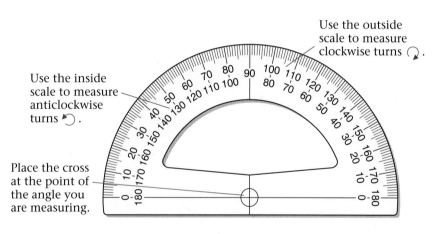

Use the outside scale to measure clockwise turns ↻.

Use the inside scale to measure anticlockwise turns ↺.

Place the cross at the point of the angle you are measuring.

Angle measurer

You can use an angle measurer instead of a protractor.

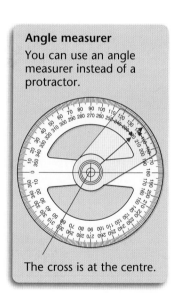

The cross is at the centre.

Example 4

Use a protractor to measure the angle *CBA*.

Here the lines of angle *CBA* are long enough to reach the outer edge of the protractor.

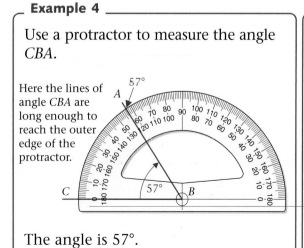

The angle is 57°.

Example 5

Use a protractor to measure the angle *BCD*.

Use the inside scale to measure angle *BCD*.

When the line is too short to reach the scale, extend it with a straight edge like this piece of paper.

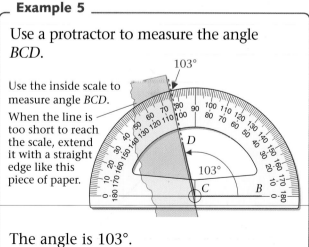

The angle is 103°.

Exercise 6D

Measure and name the angles in each diagram.

1

2

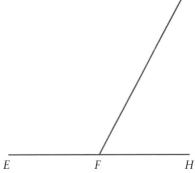

3

4

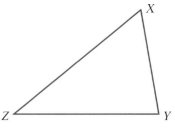

5

6

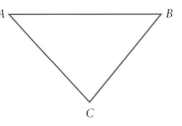

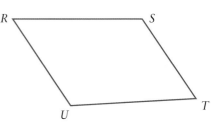

7

8

9

10

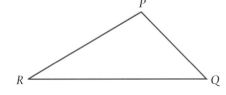

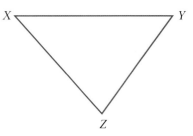

6.5 Drawing angles

You need to be able to draw angles which are accurate to within 2°.

Example 6

Draw these two angles on a line DE which is 8 cm long:

(a) a clockwise angle *DEF* = 79°   (b) an anticlockwise angle *EDC* = 123°

(a) Drawing angle *DEF*:

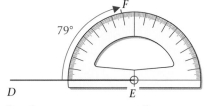

D ——— E   Draw *DE* 8 cm long.

Put the protractor cross at *E*. Mark the point *F* at a clockwise turn of 79°.

Join the points *E* and *F* to give the angle *DEF*.

(b) Drawing angle *EDC*:

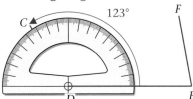

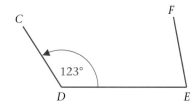

Put the protractor cross at *D*. Mark the point *C* at an anticlockwise turn of 123°.

Join the points *D* and *C* to give the angle *EDC*.

When you have to draw a reflex angle it is a good idea to use a circular protractor.

Example 7

Draw angle *CBA* = 270°

Step 1 Put the circular protractor with centre on *B* and 0° on the line *BC*.

Step 2 Count around to 270°.

Step 3 Mark the point *A*.

Step 4 Join *A* to *B*.

Example 8

Draw angle $PQR = 300°$

Step 1   360 − 300 = 60

Step 2   Draw an angle of 60°.

Step 3   Mark the 300° angle.

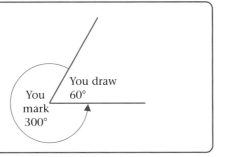

You mark 300°
You draw 60°

Exercise 6E

You need a protractor, ruler and pencil.

1   Draw and label these angles:
   (a) $ABC = 40°$ (b) $DEF = 65°$ (c) $GHK = 125°$ (d) $LMN = 34°$
   (e) $OPQ = 136°$ (f) $RST = 162°$ (g) $UVW = 78°$ (h) $XYZ = 97°$
   (i) $PQR = 185°$ (j) $XYZ = 330°$ (k) $ABC = 240°$ (l) $RST = 305°$

2   Make accurate drawings of these diagrams:

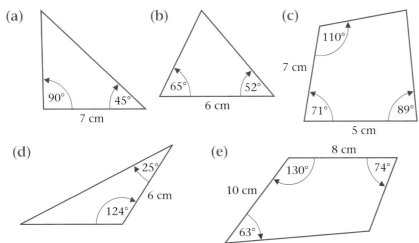

(a) 90° 45° 7 cm
(b) 65° 52° 6 cm
(c) 110° 7 cm 71° 89° 5 cm

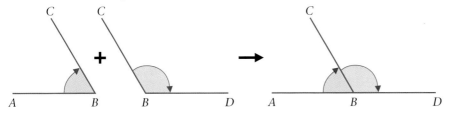

(d) 25° 6 cm 124°
(e) 8 cm 130° 74° 10 cm 63°

6.6 Angles on a straight line

Here are two angles ABC and CBD:

Joined together they make the angle ABD which is a straight line.
These two angles add up to 180°:
   angle ABC + angle $CBD = 180°$

The angles on a straight line add up to 180°.

Example 9

(a) What size is angle a?   (b) What size is angle b?

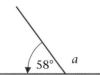   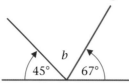

(a) The angles make a
straight line so:
$58° + a = 180°$
$a = 180° - 58° = 122°$

(b) The 3 angles make a
straight line so:
$45° + b + 67° = 180°$
$b = 180° - (45° + 67°) = 68°$

The letter a must equal 122
because $58 + 122 = 180°$

The letter b must equal 68
because $45 + 68 + 67 = 180°$

Exercise 6F

Find the angles represented by letters in these questions.
Give reasons for your answers.

1 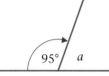   **2** 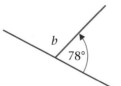   **3**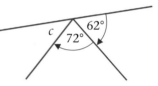

4 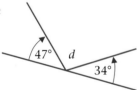   **5** 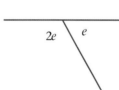   **6**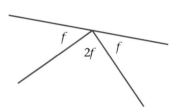

6.7 Angles meeting at a point

The angles at a point add up to 360°.

Where two straight lines cross, the
opposite angles are equal. They are
called **vertically opposite angles**.

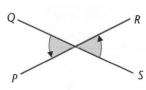

The shaded angles opposite
each other are the same.

To see why, imagine that
line *QS* has turned
anticlockwise to give line
PR. Both 'ends' of the line
have moved through the
same angle.

Example 10

Find all the angles in this diagram. Give reasons for your answers.

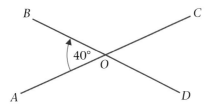

Angle $AOB = 40°$

So angle $COD = 40°$ (vertically opposite angle AOB)

Angle $AOD = 180 - 40 = 140°$ (the angles make a straight line)

So angle $BOC = 140°$ (vertically opposite angle AOD)

> Give reasons for your answers when you can.

Exercise 6G

Find the angles represented by letters in these questions.
Give reasons for your answers.

1

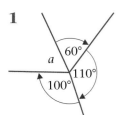

2

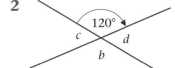

3

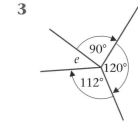

4

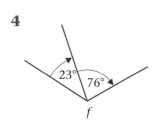

5

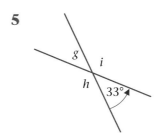

6

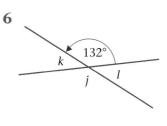

7

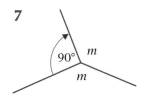

8

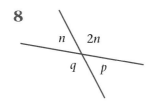

9

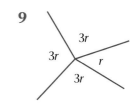

6.8 Sums of angles for triangles and quadrilaterals

The interior angles of a triangle always add up to 180°.

You can see this by checking that the angles in these triangles add up to 180°.

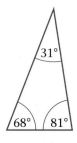 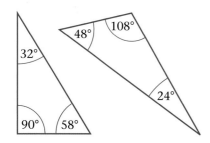

Another way to see this is to cut out a triangle and tear the corners off like this:

Tear these corners off.   Put all three corners together. They make a straight line which is an angle of 180°.

The interior angles of a quadrilateral (a four-sided shape) always add up to 360°.

You can see this by measuring the angles...

… or by dividing the quadrilateral into two triangles…

The interior angles of the two triangles add up to 180° + 180° = 360°

… or by tearing off the four corners:

Put the angles together. They make a full turn of 360°.

Example 11

(a) Work out the missing angle in this triangle:

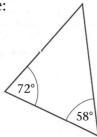

(b) Find the missing angle of this quadrilateral:

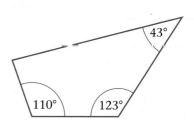

(a) Two of the angles add up to 130°. The third angle must be
180° − 130° = 50°

(b) The 3 angles marked add up to 276°
So the missing angle must be
360° − 276° = 84°

Exercise 6H

Work out the missing angles in these triangles and quadrilaterals. Give reasons for your answers.

1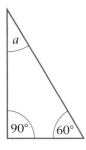

2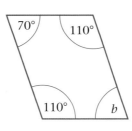

3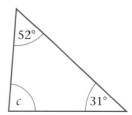

4

5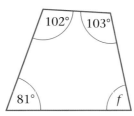

6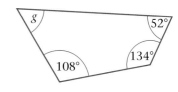

7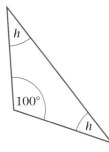

8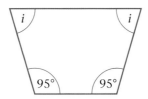

9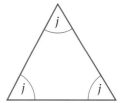

Worked examination question 1

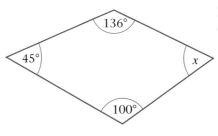

Diagram NOT accurately drawn ●

This means that you cannot measure the angles with a protractor.

Work out the value of x. [E]

$x + 136° + 45° + 100° = 360°$ (sum of angles of quadrilateral)

$x + 281° = 360°$

so $x = 360° - 281° = 79°$

Worked examination question 2

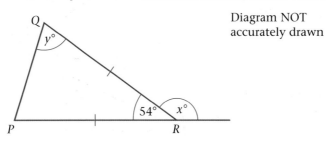

Diagram NOT
accurately drawn

$PR = QR$ and angle $PRQ = 54°$.

(a) Work out the value of x.

Triangle PQR is a special type of triangle.

(b) Write down the mathematical name of this type of triangle.

(c) Work out the value of y.   [E]

(a) $x° = 180° - 54°$ (angles on a straight line)
    $x = 126$

(b) Triangle PQR has two equal sides so it is an isosceles triangle.

(c) angle $P + y° + 54° = 180°$ (sum of angles of triangle)
    so   angle $P + y° = 180° - 54° = 126°$
    angle $P = y°$ (base angles of isosceles triangle)
    so $y° = 126° ÷ 2$
         $y = 63$

Remember:
Sides marked in the same way are the same length.

The base angles of an isosceles triangle are equal.

For more about isosceles triangles see Section 7.1.

Exercise 6I

Work out the lettered angles, giving reasons for your answers.

1

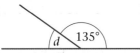

2

3

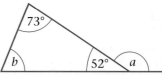

4

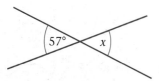

5

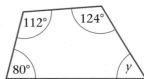

6   In triangle ABC, $AC = BC$ and angle $CAB = 25°$.
        Work out

(a)   angle CBA

(b)   angle ACB.

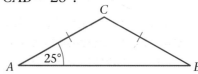

7   In triangle *PQR*, *PQ* = *QR* and angle *PQR* = 116°. Work out the size of angle *QPR*.

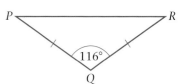

8   The arrowhead shape *PQRS* is a type of kite. *PQ* = *QR* and *PS* = *SR*. Angle *PSQ* = 115° and angle *QPS* = 23°. Calculate angle *PQR*.

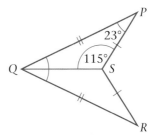

9   *ABCD* is a kite in the shape of an arrowhead. *AD* = *DC* = *BD* and *AB* = *BC*. Angle *DBC* = 34°.
    Calculate
    (a) angle *ABC*
    (b) angle *BDC*
    (c) angle *ADC*.

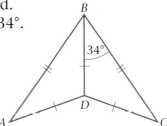

10 Work out the sizes of all the angles marked with letters.

(a)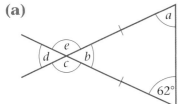

(b)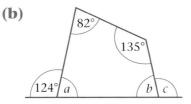

(c)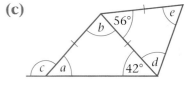

(d)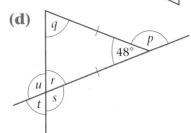

(e)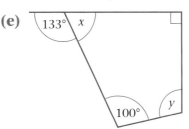

(f)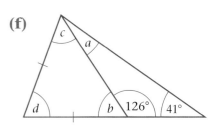

6.9 Alternate and corresponding angles

Parallel lines

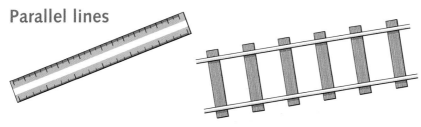

The distance between the two edges of a ruler is the same all the way along it. Similarly the distance between the two rails of a train track is the same wherever it is measured.

Lines which remain the same distance apart are called **parallel lines**. On diagrams this is shown by marking the parallel lines with arrows.

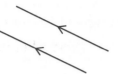

If there is a second pair of parallel lines in one diagram these are marked with double arrows.

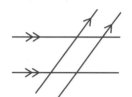

When a straight line crosses a pair of parallel lines it makes angles which are the same size.

Alternate angles

The shaded angles are equal.
They are called **alternate angles**.

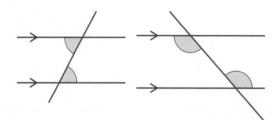

Alternate angles are sometimes called 'Z' angles.

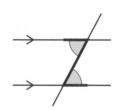

Corresponding angles

The shaded angles are equal.
They are called **corresponding angles**.

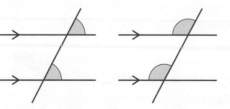

Corresponding angles are sometimes called 'F' angles.

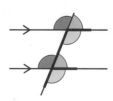

Exercise 6J

1 Find and name as many pairs of parallel lines as you can in this diagram:

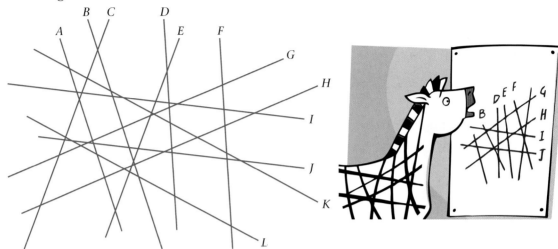

2 Here is the logo of the 'Flying A' pizza company. On a copy of the drawing mark

(a) a right angle with an R

(b) two parallel lines each with a P

(c) an obtuse angle with an O.

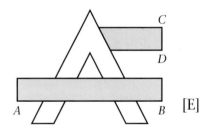

[E]

3 In the diagram, which pair of angles are alternate angles?

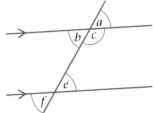

4 In the diagram, which pair of angles are corresponding angles?

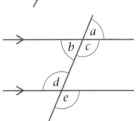

5 Find the size of each angle marked with a letter. Give reasons for your answers.

(a)

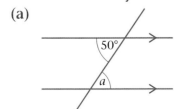

(b)

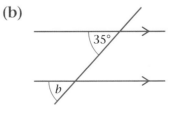

(c)

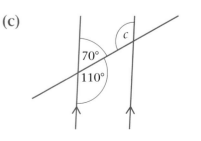

(d)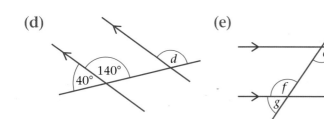

(e)

(f)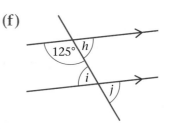

6 Calculate the named angles, giving reasons for your answers.

(a)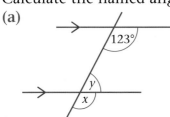

(b)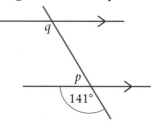

(c)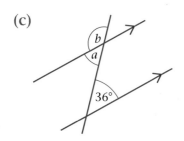

(d)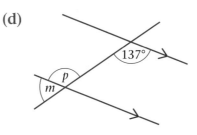

(e)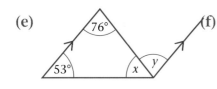

(f)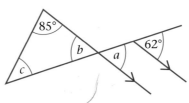

(g)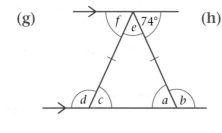

(h)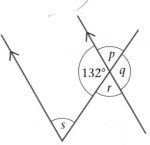

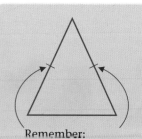

Remember:
Sides marked in the same way are the same length.

7 The diagram shows the following information:
BA is parallel to *CD*, *CA* = *CB*, angle *ACD* = 64°.
Find the size of **(a)** angle *BAC* **(b)** angle *BCA*.

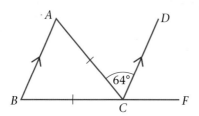

[E]

8

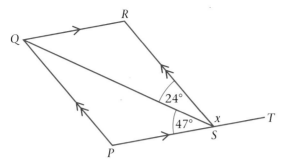

PQRS is a parallelogram
Angle *QSP* = 47°   Angle *QSR* = 24°   *PST* is a straight line.

(a) (i) Find the size of the angle marked *x*.
     (ii) Give a reason for your answer.
(b) (i) Work out the size of angle *PQS*.
     (ii) Give a reason for your answer.   [E]

6.10 Proof in geometry

Extend each side of a triangle.

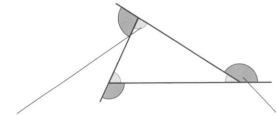

The angles inside are called the **interior angles**.

The angles outside are called the **exterior angles**.

You need to be able to prove that the exterior angle is the sum of the two interior and opposite angles:

> To prove something in maths you have to explain *why it is true*.

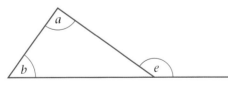

$$e = a + b$$

Through the point of angle *e* draw a line parallel to the opposite side of the triangle.
Angle *e* is now divided into two angles, *c* and *d*.

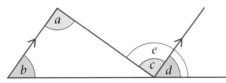

$a = c$ (alternate angles)
$b = d$ (corresponding angles)

So $a + b = c + d = e$

Proving that the angles of a triangle add up to 180°

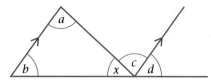

You might be asked to do this in your exam.

The angles of the triangle are a, b and x.

Angle a = angle c (alternate angles)
Angle b = angle d (corresponding angles)
$c + d + x = 180°$ (sum of angles in a straight line is 180°)
$a + b + x = 180°$ (replace c with a and d with b)

Therefore the angle sum of a triangle is 180°.

Exercise 6K

1 Prove that the angle marked x is 45° in each diagram.

(a)

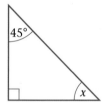

(b)

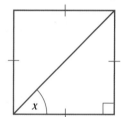

2 Prove that the angle marked y is 30° in each diagram.

(a)

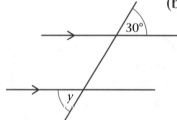

(b)

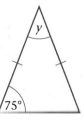

3 Prove that triangle ABC is isosceles in each diagram.

(a)

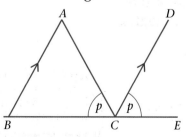

(b)

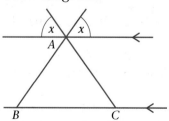

6.11 Calculating angles in polygons

Sum of exterior angles

Step 1 Draw a polygon (with each angle less than 180°) on paper.
Step 2 Extend each side of the polygon to form the exterior angles.
Step 3 Label each exterior angle with a different letter.
Step 4 Cut out each exterior angle leaving some extra paper.
Step 5 Place the angles together at a point.
Step 6 Write down what you notice.

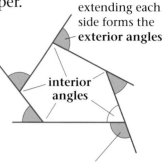

extending each side forms the **exterior angles**

interior angles

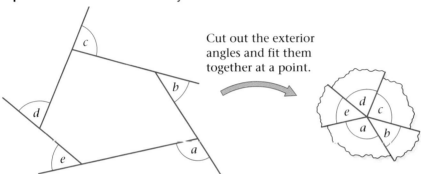

Cut out the exterior angles and fit them together at a point.

At each vertex: interior angle + exterior angle = 180°

The exterior angles fit together at a point with no gaps, so they add to 360°.

Try this yourself with a polygon with a different number of sides.

> The sum of the exterior angles of any polygon is 360°.

> At each vertex (point) of a polygon the sum of the interior angle and the exterior angle is 180°.

Sum of interior angles

In this hexagon the six vertices are joined to a point inside to make six triangles.

The sum of the interior angles of the hexagon and the angles at the point inside equals the sum of the angles of six triangles, so

sum of interior angles of a hexagon + 360° = 6 × 180°

so   sum of interior angles of a hexagon = (6 × 180°) − 360°
= 720°

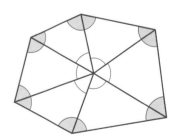

To find the sum of the interior angles of a polygon with n sides join all the vertices to a point in the centre to make n triangles.

> The sum of the interior angles of a polygon with n sides is
> $(n \times 180°) - 360°$,   usually written $(n - 2) \times 180°$

If the polygon is regular, each interior angle is the sum of all the interior angles divided by the number of sides.

A polygon is regular if its sides are all the same length and its angles are all the same size.

Example 12

Work out the size of an interior angle of a regular nonagon.

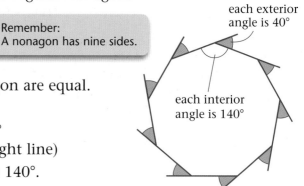

each exterior angle is 40°

Remember:
A nonagon has nine sides.

each interior angle is 140°

Method 1: Using exterior angles

The nine exterior angles add to 360°.

All the exterior angles of a regular nonagon are equal.

One exterior angle is 360° ÷ 9 = 40°.

So one interior angle is 180° − 40° = 140°
                    (angles on a straight line)

An interior angle of a regular nonagon is 140°.

Method 2: Using interior angles

A regular nonagon has nine equal sides.

Join all the vertices to the centre, O, of the nonagon.

The sum of all the angles at O is 360°

so   angle AOB = 360° ÷ 9 = 40°

    Angle ABO + angle BAO = 180° − 40° = 140°
                    (sum of angles of triangle)

    Angle ABO = angle BAO = 140° ÷ 2 = 70°
                    (base angles of isosceles triangle)

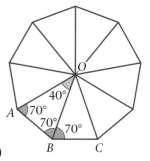

Angle CBO = 70° (by symmetry) so angle ABC is 140°.

An interior angle of a regular nonagon is 140°.

Method 3: Using the formula

A regular nonagon has 9 equal sides, so $n = 9$.

Sum of 9 interior angles = $(n − 2) \times 180°$

$$= (9 − 2) \times 180°$$
$$= 7 \times 180°$$
$$= 1260°$$

One interior angle = 1260° ÷ 9 = 140°

Example 13

Calculate x.

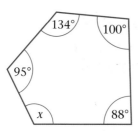

Method 1: Using exterior angles

Four of the exterior angles are:

$180° - 88° = 92°$ $180° - 100° = 80°$
$180° - 134° = 46°$ $180° - 95° = 85°$

These four angles add to 303°.
The exterior angles of a polygon add to 360°.
So the exterior angle next to x is $360° - 303° = 57°$
and $x = 180° - 57° = 123°$.

interior angle + exterior angle = 180°

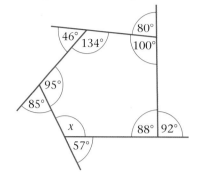

Method 2: Using interior angles

Join all the vertices to a point inside the pentagon to make five triangles.

The sum of all the angles in five triangles is
     $5 \times 180° = 900°$.
This includes 360° at the point.

So the sum of all the interior angles of the pentagon is
     $900° - 360° = 540°$.

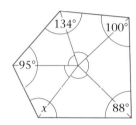

Adding all the interior angles:

     $88° + 100° + 134° + 95° + x = 540°$

so $x = 540° - 417° = 123°$

Exercise 6L

1 Work out the size of each of the exterior angles of a
   (a) regular pentagon   (b) regular hexagon
   (c) regular octagon.

2 Work out the size of each of the interior angles of a
   (a) regular pentagon   (b) regular hexagon
   (c) regular octagon.

3 The diagrams show the exterior angles of some regular
   polygons. How many sides has each of the polygons?
   (a)   (b)   (c)

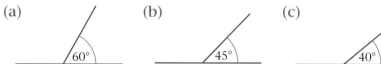

4 The diagrams show the interior angles of some regular
   polygons. How many sides has each of the polygons?
   (a)   (b)   (c)

In questions **5–7** give reasons for your answers.

5 Calculate: **(a)** *p*   **(b)** *q*.

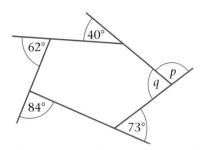

6 Calculate *m*.

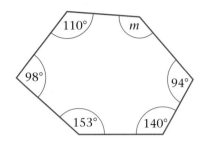

7 Calculate the size of one interior angle of a regular decagon.

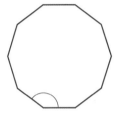

6.12 Bearings

Bearings are used to describe directions with angles.

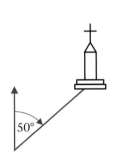

If you begin facing North and then turn clockwise until you face the monument, you have turned through 50°.

The angle you turn is called the **bearing**.

It is always written as a three-figure number.

> When there are less than three digits in the angle you need to add zeros to make a three-figure number. For example a bearing of 9° is written 009°.

You write the bearing of the monument as 050°.

On the map the bearing of Birmingham from London is 315°. The bearing of London from Birmingham is 135°.

A **bearing** is the angle measured from facing North and turning clockwise. It is always a three-figure number.

When you measure a bearing you always put the centre of your protractor on the point where the bearing is taken *from*. You put the zero of the protractor on the North line and measure the angle clockwise. It is a good idea to use a circular protractor to do this.

Example 14

Find the bearing of B from A.

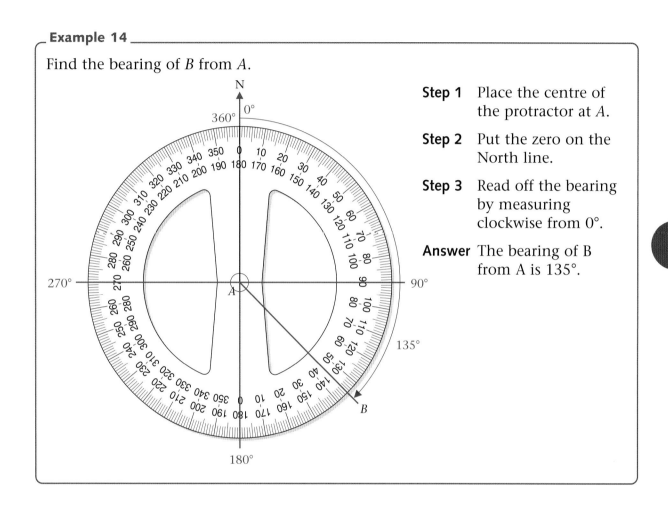

Step 1 Place the centre of the protractor at A.

Step 2 Put the zero on the North line.

Step 3 Read off the bearing by measuring clockwise from 0°.

Answer The bearing of B from A is 135°.

Exercise 6M

1 Write down the bearing of B from A.

(a)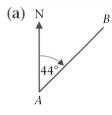

(b)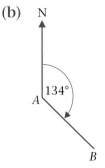

(c)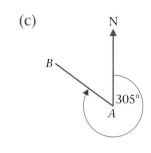

(d)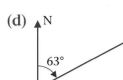
63°

(e)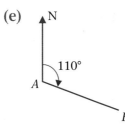
110°

(f)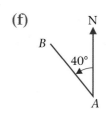
40°

(g)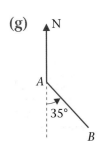
35°

(h)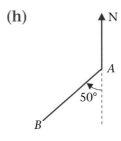
50°

(i)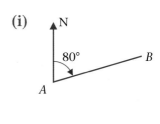
80°

2 Measure and write down the bearing of *B* from *A*.

(a)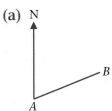

(b)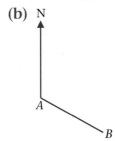

(c)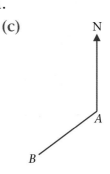

3 Draw these bearings of *B* from *A*.

(a) 050°   (b) 125°   (c) 300°   (d) 250°

4 Work out the bearing of
(a) *B* from *A*
(b) *A* from *B*
(c) *C* from *B*
(d) *B* from *C*.

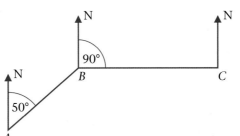

N lines are parallel.

Mixed exercise 6

1 The lines in the diagram are straight.
(a) Mark with arrows (>>)
   a pair of parallel lines.
(b) Mark with the letter *R*,
   a right angle.
(c) What type of angle is
   shown by the letter?
   (i) *x*   (ii) *y*?

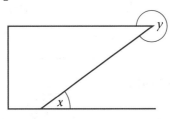

[E]

2 *PQ* is a straight line.

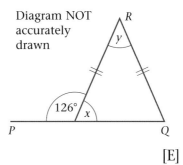

Diagram NOT accurately drawn

  (a) Work out the size of the angle marked *x*.

  (b) **(i)** Work out the size of the angle marked *y*.

   (ii) Give reasons for your answer.

[E]

3 **(a)** Find the size of angle *C*.

  (b) Triangle ABC is equilateral. Explain why.

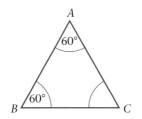

Remember:
An equilateral triangle has all three sides the same length and all three angles the same size.

[E]

4 *PQR* is a straight line.
SQ = SR

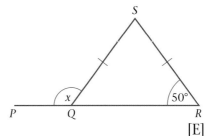

  (a) Work out the size of the angle marked *x*.

  (b) Give reasons for your answer.

[E]

5 *DE* is parallel to *FG*.
Find the size of the angle marked *y*.
Give the reason for your answer.

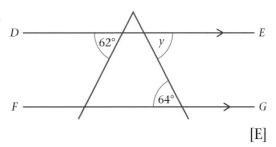

[E]

6 Here is a regular polygon.

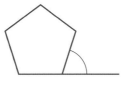

  (a) Write down the name of the polygon.

  (b) Work out the number of degrees in the exterior angle.

[E]

7 **(a)** Write down the special name for these types of angles:

  (i) **(ii)** **(iii)**

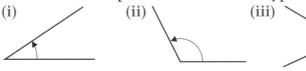

  (b) This diagram is wrong. Explain why.

[E]

8 Use a protractor to find the bearing of:

   (a) Q from P

   (b) P from R

   (c) R from Q.

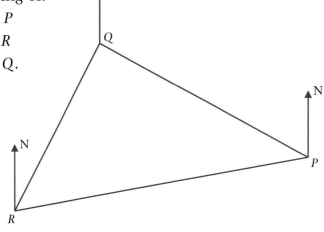

Summary of key points

1   An **angle** is a measure of *turn*. It is a change of direction. There is no change of position.

2   There are 360 degrees or 360° in a full turn. The sign for a degree is °.

3   An angle that is a $\frac{1}{4}$ turn is called a **right angle**. A right angle has 90°.

4   An angle that is less than a $\frac{1}{4}$ turn or 90° is called an **acute angle**.

5   An angle that is more than a $\frac{1}{4}$ turn or 90° and less than a $\frac{1}{2}$ turn or 180° is called an **obtuse angle**.

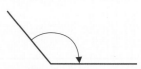

6   An angle that is a $\frac{1}{2}$ turn or 180° is called a **straight line** or **straight angle**.

7   An angle that is more than a $\frac{1}{2}$ turn or 180° and less than a full turn or 360° is called a **reflex angle**.

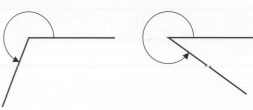

8   The angles on a straight line add up to 180°.

9   The angles at a point add up to 360°.

10   Where two straight lines cross, the opposite angles are equal.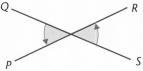
     They are called **vertically opposite angles**.

11   The interior angles of a triangle always add up to 180°.

12   The interior angles of a quadrilateral always add up to 360°.

13   Lines which remain the same distance apart are called **parallel lines**.
     On diagrams this is shown by marking the parallel lines with arrows.

14   The shaded angles are equal.
     They are called **alternate angles**.

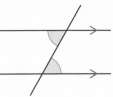

15   The shaded angles are equal.
     They are called **corresponding angles**.

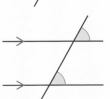

16   The sum of the exterior angles of any
     polygon is 360°.

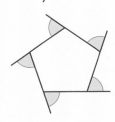

17   At each vertex (point) of a polygon the sum of the interior angle and the exterior
     angle is 180°.

18   The sum of the interior angles of a polygon with n sides is $(n \times 180°) - 360°$,
     usually written $(n - 2) \times 180°$

19   A **bearing** is the angle measured from
     facing North and turning clockwise.
     It is always a three-figure number.

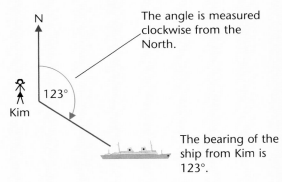

The angle is measured clockwise from the North.

The bearing of the ship from Kim is 123°.

7 2-D shapes

This chapter looks at 2-D shapes. It shows you how to use their properties to solve problems.

You should know some of these properties already:

A straight line is **one-dimensional** (1-D). It has only **length**.

A **line segment** is a section of a line. It is named using letters, for example, the line segment *AB*:

A —————————————— B

An **angle** is a measure of *turn* (or change of direction).

The darker geo strip has turned through an angle.

A rectangle and a circle are **two-dimensional** (2-D) shapes. They have *area*.
All points on 2-D shapes are in the same **plane** (or flat surface).

Two lines are **parallel** if they are in the same direction.

The arrows mean the lines are parallel.

A cube and a football are **three-dimensional** (3-D) objects. They have *volume* (or capacity).

Two lines are **perpendicular** if they are at right angles to each other.

This line is horizontal. | This line is vertical.

The square sign means the lines are perpendicular because this is a right angle.

7.1 Some reminders about polygons

A **polygon** is a 2-D shape with any number of straight sides.

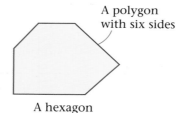

A polygon with six sides

A hexagon

Number of sides	Name of polygon
3	triangle
4	quadrilateral
5	pentagon
6	hexagon
7	heptagon
8	octagon
9	nonagon
10	decagon

The table shows the special names used for polygons with different numbers of sides.

A polygon is **regular** if all its sides and all its angles are equal.

You can show that sides are equal on a shape by using the same mark on the equal sides.

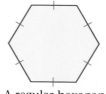

A regular hexagon

The marks show this shape has six equal sides

- The point where two sides meet is called a corner or **vertex**. The plural of vertex is **vertices**.
- The **angle** at a vertex is a measure of the turn between the two sides that meet there. Angles are usually measured in **degrees**.

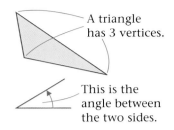

A triangle has 3 vertices.

This is the angle between the two sides.

Special triangles

Name	Shape	Properties
Triangle		• three sides • angles that add up to 180°
Isosceles triangle	2 equal sides · 2 equal angles	• two equal sides • two equal angles
Equilateral triangle	3 equal sides · The 3 angles are each 60°	• three equal sides • three 60° angles
Right-angled triangle		• a right angle as one of its angles
Scalene triangle		• no equal sides • no equal angles
Obtuse-angled triangle		• one obtuse angle

Special quadrilaterals

Name	Shape	Properties
Quadrilateral		• four sides • angles that add up to 360°
Trapezium	parallel sides	• one pair of opposite sides parallel

Name	Shape	Properties
Parallelogram		• both pairs of opposite sides parallel • opposite sides equal • opposite angles equal • diagonals that bisect each other Bisect means 'divides exactly into two equal parts'.
Rhombus		• all sides equal • both pairs of opposite sides parallel • opposite angles equal • diagonals that bisect each other at right angles • diagonals that bisect the angles at the vertices
Rectangle		• both pairs of opposite sides parallel • four 90° angles • equal diagonals that bisect each other • opposite sides equal
Square		• all sides equal • four 90° angles • both pairs of opposite sides parallel • equal diagonals that bisect each other at right angles • diagonals that bisect the angles at the vertices
Kite		• two pairs of adjacent sides equal • one pair of opposite angles equal • diagonals that cross at right angles • one of its diagonals bisected by the other diagonal

Naming angles

Angles can be named using letters. For example:

The angle marked is angle *BAC* or in short form *B$\hat{A}$C* or ∠*BAC*.
It could also be called angle *CAB* or in short *C$\hat{A}$B* or ∠*CAB*.

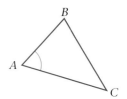

Exercise 7A

1 Copy and complete these sentences. Use numbers and/or the correct word chosen from these:

  equal   opposite   parallel   sides

The first two have been done for you.

(a) A triangle has __3__ sides and __3__ angles.

(b) An **equilateral triangle** has equal sides. Each angle measures 60°.

(c) An **isosceles triangle** has ____ equal sides and ____ angles which are equal.

(d) The largest angle in a **right-angled triangle** always measures ____ .

(e) **Quadrilaterals** have ____ sides and angles.

(f) The angles in a rectangle are all ____ . Opposite sides are ____ .

(g) All the sides of a **square** are ____ and the angles are all ____ .

(h) A **kite** has two pairs of equal ____ and one pair of ____ angles.

(i) ____ sides and angles of a **parallelogram** are ____ . ____ sides are parallel.

(j) A **rhombus** has four equal ____ and opposite angles are ____ . ____ sides are parallel.

(k) A **trapezium** has one pair of ____ sides.

Patterns in a 19th century rug, woven by Navajo Native Americans.

2 Name these special quadrilaterals:

(a)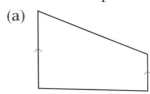

(b)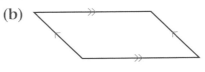

(c)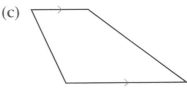

(d)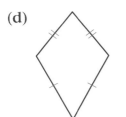

(e)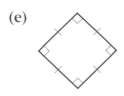

(f)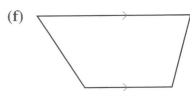

3 You will need a ruler and a protractor.

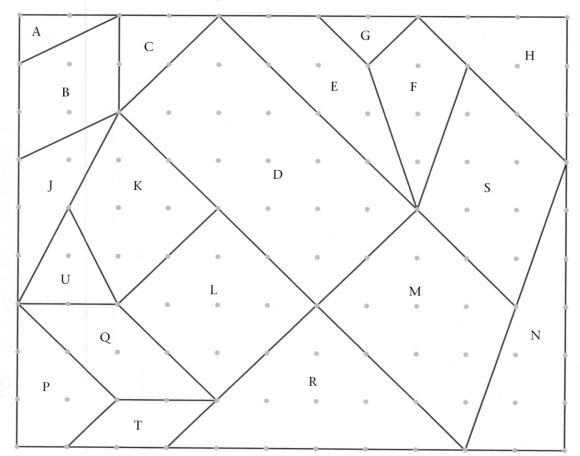

Copy and complete these statements about the 2-D shapes in the diagram.

Use a ruler and protractor to help you.

The first one has been done for you.

(a) Shapes <u>A, C, G, H, N and R</u> are all right-angled triangles.

(b) Shape ____ is a square.

(c) Shapes ____ are all parallelograms.

(d) Shape D is a ____ .

(e) Shapes ____ and ____ are trapeziums.

(f) The kites are shapes ____ and ____ .

(g) Shape ____ is an ordinary quadrilateral.

(h) Shape U is an ____ triangle.

(i) The only square in the picture is shape ____ .

(j) Shapes ____ are isosceles triangles.

4 Here is a list of the names of some shapes:

    hexagon   rhombus   isosceles triangle
    rectangle   trapezium   parallelogram
    octagon   pentagon   right-angled triangle
    square   kite   equilateral triangle

Use the list to help you write down the names of these:

(a)   **(b)**    **(c)**

(d)    **(e)**    **(f)**

(g) 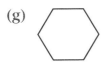   **(h)**   **(i)**

5 Write down the special names of these shapes.
  (a) a triangle with all its sides equal
  (b) a polygon with five sides
  (c) a polygon with eight equal sides and all its angles equal
  (d) a triangle with two of its sides equal
  (e) a polygon with ten vertices.

6 Write down the name of a quadrilateral with
  (a) all its sides and all its angles equal
  (b) only one pair of opposite sides parallel
  (c) only one diagonal bisected by the other diagonal.

7 Write down the names of all the quadrilaterals which have
  (a) all their angles equal
  (b) two pairs of opposite sides parallel
  (c) all their sides equal
  (d) two pairs of equal sides but not all their sides equal.

8 Write down the names of all the quadrilaterals which have
  (a) the diagonals equal
  (b) the diagonals bisecting each other
  (c) the diagonals meeting at right angles
  (d) the diagonals bisecting each other at right angles
  (e) at least one pair of opposite sides parallel.

9 In the parallelogram
  (a) write down the value of a
  (b) calculate
    (i) b **(ii)** c.

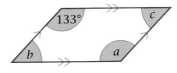

Remember:
The angles of a quadrilateral add to 360°.

10 In the kite *PQRS* angle *QPR* = 58°.
    Calculate
    (a) angle *PQS*
    (b) angle *PQR*.

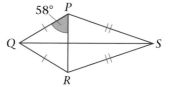

11 In the rhombus, *AC* = 6 cm and
    BD = 10 cm.
    Work out the area of
    (a) triangle *ABD*
    (b) the rhombus *ABCD*.

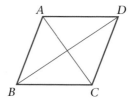

> **Note:**
> The area of a triangle is
> $\frac{1}{2} \times$ base $\times$ height. You
> can read more about this
> in Chapter 19.

7.2 Drawing 2-D shapes on grid paper

There are occasions when it is a good idea to use grid paper to
draw shapes.
Squared paper is very common but you may also use
isometric grid paper. The grid on isomeric paper is made up
from equilateral triangles.

Shapes based on right angles are easy to draw on squared paper.

Example 1

Draw a parallelogram, a square and a right-angled triangle on squared paper.

Parallelogram   Square   Right-angled triangle

You can see the sloping sides
are parallel and equal because
they are both diagonals of
2 by 1 rectangles.

You can easily see the
right angles because
of the square grid.

Shapes based on equilateral triangles or with 60° angles are
easier to draw on isometric paper.

Example 2

Draw an equilateral triangle, a regular hexagon and an arrowhead on isometric paper.

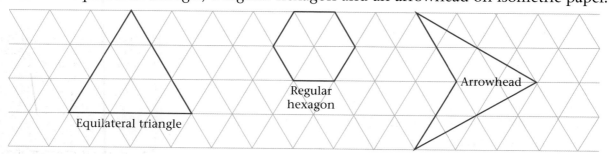

Equilateral triangle   Regular hexagon   Arrowhead

Exercise 7B

You will need squared paper and isometric paper.

1 On squared paper draw
  (a) a rectangle with sides 2 cm and 3 cm
  (b) a right-angled triangle with base 3 cm and height 2 cm
  (c) a square with sides 3 cm long.

2 On squared paper draw
  (a) an isosceles triangle with a base of 5 cm and a height of 3 cm
  (b) a parallelogram with the longest sides 5 cm
  (c) a trapezium with parallel sides that add up to 9 cm and with height 3 cm.

3 On isometric paper draw
  (a) an equilateral triangle with sides of 5 cm
  (b) a regular hexagon with sides of 4 cm
  (c) a parallelogram with opposite sides of 5 cm and 3 cm
  (d) an isosceles trapezium with parallel sides of 5 cm and 7 cm and slant sides 3 cm.

An isosceles trapezium has equal base angles.

4 Design some square tiles using quadrilaterals and triangles. Do not use too many different shapes in any one design.

Here are two designs from the floor of a Roman villa.

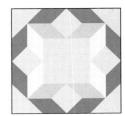

7.3 Congruent shapes

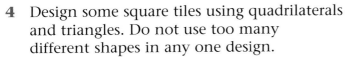

These three shapes are facing different ways but their sides are the same length and their angles are the same size.

Shapes which are exactly the same size and shape are **congruent**.

___ **Example 3** ___

Which of these shapes are congruent?

A B C D

Shapes **A** and **C** are **congruent**. They have the same length sides and the same size angles.

Reflected shapes are still the same size and shape. These shapes are congruent.

Exercise 7C

Write down the letters of the shapes which are congruent.

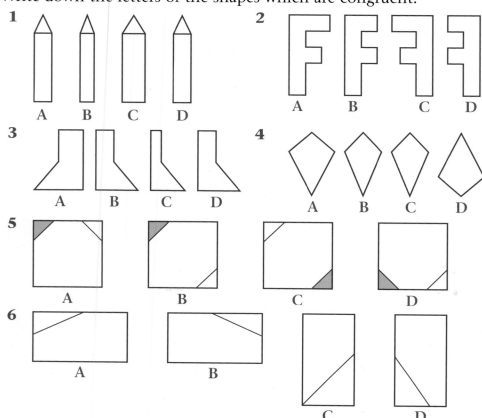

You need a ruler, protractor and squared paper to answer questions **7–8**.

7   Copy the shape on to squared paper. On the same paper draw two shapes that are congruent to the given one, but turned round into a different position.

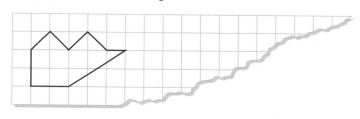

8

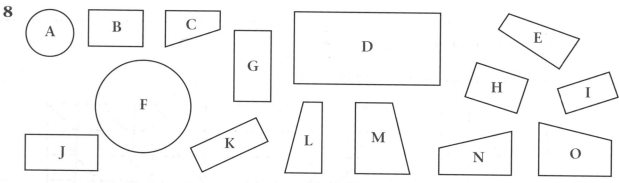

Write down the letters of two pairs of congruent shapes.

7.4 Tessellations

A pattern of shapes which fit together without leaving gaps or overlapping is called a **tessellation**.

Tessellating shapes are often used to make tiles or patterns.

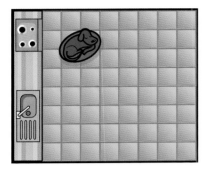

Square floor tiles

Squares rotated

Rectangular bricks

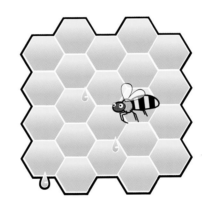

Hexagons

Example 4

Tessellate this trapezium on a grid.

There are three possible ways of doing this

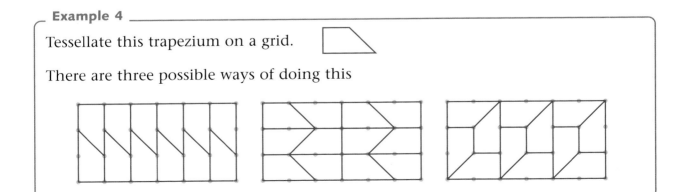

Exercise 7D

You will need dotted grid paper.

1 Show how each of these shapes tessellates.

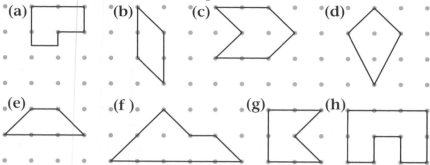

2 Using an isometric grid or dotted isometric paper show how these shapes tessellate.

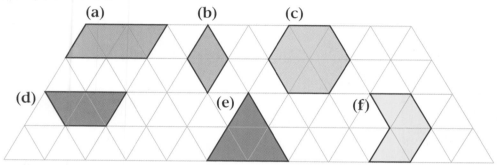

3 Show how you can make a regular octagon and a square tessellate. See if you find two other regular polygons that tessellate together.

4 Here is one shape with curved sides that tessellates. Find three more shapes with curved sides that tessellate. You must show at least eight of your shapes tessellating.

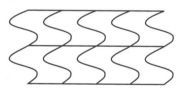

5 Make some interesting patterns using combinations of different shapes that tessellate.

7.5 Making accurate drawings

Line segments

A straight line can be continued forever in both directions. It has infinite length.

The part of the straight line that is between X and Y is called the **line segment** XY.

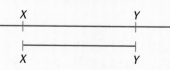

Sometimes you will be asked to make an accurate drawing from given measurements.

Example 5

Make an accurate drawing of triangle *ABC* with *AB* = 6 cm, *BC* = 5 cm and *CA* = 4 cm.

Make a rough sketch first, to get an idea of what your finished drawing should be like.

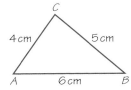

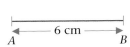

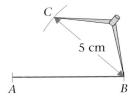

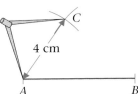

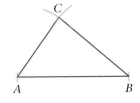

Start with the longest side. Draw a line segment 6 cm long and label its ends *A* and *B*.

Set your compasses to a radius of 5 cm. Put the point at *B* and draw an arc near where you think *C* will be.

Set your compasses to 4 cm. Put the point at *B* and draw a second arc. Point *C* is where the two arcs cross.

Join *C* to *A* and *B* to complete the triangle.

Leave in the arcs.

Example 6

Make an accurate drawing of triangle *PQR* with *PQ* = 5 cm, angle *P* = 40° and angle *Q* = 60°.

Make a rough sketch first.

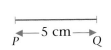

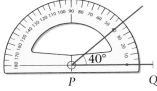

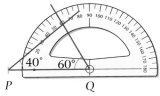

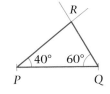

Draw a line segment 5 cm long and label its ends *P* and *Q*.

Place your protractor over point *P*. Mark a point at 40° (anticlockwise) and join it to *P* with a line.

Place your protractor over point *Q*. Mark a point at 60° (clockwise) and join it to *Q* with a line.

The new lines cross at *R* completing the triangle *PQR*.

Example 7

(a) Make an accurate drawing of quadrilateral *PQRS* with *PQ* = 6.4 cm, *PS* = 3.5 cm, *SR* = 4.7 cm, *QR* = 5.3 cm and angle *P* = 112°.

(b) Measure angle *QRS*.

(a) Make a rough sketch with the longest side at the bottom. The vertices *P*, *Q*, *R* and *S* should be in that order around the quadrilateral.

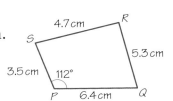

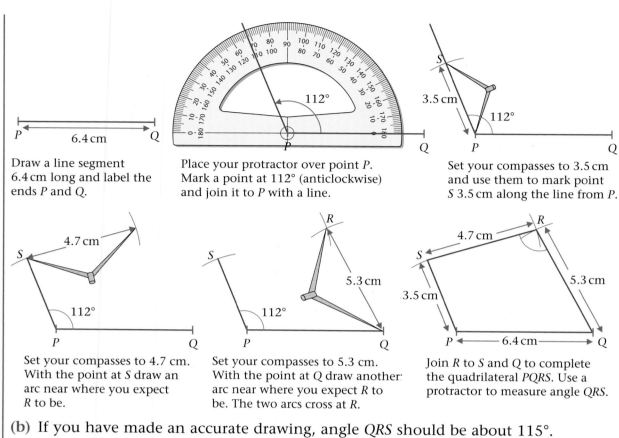

Draw a line segment
6.4 cm long and label the
ends P and Q.

Place your protractor over point P.
Mark a point at 112° (anticlockwise)
and join it to P with a line.

Set your compasses to 3.5 cm
and use them to mark point
S 3.5 cm along the line from P.

Set your compasses to 4.7 cm.
With the point at S draw an
arc near where you expect
R to be.

Set your compasses to 5.3 cm.
With the point at Q draw another
arc near where you expect R to
be. The two arcs cross at R.

Join R to S and Q to complete
the quadrilateral $PQRS$. Use a
protractor to measure angle QRS.

(b) If you have made an accurate drawing, angle QRS should be about 115°.

You can construct regular polygons inscribed in a circle
by dividing the circle equally.

This means a polygon
whose vertices all touch
the circle's circumference.

Example 8

Draw a circle with radius 5 cm.
Construct an inscribed regular polygon with nine sides.
The polygon is regular, so the angles at the centre are equal.
$9a = 360°$ so $a = 360° \div 9 = 40°$
Draw a sketch to help you.

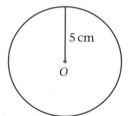
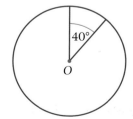
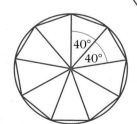

Draw a circle with radius
5 cm. Draw any radius.

Draw another radius at 40°
to the first radius. Continue
drawing radii at 40° to the
previous radius.

Join up the points where
the radii meet the circle with
nine lines. These lines will
form the regular polygon.

Exercise 7E

You need a ruler, compasses and a protractor.

1 Make accurate full-size drawings of these triangles:

(a)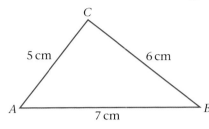

(b)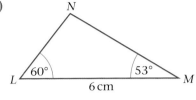

(c)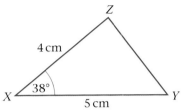

(d)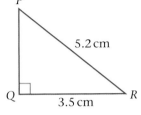

2 (a) Make an accurate drawing of the quadrilateral *ABCD*.
  (b) Measure and write down the size of angle *BAD*.

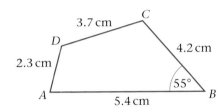

3 (a) Make an accurate drawing of the quadrilateral *PQRS*.
  (b) Measure and write down the length of *RS*.

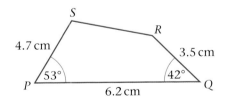

4 Draw a circle with radius 6 cm. Construct an inscribed regular polygon with nine sides.

5 Try to make accurate drawings of triangles with these measurements:
  (a) *ABC* with *AB* = 9 cm, angle *A* = 30° and *BC* = 3 cm
  (b) *LMN* with LM = 9 cm, angle *L* = 30° and *MN* = 5 cm
  (c) *XYZ* with *XY* = 9 cm, angle *X* = 30° and *YZ* = 4.5 cm.

It may be possible to draw more than one triangle, or no triangle at all for some measurements.

7.6 Using scales in accurate drawings

Maps and plans are accurate drawings from
which measurements can be made.

> There is more about ratios
> in Chapter 17.

A **scale** is a ratio which shows the
relationship between a length on a
drawing and the actual length in real life.

It didn't look that
far on the map.

Campsite 16 km

Ordnance Survey Pathfinder maps used by
hill walkers are on a scale of 1 to 25 000,
written 1 : 25 000.

1 cm on the map represents 25 000 cm
in real life, which is 250 m or a quarter
of a kilometre.

Example 9

The scale on a road map is
1 : 200 000.
Preston and Blackburn are
8 cm apart on the map.
(a) Work out the real distance,
    in km, between Preston
    and Blackburn.

York is 37 km in a straight line
from Leeds.
(b) Work out the distance of
    York from Leeds on the
    map.

Preston

Blackburn

(a) The distance on the map is 8 cm.
    The real distance is 8 cm × 200 000 = 1 600 000 cm
    Divide by 100 to change cm to m:

    real distance = 16 000 m

> Remember:
> 1 m = 100 cm
> 1 km = 1000 m

Divide by 1000 to change m to km:
The real distance between Preston and Blackburn is 16 km.

(b) The real distance is 37 km.
    Multiply by 1000 to change km to m:

    real distance = 37 × 1000 = 37 000 m

Multiply by 100 to change m to cm:
    real distance = 37 000 × 100 = 3 700 000 cm
Divide by 200 000 to find the distance on the map:

Distance on the map $= \dfrac{3\,700\,000}{200\,000} = 18.5$ cm

Scale drawings and bearings

Sometimes you will have to draw diagrams to scale and use bearings so that you can measure and calculate missing angles and distances.

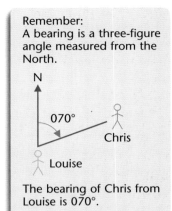
___ **Example 10** ___

Sam walks for 2 miles on a bearing of 060° from home.
He then walks a further 4 miles on a bearing of 300°.
How far is Sam from home? What bearing must Sam walk on to get back home? Use a scale of 2 cm to represent 1 mile.

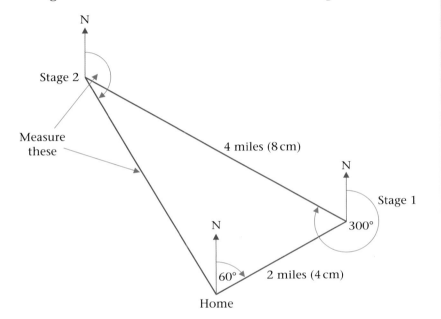

Step 1 Draw the bearing of 060° from home.
Step 2 Make the line 4 cm long. ● ─────────────
Step 3 Put in a new North line at the end of Stage 1.
Step 4 Draw the bearing of 300° from Stage 1.
Step 5 Make the line 8 cm long (4 miles is 4 × 2 cm).
Step 6 Put in a new North line at the end of Stage 2.
Step 7 Measure the distance from Stage 2 to home.
Step 8 Measure the bearing from Stage 2 to home.
Answer Sam is about 3.5 miles from home and must walk on a bearing of 150°.

> As the scale is 2 cm for 1 mile, you need to draw a line that is 4 cm long.

Exercise 7F

You will need a ruler and protractor.

1   The scale of a map is 1 cm to 2 km.
    The distance between Axton and Dixiville is 5.5 cm on the map.
    How many kilometres apart are Axton and Dixiville in real life?

2 A map is drawn on a scale of 3 cm to 1 km.

  (a) Work out the real length of a lake which is 4.2 cm long on the map.

  (b) The distance between the church in Canwick and the town hall in Barnton is 5.8 km. Work out the distance between them on the map.

> **Scale: 3 cm to 1 km**
> This means that a real length of 1 km is represented on the map by a length of 3 cm.

3 Jane walks for 10 miles on a bearing of 060°. Use a scale of 1 cm to represent 1 mile to show the journey.

4 Sam runs for 4 km on a bearing of 120°. Use a scale of 1 cm to represent 2 km to show the journey.

5 A plan of a rectangular playing field is drawn using a scale of 1 : 2500.

The width of the field on the plan is 5 cm.

  (a) **(i)** Work out the real width of the field in centimetres.

  (ii) Change your answer to metres.

The area of the field on the plan is 31.5 cm².

  (b) **(i)** Work out the length, in centimetres, of the playing field on the plan.

  (ii) Work out the real length, in metres, of the playing field.

6 On the map the scale is 1 : 50 000. Use the map to find

  (a) the distance of the church with a tower at Rampton from the church with a tower at Cottenham

  (b) the bearing of the church at Rampton from the church with a tower at Cottenham.

> The sign ✠ on this map represents a church with a tower.

> Use the straight edge of a piece of paper to join the two churches to help you measure the bearing. (See Example 5 on page 100).

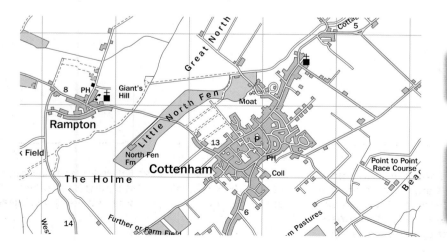

7   Witley is 2 km due South of Milford. The bearing of
    Hydestile from Milford is 125° and the distance from
    Milford to Hydestile is 2.8 km.
    (a) Make a scale drawing to show the three villages.
         Use a scale of 1 : 25 000.
    (b) Use your drawing to find
         (i) the distance of Hydestile from Witley
         (ii) the bearing of Hydestile from Witley.

> **Scale: 1 : 25 000**
> This means that 1 cm on
> the scale drawing
> represents a real length of
> 25 000 cm. This is the
> scale on maps often used
> by walkers.

8   Ian sails his boat from the Isle of Wight for 20 km on a
    bearing of 135°. He then sails on a bearing of 240° for
    10 km. How far is Ian from his starting point? What
    bearing does he need to sail on to get back to the start?
    Use a scale of 1 cm to represent 2 km.

9   Peg Leg the pirate buried his treasure 100 yards from
    the big tree on a bearing of 045°. One-Eyed Rick dug up
    the treasure and moved it 50 yards on a bearing of 310°
    from where it had been buried.
    How far is the treasure from the big tree now?
    What bearing is the new hiding place of the treasure?
    Use a scale of 1 cm to represent 10 yards.

10 Ray flew his plane on a bearing of 300° for 200 km.
    He then changed direction and flew on a bearing of 150°
    for 100 km. What bearing must Ray fly on to get back to
    the start? How far is he away from the start?

7.7 Constructing angles without a protractor

You will be expected to be able to draw some angles without
using a protractor. You will need a pair of compasses and a
straight edge (ruler).

Angle of 60°

Draw a line segment
AB.

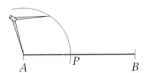

Put your compass point
at *A* and draw an arc that
crosses the line segment.
Make sure your compass
setting does not change.

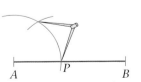

Put your compass point
at *P* and draw an arc to
cut the first arc.

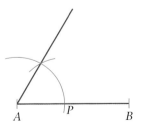

Then draw a line from
A through the point
where the two arcs meet.

Bisecting an angle (cutting an angle in half)

Put your compass point at A. Draw an arc that crosses both lines.

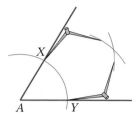

Put your compass point at X and then Y and draw two arcs that cross.

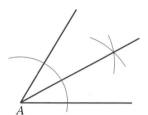

Draw a line to bisect the angle.

You can now use this technique of bisecting an angle to bisect a 60° angle and get a 30° angle.

Drawing an angle of 90°

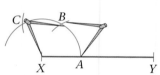

Draw a line segment XY. Put your compass point at X. Draw an arc that crosses XY at A. Move the compass point to A. Draw an arc at B

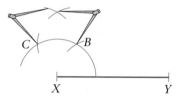

Put your compass point at B and then C. Draw arcs to cross above X.

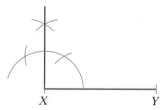

Draw a line from X through the point where the two arcs cross.

Bisecting a line

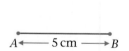

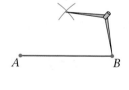

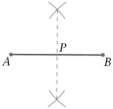

Draw a line segment 5 cm long and label its ends A and B.

Set your compasses to any radius greater than 2.5 cm (5 cm ÷ 2). With the point at A draw arcs on each side of the line segment where you expect the bisector to be.

Keep the compasses at the same radius but move the point to B and draw two new arcs.

Draw a line segment joining the points where the arcs cross. This is the perpendicular bisector of AB. Mark with a P the point where this perpendicular bisector crosses the line segment AB.

Exercise 7G

Use the ideas of starting with 60° and bisecting angles to construct the angles in questions 1–8.

1	60°	**2**	30°	**3**	120°	**4**	90°
5	45°	**6**	75°	**7**	15°	**8**	135°

9 Draw a line that is 6 cm long and bisect it.
Check that each part is 3 cm long.

10 Draw a triangle that has sides 10 cm, 8 cm and 8 cm.
Bisect each of the sides. The bisectors should meet at a point. Use that point as the centre to draw a circle. The circle should pass through all the vertices of the triangle.

11 Draw a triangle that has sides 15 cm, 10 cm and 8 cm.
Bisect each of the angles. The bisectors should meet at a point. Use that point as the centre to draw a circle. The circle should touch each of the sides of the triangle.

7.8 Finding the locus of a point

To enter the harbour safely this boat must follow the path shown by the red dotted line.

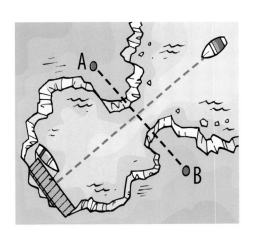

All the points on the path obey a rule:

Each point is always equidistant (the same distance) from *A* and *B*.

This path is called the **locus** of the points.

A **locus** is a set of points that obey a given rule.

Here are the main ideas behind the loci you need to know.

Loci is the plural of locus.

The locus of points equidistant from **one point** is a circle.

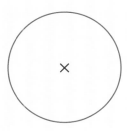

The locus of points equidistant from **two points** is the perpendicular bisector of the line joining the two points.

The locus of points equidistant from **one line** is made from two semicircles and two parallel lines.

The locus of points equidistant from **two lines** is made by bisecting the angles formed by *AB* and *CD*.

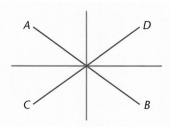

Regions

Sometimes the locus is a **region** of space.

The key words here are 'greater than', 'less than', 'nearer to'.

> Remember these signs:
> $<$ less than
> $>$ greater than

___ **Example 11** _____

(a) Shade the region that is less than 3 cm from *A*.

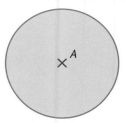

Draw the locus of the points 3 cm from *A* and shade inside the circle.

(b) Shade the region that is nearer to *BC* than to *AB*.

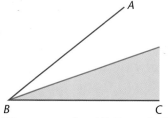

Bisect angle *ABC* and shade the part that is nearer to *BC* than it is to *AB*.

___ **Worked examination question** _____

A, *B* and *C* represent three radio masts on a plan.

Signals from mast *A* can be received 300 km away, those from mast *B* 350 km away and those from mast *C* 200 km away.

Show, by shading, the region in which signals can be received from all three masts.   [E]

B •

• A

• C

Scale: 1 cm represents 100 km

Signals from *A* can be received inside a circle with centre *A* and radius 300 km.

1 cm represents 100 km so 3 cm represents 300 km. Draw a circle with centre *A* and radius 3 cm.

In the same way draw circles with centre *B* and radius 3.5 cm and with centre *C* and radius 2 cm.

The region in which all three signals can be received must be inside all the circles, so it is the region shaded in the diagram.

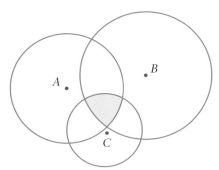

This is a scaled-down sketch.

Exercise 7H

1 Draw the locus of all points that are 5 cm from a point *P*.

2 Draw the locus of all points that are 5 cm from a line *AB* that is 8 cm long.

3 Points *P* and *Q* are 8 cm apart. Draw the locus of all points that are the same distance from *P* as they are from *Q*.

4 *AB* and *CD* are two perpendicular lines. Draw the locus of all points that are the same distance from *AB* as they are from *CD*.

5 Draw a square with sides of length 4 cm. Draw the locus of all points that are 5 cm from the sides of the square.

6 Here is a diagram of a rectangular garden. Copy it into your book using a scale of 1 cm to 1 m.

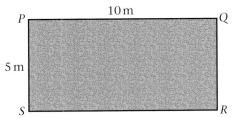

A tree is to be planted nearer to *PQ* than to *PS* and less than 4 metres from *P*. Shade the region within the garden where the tree could be planted.

7 Two marker buoys *A* and *B* are in the sea near the town of Barry. *B* is 250 m due East of *A*.
   (a) Using a scale of 1 cm to 50 m make an accurate drawing to show the positions of *A* and *B*.

Juliet sails her boat so that she is always the same distance from *A* as from *B*.
   (b) Construct accurately the course along which Juliet sails.

8 In triangle *DEF*, *DE* = 7 cm, angle *D* = 42° and angle *E* = 57°.
   (a) Make an accurate drawing of triangle *DEF*.
   (b) Draw accurately the locus of all points that are the same distance from *D* as from *E*.
   (c) Draw the locus of all points that are 4 cm from *D*.
   (d) Mark the points *P* and *Q* which are on both loci.

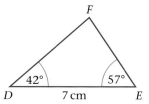

9 The map shows part of a coastline and a coastguard station. 1 cm on the map represents 2 km.
   A ship is 12 km from the coastguard station on a bearing of 160°.
   (a) Use tracing paper to make a copy of the map. Plot the position of the ship from the coastguard station.
   It is not safe for ships to come within 6 km of the coastguard station.
   (b) Shade the area on the map which is less than 6 km from the coastguard station.

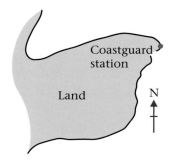

Mixed exercise 7

1 Write down the name of each of these shapes:
   (a)  **(b)** 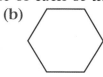 **(c)**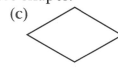

2 Write down the letters of the shapes that are congruent.

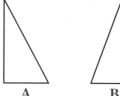   

A   B   C   D   E

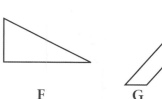 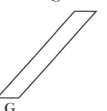

F   G   H

Floor pattern in an Italian church.

3 Use a grid made of centimetre squares to show how these shapes will tessellate. You must draw at least eight shapes.
   (a) 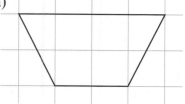 **(b)** 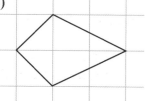 **(c)**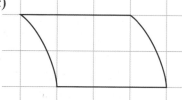

4 The diagram shows a sketch of triangle *ABC*.
$BC = 7.3$ cm
$AC = 8$ cm
Angle $C = 38°$
(a) Make an accurate drawing of triangle *ABC*.
(b) Measure the size of angle *A* on your diagram.   [E]

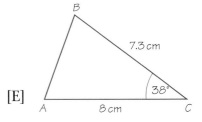

5 On a copy of the grid below, draw a line from the point *C* perpendicular to the line *AB*.

[E]

6 This is a map of Northern England.

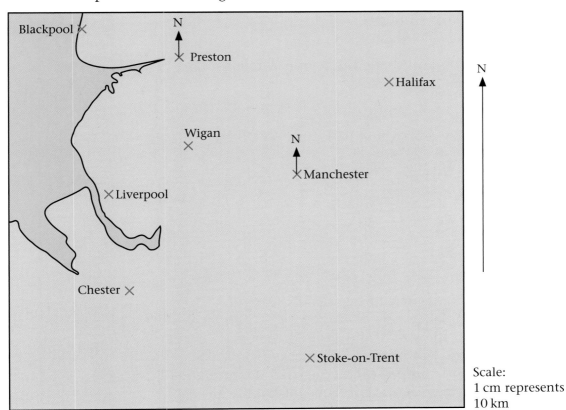

Scale:
1 cm represents
10 km

A plane flies in a straight line from Preston to Stoke-on-Trent.
(a) How far does it fly?
    Give your answer in kilometres.
(b) Measure and write down the bearing of Preston from Manchester.   [E]

7 Using ruler and compasses **construct** an angle of 45°.
You must show **all** construction lines.   [E]

8 The diagram represents a triangular garden *ABC*.

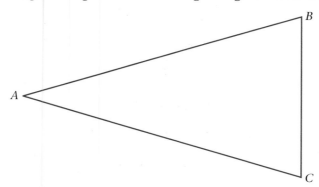

The scale of the diagram is 1 cm to represent 1 m. A tree
is to be planted in the garden so that it is

> nearer to *AB* than to *AC*
> within 5 m of point *A*.

Trace the diagram and shade the region where the tree
may be planted.   [E]

9 This is part of the design of a pattern found at the
theatre of Diana at Alexandria.

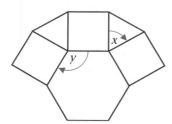

It is made up of a regular hexagon, squares and
equilateral triangles.
(a) Write down the size of the angle marked *x*.
(b) Work out the size of the angle marked *y*.
(c) Use ruler and compasses to **construct** an equilateral
triangle with sides of 4 cm. You must show all
construction lines.

10 Draw triangle *PQR* with *PQ* = 10 cm, *QR* = 8 cm and
RP = 6 cm.
Bisect the lines *PQ*, *QR* and *RP*.

Summary of key points

1 A **polygon** is a 2-D shape with any number of straight sides.

A pentagon

2 A polygon is **regular** if all its sides and all its angles are equal.

A regular pentagon

3 Shapes which are exactly the same size and shape are **congruent**.

These shapes are congruent

4 A pattern of shapes which fit together without leaving gaps or overlapping is called a **tessellation**.

5 A straight line can be continued forever in both directions. It has infinite length. The part of the straight line that is between X and Y is called the **line segment** XY.

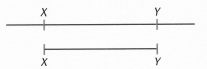

6 A **scale** is a ratio which shows the relationship between a length on a drawing and the actual length in real life.

7 Using a pair of compasses and a ruler you can construct an angle of 60°, bisect an angle and bisect a line without using a protractor.

8 A **locus** is a set of points that obey a given rule.

9 The locus of points equidistant from **one point** is a circle.

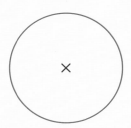

10 The locus of points equidistant from **two points** is the perpendicular bisector.

11 The locus of points equidistant from **one line** is made from two semicircles and two parallel lines.

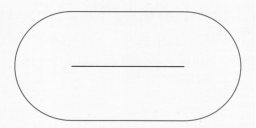

12 The locus of points equidistant from **two lines** is made by bisecting the angles formed by *AB* and *CD*.

13 Sometimes the locus is a **region** of space.

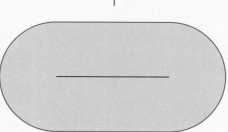

⑧ Fractions

8.1 Fractions from pictures

All these things can be divided into parts called **fractions**:

This football pitch has two halves.

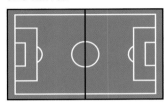

One part is **one half** or $\frac{1}{2}$ of the pitch.

This DVD has eight sectors.

One part is **one eighth** or $\frac{1}{8}$ of the DVD.

This chessboard has 64 small squares.

One part is **one sixty-fourth** or $\frac{1}{64}$ of the board.

Using numbers to represent fractions

I am going to eat three quarters or $\frac{3}{4}$ of this omelette.

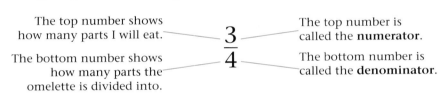

The top number shows how many parts I will eat.

The bottom number shows how many parts the omelette is divided into.

$$\frac{3}{4}$$

The top number is called the **numerator**.

The bottom number is called the **denominator**.

Two thirds or $\frac{2}{3}$ of these parking spaces are occupied.

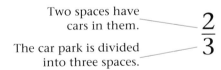

Two spaces have cars in them.

The car park is divided into three spaces.

$$\frac{2}{3}$$

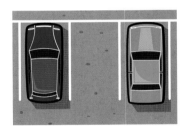

Exercise 8A

1 Copy these shapes into a table like the one on the right. Complete the table. The first shape has been done for you.

Shape	Fraction shaded	Fraction not shaded
⊘	$\frac{1}{2}$	$\frac{1}{2}$

2 Make four copies of this rectangle.
Shade them to show these fractions:

(a) $\frac{1}{16}$ (b) $\frac{3}{16}$ (c) $\frac{8}{16}$ (d) $\frac{16}{16}$

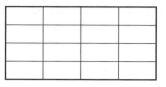

3 Make three copies of this circle.
Shade them to show these fractions:

(a) $\frac{1}{6}$ (b) $\frac{3}{6}$ (c) $\frac{1}{2}$

4 Here is a counting stick with an arrow showing $\frac{7}{10}$:

Draw three more sticks with length 10 cm. Use them to show

(a) $\frac{3}{10}$ (b) $\frac{1}{10}$ (c) $\frac{5}{10}$

8.2 Fractions from words

Sometimes you will need to use fractions to solve problems given in words.

Example 1

John has a collection of 1000 stamps.
113 are British stamps. The others are foreign.

What fraction of John's collection is

(a) British   (b) foreign?

(a) 113 of the 1000 stamps are British.
The fraction is $\frac{113}{1000}$

(b) 1000 − 113 = 887 stamps are foreign.
The fraction is $\frac{887}{1000}$

Exercise 8B

1 There are 28 people on a martial arts course. 13 are female and 15 are male. What fraction of the people are

(a) male   (b) female?

2 28 competitors took part in a surfing competition on a Saturday, and a further 47 took part on Sunday.

(a) How many surfers were there altogether?

(b) What fraction of the surfers competed on Saturday?

(c) What fraction of the surfers competed only on Sunday?

3 A transport company has a fleet of 51 vehicles.
37 are lorries, 10 are vans and 4 are cars.
What fraction of the fleet is

    (a) lorries   **(b)** vans   **(c)** cars?

4 A plumber's weekly earnings are £317 per week.
£298 is basic pay and £19 is bonus pay.
What fraction of his weekly earnings is

    (a) basic pay   **(b)** bonus pay?

5 In the safari section of the zoo there are 7 zebras, 3 lions,
5 hippos and 1 giraffe.
    (a) How many animals are there altogether?
What fraction of the entries are

    (b) zebras   **(c)** lions   **(d)** hippos   **(e)** giraffes?

6 An electrical superstore sold 5 CD players, 6 DVD players,
4 refrigerators and 2 freezers.
    (a) How many items were sold altogether?
What fraction of the items sold were

    (b) CD players   **(c)** DVD players
    (d) refrigerators   **(e)** freezers?

7 A taxi driver works 11 hours a day.
She spends 6 hours driving, 4 hours waiting for
passengers and 1 hour on paperwork.
What fraction of her working day is spent

    (a) driving   **(b)** waiting   **(c)** on paperwork?

8.3 Improper fractions and mixed numbers

These fractions are **top heavy**:

    $\frac{5}{4}$ is top heavy because 5 is bigger than 4

    $\frac{11}{9}$ is top heavy because 11 is bigger than 9

Top heavy fractions are also called **improper fractions**.

An improper fraction can also be written as a **mixed number**
(a mixture of a whole number and a fraction, and a mixed
number can also be written as an improper fraction.

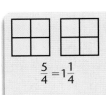

$$\text{improper fraction} \longrightarrow \frac{11}{9} = \frac{9}{9} + \frac{2}{9} = 1\frac{2}{9} \longleftarrow \text{mixed number}$$

Example 2

Change the mixed number $1\frac{4}{7}$ to an improper fraction.

1 can be written as $\frac{7}{7}$ so $1\frac{4}{7} = \frac{7}{7} + \frac{4}{7} = \frac{11}{7}$

Example 3

Write $5\frac{3}{7}$ as an improper fraction.

5 can be written as $\frac{5 \times 7}{7} = \frac{35}{7}$ so $5\frac{3}{7} = \frac{35}{7} + \frac{3}{7} = \frac{38}{7}$

Exercise 8C

1 Change these improper fractions to mixed numbers.

(a) $\frac{5}{2}$ (b) $\frac{7}{4}$ (c) $\frac{9}{7}$ (d) $\frac{11}{8}$

(e) $\frac{9}{8}$ (f) $\frac{16}{5}$ (g) $\frac{23}{10}$ (h) $\frac{24}{5}$

(i) $\frac{16}{7}$ (j) $\frac{12}{5}$ (k) $\frac{20}{3}$ (l) $\frac{16}{9}$

(m) $\frac{39}{4}$ (n) $\frac{27}{5}$ (o) $\frac{26}{9}$ (p) $\frac{17}{10}$

> Divide the bottom number into the top number,
> e.g. $\frac{7}{2} = 7 \div 2 = 3\frac{1}{2}$

2 Change these mixed numbers to improper fractions.

(a) $1\frac{1}{2}$ (b) $5\frac{1}{2}$ (c) $2\frac{3}{4}$ (d) $1\frac{2}{3}$

(e) $3\frac{1}{4}$ (f) $4\frac{2}{5}$ (g) $3\frac{7}{10}$ (h) $5\frac{1}{5}$

(i) $7\frac{3}{4}$ (j) $2\frac{1}{4}$ (k) $1\frac{9}{10}$ (l) $9\frac{1}{3}$

(m) $2\frac{5}{6}$ (n) $5\frac{3}{8}$ (o) $3\frac{5}{8}$ (p) $1\frac{9}{100}$

8.4 Finding a fraction of a quantity

You need to be able to do calculations like these:

$\frac{3}{4}$ of £60 $\frac{5}{8}$ of 160

> $\frac{3}{4} = 3 \div 4$

Example 4

Find $\frac{3}{4}$ of £60.

Multiply the numerator 3 by the quantity 60: $\frac{3 \times 60}{4} = \frac{180}{4}$

Divide the result 180 by the denominator 4: $\frac{180}{4} = 45$

So $\frac{3}{4}$ of £60 is £45.

> Another method:
> one quarter is
> $\frac{60}{4} = 15$
> three quarters is
> $3 \times 15 = 45$

If you are dealing with small numbers then you can use this more practical approach:

Example 5

Find $\frac{5}{6}$ of £48.

You make 6 boxes and count out the 48 pounds between them:

You end up with 8 in each box.

Then count how many there are in 5 of the boxes.

The answer is £40.

Exercise 8D

1 Find

    (a) $\frac{1}{2}$ of 70   (b) $\frac{2}{5}$ of £65   (c) $\frac{3}{10}$ of 80 kg

    (d) $\frac{2}{3}$ of 96   (e) $\frac{3}{8}$ of £56   (f) $\frac{3}{4}$ of 60p

    (g) $\frac{1}{4}$ of £6.80   (h) $\frac{7}{10}$ of 90p   (i) $\frac{7}{8}$ of £3.20

2 Work out

    (a) $\frac{1}{8}$ of 72   (b) $\frac{5}{6}$ of 36

    (c) $\frac{4}{9}$ of 63 litres   (d) $\frac{7}{16}$ of 48 pints

3 Work out

    (a) $\frac{3}{4}$ of 36 lb   (b) $\frac{2}{5}$ of £5.55

    (c) $\frac{11}{12}$ of 720 km   (d) $\frac{4}{7}$ of 490 people

4 A superstore employs 85 people. $\frac{2}{5}$ are men.

    (a) How many men does the store employ?

    (b) How many women does the store employ?

5 A chain store closed $\frac{2}{15}$ of its 345 shops.
How many shops were closed?

6 Out of 186 pupils in Year 10 of Angel High School, $\frac{1}{3}$ have an MP3 player. How many is this?

7 The metal parts of a car weigh 1250 kg. $\frac{3}{10}$ of the metal is recycled. How much does the recycled metal weigh?

8 Stan sold 560 sandwiches today. $\frac{1}{4}$ were ham sandwiches, $\frac{2}{5}$ were salad, $\frac{1}{8}$ were tuna and the rest were cheese. How many of each type did Stan sell?

9 In a survey conducted by a local newspaper, 3500 people were questioned about the construction of a new skate park. $\frac{1}{10}$ were against the project, $\frac{7}{10}$ were in favour and the rest abstained. How many people

(a) were against the project

(b) were in favour of the project

(c) abstained?

10 A department store had 480 customers last Saturday. $\frac{2}{3}$ paid by credit card, $\frac{1}{4}$ paid by cheque and the others paid in cash.
How many customers paid

(a) by credit card

(b) by cheque

(c) in cash?

11 During a 28-week holiday season, $\frac{2}{7}$ of the days were wet. How many dry days were there?

12 Jomo delivers 56 newspapers on his round. On Fridays $\frac{3}{8}$ of the newspapers have a magazine supplement. How many supplements does he deliver?

8.5 Simplifying fractions

Fractions can be **simplified** if the numerator (top) and denominator (bottom) have a common factor.

> Simplifying fractions means writing them in their lowest terms. This is also called cancelling fractions.

For example:

$\dfrac{4}{8}$ The numerator will divide by 4

        The denominator will divide by 4

4 is a common factor.

$\dfrac{4}{8}$ 4 divided by 4 is 1   8 divided by 4 is 2 $\dfrac{1}{2}$ so $\frac{4}{8}$ can be simplified to $\frac{1}{2}$

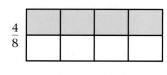

$\frac{4}{8}$ and $\frac{1}{2}$ are **equivalent fractions**. They represent the same value. To simplify a fraction you find an equivalent fraction that has smaller numbers on the top and bottom.

Example 6

Simplify $\frac{9}{15}$ by finding a common factor.

3 is a common factor of 9 and 15.

$$\frac{9}{15} \quad \boxed{\text{9 divided by 3 is 3}} \quad \boxed{\text{15 divided by 3 is 5}} \Rightarrow \frac{3}{5}$$

Factors of 9 are: 1, 3, 9
Factors of 15 are: 1, 3, 5, 15

3 is a common factor

$\frac{9}{15}$  is the same as $\frac{3}{5}$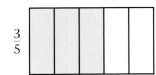

Example 7

Simplify $\frac{24}{30}$ by finding a common factor.

3 is a common factor of 24 and 30.

$$\frac{24}{30} \quad \boxed{\text{24 divided by 3 is 8}} \quad \boxed{\text{30 divided by 3 is 10}} \Rightarrow \frac{8}{10}$$

$\frac{8}{10}$ can also be simplified. 2 is a common factor of 8 and 10.

$$\frac{8}{10} \quad \boxed{\text{8 divided by 2 is 4}} \quad \boxed{\text{10 divided by 2 is 5}} \Rightarrow \frac{4}{5}$$

$\frac{4}{5}$ cannot be simplified any more. This fraction is in its **simplest form**.

Exercise 8E

1 Write each fraction in its simplest form.
   (a) $\frac{12}{18}$ (b) $\frac{9}{15}$ (c) $\frac{20}{35}$ (d) $\frac{18}{24}$ (e) $\frac{14}{21}$

2 Write these in their simplest form.
   (a) $\frac{6}{8}$ (b) $\frac{30}{36}$ (c) $\frac{40}{48}$ (d) $\frac{35}{49}$ (e) $\frac{25}{45}$

3 Write these in their simplest form.
   (a) $\frac{20}{32}$ (b) $\frac{48}{64}$ (c) $\frac{21}{27}$ (d) $\frac{24}{60}$ (e) $\frac{48}{72}$

4 Simplify these fractions by finding common factors.
   (a) $\frac{4}{6}$ (b) $\frac{3}{6}$ (c) $\frac{2}{4}$ (d) $\frac{3}{9}$
   (e) $\frac{4}{10}$ (f) $\frac{8}{12}$ (g) $\frac{14}{21}$ (h) $\frac{15}{20}$
   (i) $\frac{14}{22}$ (i) $\frac{24}{28}$ (k) $\frac{27}{36}$ (l) $\frac{25}{30}$

5 Copy these shapes into a table like the one on the right.
For each shape use two equivalent
fractions to describe how much is shaded.
The first shape has been done for you.

Shape	Fraction	Fraction
⊕	$\frac{2}{4}$	$\frac{1}{2}$

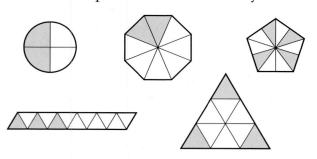

In questions **6**, **7** and **8** write your answers as fractions in
their simplest form.

6 A car salesman sold 6 new cars and 15 secondhand cars.
What fraction of the cars were

   (a) new   (b) secondhand?

7 Siân has collected autographs from 16 pop stars,
28 footballers and 12 athletes.
What fraction of her autographs are from

   (a) pop stars   (b) footballers

   (c) athletes?

8 Form 11B were surveyed about
their favourite type of movies.
What fraction chose

   (a) comedy   (b) action

   (c) musical   (d) other?

Movie Survey Results	
Comedy	13
Action	5
Musical	3
Other	7

8.6 Equivalent fractions

This circle is divided into 8 parts.

Each part is $\frac{1}{8}$ (or one eighth) of the whole circle.

The shaded area is $\frac{2}{8}$ of the whole circle.

The shaded area is also $\frac{1}{4}$ (or one quarter) of the whole circle.

$\frac{2}{8}$ and $\frac{1}{4}$ represent the same area of the circle. They are called
equivalent fractions.

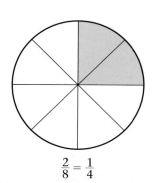

$$\frac{2}{8} = \frac{1}{4}$$

Equivalent fractions are fractions that have the same value.

Example 8

Make a list of fractions equivalent to $\frac{2}{3}$

$$\frac{2}{3} = \frac{4}{6} = \frac{6}{9} = \frac{8}{12} = \frac{10}{15} = \frac{12}{18} \cdots$$

— The top row goes up in the 2 time table.

— The bottom row goes up in the 3 times table.

Example 9

Change $\frac{5}{8}$ to an equivalent fraction with the denominator 48.

2 To get an equivalent fraction, multiply the numerator 5 by 6 too.

$$\frac{5}{8} = \frac{5 \times 6}{8 \times 6} = \frac{30}{48}$$

1 To change the denominator from 8 to 48, multiply 8 by 6.

So $\frac{5}{8}$ and $\frac{30}{48}$ are equivalent fractions.

Exercise 8F

For each of these diagrams write down at least two equivalent fractions that describe the shaded fraction.

1 (a)   **(b)** 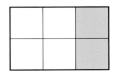   **(c)**   **(d)**

(e) 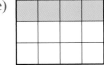   **(f)**   **(g)**   **(h)**

(i)   **(j)**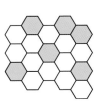

Copy and complete each set of equivalent fractions.

2 (a) $\dfrac{3}{4} = \dfrac{}{8} = \dfrac{}{12} = \dfrac{}{16} = \dfrac{}{20} = \dfrac{}{24}$

(b) $\dfrac{2}{7} = \dfrac{}{14} = \dfrac{}{21} = \dfrac{}{28} = \dfrac{}{35} = \dfrac{}{42}$

(c) $\dfrac{4}{5} = \dfrac{}{10} = \dfrac{}{15} = \dfrac{}{20} = \dfrac{}{25} = \dfrac{}{30}$

(d) $\dfrac{1}{3} = \dfrac{}{9} = \dfrac{}{18} = \dfrac{}{27} = \dfrac{}{36} = \dfrac{}{45}$

3 (a) $\dfrac{1}{6} = \dfrac{}{18}$ (b) $\dfrac{3}{7} = \dfrac{}{14}$ (c) $\dfrac{3}{8} = \dfrac{}{48}$ (d) $\dfrac{4}{7} = \dfrac{}{21}$

(e) $\dfrac{5}{6} = \dfrac{}{36}$ (f) $\dfrac{2}{3} = \dfrac{6}{}$ (g) $\dfrac{4}{9} = \dfrac{24}{}$ (h) $\dfrac{5}{7} = \dfrac{}{56}$

(i) $\dfrac{9}{10} = \dfrac{90}{}$ (j) $\dfrac{7}{12} = \dfrac{84}{}$ (k) $\dfrac{7}{8} = \dfrac{49}{}$ (l) $\dfrac{2}{9} = \dfrac{}{81}$

4 (a) Find a fraction equivalent to $\frac{1}{2}$ and a fraction equivalent to $\frac{1}{3}$ so that the denominators of the two new fractions are equal.

(b) Repeat part **(a)** for

    (i) $\frac{2}{5}$ and $\frac{3}{6}$ (ii) $\frac{1}{10}$ and $\frac{1}{7}$ (iii) $\frac{1}{4}$ and $\frac{5}{6}$

    (iv) $\frac{1}{2}$ and $\frac{3}{5}$ (v) $\frac{2}{3}$ and $\frac{1}{8}$ (vi) $\frac{3}{4}$ and $\frac{3}{5}$

8.7 Putting fractions in order of size

Which is larger, $\frac{3}{4}$ or $\frac{3}{5}$? Equivalent fractions can help you decide.

First make lists of equivalent fractions for $\frac{3}{4}$ and $\frac{3}{5}$:

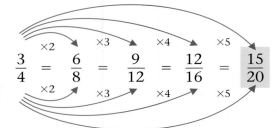 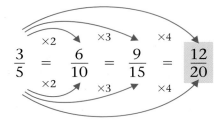

> Compare the lists. Find fractions with the same denominator (bottom).

$\frac{15}{20}$ is larger than $\frac{12}{20}$ (imagine a cake divided into 20 parts and getting either 12 or 15 slices).

As $\frac{15}{20}$ is equivalent to $\frac{3}{4}$ and $\frac{12}{20}$ is equivalent to $\frac{3}{5}$,

$\frac{3}{4}$ must be *larger* than $\frac{3}{5}$

Another way of checking which of two fractions is bigger is to represent them as parts of a rectangle.

For $\frac{2}{3}$ and $\frac{3}{4}$ you need to split a rectangle into 3 and 4 (thirds and quarters).

You split the rectangle in two directions so that you can compare the fractions you have shaded.

8 parts are shaded for $\frac{2}{3}$ and 9 for $\frac{3}{4}$, so $\frac{3}{4}$ is bigger.

Thirds   Quarters

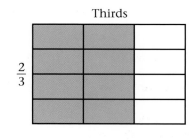 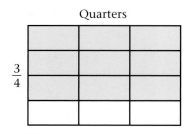

Exercise 8G

1 By shading rectangles show which of each pair of
   fractions is the larger.
   (a) $\frac{3}{4}$ or $\frac{1}{2}$ (b) $\frac{1}{3}$ or $\frac{1}{4}$ (c) $\frac{4}{5}$ or $\frac{3}{4}$ (d) $\frac{5}{6}$ or $\frac{4}{5}$

2 By writing equivalent fractions find the smaller fraction.
   (a) $\frac{2}{5}$ or $\frac{1}{4}$ (b) $\frac{3}{4}$ or $\frac{4}{5}$ (c) $\frac{2}{3}$ or $\frac{3}{4}$ (d) $\frac{3}{5}$ or $\frac{7}{10}$

3 Which is larger:
   (a) $\frac{2}{5}$ or $\frac{3}{6}$ (b) $\frac{1}{10}$ or $\frac{1}{7}$ (c) $\frac{1}{4}$ or $\frac{5}{6}$
   (d) $\frac{1}{2}$ or $\frac{3}{5}$ (e) $\frac{2}{3}$ or $\frac{1}{8}$ (f) $\frac{3}{4}$ or $\frac{3}{5}$?

4 Write these fractions in order of size. Put the smallest one
   first.
   (a) $\frac{1}{2}, \frac{3}{4}, \frac{2}{3}$ (b) $\frac{4}{5}, \frac{5}{6}, \frac{7}{15}$ (c) $\frac{3}{4}, \frac{4}{5}, \frac{1}{2}$ (d) $\frac{3}{7}, \frac{5}{14}, \frac{1}{2}, \frac{4}{7}$

5 Put these fractions in order of size, starting with the largest:
   $\frac{2}{5}$ $\frac{1}{2}$ $\frac{7}{8}$ $\frac{3}{4}$ $\frac{2}{10}$

Using fractions in your exam

In your exam, fractions will usually appear in the context of a
number problem or in questions on probability, areas or
volumes. You need to be able to add, subtract, multiply and
divide fractions in such problems. The rest of this chapter
shows you how to do this.

8.8 Adding fractions

It is easy to add fractions when the denominators (bottom)
are the same:

Easy to add:

$$\frac{1}{4} + \frac{2}{4} = \frac{3}{4}$$

Denominators are the same.

Harder to add:

$$\frac{1}{2} + \frac{2}{3} = ?$$

Denominators are different.

Adding fractions with the same denominator

$$\frac{7}{10} + \frac{2}{10} = \frac{9}{10}$$

Add the numerators (top).

Write them over the
same denominator (bottom).

Adding fractions with different denominators

$$\frac{1}{2} + \frac{2}{3} = ?$$

First find equivalent fractions to these that have the same denominator (bottom):

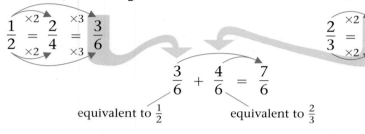

Fractions equivalent to $\frac{1}{2}$

Fractions equivalent to $\frac{2}{3}$

$$\frac{3}{6} + \frac{4}{6} = \frac{7}{6}$$

equivalent to $\frac{1}{2}$ equivalent to $\frac{2}{3}$

These fractions have the same denominator (bottom). Now they are easy to add.

So $\frac{1}{2} + \frac{2}{3} = \frac{7}{6}$

$\frac{7}{6}$ is top heavy. You can write it as a mixed number: $1\frac{1}{6}$

> To **add** fractions, find equivalent fractions that have the same denominator (bottom).

Example 10

Work out $\frac{2}{3} + \frac{7}{12}$

Find equivalent fractions to these that have the same denominator (bottom):

$$\frac{2}{3} + \frac{7}{12} = ?$$

Notice that
$3 \times 4 = 12$

So you only need to change one of the fractions:

$$\frac{2}{3} \xrightarrow[\times 4]{\times 4} \frac{8}{12}$$

Now both have the same denominator:

$$\frac{8}{12} + \frac{7}{12} = \frac{15}{12}$$

equivalent to $\frac{2}{3}$

So $\frac{8}{12} + \frac{7}{12} = \frac{15}{12}$

$\frac{15}{12}$ is top heavy. It is usually written as a mixed number: $1\frac{3}{12}$

This simplifies to $1\frac{1}{4}$.

Example 11

Work out $\frac{5}{8} + \frac{3}{7}$

Find equivalent fractions to these that have the same denominator (bottom).

$\frac{5}{8} \xrightarrow{\times 7} = \frac{35}{56}$ $\frac{3}{7} \xrightarrow{\times 8} = \frac{24}{56}$

Notice that $7 \times 8 = 56$
56 is the lowest common multiple of 7 and 8.

$\frac{35}{56} + \frac{24}{56} = \frac{59}{56}$ Same denominator – now you can add the numerators.

So $\frac{5}{8} + \frac{3}{7} = \frac{59}{56}$

$\frac{59}{56}$ is top heavy. It is usually written as a mixed number: $1\frac{3}{56}$

Example 12

Work out $2\frac{1}{4} + 3\frac{1}{5}$

These are **mixed numbers**. First add the whole numbers: $2 + 3 = 5$

Then add the fractions:

$\frac{1}{4} + \frac{1}{5} = ?$

Change both denominators (bottom) to 20 because $4 \times 5 = 20$:

$\frac{1}{4} \xrightarrow{\times 5} = \frac{5}{20}$ $\frac{1}{5} \xrightarrow{\times 4} = \frac{4}{20}$

$\frac{5}{20} + \frac{4}{20} = \frac{9}{20}$ Same denominator – now you can add the numerators.

Now put the whole numbers and the fractions back together:

5 and $\frac{9}{20}$ is $5\frac{9}{20}$

So $2\frac{1}{4} + 3\frac{1}{5} = 5\frac{9}{20}$

Exercise 8H

1 Work out

(a) $\frac{3}{8} + \frac{4}{8}$ (b) $\frac{2}{9} + \frac{5}{9}$ (c) $\frac{5}{12} + \frac{1}{12}$ (d) $\frac{5}{18} + \frac{11}{18}$

(e) $\frac{1}{2} + \frac{1}{4}$ (f) $\frac{1}{4} + \frac{3}{8}$ (g) $\frac{1}{2} + \frac{7}{8}$ (h) $\frac{2}{3} + \frac{1}{6}$

(i) $\frac{5}{6} + \frac{1}{3}$ (j) $\frac{2}{5} + \frac{3}{10}$ (k) $\frac{7}{12} + \frac{3}{4}$ (l) $\frac{3}{4} + \frac{7}{20}$

(m) $\frac{1}{8} + \frac{3}{8}$ (n) $\frac{2}{7} + \frac{4}{7}$ (o) $\frac{2}{5} + \frac{4}{5}$ (p) $\frac{9}{10} + \frac{7}{10}$

(q) $\frac{7}{9} + 2\frac{4}{9}$ (r) $\frac{5}{6} + 1\frac{5}{6}$ (s) $\frac{3}{4} + \frac{3}{4} + \frac{1}{4}$ (t) $\frac{3}{8} + \frac{5}{8} + \frac{7}{8}$

2 Work out

(a) $\frac{1}{2} + \frac{7}{8}$ (b) $\frac{3}{4} + \frac{1}{10}$ (c) $\frac{4}{9} + \frac{5}{12}$ (d) $\frac{7}{8} + \frac{9}{10}$

(e) $\frac{3}{10} + \frac{4}{15}$ (f) $\frac{5}{6} + \frac{1}{4}$ (g) $\frac{3}{8} + \frac{7}{12}$ (h) $\frac{1}{6} + \frac{8}{9}$

(i) $\frac{5}{8} + \frac{1}{4}$ (j) $1\frac{1}{2} + 2\frac{1}{8}$ (k) $\frac{1}{6} + \frac{5}{8}$ (l) $2\frac{3}{4} + 3\frac{7}{8}$

(m) $1\frac{3}{4} + 2\frac{5}{16}$ (n) $\frac{3}{4} + 3\frac{5}{8}$ (o) $\frac{3}{8} + \frac{11}{16}$ (p) $2\frac{9}{16} + 1\frac{5}{8}$

3 Work out

(a) $\frac{1}{2} + \frac{1}{3}$ (b) $\frac{2}{5} + \frac{1}{6}$ (c) $\frac{5}{8} + \frac{1}{5}$ (d) $\frac{3}{4} + \frac{1}{9}$

(e) $\frac{5}{6} + \frac{3}{7}$ (f) $\frac{9}{10} + \frac{2}{7}$ (g) $\frac{2}{3} + \frac{7}{10}$ (h) $\frac{3}{5} + \frac{3}{4}$

(i) $\frac{1}{5} + \frac{3}{8}$ (j) $\frac{1}{5} + \frac{1}{6}$ (k) $1\frac{3}{10} + 1\frac{2}{3}$ (l) $\frac{2}{3} + \frac{2}{7}$

(m) $3\frac{1}{6} + \frac{2}{7}$ (n) $2\frac{5}{6} + 1\frac{1}{7}$ (o) $3\frac{2}{5} + 2\frac{7}{15}$ (p) $1\frac{2}{3} + 1\frac{2}{9}$

4 Jo cycled $2\frac{3}{4}$ miles to one village and
then a further $4\frac{1}{3}$ miles to her home.
What is the total distance Jo travelled?

5 Work out

(a) $3\frac{1}{4} + 2\frac{1}{2}$ (b) $2\frac{1}{2} + \frac{2}{3}$ (c) $1\frac{1}{4} + 2\frac{7}{8}$ (d) $3\frac{1}{3} + 5\frac{3}{4}$

(e) $3\frac{5}{16} + 1\frac{7}{8}$ (f) $2\frac{11}{12} + \frac{3}{4}$ (g) $\frac{5}{6} + 6\frac{1}{3}$ (h) $2\frac{2}{3} + 4\frac{3}{5}$

6 In a market garden $\frac{1}{4}$ of the garden is used for potatoes,
$\frac{3}{20}$ is used for beans and $\frac{1}{10}$ is used for cabbages.
What fraction of the garden is used to grow these
vegetables altogether?

7 John gave away his old CD collection to his brother and
two sisters. The elder sister received $\frac{3}{10}$ of them and the
younger sister $\frac{5}{16}$ of them. The brother received the rest.
What fraction of the collection did the sisters receive
altogether?

8 Work out the perimeter of this photograph.

9 Two pieces of wood are fixed together. One piece has
thickness $2\frac{3}{8}$ inch and the other has thickness $1\frac{5}{16}$ inch.
What is the total thickness of the two pieces of wood?

10 In a class, $\frac{1}{6}$ of the students own one pet, and $\frac{2}{5}$ of the
students own more than one pet.
What total fraction of the students own at least one pet?

11 A bag weighs $\frac{3}{7}$ lb. The contents weigh $1\frac{1}{5}$ lb.
What is the total weight of the bag and its contents?

$5\frac{1}{4}$ in

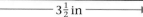

$3\frac{1}{2}$ in

8.9 Subtracting fractions

It is easy to subtract fractions when the denominators (bottom) are the same:

Easy to subtract:

$$\frac{7}{12} - \frac{2}{12} = \frac{5}{12}$$

Denominators are the same.

Harder to subtract:

$$\frac{5}{9} - \frac{1}{4} = ?$$

Denominators are different.

Example 13

Work out $\frac{5}{9} - \frac{1}{4}$

Find equivalent fractions to these that have the same denominator (bottom).

An easy way is to change both denominators to 36 because $9 \times 4 = 36$.

$$\frac{5}{9} \xrightarrow[\times 4]{\times 4} \frac{20}{36} \qquad \frac{1}{4} \xrightarrow[\times 9]{\times 9} \frac{9}{36}$$

$$\frac{20}{36} - \frac{9}{36} = \frac{11}{36}$$

Same denominator – easy to subtract

equivalent to $\frac{5}{9}$ equivalent to $\frac{1}{4}$

So $\frac{5}{9} - \frac{1}{4} = \frac{11}{36}$

Example 14

Work out $4\frac{1}{2} - 1\frac{5}{11}$

These are **mixed numbers**.

First subtract the whole numbers: $4 - 1 = 3$

$4\frac{1}{2} - 1\frac{5}{11}$ is the same as $3\frac{1}{2} - \frac{5}{11}$

Then find equivalent fractions to $\frac{1}{2}$ and $\frac{5}{11}$ that have the same denominator (bottom).

Change both denominators to 22 because $2 \times 11 = 22$:

$$\frac{1}{2} \xrightarrow[\times 11]{\times 11} \frac{11}{22} \qquad \frac{5}{11} \xrightarrow[\times 2]{\times 2} \frac{10}{22}$$

$$\frac{11}{22} - \frac{10}{22} = \frac{1}{22}$$

Same denominator – easy to subtract

Now put the whole numbers and fractions back together: 3 and $\frac{1}{22}$ is $3\frac{1}{22}$

So $4\frac{1}{2} - 1\frac{5}{11} = 3\frac{1}{22}$

Example 15

Work out $2\frac{3}{12} - \frac{8}{12}$

$\frac{3}{12}$ is smaller than $\frac{8}{12}$ so you can't just subtract the fractions on their own.

Change the mixed number $2\frac{3}{12}$ into a top heavy (or improper) fraction:

$$2\frac{3}{12} = \frac{24}{12} + \frac{3}{12} = \frac{27}{12}$$

So $2\frac{3}{12} - \frac{8}{12} = \frac{27}{12} - \frac{8}{12}$

$$= \frac{19}{12}$$

This is usually written as a mixed number: $1\frac{7}{12}$

To **subtract** fractions, find equivalent fractions that have the same denominator (bottom).

Exercise 8I

1 Work out

   (a) $\frac{5}{11} - \frac{3}{11}$ (b) $\frac{7}{9} - \frac{5}{9}$ (c) $\frac{7}{8} - \frac{1}{8}$ (d) $\frac{7}{12} - \frac{5}{12}$

   (e) $\frac{3}{4} - \frac{1}{4}$ (f) $\frac{5}{8} - \frac{3}{8}$ (g) $\frac{15}{16} - \frac{7}{16}$ (h) $\frac{6}{7} - \frac{3}{7}$

2 Work out

   (a) $\frac{1}{2} - \frac{1}{4}$ (b) $\frac{7}{8} - \frac{3}{4}$ (c) $\frac{5}{8} - \frac{1}{2}$ (d) $\frac{3}{4} - \frac{1}{8}$

   (e) $\frac{5}{6} - \frac{1}{3}$ (f) $\frac{7}{12} - \frac{1}{3}$ (g) $\frac{9}{10} - \frac{2}{5}$ (h) $\frac{1}{4} - \frac{1}{20}$

   (i) $\frac{1}{2} - \frac{3}{8}$ (j) $\frac{7}{8} - \frac{1}{2}$ (k) $\frac{11}{12} - \frac{3}{4}$ (l) $4\frac{5}{8} - 2\frac{1}{4}$

3 Work out

   (a) $\frac{2}{3} - \frac{1}{2}$ (b) $\frac{5}{8} - \frac{1}{3}$ (c) $\frac{1}{5} - \frac{1}{6}$ (d) $\frac{3}{5} - \frac{1}{6}$

   (e) $\frac{4}{5} - \frac{2}{3}$ (f) $\frac{3}{4} - \frac{3}{5}$ (g) $\frac{7}{10} - \frac{1}{3}$ (h) $\frac{9}{10} - \frac{3}{4}$

4 Work out

   (a) $5\frac{1}{4} - \frac{1}{10}$ (b) $7\frac{1}{2} - \frac{1}{3}$ (c) $6\frac{1}{2} - 5\frac{1}{4}$ (d) $9\frac{1}{2} - 7\frac{3}{10}$

   (e) $4 - 1\frac{3}{10}$ (f) $4\frac{4}{5} - 3\frac{9}{10}$ (g) $1\frac{2}{3} - \frac{11}{12}$ (h) $5\frac{3}{4} - 2\frac{19}{20}$

   (i) $4\frac{7}{8} - 1\frac{2}{3}$ (j) $5\frac{7}{9} - 3\frac{1}{3}$ (k) $3\frac{4}{5} - \frac{3}{8}$ (l) $7\frac{4}{7} - 4\frac{2}{5}$

5 In a school, $\frac{7}{16}$ of the students are girls.
   What fraction of the students are boys?

6 $\frac{2}{5}$ of the students at Hay College wear contact lenses.
   What fraction of the students do not wear them?

7 The garden of Granny Smith's house measures $1\frac{1}{3}$ acres. Sharky Estates buy $1\frac{1}{4}$ acres of the garden to build new homes. How much garden does Granny Smith have left?

8 A box containing tomatoes has a total weight of $5\frac{7}{8}$ kg. The empty box has a weight of $1\frac{1}{4}$ kg. What is the weight of the tomatoes?

9 In the first week of its run, the TV drama 'New Heights' had a respectable $7\frac{1}{2}$ million viewers. Unfortunately after three weeks $4\frac{3}{8}$ million had deserted. How many viewers now remained?

10 A plank of wood is $6\frac{1}{2}$ feet long. A $4\frac{3}{8}$ foot length is cut from one end of the plank. What length of wood remains?

11 Carol spends $\frac{2}{3}$ of her salary on food. She spends $\frac{1}{4}$ of her salary on bills. What fraction of her salary is left?

8.10 Multiplying fractions

How to multiply two fractions

To **multiply** two fractions, multiply the numerators together and multiply the denominators together.

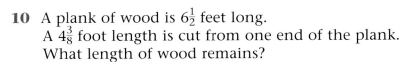

$$\frac{5}{8} \times \frac{7}{10} = \frac{35}{80}$$

Multiply the numerators (top)

Multiply the denominators (bottom)

You can simplify this to $\frac{7}{16}$ (by dividing the top and bottom of $\frac{35}{80}$ by 5).

Another way of doing this is to simplify the fractions *before* you multiply them:

$$\frac{5}{8} \times \frac{7}{10} = \frac{5 \times 7}{8 \times 10}$$

5 is a common factor of 5 and 10, so you can simplify here by dividing the top and the bottom by 5.

$$\frac{(5 \times 7) \div 5}{(8 \times 10) \div 5} = \frac{7}{8 \times 2} = \frac{7}{16}$$

This method is less obvious than the first one.

This gives the same answer $\frac{7}{16}$ as the first method.

How to multiply a fraction by a whole number

$$\frac{7}{10} \times 4 = ?$$

You can write 4 as the **top heavy** (or improper) fraction $\frac{4}{1}$

$$\frac{7}{10} \times \frac{4}{1} = \frac{28}{10}$$

Multiply the numerators (top)

Multiply the denominators (bottom)

So $\frac{7}{10} \times 4 = \frac{28}{10}$ This is usually written as a mixed number: $2\frac{8}{10}$

The fraction part of $2\frac{8}{10}$ simplifies (by dividing top and bottom by 2) so $2\frac{8}{10} = 2\frac{4}{5}$

How to multiply two mixed numbers

$$3\frac{1}{4} \times 2\frac{4}{5} = ?$$

Change both mixed numbers to top heavy (or improper) fractions:

$$3\frac{1}{4} = \frac{12}{4} + \frac{1}{4} = \frac{13}{4} \qquad\qquad 2\frac{4}{5} = \frac{10}{5} + \frac{4}{5} = \frac{14}{5}$$

$$\frac{13}{4} \times \frac{14}{5} = \frac{182}{20}$$

Multiply

Multiply

So $3\frac{1}{4} \times 2\frac{4}{5} = \frac{182}{20}$ This is usually written as a mixed number: $9\frac{2}{20}$

The fraction part of $9\frac{2}{20}$ simplifies (by dividing top and bottom by 2) so $9\frac{2}{20} = 9\frac{1}{10}$

Exercise 8J

1 Work out

(a) $\frac{1}{2} \times \frac{3}{4}$ (b) $\frac{3}{8} \times \frac{1}{4}$ (c) $\frac{2}{5} \times \frac{4}{5}$ (d) $\frac{3}{8} \times \frac{3}{4}$

(e) $\frac{5}{12} \times \frac{1}{3}$ (f) $\frac{7}{10} \times \frac{3}{4}$ (g) $\frac{3}{10} \times \frac{3}{5}$ (h) $\frac{2}{3} \times \frac{2}{3}$

(i) $\frac{1}{2} \times \frac{3}{8}$ (j) $\frac{4}{5} \times \frac{2}{3}$ (k) $\frac{4}{7} \times \frac{1}{3}$ (l) $\frac{2}{3} \times \frac{2}{5}$

(m) $\frac{2}{7} \times \frac{1}{5}$ (n) $\frac{2}{3} \times \frac{5}{7}$ (o) $\frac{1}{2} \times \frac{3}{4}$ (p) $\frac{3}{5} \times \frac{1}{3}$

2 Work out

(a) $\frac{1}{2} \times \frac{4}{5}$ (b) $\frac{3}{4} \times \frac{4}{5}$ (c) $\frac{5}{6} \times \frac{3}{5}$ (d) $\frac{4}{5} \times \frac{3}{10}$

(e) $\frac{5}{6} \times \frac{3}{4}$ (f) $\frac{7}{12} \times \frac{3}{14}$ (g) $\frac{8}{9} \times \frac{3}{10}$ (h) $\frac{3}{4} \times \frac{16}{21}$

(i) $\frac{1}{3} \times \frac{6}{7}$ (j) $\frac{6}{7} \times \frac{5}{12}$ (k) $\frac{1}{2} \times \frac{4}{5}$ (l) $\frac{2}{3} \times \frac{1}{4}$

(m) $\frac{3}{7} \times \frac{2}{6}$ (n) $\frac{6}{5} \times \frac{1}{3}$ (o) $5 \times \frac{7}{10}$ (p) $\frac{9}{10} \times \frac{13}{18}$

3 Work out

(a) $\frac{1}{2} \times 7$ (b) $\frac{2}{3} \times 5$ (c) $6 \times \frac{4}{5}$ (d) $8 \times \frac{3}{4}$

(e) $\frac{7}{10} \times 20$ (f) $9 \times \frac{2}{3}$ (g) $10 \times \frac{2}{5}$ (h) $\frac{5}{6} \times 12$

(i) $\frac{2}{3} \times 1\frac{1}{3}$ (j) $\frac{2}{5} \times 2\frac{1}{3}$ (k) $1\frac{1}{2} \times \frac{1}{4}$ (l) $1\frac{1}{2} \times 2\frac{1}{2}$

4 Work out

(a) $3\frac{1}{4} \times \frac{1}{2}$ (b) $\frac{2}{3} \times 4\frac{1}{2}$ (c) $\frac{5}{6} \times 1\frac{1}{3}$ (d) $2\frac{1}{2} \times \frac{7}{10}$

(e) $3\frac{1}{2} \times 1\frac{1}{2}$ (f) $2\frac{1}{3} \times 2\frac{3}{8}$ (g) $1\frac{4}{5} \times 2\frac{1}{3}$ (h) $3\frac{3}{4} \times 1\frac{2}{5}$

(i) $2\frac{1}{2} \times \frac{1}{4}$ (j) $1\frac{2}{5} \times 1\frac{1}{3}$ (k) $6 \times 2\frac{2}{3}$ (l) $2\frac{1}{7} \times 1\frac{2}{5}$

5 On Monday to Friday inclusive Jamie spends $2\frac{1}{4}$ hours on his homework but his sister Claire spends only $1\frac{3}{4}$ hours each day on hers.
How long in a week does each one spend on homework?

6 A machine takes $5\frac{1}{2}$ minutes to produce a special type of container. How long would the machine take to produce 15 containers?

7 Calculate the area of a rectangle of length $3\frac{1}{4}$ cm and width $2\frac{1}{4}$ cm.

> Area of rectangle is length × width

8 A melon weighs $2\frac{1}{2}$ lb. Work out the total weight of $8\frac{1}{4}$ melons.

9 Ivor takes $2\frac{1}{4}$ minutes to clean one window. How long will it take him to clean $6\frac{1}{2}$ windows of a similar size?

10 On average it takes Kieran $1\frac{1}{3}$ minutes to complete a lap at the Go Kart Centre.
How long will 15 laps take him?

11 Sharon can paint a garage door in $1\frac{2}{5}$ hours. How long will it take her to paint 7 garage doors?

12 Find the area of
this rectangle.
Leave your answer
as a fraction.

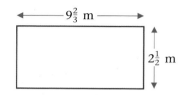

8.11 Dividing fractions

How to divide fractions

To **divide** fractions, invert the dividing fraction (turn it upside down) and multiply.

$$\frac{1}{4} \div \frac{3}{5} = ?$$

Turn the ÷
sign into
a × sign.

Turn the fraction you are
dividing by upside down.

This is called **inverting**
the fraction.

$$\frac{1}{4} \times \frac{5}{3} = \frac{5}{12}$$

So $\frac{1}{4} \div \frac{3}{5} = \frac{5}{12}$

Why inverting works
A fraction like $\frac{3}{4}$ is the
same as:

$$3 \div 4 \quad \text{or} \quad 3 \times \frac{1}{4}$$

But $\frac{1}{4}$ is $\frac{4}{1}$ inverted.
So dividing is the same as
multiplying by the
inverted number:

$$12 \div 3 = 4$$
$$12 \times \frac{1}{3} = 4 \quad \text{too}$$

How to divide a fraction by a whole number

$$\frac{15}{16} \div 5 = ?$$

Turn ÷
into ×

Invert the dividing
number.

$$\frac{15}{16} \times \frac{1}{5} = \frac{15}{80}$$

So $\frac{15}{16} \div 5 = \frac{15}{80}$
This simplifies to $\frac{3}{16}$ (by dividing top and bottom by 5).

Remember:
$$5 = \frac{5}{1}$$
so inverting gives
$$\frac{1}{5}$$

How to divide mixed numbers:

$$3\frac{1}{2} \div 4\frac{3}{4} = ?$$

Change mixed numbers to top
heavy (or improper) fractions.

$$\frac{7}{2} \div \frac{19}{4}$$

Turn ÷
into ×

Invert the dividing fraction.

$$\frac{7}{2} \times \frac{4}{19} = \frac{28}{38}$$

So $3\frac{1}{2} \div 4\frac{3}{4} = \frac{28}{38}$
This simplifies to $\frac{14}{19}$ (by dividing top and bottom by 2).

Exercise 8K

1 Work out
   (a) $\frac{1}{3} \div \frac{1}{4}$ (b) $\frac{1}{4} \div \frac{1}{3}$ (c) $\frac{3}{4} \div \frac{1}{2}$ (d) $\frac{1}{2} \div \frac{7}{10}$
   (e) $\frac{2}{3} \div \frac{1}{5}$ (f) $\frac{5}{8} \div \frac{1}{3}$ (g) $\frac{5}{6} \div \frac{3}{4}$ (h) $\frac{7}{10} \div \frac{4}{5}$
   (i) $\frac{2}{9} \div \frac{1}{2}$ (j) $\frac{2}{5} \div \frac{3}{4}$ (k) $\frac{3}{8} \div \frac{2}{3}$ (l) $\frac{1}{2} \div \frac{1}{4}$

2 Work out
   (a) $2\frac{1}{2} \div \frac{1}{2}$ (b) $3\frac{1}{4} \div 2\frac{1}{2}$ (c) $3\frac{3}{4} \div 2\frac{1}{4}$ (d) $1\frac{5}{8} \div 3\frac{1}{6}$
   (e) $3\frac{2}{3} \div 7\frac{1}{3}$ (f) $5\frac{1}{2} \div 2\frac{3}{4}$ (g) $1\frac{7}{10} \div 2\frac{7}{10}$ (h) $\frac{7}{8} \div 1\frac{2}{3}$

3 Work out
   (a) $\frac{3}{4} \div 8$ (b) $\frac{5}{6} \div 2$ (c) $\frac{3}{5} \div 6$ (d) $\frac{4}{5} \div 5$
   (e) $1\frac{1}{3} \div 4$ (f) $3\frac{1}{4} \div 6$ (g) $2\frac{5}{6} \div 10$ (h) $2\frac{1}{2} \div 15$
   (i) $\frac{8}{9} \div 4$ (j) $\frac{2}{3} \div 6$ (k) $4\frac{2}{3} \div 4$ (l) $5\frac{1}{4} \div 3$

4 Work out
   (a) $8 \div \frac{1}{2}$ (b) $12 \div \frac{3}{4}$ (c) $6 \div \frac{3}{5}$ (d) $8 \div \frac{7}{8}$
   (e) $4 \div \frac{4}{5}$ (f) $1 \div \frac{7}{12}$ (g) $5 \div \frac{1}{3}$ (h) $6 \div \frac{1}{4}$

5 Work out
   (a) $1\frac{1}{3} \div 1\frac{1}{2}$ (b) $2\frac{1}{2} \div \frac{1}{3}$ (c) $4\frac{3}{5} \div \frac{2}{3}$ (d) $2\frac{1}{5} \div 1\frac{1}{3}$
   (e) $1\frac{1}{3} \div 2\frac{2}{9}$ (f) $2\frac{2}{3} \div 2\frac{2}{5}$ (g) $3\frac{1}{3} \div 7\frac{1}{2}$ (h) $4\frac{4}{5} \div 5\frac{1}{3}$

6 A tin holds $10\frac{2}{3}$ litres of methylated spirit for a lamp. How many times will it fill a lamp holding $\frac{2}{3}$ litre?

7 A newly built swimming pool is $10\frac{4}{5}$ metres long. A tile is $\frac{3}{10}$ metres long. Work out how many tiles are needed for one row along the length of the pool.

8 Tar & Stone Ltd can resurface $2\frac{1}{5}$ km of road in a day. How many days will it take them to resurface a road of length $24\frac{3}{5}$ km?

8.12 Solving problems involving fractions

In this section you are given various problems to solve. Fractions are used in many different situations and these problems introduce you to the types of question that are included in GCSE exams.

Example 16

A bag of flour weighs 2.25 kg. More flour is added, and the weight of the bag of flour is increased by three fifths.

What is the new weight of the bag of flour?

$$\frac{3}{5} \text{ of } 2.25 \text{ kg is } \frac{3}{5} \times 2.25 = \frac{3 \times 2.25}{5} = \frac{6.75}{5} = 1.35 \text{ kg}$$

× can be read as 'of'

The new weight is 2.25 kg + 1.35 kg = 3.6 kg

Example 17

A 5 litre tin of paint is filled with blue and yellow paint to make a shade of green. The tin contains $1\frac{1}{2}$ litres of blue paint.

What fraction of the paint in the 5 litre tin is blue?

The fraction of paint that is blue is

$$\frac{\text{blue paint}}{\text{whole tin}} = \frac{1\frac{1}{2}}{5} = 1\frac{1}{2} \div \frac{5}{1} = \frac{3}{2} \times \frac{1}{5} = \frac{3}{10}$$

Exercise 8L

1   A loaded lorry has a total weight of 13.2 tonnes. This weight is decreased by five eighths when the load is removed.
    Find the weight of the lorry without the load.

2   Last year 204 cars were imported by a garage. This year the number of cars imported has increased by five twelfths.
    How many cars have been imported this year?

3   Of 144 rail passengers surveyed, 32 claimed their train was regularly late.
    What fraction of the total number of passengers was this?

4   There are 225 houses on an estate. Of these houses, 85 have no garage.
    What fraction of houses have no garage?

5   Find the difference between $\frac{3}{5}$ of 36 miles and $\frac{2}{3}$ of 30 miles.

6   A tin contains approximately 440 beans. The manufacturer
    increases the volume of the tin by three eighths.
    Approximately how many beans would you expect to
    find in the larger tin?

7   A newspaper has 14 columns of photographs
    and 18 columns of advertisements.
    What fraction of the paper is advertisements?

8   144 men, 80 women and 216 children went on the
    rollercoaster.
    What fraction of the total number is made up of children?

8.13 Fractions and decimals

Fractions can be changed into **decimals** by dividing the
numerator by the denominator.

___Example 18___

Change $\frac{3}{4}$ into a decimal.

$\frac{3}{4}$ means $3 \div 4$ (numerator ÷ denominator)

$$\begin{array}{r} 0.\ 7\ 5 \\ \hline 4 \overline{)3.\ ^30^20} \end{array}$$ ——— Put two extra '0's here.

$\frac{3}{4} = 0.75$

Some fractions which you often use are shown in this table,
along with their decimal equivalents:

Fraction	Decimal
$\frac{3}{10}$	0.3
$\frac{2}{5}$	0.4
$\frac{1}{4}$	0.25
$\frac{1}{2}$	0.5
$\frac{3}{4}$	0.75
$\frac{1}{8}$	0.125
$\frac{1}{3}$	0.3333 …

Decimals can be changed into **fractions** by using a place
value table.

Example 19

Change 0.763 into a fraction.

The place value table shows that 0.763 is 7 tenths, 6 hundredths and 3 thousandths. This is the same as 763 thousandths, so you can write the decimal as a fraction like this:

$$\frac{763}{1000}$$

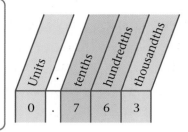

Example 20

Write as a fraction   (a) 0.7   (b) 0.59   (c) 0.071

Using the place value table:

(a) 7 tenths $= \frac{7}{10}$

(b) 59 hundredths $= \frac{59}{100}$

(c) 71 thousandths $= \frac{71}{1000}$

Exercise 8M

1 Change these fractions to decimals. Show your working.

(a) $\frac{3}{5}$ (b) $\frac{1}{2}$ (c) $\frac{7}{10}$ (d) $\frac{7}{20}$

(e) $\frac{4}{25}$ (f) $\frac{3}{50}$ (g) $\frac{7}{8}$ (h) $\frac{9}{20}$

(i) $\frac{19}{25}$ (j) $\frac{5}{16}$ (k) $\frac{1}{8}$ (l) $\frac{27}{50}$

(m) $\frac{9}{100}$ (n) $\frac{13}{200}$ (o) $\frac{2}{3}$ (p) $\frac{19}{20}$

2 Change these decimals to fractions.

(a) 0.3   (b) 0.37   (c) 0.93   (d) 0.137

(e) 0.293   (f) 0.07   (g) 0.59   (h) 0.003

(i) 0.000 03   (j) 0.0013   (k) 0.77   (l) 0.077

(m) 0.39   (n) 0.0041   (o) 0.019   (p) 0.031

3 Write as decimals:

(a) $\frac{4}{5}$ (b) $\frac{3}{4}$ (c) $1\frac{1}{8}$ (d) $\frac{19}{100}$

(e) $3\frac{3}{5}$ (f) $\frac{13}{25}$ (g) $\frac{5}{8}$ (h) $3\frac{17}{40}$

(i) $\frac{7}{50}$ (j) $4\frac{3}{16}$ (k) $3\frac{3}{20}$ (l) $4\frac{5}{16}$

(m) $\frac{7}{1000}$ (n) $1\frac{7}{25}$ (o) $15\frac{15}{16}$ (p) $2\frac{7}{20}$

4 Write as fractions in their simplest form:

(a) 0.48   (b) 0.25   (c) 1.7   (d) 3.406

(e) 4.003   (f) 2.025   (g) 0.049   (h) 4.875

(i) 3.75   (j) 10.101   (k) 0.625   (l) 2.512

(m) 0.8125   (n) 14.14   (o) 9.1875   (p) 60.065

8.14 Recurring decimals

Not all fractions have an exact equivalent decimal.

The fraction $\frac{2}{3}$ is $2 \div 3 = 0.666\,666\,6\ldots$ This is called a *recurring* decimal since one of the digits recurs (repeats).

You usually put a dot over the digits that repeat:

$\frac{2}{3} = 0.6666666\ldots = 0.\dot{6}$ $\frac{5}{12} = 0.4166666\ldots = 0.41\dot{6}$

$\frac{1}{3} = 0.3333333\ldots = 0.\dot{3}$ $\frac{3}{11} = 0.2727272\ldots = 0.\dot{2}\dot{7}$

$\frac{7}{9} = 0.7777777\ldots = 0.\dot{7}$

$\frac{1}{7} = 0.142\,857142857142857\ldots = 0.\dot{1}4285\dot{7}$

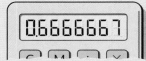

If you work out $2 \div 3$ or $\frac{2}{3}$ on a calculator the result on the display could be 0.6666667. The result has been corrected to 7 s.f. by the calculator.

You need two dots here since both the 2 and the 7 repeat.

The two dots show that this group of digits repeats.

Recurring decimal notation:
$0.\dot{3}$ means $0.3333333\ldots$ recurring and
$0.\dot{1}\dot{7}$ means $0.17171717\ldots$ recurring.

Example 21

Write these fractions as recurring decimals.

(a) $\frac{6}{11}$ (b) $3\frac{8}{9}$

Write your answers
 (i) as shown on the calculator display
(ii) using recurring decimal notation.

(a) (i) $\frac{6}{11} = 6 \div 11 = 0.5454545$ (ii) $0.\dot{5}\dot{4}$

(b) (i) $3\frac{8}{9} = 3 + (8 \div 9) = 3.8888888$ (or 3.8888889)
      (ii) $3.\dot{8}$

Your calculator may round 3.8888888 to 3.8888889

Exercise 8N

Write the fractions in questions 1–10 as recurring decimals.

Write your answers
 (i) as shown on the calculator display
(ii) using recurring decimal notation.

1 $\frac{5}{6}$ **2** $1\frac{2}{9}$ **3** $3\frac{1}{6}$ **4** $\frac{11}{12}$ **5** $5\frac{5}{9}$

6 $4\frac{9}{11}$ **7** $\frac{3}{44}$ **8** $2\frac{7}{11}$ **9** $9\frac{21}{22}$ **10** $\frac{25}{30}$

11 Write these fractions as recurring decimals:
$\frac{1}{7}, \frac{2}{7}, \frac{3}{7}, \frac{4}{7}, \frac{5}{7}, \frac{6}{7}$ What do you notice?

12 Write these fractions as recurring decimals:
$\frac{1}{9}, \frac{2}{9}, \frac{3}{9}, \frac{4}{9}, \frac{5}{9}, \frac{6}{9}, \frac{7}{9}, \frac{8}{9}$ What do you notice?

8.15 Reciprocals

The **reciprocal** of a number is made dividing the number into 1.

Reciprocal of $5 = 1 \div 5 = \frac{1}{5}$

Example 22

(a) The reciprocal of 2 is $\frac{1}{2}$ or a half or 0.5

(b) The reciprocal of 3 is $\frac{1}{3}$ or a third or 0.3333333...

(c) The reciprocal of $\frac{2}{3}$ is $\frac{3}{2}$

(d) The reciprocal of $\frac{1}{2}$ is $\frac{2}{1}$ or 2

You can use the reciprocal function on your calculator. On some calculators it is shown as **1/x** or **x⁻¹**.

Exercise 80

1 Find the reciprocals of these numbers without using a calculator.

(a) 5   (b) 4   (c) 6   (d) 8   (e) 10

(f) $\frac{1}{4}$ (g) $\frac{1}{8}$ (h) $\frac{3}{5}$ (i) $\frac{5}{6}$ (j) $\frac{5}{3}$

2 Use your calculator to find the reciprocals of these numbers.

(a) 25   (b) 50   (c) 3   (d) 7   (e) 9

(f) 75   (g) 100   (h) $\frac{1}{40}$ (i) 0.125   (j) 0.05

(k) 0.001   (l) 0.003   (m) 0.0002   (n) $\frac{2}{7}$ (o) $\frac{7}{5}$

Mixed exercise 8

1 (a) Write down the fraction of this shape that is shaded. Write your fraction in its simplest form.

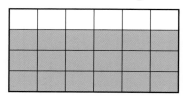

(b) Copy the shape. Shade $\frac{2}{3}$ of this shape.

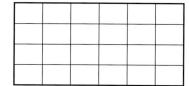

[E]

2   Here are two fractions: $\frac{3}{5}$ and $\frac{2}{3}$.

Explain which is the larger fraction.
You may use grids like these to help with your explanation.

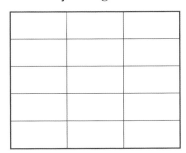 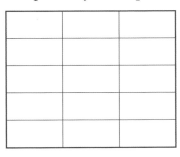

[E]

3   Write these fractions in order of size: $\frac{1}{2}, \frac{2}{3}, \frac{2}{5}, \frac{3}{4}$ [E]

4   Write down a fraction that is greater than a half and less than two thirds.

5   Ted spent $\frac{1}{4}$ of his pocket money on a new computer game. He spent $\frac{2}{5}$ of his pocket money on a ticket for a football match.
Work out the fraction of his pocket money that he had left.

6   Work out
(a) $\frac{2}{5} + \frac{2}{3}$ (b) $4\frac{3}{4} - 1\frac{2}{3}$ (c) $5\frac{2}{3} - 1\frac{3}{4}$
(d) $\frac{11}{14} - \frac{5}{7}$ (e) $1\frac{2}{3} + 3\frac{1}{2}$ (f) $4\frac{3}{5} + 1\frac{1}{4}$

7   One glass of Summer Spring water holds $\frac{1}{6}$ of a whole bottle. How many bottles are needed for 54 glasses of Summer Spring?

8   Write the following improper fractions as mixed numbers.
(a) $\frac{16}{3}$ (b) $\frac{35}{4}$ (c) $\frac{11}{2}$ (d) $\frac{19}{3}$ (e) $\frac{55}{13}$

9   Write the following mixed numbers as improper fractions.
(a) $1\frac{9}{11}$ (b) $3\frac{1}{6}$ (c) $4\frac{16}{25}$ (d) $3\frac{3}{4}$ (e) $10\frac{1}{10}$

10   Work out
(a) $\frac{2}{5} \times \frac{2}{3}$ (b) $3\frac{3}{4} \div 1\frac{2}{3}$ (c) $5\frac{1}{3} \times 1\frac{3}{4}$
(d) $\frac{11}{14} \div \frac{5}{7}$ (e) $1\frac{2}{7} \times 3\frac{1}{2}$ (f) $4\frac{4}{5} \div 1\frac{1}{5}$

11   Work out
(a) $\frac{3}{4}$ of £60   (b) $\frac{5}{6}$ of 54 km   (c) $\frac{2}{3}$ of 48 kg

12 Here is part of a map.

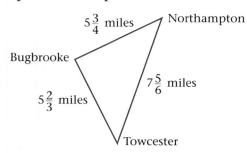

Fran drives from Bugbrooke to Northampton via Towcester.
Rea drives from Bugbrooke to Northampton directly.

How many miles further does Fran drive than Rea?

13 Seamus buys petrol from his local garage.
On Monday he filled up his petrol tank.

On Tuesday his tank was $\frac{4}{5}$ full.

(a) What fraction of a full tank had he used?

(b) Write $\frac{4}{5}$ as a decimal.

(c) Write $\frac{4}{5}$ as a percentage.

14 Change these fractions into decimals.

(a) $\frac{1}{2}$ (b) $\frac{1}{4}$ (c) $\frac{3}{4}$ (d) a third

(e) $\frac{3}{5}$ (f) $\frac{3}{7}$ (g) $\frac{2}{9}$

15 Change these decimals into fractions.

(a) 0.2   (b) 0.35   (c) 0.075   (d) 0.125

16 Work out the reciprocals of these numbers.

(a) $\frac{1}{2}$ (b) $\frac{3}{4}$ (c) 5   (d) 0.125

(e) 500   (f) 0.05   (g) 0.2   (h) 25

17 Find two equivalent fractions for each of the following:

(a) $\frac{6}{9}$ (b) $\frac{13}{25}$ (c) $\frac{1}{3}$ (d) $\frac{5}{17}$

18 Express the following fractions in their simplest form.

(a) $\frac{9}{12}$ (b) $\frac{15}{25}$ (c) $\frac{98}{100}$ (d) $\frac{35}{49}$

19 Write these fractions as recurring decimals. Write your answers

  (i) as shown on the calculator display

  (ii) using recurring decimal notation.

(a) $\frac{4}{9}$ (b) $\frac{3}{7}$ (c) $2\frac{1}{7}$ (d) $5\frac{6}{11}$ (e) $4\frac{16}{26}$

Summary of key points

1   Top heavy fractions, e.g. $\frac{11}{9}$, are also called **improper fractions**.

2   An improper fraction can also be written as a **mixed number** (a mixture of a whole number and a fraction), and a mixed number can also be written as an improper fraction.

$$\text{improper fraction} \quad\rule{1cm}{0.4pt}\quad \frac{11}{9} = \frac{9}{9} + \frac{2}{9} = 1\frac{2}{9} \quad\rule{1cm}{0.4pt}\quad \text{mixed number}$$

3   Fractions can be **simplified** if the numerator (top) and denominator (bottom) have a common factor.

$$\frac{8}{12} \quad\text{simplifies to}\quad \overset{\div 4}{\underset{\div 4}{\longrightarrow}} \quad \frac{2}{3} \qquad \text{The common factor is 4}$$

4   **Equivalent fractions** are fractions that have the same value.

$$\frac{8}{12} = \frac{4}{6} = \frac{2}{3}$$

5   To **add** fractions, find equivalent fractions that have the same denominator (bottom).

$$\overset{\times 3}{\underset{\times 3}{\frac{1}{2}}} + \frac{4}{6} = \frac{3}{6} + \frac{4}{6} = \frac{7}{6}$$

6   To **subtract** fractions, find equivalent fractions that have the same denominator (bottom).

$$\frac{4}{6} - \overset{\times 3}{\underset{\times 3}{\frac{1}{2}}} = \frac{4}{6} - \frac{3}{6} = \frac{1}{6}$$

7   To **multiply** two fractions, multiply the numerators together and multiply the denominators together.

$$\frac{3}{4} \times \frac{4}{7} = \frac{12}{28}$$

Multiply the numerators (top)

Multiply the denominators (bottom)

8 To **divide** fractions, invert the dividing fraction (turn it upside down) and multiply.

Turn ÷ into ×

$$\frac{1}{4} \div \frac{2}{5} = \frac{1}{4} \times \frac{5}{2} = \frac{5}{8}$$

Invert (turn upside down)

9 Fractions can be changed into **decimals** by dividing the numerator by the denominator.

10 Decimals can be changed into **fractions** by using a place value table.

11 A **recurring decimal** is one where a group of digits after the decimal place continually repeat themselves.

Recurring decimal notation:
$0.\dot{3}$ means 0.3333333... recurring
$0.\dot{1}\dot{7}$ means 0.1717171717... recurring.

12 The **reciprocal** of a number is made by dividing the number into 1.
For example, the reciprocal of 2 is $1 \div 2 = \frac{1}{2}$ and the reciprocal of $\frac{1}{3}$ is $1 \div \frac{1}{3} = 3$.

9 Estimating and using measures

9.1 Estimating

In real life people estimate all the time. How long will it take me to walk to the shops? Have I got time for a cup of tea? Is there enough milk in the fridge for the rest of the week?

Here are some measures that you have to estimate in real life:

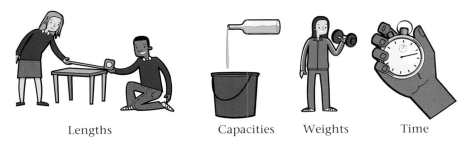

Lengths   Capacities   Weights   Time

Some imperial measures
12 inches = 1 foot
3 feet = 1 yard
1760 yards = 1 mile
8 pints = 1 gallon

You need to be able to estimate measurements in metric units and in imperial units such as gallons, miles and pounds.

9.2 Estimating lengths

Lengths and **distances** are measured in these metric and imperial units:

metric: kilometres (km), metres (m), centimetres (cm), millimetres (mm)

imperial: miles, yards, feet, inches

Example 1 shows some estimates of distances in real life.

Example 1

A 30 cm ruler is about 1 foot long.

A door is 2 m high or about $6\frac{1}{2}$ feet.

A long stride is 1 m long or about 3 feet.

$2\frac{1}{2}$ times around the track is 1 km or about $\frac{5}{8}$ mile.

Exercise 9A

Look at this picture, then write down an estimate for each
of the following in real life.

1 The height of the **(a)** man **(b)** girl **(c)** bus **(d)** car.
2 The length of the **(a)** car **(b)** bus.
3 The height of the **(a)** house **(b)** tree.
4 The width of the **(a)** drive **(b)** garage **(c)** house.

9.3 Estimating capacities

Capacity is a measure of the amount a container can hold.
It is measured in these units:

metric:	litres (*l*), centilitres (c*l*), millilitres (m*l*)
imperial:	gallons, pints, fluid ounces

> 20 fluid ounces = 1 pint
> 8 pints = 1 gallon

Example 2

This milk carton holds
1 pint or about 570 m*l*.

This petrol can holds
1 gallon or about 4.5 litres.

A mug and a can of cola hold
about $\frac{1}{2}$ pint or about 300 m*l*.

Exercise 9B

Look at this picture, then copy and complete the table with
your estimates for each of the following in real life.

	Amount of	Metric	Imperial
1	milk in a full carton		
2	cola in a full can		
3	lemonade in the bottle		
4	lemonade in the glass		
5	coffee in the jug		
6	water in a full bucket		
7	water in a full paddling pool		

9.4 Estimating weights (masses)

Weight is measured in these units:

metric: tonnes (t), kilograms (kg),
          grams (g), milligrams (mg)
imperial: tons, hundredweight,
          stones, pounds (lb), ounces (oz)

16 ounces = 1 pound
14 pounds = 1 stone
8 stones = 1 hundredweight
20 hundredweights = 1 ton

Example 3

A 125g packet of tea weighs about $\frac{1}{4}$ pound.

A 1 kg bag of sugar weighs about 2.2 pounds.

A 50 kg bag of cement weighs about 110 pounds.

You are really dealing with the *mass* of these quantities. However, in everyday life we talk about the *weight* of a quantity so that word is used here.

Exercise 9C

Look at this picture, then copy and complete the table with your estimates for the items in real life.

	Weight of the	Metric	Imperial
1	bag of potatoes		
2	block of butter		
3	bag of apples		
4	packet of coffee		
5	loaf of bread		
6	packet of cereal		
7	bottle of squash		
8	packet of biscuits		
9	packet of crisps		
10	box of soap powder		

9.5 Choosing appropriate units of measure

When you want to measure something you have to choose the most appropriate units to use. For example, to measure how long it takes to run 100 m you use seconds. But to measure how long it takes to run a 26 mile marathon you would need to use hours, minutes and seconds.

Should I use hours, minutes or seconds to time the 400 metre race?

Exercise 9D

Copy and complete this table with appropriate units for each measurement.

		Metric	Imperial
1	The length of your classroom		
2	The width of this book		
3	The distance from Edinburgh to London		
4	The length of a double decker bus		
5	The weight of a sack of potatoes		
6	The weight of a packet of sweets		
7	The weight of a lorry full of sand		
8	The amount of petrol in a car's petrol tank		
9	The amount of liquid in a full cup of tea		
10	The amount of medicine in a medicine spoon		
11	The amount of water in a raindrop		
12	The amount of water in a reservoir		
13	The time it takes to boil an egg		
14	The time it takes to run 400 metres		
15	The time it takes to walk 20 miles		
16	The time it takes to sail from Southampton to New York		
17	The length of a ballpoint pen		
18	The thickness of a page in this book		
19	The weight of 30 of these books		
20	The time it takes to travel from the Earth to Mars		

Sensible estimates

Example 4

Julie says 'My car is 20 m long.' Is this estimate sensible?

This is not a sensible statement because it means the car would be over 20 paces long, or about as long as an articulated lorry.

A sensible answer would be about 4 or 5 m.

Exercise 9E

For each of these statements say whether the measurement is sensible or not. If the statement is not sensible then give a reasonable estimate for the measurement.

1 (a) My teacher is 20 m tall.
   (b) My father is 20 cm tall.
   (c) The classroom measures 2 m by 3 m.
   (d) I bought 2 g of potatoes at the supermarket.
   (e) A can of cola holds 3 *l* of liquid.
   (f) A house is 10 m high.

2 (a) The tallest boy in school is 2 m tall.
   (b) John can just lift 50 kg.
   (c) Jane has to walk 1 km to school each day.
   (d) A cup full of tea contains 2 *l* of liquid.
   (e) The river Thames is 20 km long.
   (f) A 50p piece weighs 0.5 kg.

3 (a) A box of chocolates weighs 500 g.
   (b) A pint glass will hold 1 *l* of liquid.
   (c) The capacity of the petrol tank in my car is 5 *l*.

4 (a) The Eiffel Tower in Paris is more than 200 m high.
   (b) The capacity of the petrol tank in my car is 50 gallons.
   (c) A packet of tea weighs 50 g.
   (d) A kilogram bag of sugar weighs 2 pounds.

9.6 Measuring time

You need to be able to

- read the time using digital and analogue clocks
- use 12-hour and 24-hour clock times and convert from one type to the other.

Digital clocks have a number display:

Analogue clocks have hands:

Reading the time from an analogue clock

When you *say* the time you can use phrases such as 'half past four' and 'ten to five'.

This clock shows the key phrases you need to know:

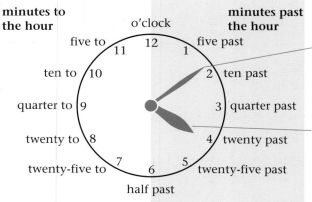

For the long 'minute' hand the journey from one number to the next takes 5 minutes.

For the short 'hour' hand the journey from one number to the next takes 1 hour.

Remember: 60 minutes = 1 hour

Two of the four clock faces of Big Ben, illuminated at night.

Exercise 9F

1   Write down in words the times shown by these clocks as you would say them.

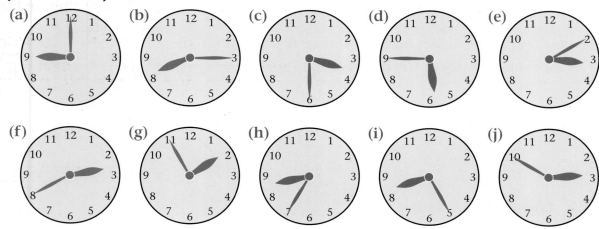

2   Draw six clock faces and mark these times on them.

(a) seven o'clock

(b) ten past eight

(c) quarter to five

(d) twenty to three

(e) quarter past nine

(f) twenty-five past four

Reading the time from a digital clock

Example 5

Write these times as you would say them, in two different ways.

09:20 The colon keeps the hours and minutes apart.

20 minutes past 9 or nine twenty

09:40 40 minutes past 9 = 20 minutes to 10.

20 minutes to 10 or nine forty.

Exercise 9G

1 Write these times as you would *say* them, in two different ways.
(a) 08 30   (b) 10 10   (c) 11 05   (d) 04 45   (e) 03 55

2 Draw five digital watches and show the following times on them:
(a) quarter past 9   (b) half past 3   (c) twenty to 5
(d) quarter to 7   (e) five o'clock

12-hour and 24-hour clock times

You need to be able to tell the difference between times such as 2 o'clock in the morning and 2 o'clock in the afternoon. There are two ways of doing this.

12-hour clock times use **am** or **pm** to show whether a time is before or after midday:

| 12 midnight yesterday | 3 am | ante meridiem before midday am | midday or noon today | 3 pm | post meridiem after midday pm | 12 midnight today |

12 1 2 3 4 5 6 7 8 9 10 11 12 1 2 3 4 5 6 7 8 9 10 11 12

24-hour clock times number the hours from **1 to 24**:

3 o'clock in the morning   3 o'clock in the afternoon

00:00 01:00 02:00 03:00 04:00 05:00 06:00 07:00 08:00 09:00 10:00 11:00 12:00 13:00 14:00 15:00 16:00 17:00 18:00 19:00 20:00 21:00 22:00 23:00 24:00

Example 6

Write down the times shown.

Morning

 **09:25**

The time shown by these clocks is 9:25 am or 09 25

Afternoon

 **13:35**

The time shown by these clocks is 1:35 pm or 13 35

Changing 12-hour clock times to 24-hour clock times

Up to 12 noon the times are the same:

12-hour → 24-hour

9:35 am → 09 35

A 24-hour digital clock shows a zero here.

After 12 noon add 12 to the hour number:

12-hour → 24-hour

1:45 pm → 13 45

+12

Exercise 9H

1 Change these times from 12-hour clock times (am and pm) to 24-hour clock times.
(a) 10:00 am (b) 10:00 pm (c) 9:30 am (d) 9:30 pm
(e) 8:20 pm (f) 8:20 am (g) 7 am (h) 8 pm
(i) 3:30 pm (j) 4:40 am (k) 1:08 am (l) 1:08 pm
(m) 5:50 pm (n) 5:50 am (o) 11 pm (p) 8 am
(q) quarter past 8 in the morning
(r) quarter to 9 in the evening
(s) five to three in the afternoon
(t) twenty to seven in the morning

2 Change these times from 24-hour clock times to 12-hour clock times (am or pm).
(a) 08:00 (b) 09:20 (c) 21:30 (d) 13:10
(e) 12:10 (f) 00:20 (g) 01:40 (h) 08:00
(i) 15:45 (j) 18:00 (k) 16:30 (l) 21:10
(m) 23:55 (n) 14:02 (o) 06:25 (p) 00:00
(q) 24:00 (r) 12:00 (s) 10:55 (t) 20:55

9.7 Reading scales

You need to be able to read these types of scales:

• a ruler to measure lengths • weighing scales • a measuring cylinder to measure amounts of liquid.

Example 7

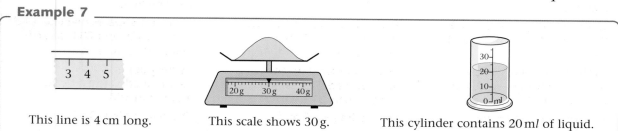

3 4 5

This line is 4 cm long.

This scale shows 30 g.

This cylinder contains 20 ml of liquid.

Exercise 9I

1 Write down the readings on these scales.

(a)

(b)

(c) (d)

(e)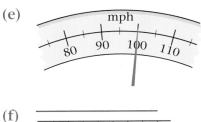

(f)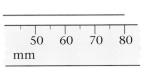

2 Draw diagrams to show these readings on a scale.

    (a) 5 cm   (b) 20 ml   (c) 50 g

    (d) 3 cm   (e) 25 ml   (f) 250 g

Using the marks on a scale

Example 8

Write down the measurements shown on these scales.

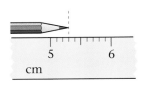 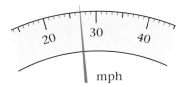 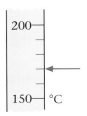

This pencil ends between the 5 and the 6.

There are 10 spaces between the 5 and the 6 so each mark shows $\frac{1}{10}$ or 0.1

As the pencil ends on the third mark it must be 0.3 or $\frac{3}{10}$ more than 5.

The pencil is 5.3 cm long.

This pointer is between 20 and 30.

There are 10 spaces between 20 and 30 so each mark shows 1 unit.

As the pointer is on the seventh mark it must be 7 more than 20.

The reading is 27 mph.

This reading is between 150 and 200.

There are 5 spaces marked between 150 and 200 so each mark shows 10 units.

As the pointer is on the second mark it must be 20 more than 150.

The reading is 170 °C.

Exercise 9J

Write down the readings on these scales.

1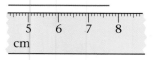

2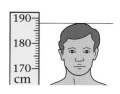

3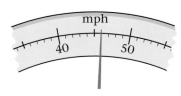

4

5

6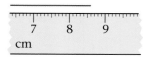

Estimating from a scale

Some scales have no helpful marks on them so you have to estimate a reading.

Example 9

Estimate the reading shown.

The middle mark on this scale is halfway between 4 and 5 at 4.5.

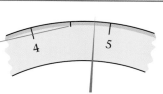

The pointer is a little more than halfway between 4.5 and 5. So a good estimate is 4.8 units.

Exercise 9K

Estimate the measurements on these scales.

1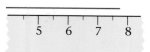

2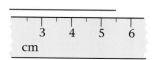

3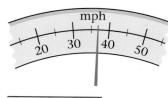

4

5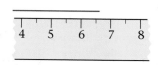

6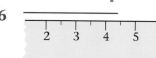

Measuring lines accurately

When you measure the length of a line, remember to start measuring from the 0 on the scale you are using, *not the end of the ruler.*

Example 10

Write down the length of this line in cm.

Start measuring from the zero mark.

This line measures 3.7 cm.

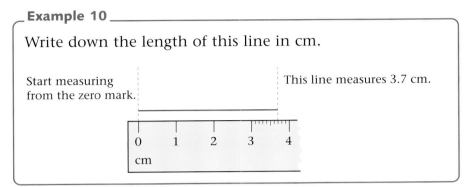

Exercise 9L

1   Measure and write down the lengths of these lines in centimetres.

(a) ─────────

(b) ─────────────

(c) ───────────────────

(d) ──────────────────────────────

(f)

(g) ─────────

(e)

(h) ─────────────────────

2   Draw and label lines with lengths

(a) 4 cm   (b) 6 cm   (c) 2.5 cm

(d) 5.7 cm   (e) 4.8 cm   (f) 3.2 cm

(g) 8.3 cm   (h) 10.2 cm   (i) 4.6 cm

(j) 3.9 cm   (k) 6.4 cm   (l) 7.2 cm

3   Draw and label lines with lengths

(a) 20 mm   (b) 35 mm   (c) 55 mm

(d) 100 mm   (e) 74 mm   (f) 8 mm

(g) 18 mm   (h) 68 mm

Marking part way along a line

Sometimes you will have to measure or draw a line and mark a point that is half, a third or a quarter of the way along your line.

Example 11

Draw a line 8 cm long and mark the point halfway along it. Divide 8 cm by 2, 8 cm ÷ 2 = 4 cm. Measure 4 cm from one end and put a cross to show halfway.

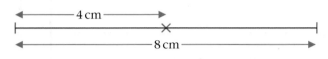

Exercise 9M

1   Copy these lines. Mark the halfway point of each.

    (a) ————————————————————

    (b) ——————————————————

    (c) ——————————————————————

    (d) ——————————

2   Copy these lines. On each mark the point a quarter of the way along the line.

    (a) ————————————————————

    (b) —————————————————————————

    (c) ——————————

3   Draw two lines that are 6 cm long.

    (a)   Mark a point one third of the way along the first line.

    (b)   Mark a point two thirds of the way along the second line.

4   Draw two lines that are 12 cm long.

    (a)   Mark a point one quarter of the way along the first line.

    (b)   Mark a point three quarters of the way along the second line.

5   Draw four lines that are 10 cm long.

    (a)   Mark a point one tenth of the way along the first line.

    (b)   Mark a point three tenths of the way along the second line.

    (c)   Mark a point seven tenths of the way along the third line.

    (d)   Mark a point nine tenths of the way along the fourth line.

Mixed exercise 9

1   Copy and complete this table.
    Write a sensible unit for each measurement.

	Metric	Imperial
The weight of a turkey		pounds
The volume of water in a swimming pool		gallons
The width of this page	centimetres	

[E]

2   A petrol station has a diagram for converting gallons to
    litres.

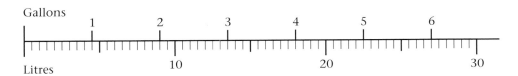

Use the diagram to convert

(a) 4 gallons to litres   (b) 3 gallons to litres

(c) 27 litres to gallons   (d) 20 litres to gallons.

3   (a) Draw a line *AB* with length 10 cm.

    (b) Mark a point *P* halfway along the line.

4   (a) What metric unit of length would you use
        to measure the length of a large coach?

    (b) Using the unit in part (a) estimate the
        length of a large coach.

5   It takes a world-class athlete about 10 seconds to run
    100 metres.

    (a) Estimate the time an average 16 year old would take
        to run 100 metres.

    (b) Estimate the time your maths teacher would take to
        run 100 metres.

6   Draw clock faces to show these times:

    (a) 7 pm   (b) 08 30   (c) a quarter to 4

7 The scale diagram shows a man and a dinosaur called a *Tyrannosaurus rex*.

The man is 6 ft or approximately 2 metres tall.
Estimate the height of the *Tyrannosaurus rex*:

(a) in feet

(b) in metres.

Tyrannosaurus rex   Man (to scale)

Summary of key points

1 **Lengths** and **distances** are measured in these metric and imperial units:

metric: kilometres (km), metres (m), centimetres (cm), millimetres (mm)

imperial: miles, yards, feet, inches

2 **Capacity** is a measure of the amount a container can hold. It is measured in these units:

metric: litres (*l*), centilitres (c*l*), millilitres (m*l*)

imperial: gallons, pints, fluid ounces

3 **Weight** is measured in these units:

metric: tonnes (t), kilograms (kg), grams (g), milligrams (mg)

imperial: tons, hundredweight, stones, pounds (lb), ounces (oz)

4 **Digital** clocks have a number display:

5 **Analogue** clocks have hands:

6 Up to 12 noon the times are the same: After 12 noon add 12 to the hour number:

12-hour → 24-hour
9:35 am → 09 35

A 24-hour digital clock shows a zero here.

12-hour → 24-hour
1:45 pm → 13 45

+12

10 Collecting and recording data

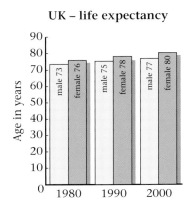

UK – life expectancy

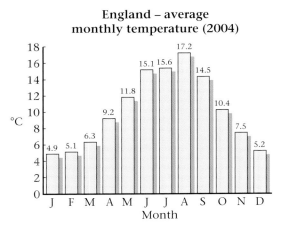

England – average monthly temperature (2004)

2012 Olympics – First round voting

You often see charts and tables like this in the press and on TV. They give you information or **data** as it is usually called. Sometimes you can use this data to make forecasts and plan for the future.

For example, the number of babies born this year helps councils to plan the number of school places needed in five years' time.

Statistics is the branch of mathematics concerned with
- **collecting** and **recording** data
- **sorting** and **tabulating** that data
- presenting data visually in **charts** and **diagrams**
- making **calculations**
- **interpreting** results.

This chapter shows you how to start collecting and recording data.

There were four rounds of voting before London was chosen to host the 2012 Olympic Games.
One city was eliminated in each round.

10.1 Ways of collecting data

You can collect data
- by using a questionnaire
- by making observations and recording the results
- by carrying out an experiment
- from records or a database
- from the internet.

You must be careful how you collect data. If you want to find out what people think about marriage, for example, it is not sensible just to ask people at a wedding. They are interested in marriage and you might be led to the wrong conclusions!

10.2 Designing questions to collect data

When you are writing questions for a **questionnaire**:
- be clear what you want to find out, and what data you need
- ask short, simple questions
- provide tick boxes with possible answers.

Here are some good examples:

Are you:

Male ☐ ———— This has a clear choice of two answers.

Female ☐

What age are you?

Under 17 ☐

17–20 ☐

21–30 ☐

Over 30 ☐

Which of these styles of music do you like?
(Tick as many boxes as you want)

Metal ☐

House ☐

Grunge ☐

Pop ☐

These both offer four choices.

Avoid questions which are too vague, too personal, or which may influence the answer.

How often do you go swimming?

Sometimes ☐   Occasionally ☐   Often ☐

Sometimes, occasionally and *often* may mean different things to different people.

Have you ever stolen anything from a shop?

Yes ☐   No ☐

Even a hardened criminal is unlikely to answer this question honestly!

Do you agree that the UK should have the euro?

Yes ☐   No ☐

This question suggests that the right answer is Yes. It is **biased**.

Test your questionnaire on a few people first to see if it works or needs to be improved. This is called a **pilot survey**.

Exercise 10A

1   Look at these pairs of questions. Decide whether Question X
     or Question Y is better to do the job in the *To find out* column.

	To find out:	Question X	Question Y
(a)	if people like the Labour party	Do you like the Labour party? Yes/No	Do you agree that New Labour is the best party? Yes/No
(b)	which age group a person is in	How old are you?	Are you under 21, 21 to 40, 41 to 60, over 60?
(c)	the most popular soap on TV	Do you watch Eastenders? Yes/No	Do you watch Eastenders/ Coronation Street/ Emmerdale/Hollyoaks/ Other?
(d)	if they watched the film	Did you see the film *War of the Worlds*? Yes/No	Do you like Steven Spielberg?
(e)	if someone is short sighted	How good is your eyesight?	Can you read that sign without glasses? Yes/No
(f)	if people give money to charity	Do you give money to charity? Yes/No	Everyone gives money to charity, don't they? Yes/No
(g)	if the hotel was satisfactory	Was everything all right? Yes/No	Did you enjoy your stay? Yes/No
(h)	if newspapers should be censored	Newspapers should be censored: Agree/Disagree/Don't know	What do you think about censoring newspapers?

Example 1

Decide if the following question is suitable for use in a questionnaire.
If it is not, give a reason and rewrite the question to improve it.

> How much pocket money do you get?
>
> a little ☐   some ☐   a lot ☐

A little to some people may be *a lot* to others. Also the word *some* means different
amounts to different people. It would be better to be more precise. A better
question would be:

> How much pocket money do you get each month?
>
> 0–£14.99 ☐   £15–£24.99 ☐   £25–£34.99 ☐   over £35 ☐

Exercise 10B

1   Here are some questions that are not suitable for a
    questionnaire. For each one, say why and write a more
    suitable question.
    (a) Do you agree that the UK should have a monarchy?
         Yes ☐   No ☐   Don't know ☐
    (b) What was the weather like on your holiday?
         Terrible ☐   Quite good ☐   OK ☐
    (c) Most people approve of corporal punishment. Do you?
         Yes ☐   No ☐
    (d) Do you still play football?
         Yes ☐   No ☐
    (e) How many hours of television do you watch?
         1 ☐   2 ☐   3 ☐
    (f) Does your local library have wheelchair access?

2   Finn wants to find out about people's mobile phones. He
    has designed the following questionnaire for his web page.

Questionnaire: Mobile phones

1 Do you have a mobile phone?
    Yes ☐   No ☐

2 Who is your service provider?
    Mobile P ☐ H_4 ☐   Five ☐
    Fonavode ☐   Pineapple ☐   Other ☐

3 Do you: Pay monthly   ☐
                 Pay-As-You-Go   ☐

4 How much do you spend on your phone each month?
    £5 ☐   £10 ☐   £15 ☐   £20 ☐

    (a) How could you improve part **4** of the questionnaire?
    (b) Finn also wants to write a question about how people
         buy their call time. Design a question he could use.
         Include tick boxes for a response.

Activity – Holidays

- Design a questionnaire to find out about the kind of holidays people had last year.
- Test your questions by asking some of your friends.

10.3 Collecting data by sampling

If you carry out a survey in a mixed school, but only question the first five students on each form register, you could end up asking all boys or all girls.

Ideally you should ask everyone in the school – but this is usually not practical. Instead you ask a limited number of students – a **sample**.

You need to make sure each student in the school has an equal chance of being picked to be part of the sample. You might question six students from each class, drawing their names out of a hat. This is called a **random sample**. Then questioning your sample should give a similar result to questioning the whole school.

If your sample is not random your answers may be **biased**. In a survey to find out which sports a typical teenager watches, choosing a sample from teenagers at a football match will **bias** your answers – there will be more football lovers than in a random sample.

A **random sample** helps this market researcher find out what a typical person thinks without asking them all. For a fair survey you may need to ask people of different ages, genders, jobs, nationalities, and so on.

> When you carry out a survey, select a **random sample** to avoid **bias**.

Exercise 10C

For each question, select the most appropriate group of people to ask, **A**, **B** or **C**.

	Data needed	Who to ask
1	How people get to work	A Every fifth person near a bus stop B A group of people arriving together C A group of people during a tea break
2	If people think Coldplay is a good group	A People in a library B People going to a Coldplay concert C People in your class
3	If people think private healthcare is a good idea	A Unemployed people B Doctors C People in a town centre
4	If people are in favour of a new pedestrian crossing	A Car drivers using the road B Local residents C Pedestrians crossing the road
5	If people want harsher prison sentences for criminals	A The police B People in a shopping centre C Prisoners

10.4 Collecting data by observation

You could do a traffic survey by counting vehicles and recording what type they are as they pass you.

You would have to decide where, how and for how long to carry out your survey.

For example, if you did your survey during rush hour the results would be different from a survey early one Sunday morning.

Here is a **data capture sheet** from a traffic survey:

Traffic survey by H. Short on 5/6/05 at Main Street, Ash 9.00–9.30 am.

Type of vehicle	Tally	How many
Bus	卌 卌 ‖	12
Car	卌 卌 卌 卌 ‖	22
Lorry	卌 ‖	7
Van	卌 卌	10
Motorcycle	卌 卌 卌	16

Remember to record 5 in a tally chart like this:

卌

Exercise 10D

1   Prepare data capture sheets for surveys to find out two of the following by observation
    (a)   the make of people's MP3 players
    (b)   the colour of people's eyes
    (c)   the CPU speed and hard disk space on people's computers
    (d)   the age and sex of people entering a supermarket.

10.5 Collecting data by experiment

When you carry out an experiment you can use a **data capture sheet** to record your results.

Example 2

Greta has a six-sided dice. She throws it 60 times and records her results in a data capture sheet.

Score	Tally	Frequency
1	ЖІ ІІІІ	9
2	ЖІ ЖІ І	11
3	ЖІ ЖІ ІІ	12
4	ЖІ ІІІІ	9
5	ЖІ ЖІ	10
6	ЖІ ІІІІ	9

From Greta's data, do you think the dice is fair?
The dice seems to be fair as the results for each score are about the same.

Exercise 10E

Carry out the following experiments.

1   Find out how accurate people are at estimating.
    Ask people to estimate
    (a)   the length in centimetres of a piece of wood
    (b)   the number of sweets in a jar
    (c)   the weight in grams of a piece of metal.

2   Find out whether a typical science textbook has longer words than a typical English textbook.
    • Choose two passages of about 50 words from each book.
    • For each passage make a data collection table like the one on the right and complete it.
    • Compare the results.

Number of letters in a word	Tally	Frequency
1		
2		
3		
4		

3   Find two newspapers, one 'serious' and one 'lightweight'. Find an article in each paper about the same story. Carry out an experiment to find out which paper has the greater average word length by counting the length of the first 100 words in each article in each paper.

10.6 Secondary data

Data you collect is called **primary data**. Data that has been collected by other people is called **secondary data**.

> The **National Census** is carried out every 10 years and provides information about people in the UK.

Two-way tables are used to record or display information that is grouped in two different catergories.

Example 3

Here is an extract from a table in the 1991 Census which shows information about residents in some London boroughs. The figures are percentages.

	Bexley	Brent	Bromley	Camden	Croydon	Newham	Greenwich	Average London
Retired	17.4	14.3	19.6	17.3	16.1	14.2	17.6	16.8
Birth rate	13.8	17.0	12.8	13.5	15.1	20.2	15.9	15.4
Unemployment	38.1	41.6	35.5	40.6	40.2	43.6	44.6	40.8
2-car families	26.1	16.0	28.9	9.4	24.6	8.8	14.8	18.2
No-car families	26.7	43.4	25.6	55.8	30.5	53.5	43.6	40.7

(a) Which borough has the highest percentage
   (i) birth rate   (ii) unemployment?

> In this two-way table data is grouped by
> 1 type of resident
> 2 area of London

(b) What percentage of families have two cars in
   (i) Bromley   (ii) Brent?
(c) Use information from the table to suggest a reason why Camden has a large percentage of families with no car.
(d) Which boroughs have a higher percentage of families with two cars than the average figure for all of London?

(a) (i) Newham   (ii) Greenwich
(b) (i) 28.9   (ii) 16.0
(c) High unemployment
(d) Bexley, Bromley and Croydon

Exercise 10F

1   The table shows the percentage unemployment figures for August.

Year	1999	2000	2001	2002	2003	2004	2005
Male	5.2	4.7	4.0	3.6	3.7	3.4	3.3
Female	4.7	4.1	3.8	3.0	3.0	2.7	2.5

(a) What was the female unemployment rate in 2004?

(b) Which year had the
    (i) highest (ii) lowest percentage total unemployment?

(c) Between which two years did male unemployment
    fall the most?

2 This table shows the money spent or collected, in pounds per
   person, in different London boroughs:

	Camden	Barnet	Haringey	Islington	Lambeth	Redbridge	Richmond	Southwark
Average weekly rent	106	102	112	100	82	122	96	88
Management	36	26	28	32	32	32	24	46
Repairs	18	22	20	26	28	40	24	28
Bad debts	8	0.08	6	1.54	0.96	0.46	0.28	3.52
Rent rebates	64	62	82	62	48	86	54	26

(a) Which borough has
    (i) the highest (ii) the lowest average weekly rent?

(b) Which borough has a bad debts figure of 0.28?

(c) Which borough has
    (i) the highest (ii) the lowest repairs figure?

(d) What is the rent rebate per person in Richmond?

10.7 Obtaining data from a database

A **database** is an organised collection of information.
It can be stored on paper or on a computer.

Here is a spreadsheet showing part of a database stored on a
computer:

	A	B	C	D	E	F	G	H
1	Year group	Surname	Years	Months	Gender	Sport	Height (m)	Weight (kg)
2	10	Abejurouge	15	3	Male	Rugby	1.63	60
3	10	Aberdeen	15	0	Male	Rounders	1.75	45
4	11	Ableson	16	6	Female	Table Tennis	1.83	60
5	11	Acton	16	3	Female	Basketball	1.67	52
6	10	Adam	15	1	Male	Judo	1.80	49
7	10	Agha	15	7	Male	Cricket	1.66	70

A computer database allows you to obtain information quickly and in a variety of forms, for example:

- in alphabetical order
- in numerical order
- girls' results only
- males over a certain height.

> **Activity – Mayfield School database (Go to www.heinemann.co.uk/hotlinks, insert the express code 4084P and click on this activity.)**
>
> Use the Mayfield School database to answer these questions:
>
> (a) How tall is David Hazelwood (Year 9)?
>
> (b) How many KS4 pupils were born in April?
>
> (c) How many KS3 pupils said their favourite TV programme was The Simpsons? Which one of these said their favourite sport was running?
>
> (d) How many of the KS3 pupils are right handed and have dark brown eyes? Which of these said their favourite TV programme was Eastenders?
>
> (e) Which female KS4 pupil has 5 pets and said her favourite subject was PE?

Exercise 10G

1   This database contains details of some second-hand cars.

Make	Model	Colour	Insurance group	Number of doors	Year	Price (£)
BMW	3 series	Blue	11	3	2001	8845
Suzuki	Alto	Red	5	5	2003	2695
Porsche	Cayenne	Red	20	5	2003	30 795
Proton	Persona	Green	8	4	1999	1995
Citroën	C8	Silver	11	5	2002	10 295
Daewoo	Matiz	Blue	2	5	2000	1895
Volkswagen	Passat	Red	9	4	1997	3145
Seat	Ibiza	Yellow	2	3	2002	4145
Nissan	Primera	Black	9	4	2002	6345
Vauxhall	Corsa	Silver	2	3	1998	1645

Use the database to answer the following questions.
(a) Which is the oldest car?
(b) Which is the most expensive car?
(c) Which car has the highest insurance group?
(d) How many cars have 5 doors?
(e) Karen has £3000. Which cars could she buy?
(f) Which is the cheapest 5-door red car?
(g) List the models of car in order of price, most expensive first.

2 This database contains information about some African
   countries.

	A	B	C	D	E	F	G
1	Country	Religion	Currency	Population 2004 (millions)	Urban population	Fertility rate (births/woman)	Population 2015 (est.) (millions)
2	Algeria	Islam	Dinar	32.1	59%	2.0	38
3	Angola	Christianity	New Kwanza	11	36%	6.3	20.8
4	Botswana	Indigenous beliefs	Pula	1.5	52%	3.2	1.7
5	Benin	Indigenous beliefs	Franc	7.3	45%	6.0	9.4
6	Burundi	Christianity	Franc	6.2	10%	5.9	9.8
7	Chad	Islam and Christianity	Franc	9.5	25%	6.4	12.4

(a) Use the database to find out
   (i) which country has both Islam and Christianity
       as major religions
   (ii) which country has the lowest fertility rate
   (iii) which country had the highest population in
         2004
   (iv) what is the estimated population of Angola for
        2015.
(b) Compare the urban population of Burundi with
     those of other countries in the database.
(c) Write a question of your own using at least two
     pieces of data from the database.

3 Give an example of a database used in your school.
   Who uses it? What information does it contain?

10.8 Obtaining data from the internet

The internet can be a very useful source of data. But remember
that data collected from the internet may be inaccurate or out
of date.

When you collect data from the internet make sure that:
• the data comes from a reliable source
• the data is accurate – check against other sources.

Activity – Internet search

Use the internet to find the following information.
Give two reliable sources for each answer.

(a) The members of the European Union.

(b) The heights of the five highest mountains in the world.

(c) The average life expectancy of people in the UK.

(d) The number of gold, silver and bronze metals won by Great Britain in the Paralympic Games in 2004.

10.9 Using mileage charts

In books of roadmaps you often see tables that give the distances between towns.

Here is an example of how one of these tables can be built up.

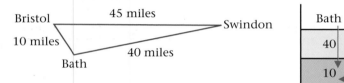

To use the mileage chart to find the distance between Bath and Bristol you follow the arrows from Bath and Bristol, and find where they meet. In this case it is 10. The distance is 10 miles.

Exercise 10H

1 Here is a mileage chart:

York				
71	Manchester			
24	44	Leeds		
91	74	110	Kendal	
211	204	201	268	London

The distance from Manchester to Kendal is 74 miles.
Use this mileage chart to find the distance between these places:

(a) London and Manchester (b) York and Kendal

(c) Leeds and York (d) Leeds and London

(e) Manchester and Leeds (f) London and York.

2 Here is a mileage chart:

Use this mileage chart to find the shortest distance between these places:

(a) London and Bristol

(b) Cardiff and Salisbury

(c) Oxford and Bristol

(d) Oxford and London

(e) Cardiff and London

(f) Bristol and Salisbury.

Bristol				
44	Cardiff			
73	107	Oxford		
52	98	70	Salisbury	
120	153	56	169	London

3 Here is a mileage chart:

Use this mileage chart to find the distance between these places:

(a) London and Glasgow

(b) Edinburgh and Glasgow

(c) Stranraer and Edinburgh

(d) Edinburgh and London

(e) Inverness and Glasgow

(f) London and Inverness.

Glasgow				
47	Edinburgh			
176	157	Inverness		
86	132	261	Stranraer	
410	413	574	420	London

4 The diagram shows the shortest distances between these four cities:

Use the distances to make up a mileage chart to show the shortest distances between these cities.

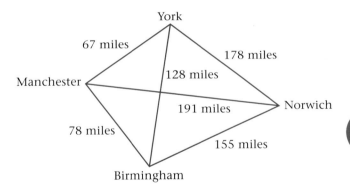

5 Here is a table showing the journey times between places.

Use the table to find the times for these journeys:

(a) London to Manchester

(b) York to Kendal

(c) Leeds to York

(d) Leeds to London

(e) Manchester to Leeds

(f) London to York.

York				
1h 22 min	Manchester			
40 min	54 min	Leeds		
2h 09 min	1h 25 min	1h 58 min	Kendal	
3h 52 min	3h 52 min	3h 38 min	4h 48 min	London

Mixed exercise 10

1 Tony decides to collect information on how people were
going to vote in an election. He uses the question 'What
do you think of the Government?'
Explain what is wrong with Tony's question.

2 Catherine wants to find out what types of DVDs her
friends own.
Draw a suitable data collection sheet she could use.

3 Daisy and Don want to know what type of music their
friends listen to.
Draw a suitable data collection sheet they could use.

4 Joe plans to carry out a traffic survey of the types of
vehicles that pass the school gate at the end of a school
day.
Draw a suitable data collection sheet he could use.

5 Shaun plans to carry out a survey into the television
viewing habits of his tutor group.
One of his questions is 'How much television do you
watch?'
Amy tells him that this is not a very good question.
Write down an improved question that Shaun could
use.

6 Lewis is going to use this data collection sheet to carry
out a survey of the age of cars in the school car park.

Age of car	Tally	Frequency
0–1		
1–2		
2–3		
4–5		
Over 5		
Over 10		

Explain two faults on Lewis's data collection sheet.

7 The headteacher in a school wants to carry out a survey
of what students think of the school. Explain how she
could select a random sample of students to use in the
survey.

8 Mr Beeton is going to open a restaurant.
He wants to know what type of restaurant people like.
He designs a questionnaire.

(a) Design a suitable question he could use to find out what type of restaurant people like.

He asks his family 'Do you agree that pizza is better than pasta?'
This is **not** a good way to find out what people who might use his restaurant like to eat.

(b) Write down **two** reasons why this is **not** a good way to find out what people who might use his restaurant like to eat.   [E]

9 (a) Explain why each of these ways of sampling is not random:

(i) Standing outside the school tuck shop when you want to find out where students buy snacks.

(ii) Telephoning people on a Friday night when you want to find out how often they go to the cinema on a Friday night.

(iii) Asking people who are shopping in an out-of-town shopping mall if they have a car.

(iv) Asking people travelling on a train, on a snowy day, what they think about the punctuality of trains.

(b) What would be a suitable sampling method to find out how London office workers get to work?

10 Here is a mileage chart:

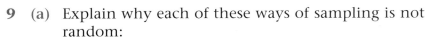

Cardiff					
232	Dover				
393	490	Edinburgh			
201	295	224	Liverpool		
152	78	403	210	London	
318	365	108	172	292	Newcastle

Use the mileage chart to find the distance between these places:

(a) London and Dover
(b) Cardiff and Liverpool
(c) Newcastle and Edinburgh
(d) Liverpool and London
(e) Cardiff and Edinburgh
(f) Newcastle and London.

Summary of key points

1 When you are writing questions for a **questionnaire**:
   - be clear what you want to find out and what data you need
   - ask short, simple questions
   - provide tick boxes with possible answers
   - avoid questions which are too vague, too personal, or which may influence the answer.

2 When you carry out a survey, select a **random sample** to avoid **bias**.
   In a random sample everyone has an equal chance of being chosen.

3 When you carry out an experiment you can use a **data capture sheet** to record your results.

4 Data you collect is called **primary data**. Data that has been collected by other people is called **secondary data**.

5 **Two-way tables** are used to record or display information that is grouped in two different catergories.

6 A **database** is an organised collection of information.
   It can be stored on paper or on a computer.

7 When you collect data from the internet make sure that:
   - the data comes from a reliable source
   - the data is accurate – check against other sources.

11 Linear equations

11.1 Simple equations

In algebra letters are used to represent numbers.

$a + 3 = 7$ The letter a must equal 4 because 4 add 3 equals 7.
$\quad a = 4$

$a - 3 = 2$ a must equal 5 because 5 take away 3 equals 2.
$\quad a = 5$

These are examples of **equations**.

Equations are used to solve real-life problems. For example, the value of t in the equation $20 = 5 + 10t$ tells a sky diver how long it takes to go from a speed of 5 metres per second to 20 metres per second.

Exercise 11A

Find the value of the letter in these equations.

1 $a + 2 = 5$	**2** $b + 1 = 4$	**3** $c + 2 = 9$
4 $w + 5 = 7$	**5** $m + 3 = 4$	**6** $y + 5 = 5$
7 $x - 2 = 3$	**8** $k - 4 = 1$	**9** $n - 3 = 3$
10 $h - 5 = 3$	**11** $g - 2 = 2$	**12** $f - 5 = 4$
13 $d + 2 = 7$	**14** $2 + e = 5$	**15** $4 + y = 7$
16 $10 + x = 14$	**17** $7 - m = 3$	**18** $5 - d = 2$
19 $k + 6 = 15$	**20** $12 = y + 2$	**21** $15 - t = 5$
22 $z - 2 = 2$	**23** $z + 2 = 2$	**24** $n - 5 = 0$

The balance method

In Exercise 11A you probably spotted the answers and then wrote them down. There is another way of looking at equations.

> An equation is a balancing act!

Example 1 shows a way of working out the value of the letter in an equation that does not rely on guessing the answer.

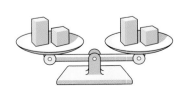

Example 1

To find a from $a + 6 = 9$:

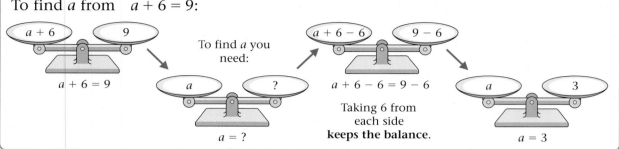

$a + 6 = 9$

To find a you need:

$a = ?$

$a + 6 - 6 = 9 - 6$

Taking 6 from each side **keeps the balance.**

$a = 3$

Example 2

To find k from $k - 7 = 13$:

$$k - 7 \qquad = 13$$
$$k - 7 + 7 = 13 + 7 \quad\text{——— Adding 7 to each side keeps}$$
$$k \qquad\quad = 20 \qquad\qquad\text{the balance.}$$

Exercise 11B

Find the value of the letter in these equations. Use the balancing method to help you.

1 $a + 6 = 7$ **2** $y + 3 = 5$ **3** $h + 2 = 9$

4 $p - 5 = 4$ **5** $q - 3 = 7$ **6** $d - 6 = 2$

7 $x + 3 = 3$ **8** $t - 4 = 0$ **9** $r + 7 = 10$

10 $k + 2 = 3$ **11** $n + 1 = 2$ **12** $x - 2 = 3$

13 $m + 7 = 12$ **14** $y - 7 = 9$ **15** $w + 5 = 5$

16 $q - 10 = 2$ **17** $5 + p = 7$ **18** $6 + t = 6$

19 $a + 19 = 31$ **20** $21 + x = 21$ **21** $p - 15 = 23$

22 $7 = a + 3$ **23** $6 = b + 5$ **24** $10 = y + 10$

Wot, no letter z?

Exercise 11C

Find the value of the letter in these equations.

1 $a + 5 = 10$ **2** $p - 4 = 7$ **3** $q - 3 = 5$

4 $x + 7 = 15$ **5** $y + 4 = 17$ **6** $s + 12 = 15$

7 $x - 7 = 15$

8 $y - 4 = 17$

9 $s - 12 = 15$

10 $a + 5 = 6$

11 $p - 5 = 6$

12 $c + 17 = 21$

13 $5 + a = 6$

14 $11 + p = 16$

15 $12 + q = 12$

16 $4 = a + 2$

17 $5 = b + 3$

18 $12 = c - 3$

19 $10 = p + 5$

20 $11 = y - 10$

21 $15 = t + 10$

22 $12 = p + 12$

23 $12 = p - 12$

24 $p + 12 = 12$

Example 3 shows how to find the value of the letter when the letter is multiplied by a number.

Example 3

$3a = 12$

This means $a \times 3 = 12$

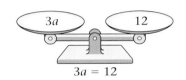

$3a = 12$

> Remember:
> $3a$ means 3 lots of a or $3 \times a$

To work out $a = ?$ you need to keep the balance in the equation.

To keep the equation balanced you must do the same to each side.

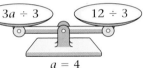

Try: $3a \div 3 = 12 \div 3$

$a = 4$

$a = 4$

> The inverse of $\times 3$ is $\div 3$.

To keep an **equation** balanced you must do the same to each side.

Exercise 11D

Find the value of the letter in these equations.

1 $3a = 6$

2 $4p = 8$

3 $5p = 15$

4 $6s = 18$

5 $2k = 10$

6 $7u = 28$

7 $2g = 14$

8 $5k = 35$

9 $6j = 12$

10 $8f = 32$

11 $3r = 27$

12 $5v = 45$

13 $2t = 42$

14 $4d = 48$

15 $7t = 63$

Example 4

$$\frac{w}{3} = 5$$

This means $w \div 3 = 5$

$$\frac{w}{3} \times 3 = 5 \times 3 \quad\text{————————} \quad \text{Multiply each side of the equation by 3.}$$

$$w = 15$$

> Look for the opposite (or inverse) operation.
> The inverse of $\div$ 3 is $\times$ 3.

Exercise 11E

Find the value of the letter in these equations.

1 $\frac{a}{2} = 5$ **2** $\frac{b}{5} = 4$ **3** $\frac{s}{4} = 3$

4 $\frac{c}{6} = 5$ **5** $\frac{t}{4} = 6$ **6** $\frac{s}{8} = 9$

7 $\frac{h}{6} = 12$ **8** $\frac{f}{4} = 7$ **9** $\frac{d}{3} = 15$

10 $\frac{a}{3} = 15$ **11** $\frac{b}{5} = 8$ **12** $\frac{r}{4} = 13$

13 $\frac{a}{12} = 5$ **14** $\frac{b}{2} = 16$ **15** $\frac{k}{3} = 16$

Exercise 11F

Solve these equations.

1 $a + 4 = 5$ **2** $b + 3 = 6$ **3** $c + 4 = 9$

4 $p - 3 = 6$ **5** $q - 2 = 2$ **6** $d - 6 = 2$

7 $2p = 6$ **8** $4r = 8$ **9** $5t = 20$

10 $\frac{a}{2} = 6$ **11** $\frac{b}{5} = 12$ **12** $\frac{s}{4} = 5$

13 $4 + r = 7$ **14** $6 + e = 7$ **15** $7 + p = 7$

> Solve means 'find the value of the letter'. So for question 1, find the value of a.

11.2 Equations combining operations

You have dealt with equations where you added or subtracted numbers and where you multiplied or divided by numbers. You are now going to look at what happens when these are combined into one equation.

> In a combined equation, deal with the + or − first.

Example 5

$$2a + 3 = 11$$
$$2a + 3 - 3 = 11 - 3 \quad\text{———— Take 3 from each side.}$$
$$2a = 8$$
$$2a \div 2 = 8 \div 2 \quad\text{———— Divide each side by 2.}$$
$$a = 4$$

> First try to get letters only on one side.

Example 6

$$5p - 3 = 7$$
$$5p - 3 + 3 = 7 + 3 \quad\text{———— Add 3 to each side.}$$
$$5p = 10$$
$$5p \div 5 = 10 \div 5 \quad\text{———— Divide each side by 5.}$$
$$p = 2$$

Example 7

$$\frac{m}{4} + 3 = 8$$
$$\frac{m}{4} + 3 - 3 = 8 - 3 \quad\text{———— Take 3 from each side.}$$
$$\frac{m}{4} = 5$$
$$\frac{m}{4} \times 4 = 5 \times 4 \quad\text{———— Multiply each side by 4.}$$
$$m = 20$$

Exercise 11G

Find the value of the letter in these equations.

1 $2a + 1 = 5$　　　**2** $2a - 1 = 5$　　　**3** $3a + 2 = 8$

4 $3a - 5 = 4$　　　**5** $3p + 7 = 7$　　　**6** $3p + 7 = 13$

7 $4q + 5 = 17$　　　**8** $5r - 6 = 4$　　　**9** $6t - 12 = 18$

10 $7f - 12 = 9$　　　**11** $2r - 11 = 15$　　　**12** $10a - 5 = 5$

13 $10a + 5 = 5$　　　**14** $4d + 7 = 19$　　　**15** $5c - 2 = 18$

16 $\dfrac{a}{3} + 2 = 3$　　　**17** $\dfrac{z}{5} + 1 = 2$　　　**18** $\dfrac{r}{6} + 4 = 7$

19 $\dfrac{s}{4} + 6 = 9$　　　**20** $\dfrac{b}{3} + 7 = 13$　　　**21** $\dfrac{c}{4} - 2 = 4$

22 $\dfrac{f}{3} - 6 = 3$　　　**23** $\dfrac{h}{2} - 4 = -2$　　　**24** $\dfrac{x}{5} - 1 = 2$

All the equations dealt with so far have had solutions that are whole numbers. Look at the following examples. You can see that solutions can be fractions or decimals as well.

Example 8

$$4p + 7 = 16$$
$$4p + 7 - 7 = 16 - 7 \qquad \text{Take 7 from each side.}$$
$$4p = 9$$
$$4p \div 4 = 9 \div 4 \qquad \text{Divide each side by 4.}$$
$$p = 2\tfrac{1}{4}$$

Example 9

$$5q - 8 = 3$$
$$5q - 8 + 8 = 3 + 8 \qquad \text{Add 8 to each side.}$$
$$5q = 11$$
$$5q \div 5 = 11 \div 5 \qquad \text{Divide each side by 5.}$$
$$q = 2.2$$

Exercise 11H

Find the value of the letter in these equations.

1 $2a + 3 = 6$	**2** $2a - 4 = 3$	**3** $3a + 7 = 15$
4 $3a - 6 = 7$	**5** $5p + 7 = 15$	**6** $5p - 7 = 15$
7 $5e + 3 = 3$	**8** $4t + 3 = 9$	**9** $8j - 7 = 5$
10 $7c - 4 = 7$	**11** $8k + 3 = 5$	**12** $3d - 7 = 3$
13 $9u + 7 = 9$	**14** $4q - 4 = 5$	**15** $7y + 6 = 15$

So far all the solutions to the equations you have looked at have been positive. Example 10 shows how to deal with equations when the solutions are negative.

Example 10

$$2a + 7 = 1$$
$$2a + 7 - 7 = 1 - 7 \qquad \text{Take 7 from each side.}$$
$$2a = -6$$
$$2a \div 2 = -6 \div 2 \qquad \text{Divide each side by 2.}$$
$$a = -3$$

Exercise 11I

Find the value of the letter in these equations.

1 $2a + 3 = 1$ **2** $2a + 5 = 1$ **3** $2a + 9 = 1$

4 $3a + 8 = 5$ **5** $3a + 7 = 1$ **6** $5p + 12 = 2$

7 $2s + 7 = -3$ **8** $5p - 2 = -12$ **9** $4k - 5 = -9$

10 $8h + 10 = 2$ **11** $4y + 12 = -8$ **12** $3e + 47 = 20$

13 $6t - 12 = -12$ **14** $3w + 4 = 1$ **15** $2c + 15 = 11$

16 $13a + 9 = 9$

Exercise 11J

Find the value of the letter in these equations.

1 $2s + 4 = 10$ **2** $5d + 3 = 18$ **3** $8m - 7 = 33$

4 $4h - 2 = 14$ **5** $4k + 7 = 43$ **6** $3y + 7 = 13$

7 $5p + 2 = 9$ **8** $4f + 4 = 17$ **9** $3s - 6 = 5$

10 $-7g - 4 = 12$ **11** $4f - 5 = 12$ **12** $5k - 12 = 6$

13 $-3s - 15 = 2$ **14** $6j - 3 = 19$ **15** $9b + 7 = 2$

16 $-2r + 12 = 5$ **17** $5t + 15 = -12$ **18** $7y - 15 = -21$

19 $3e - 5 = -6$ **20** $-4f - 7 = -2$ **21** $5g + 17 = 15$

22 $4h + 4 = 0$ **23** $-3c - 5 = 0$ **24** $8s + 9 = 4$

25 $\dfrac{z}{2} + 2 = 4$ **26** $\dfrac{x}{5} - 3 = 2$ **27** $\dfrac{p}{2} - 5 = -3$

28 $\dfrac{c}{3} + 4 = -2$ **29** $\dfrac{a}{8} - 1 = 5$ **30** $-\dfrac{e}{3} + 2 = 10$

11.3 Equations with brackets

Chapter 3 dealt with quite complicated algebraic expressions. You can use what you learned there to solve quite complicated equations.

Example 11

Find the value of p for

$$3(2p + 3) = 5$$
$$3 \times 2p + 3 \times 3 = 5$$
$$6p + 9 = 5$$
$$6p + 9 - 9 = 5 - 9$$
$$6p = -4$$
$$6p \div 6 = -4 \div 6$$
$$p = -\tfrac{4}{6} \text{ or } -\tfrac{2}{3}$$

Remember to deal with brackets first. Multiply each term inside the brackets by 3.

$3(2p + 3)$
$3 \times 2p + 3 \times 3$

In an equation with brackets, expand the brackets first.

Exercise 11K

Find the value of the letter in these equations.

1 $2(p + 4) = 10$ **2** $3(d - 2) = 9$ **3** $2(c + 5) = 16$

4 $3(b - 2) = 1$ **5** $3(g + 2) = 15$ **6** $5(g - 2) = 15$

7 $2(v + 3) = 2$ **8** $4(4 + s) = 20$ **9** $2(3d + 3) = 4$

10 $3(t - 5) = 2$ **11** $4(h - 3) = 0$ **12** $2(3h - 7) = 10$

13 $2(2s + 5) = 22$ **14** $4(2y - 3) = 16$ **15** $4(4r - 12) = 32$

Exercise 11L

Solve these equations.

1 $2(a + 2) = 6$ **2** $3(h - 4) = 12$ **3** $4(g + 5) = 8$

4 $6(f - 3) = 18$ **5** $5(q + 7) = 35$ **6** $9(k - 2) = 18$

7 $5(4 + g) = 25$ **8** $4(5 + h) = 12$ **9** $3(d + 2) = 3$

10 $2(v + 7) = 3$ **11** $3(s + 7) = 4$ **12** $5(2n - 3) = 20$

13 $4(4f + 5) = 6$ **14** $6(7d - 12) = 30$ **15** $2(5m + 11) = 0$

Equations with letters on both sides

If there are letters on both sides of an equation you have to deal with the problem slightly differently. It is a good idea always to keep the letter on the side with the most; in Example 12 this is the side with $5p$.

Example 12

Find the value of p in the equation

$$5p - 2 = 3p + 6$$
$$5p - 3p - 2 = 3p - 3p + 6 \quad\text{———— Take } 3p \text{ from both sides.}$$
$$2p - 2 = 6$$
$$2p = 6 + 2 \quad\text{———— Add 2 to both sides.}$$
$$2p = 8$$
$$p = 4 \quad\text{———— Divide by 2.}$$

Exercise 11M

Find the value of the letter in these equations.

1 $2k - 3 = k + 2$

2 $5s - 4 = 3s + 3$

3 $4p + 2 = 3p + 6$

4 $5g + 4 = 3g + 2$

5 $7t - 4 = 4t + 7$

6 $2k + 6 = 3k - 3$

7 $4d + 9 = 5d + 2$

8 $5c + 8 = 7c + 2$

9 $5z + 6 = 3z + 4$

10 $7b + 12 = 3b - 6$

11 $9p + 8 = 3p - 2$

12 $4g + 9 = 3g + 17$

Exercise 11N

Solve these equations.

1 $5h - 5 = 4h + 7$

2 $7t + 11 = 6t + 3$

3 $5d + 3 = 3d + 1$

4 $6f + 9 = 4f + 3$

5 $3s + 5 = 4s - 2$

6 $4d + 13 = 5d + 7$

7 $2a + 7 = 4a - 2$

8 $3q + 9 = 6q - 3$

9 $4y + 4 = 7y + 6$

10 $2e + 6 = 5e + 9$

11 $12s + 6 = 6s - 4$

12 $5u + 9 = 3u - 2$

13 $5t - 5 = 2t - 9$

14 $6s + 9 = 2s + 2$

15 $3q + 6 = 7q - 5$

16 $2w + 3 = 7w + 9$

17 $8h + 4 = 3h - 4$

18 $3s + 4 = 2s - 3$

19 $r + 2 = 5r + 6$

20 $5a - 7 = 2a + 4$

Equations with brackets

The most complicated equations you will be asked to solve
will have letters on both sides and perhaps brackets as well.

Example 13

$$4(2x - 3) = 2(x + 3)$$
$$8x - 12 = 2x + 6$$
$$8x - 2x - 12 = 2x - 2x + 6$$
$$6x - 12 = 6$$
$$6x - 12 + 12 = 6 + 12$$
$$6x = 18$$
$$x = 3$$

> The first step is to expand the brackets. Then sort out the equation in the usual way.

Exercise 11O

Find the value of the letters in these equations.

1 $4(2p + 3) = 2(p + 8)$ **2** $5(2h - 9) = 3(3h + 7)$

3 $6(5r - 7) = 4(3r + 7)$ **4** $7(2t + 6) = 3(5t + 7)$

5 $4(3g + 5) = 2(5g + 7)$ **6** $5(4d + 9) = 6(3d + 5)$

7 $8(2k - 6) = 5(3k - 7)$ **8** $7(2m + 3) = 4(5m - 3)$

9 $7(9d - 5) = 12(5d - 6)$ **10** $5(3j + 7) = 4(4j + 3)$

11 $4(8y + 3) = 6(7y + 5)$ **12** $3(6t + 7) = 5(4t + 7)$

Mixed exercise 11

Solve these equations.

1 $x + 8 = 13$ **2** $14 = 20 - x$

3 $5t + 7 = 3t + 10$ **5** $4g + 7 = 3g + 9$

5 $6s - 6 = 4s + 2$ **7** $5q - 5 = 3q + 7$

7 $2d + 4 = 5d - 6$ **8** $6k - 3 = 2k + 7$

9 $2(a + 3) = 7$ **10** $5(2k - 4) = 15$

11 $5 = 2(2d + 7)$ **12** $8 = 4(7p - 3)$

13 $2(3p + 2) = 5p - 7$ **14** $3(5r + 2) = 12r - 7$

15 $2(6t + 2) = 3(5t - 6)$ **16** $6(g + 7) = 3(4g + 2)$

17 $5(2a + 1) + 3(3a - 4) = 4(3a - 6)$ **18** $\dfrac{x}{4} - 2 = 3$

Summary of key points

1 In algebra letters are used to represent numbers. For example $a = 5$.

2 To keep an **equation** balanced you must do the same to each side.

$$a + 4 = 7 \quad \rightarrow \quad a + 4 - 4 = 7 - 4 \quad \rightarrow \quad a = 3$$
$$a - 3 = 1 \quad \rightarrow \quad a - 3 + 3 = 1 + 3 \quad \rightarrow \quad a = 4$$
$$5a = 30 \quad \rightarrow \quad 5a \div 5 = 30 \div 5 \rightarrow \quad a = 6$$
$$\frac{a}{2} = 7 \quad \rightarrow \quad \frac{a}{2} \times 2 = 7 \times 2 \quad \rightarrow \quad a = 14$$

3 In a combined equation, deal with the $+$ and $-$ first.

$$3a + 7 = 1 \quad \rightarrow \quad 3a + 7 - 7 = 1 - 7$$
$$3a = -6$$
$$a = -2$$

4 In an equation with brackets, expand the brackets first.

$$3(x + 1) = 4 \quad \rightarrow \quad 3x + 3 = 4$$

12 Sorting and presenting data

12.1 Some ways of presenting data

In a survey, 60 pupils were asked how many text messages they got last Saturday. Here are the results:

3 6 2 5 4 7 7 6 7 9 5 7 8 6 6 5 7 8 6 3 7 7 6 9 8 4 5 5 4 7
6 4 8 3 5 7 3 7 6 8 7 5 8 4 8 7 1 9 7 6 8 2 6 5 4 5 8 6 7 9

To see this information more clearly you can draw up a **tally chart**:

Number of messages	Tally	Frequency
0		0
1	I	1
2	II	2
3	IIII	4
4	⧸⧸⧸⧸ I	6
5	⧸⧸⧸⧸ IIII	9
6	⧸⧸⧸⧸ ⧸⧸⧸⧸ I	11
7	⧸⧸⧸⧸ ⧸⧸⧸⧸ IIII	14
8	⧸⧸⧸⧸ IIII	9
9	IIII	4

This tally chart, or frequency table, shows the frequencies of the different numbers of messages (how often each number occurred). Tally marks are grouped in fives to make them easier to count:

⧸⧸⧸⧸ ⧸⧸⧸⧸ ⧸⧸⧸⧸ III

is easier to count than

IIIIIIIIIIIIIIIII

Another way to show up any pattern in data is to draw a **bar chart**.
This bar chart shows the data from the text message survey.

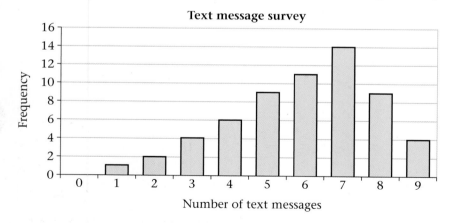

When drawing a bar chart you must make sure that
- the horizontal and vertical axes are clearly labelled
- the chart has a title
- the scale is designed so that the bar chart is a sensible size.

Activity – Text messages

Collect data for the number of text messages received by the students in your class yesterday. Draw a bar chart to show this information.

It is important always to check the scale on a bar chart carefully.

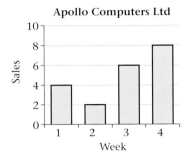

Apollo Computers Ltd

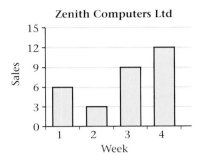

Zenith Computers Ltd

These computer sales figures look the same until you look at the scales on the vertical axes.

For Apollo Computers Ltd the number of computers sold in the four weeks was $4 + 2 + 6 + 8 = 20$

For Zenith Computers Ltd the number sold was $6 + 3 + 9 + 12 = 30$

Tally charts and **bar charts** are two ways of displaying data that can be counted.

You must leave a gap between the bars when you draw bar charts of data that can be counted.

Here is a bar chart showing what sports people watch on TV.

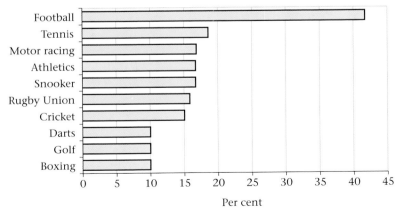

Percentages of people watching sport on TV
(Survey January 2003)

It shows that football is the most popular sport that people watch on TV.

Exercise 12A

For each of the following sets of data recorded at an island weather station, display the information in

(a) a tally chart   (b) a bar chart.

1 Hours of sunshine

5	6	0	1	3	1	4	7	5	6	6	2
4	3	1	0	7	10	9	11	5	4	7	6
9	9	11	12	12	7	9	10	11	10	9	7
8	4	6	5	7	8	10	8	6	3	6	8
3	3	4	1	10	9	11	7	2	6	10	7

2 Force of wind measured on the Beaufort scale

3	1	4	4	3	5	2	6	4	2	2	2
0	1	4	2	5	3	3	4	4	3	6	7
5	4	0	1	2	3	1	5	4	3	2	2
8	10	9	7	7	8	6	5	4	3	5	2
6	7	5	5	1	2	6	4	3	4	6	5

3 Maximum temperature in degrees Celsius

18	19	19	21	19	21	18	18	19	18	16	18
17	18	18	17	19	18	17	16	21	22	21	21
20	22	22	23	21	18	23	21	21	22	22	17
19	17	19	21	19	19	17	19	19	16	19	17
20	22	21	20	23	21	21	22	21	21	20	20

12.2 Grouping data

When there are lots of different data values, it is useful to group the data.

Here are the numbers of cars photographed by a speed camera on each of 60 days:

17	39	36	22	16	43	25	43	55	26	67	13
38	37	37	18	30	11	5	54	23	24	43	0
32	43	4	30	22	23	55	26	21	24	36	23
43	26	46	47	17	3	36	38	11	57	12	32
8	58	27	34	15	24	43	25	61	25	64	15

First group the number of photographs per day in tens and make a frequency table.

Photographs	Tally	Frequency
0–9	ⅲⅲ	5
10–19	ⅲⅲ ⅲⅲ	10
20–29	ⅲⅲ ⅲⅲ ⅲⅲ |	16
30–39	ⅲⅲ ⅲⅲ |||	13
40–49	ⅲⅲ |||	8
50–59	ⅲⅲ	5
60–69	|||	3
70+		0

The **modal class** is 20–29 because this group has the highest frequency.

The intervals 0–9, 10–19, … are called **class intervals**.

The **modal class** is the group which has the highest frequency.

Next draw a bar chart to illustrate the data.

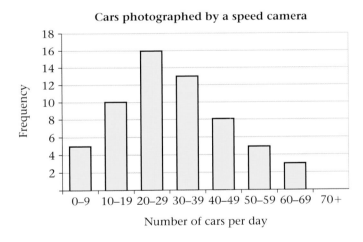

Cars photographed by a speed camera

Exercise 12B

1 In a music contest the marks awarded were:

```
15  21   13   18  22  17   9  12   7  19
24  16   11    8  14  28  17  15  18   7
 5  17   10   26   7  16  23  14  11  20
12   6   26   16  10  19  13  29  17   8
```

(a) Using class intervals 0–4, 5–9, …, draw up a frequency table.

(b) Draw a bar chart to represent your frequency table.

2 The number of people logged on at an internet café was recorded every hour over a 48-hour period.
Here are the results:

```
14 14 24  9 25 18 22  5
13  7 11 14  4 16 11 27
17 19 13 15 34 15 14  9
25  7 28  3 15 12 20 13
 1 16 10 24  6 29  7 22
20 14 29 12 24  8 16 10
```

   (a) Draw up a frequency table, using class intervals 0–5, 6–10, 11–15, … .

   (b) Draw a bar chart of the data.

   (c) What is the modal class?

3 Bowling shoes may be hired at Bronx Bowling Alley.
Here are the sizes of the shoes at the alley:

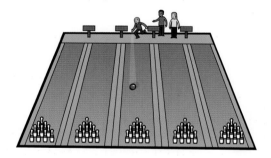

$3\frac{1}{2}$ 4   5   1   5 $9\frac{1}{2}$ $2\frac{1}{2}$ 4   5   4

5   2 $7\frac{1}{2}$ 3   6   4   7 $6\frac{1}{2}$ 3   7

4   7   5   9 $3\frac{1}{2}$ 10   5 $2\frac{1}{2}$ $4\frac{1}{2}$ $7\frac{1}{2}$

$5\frac{1}{2}$ 3 $6\frac{1}{2}$ 5   7   5   6 $6\frac{1}{2}$ 8   6

2   6 $4\frac{1}{2}$ 7   5   3   3 $5\frac{1}{2}$ $7\frac{1}{2}$ 2

   (a) Draw up a frequency table for the data. Choose classes with equal intervals.

   (b) Draw a bar chart of the data.

   (c) Comment on your findings.

12.3 Comparing data

You can use bar charts to compare different sets of data.

The numbers of patients who attended morning and evening surgeries in a doctor's practice one week are shown in the table and the following bar chart.

	Mon	Tue	Wed	Thu	Fri	Sat
Morning	145	120	96	116	125	28
Evening	81	65	43	55	64	–

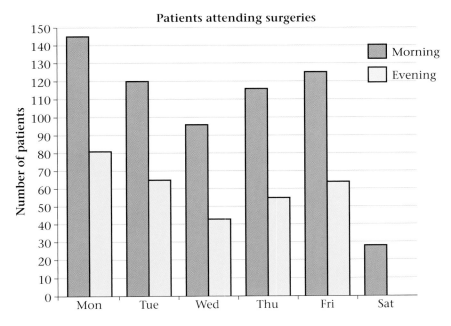

This type of graph is called a **dual bar chart** because it compares **two** sets of data. Often it is easier to see a pattern by looking at the chart rather than the table.

A **dual bar chart** is used to compare two sets of data.

Example 1

Use the table and bar chart to answer the following questions.
(a) On which day did most patients attend?
(b) On which day did fewest patients attend?
(c) On which day was there no evening surgery?
(d) On which day did 171 patients attend?
(e) How many more patients attended on Tuesday morning than on Tuesday evening?

(a) Monday——— This is clear from the bar chart
(b) Saturday——— This is clear from the bar chart
(c) Saturday——— Use the table or the bar chart
(d) Thursday——— Use the table for exact numbers
(e) 55——— Use the table

Activity – Homework time

Record the times you and a friend spend doing homework on each day during a week. Enter the results in a table and draw a dual bar chart of the data.

Example 2

Here is a bar chart showing information about applications for asylum in the UK in 2003.

Use the bar chart to answer these questions:

(a) Which is the most common age group for asylum-seekers?

(b) Which age group(s) had the same percentage of males as of females?

(a) 25–29

(b) 30–34 and 35–39

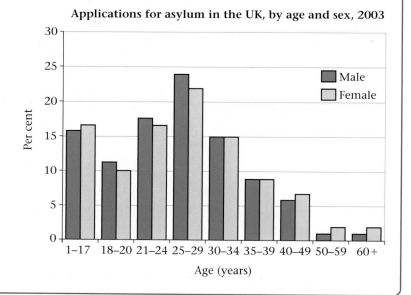

Applications for asylum in the UK, by age and sex, 2003

Exercise 12C

1 The average daily temperatures, in °F, in London and Majorca are recorded in the table.

	Oct	Nov	Dec	Jan	Feb	Mar	Apr
London	58	50	45	42	43	50	58
Majorca	71	65	58	52	58	62	68

(a) Draw a dual bar chart to illustrate the data.

(b) Write down three things you notice from your chart.

2 The prices of holiday accommodation in Majorca per person, in £ sterling per week, are given in the table.

	Oct	Nov	Dec	Jan	Feb	Mar	Apr
Hotel	260	290	270	280	295	315	330
Self catering	190	150	140	110	125	150	180

(a) Draw a dual bar chart to illustrate the data.

(b) Which months have the greatest difference in price between hotel and self catering?

(c) Write down three things you notice from your chart.

> Think carefully about the vertical scale you choose.

3   The amounts of money, in euros, spent by Norma and
    Adrian buying presents were:

	Mon	Tue	Wed	Thu	Fri	Sat
Norma	7.60	0	12.30	2.00	25.40	6.00
Adrian	5.50	7.10	2.40	20.80	6.00	4.00

(a) Represent this data by drawing a dual bar chart.
(b) Write down three statements about Norma's and
     Adrian's spending.

12.4 Pictograms

A **pictogram** is a quick, visual way of showing information by
using a symbol to represent a quantity.

For example, a primary teacher recorded the number of
students in his class who got a merit one week and drew a
pictogram for classroom display:

Rashid went round a factory car park and made a note of the
colours of the cars. His findings were:

Black	35	White	20
Red	10	Grey	15
Silver	15	Beige	2
Green	5	Other	14

He decided to use the symbol to represent 5 cars and drew this pictogram.

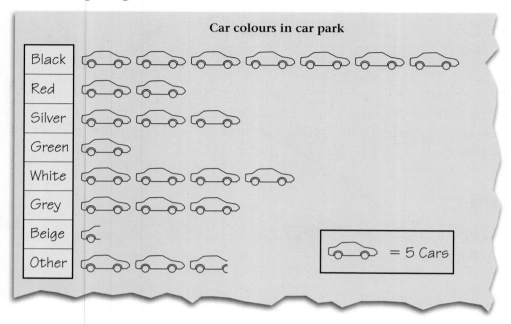

Car colours in car park

= 5 Cars

Exercise 12D

1 Draw a pictogram to illustrate each set of data. First decide what symbol you will use and what it will represent.

(a) This table shows the numbers of different types of housing in a village.

	Flats	Bungalows	Detached	Semi-detached
Number	50	80	40	60

(b) This table shows the numbers of telephone calls to an answering service between midnight and 7:00 am during a certain week.

	Mon	Tue	Wed	Thu	Fri	Sat	Sun
Calls	24	20	32	48	28	32	12

(c) This table shows the numbers of members in the European parliament for certain countries in 2004.

	Belgium	France	Germany	Ireland	Spain	UK
Members	24	78	99	13	54	78

2 The pictograms show how many drinks were sold from
   two machines.

Drinks machine sales

Dining room	
Coffee	🥤🥤🥤
Tea	🥤🥤🥤🥤
Hot chocolate	🥤🥤🥤
Soup	🥤🥤
Hot blackcurrant	🥤🥤🥤

Staff room	
Coffee	🥤🥤🥤🥤🥤🥤
Tea	
Hot chocolate	🥤🥤
Soup	🥤
Hot blackcurrant	🥤

Key: 🥤 10 drinks sold
     🥤 5 drinks sold

(a)   **(i)** Which drink was the most popular in the dining
            room?
       (ii) How many hot blackcurrants were sold in the
            dining room?
      (iii) How many hot chocolates were sold in the staff
            room?
(b) The staff room machine also sold 45 teas.
     Copy and complete the pictogram.
(c) Work out the total number of drinks sold in the
     dining room.
(d) 64 people used the machine in the dining room.
     Find the average number of drinks sold per person.
(e) Comment on the differences in sales from the
     two machines.   [E]

12.5 Discrete and continuous data, and line graphs

It is important, when drawing graphs, to know if the data is
discrete or continuous.

Data which can be counted is called **discrete data**.

For example, George has three sisters.
           Southampton beat Liverpool 2–1.
           There are ten coins in my pocket.

Data which is measured is called **continuous data**.

For example, Mike is 1.79 m tall.
           The athlete ran 100 m in 10.3 seconds.
           The weight of a bag of sugar is 1 kg.

Line graphs can be used to show continuous data.

The table shows the temperature in Leeds at midday during the first week in May.

May	1	2	3	4	5	6	7
Temperature (°C)	12	16	14	11	12	15	13

You could show this data on a **line graph**.
Here are two ways of doing this.

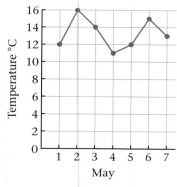

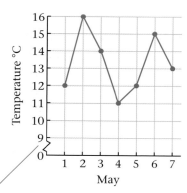

The temperature scale on this graph starts at 0 °C.

The break in the axis shows that the scale goes straight from 0 to 9.

This graph gives more space on the y-axis to values between 10 and 16 °C. This shows the pattern in the data more clearly.

The data is *continuous* so you can join the points.

This table shows the number of passengers that got off a train at each stop on a line in South-East London.

Station	London Bridge (B)	Hither Green (G)	Lee (L)	Mottingham (M)
Passengers	30	19	28	24

If you drew a graph like the one on the right, it might give the impression that people got off the train between stations!

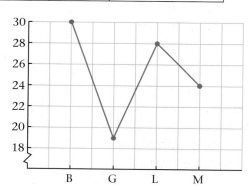

The data is *discrete* so you should not join the points.

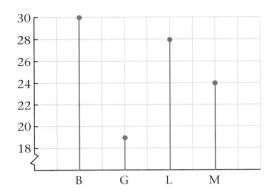

This is called a **vertical line graph** or **bar-line graph**. It is similar to a bar chart, and is used to display data that can be counted.

Activity – Sweets

Count the numbers of different colours of sweets in a packet and record the data in a suitable diagram.

Compare your findings with those from a packet of the same brand of sweet.

Example 3

Here is a line graph showing the percentage of household waste recycled in England.

Use the graph to answer these questions:
(a) What percentage of waste was recycled in England in 1998?
(b) In which year was 11.2% of waste recycled?
(c) Make a comment about what the graph shows.

(a) 9.0%
(b) 2000
(c) The percentage of waste that was recycled rose every year from 1996 to 2002 – the graph shows an increasing trend.

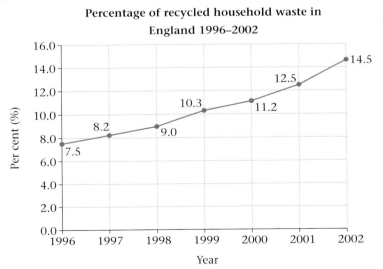

Percentage of recycled household waste in England 1996–2002

Exercise 12E

1 Which of the following are discrete data and which are continuous?

   (a) the number of pages in a book
   (b) the weight of a bag of sweets
   (c) the temperature of a bottle of milk
   (d) the number of sweets in a tube of Tasties
   (e) the Third World debt
   (f) the number of countries in the EU
   (g) the distance to the Moon
   (h) the number of people living in France
   (i) the number of questions you get right
   (j) the time it takes you to do this exercise.

2 Draw suitable graphs to represent each of the following sets of data.

   (a) The number of letters delivered to an office one week

	Sat	Sun	Mon	Tue	Wed	Thu	Fri
Letters	20	0	12	25	15	19	23

   (b) The noon temperature in Weymouth for certain days in August

August	1	2	3	4	5	6	7
Temperature (°F)	73	69	65	70	75	79	76

   (c) The lengths of some of the longest rivers in the British Isles, in km to the nearest 10 km

River	Severn	Wye	Shannon	Tay	Thames
Length	340	210	390	190	340

3 The graphs show the sales of bikes from January to May.

(a) (i) Look quickly at the graphs. Which shop appears to sell more bikes?

(ii) Look at the scales carefully.

Which shop sells more bikes?

(b) How many bikes did Cycleshop sell in March?

(c) How many bikes were sold altogether by

(i) Cycleshop　(ii) Bikeshop?

(d) In which month did both shops sell the same number of bikes?

4　The graphs show the numbers of vehicles coming for petrol at two garages during a week.

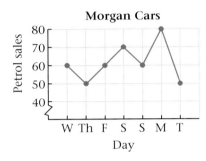

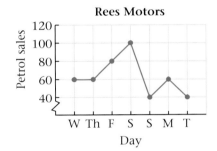

(a) Copy and complete the table below.

Petrol Sales	Wed	Thu	Fri	Sat	Sun	Mon	Tue
Morgan Cars							
Rees Motors							

(b) Draw a dual bar chart for this information.

(c) Use your chart to make three comments about the sales.

12.6 Time series

A line graph used to illustrate data collected at intervals in time (e.g. hourly, daily, weekly, …) is called a **time series** graph.

By observing results over time, you can predict what may happen in the future.

___ **Example 4** ___

This graph shows the temperature, in degrees Celsius, at noon during the first ten days of June in Llangrannog.

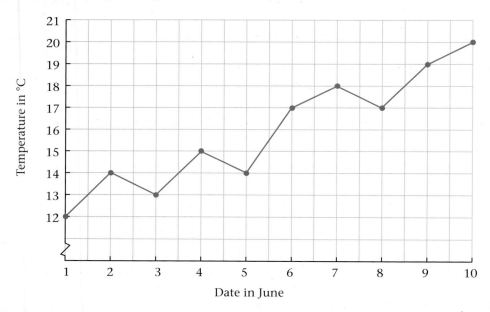

(a) What was the highest temperature recorded?

(b) What do you think the temperature might be over the next few days?

(c) Give a reason why your prediction might be wrong.

(a) 20 °C   (b) 20–21 °C

(c) The weather may change very suddenly.

Exercise 12F

1 This table shows the numbers of anglers fishing in Richmond Pond each year from 1998 to 2005.

Year	1998	1999	2000	2001	2002	2003	2004	2005
Number	279	268	272	240	228	212	209	195

(a) Draw a time series graph to represent this data.

(b) Comment on your graph.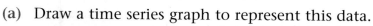

(c) Make a prediction for the number of anglers in 2006.

Hint: You could say what the highest and lowest values were, whether the graph has gone up or down, or if there is a repeating pattern in the data.

2   This table shows the values, in pence, of shares in two companies on the last day of each month last year.

	Jan	Feb	Mar	Apr	May	Jun	Jul	Aug	Sep
UXP	74	75	74	72	70	68	69	67	66
HCOR	35	36	40	41	39	42	41	43	44

(a) Using the same axes, draw a time series graph for each of these companies.

(b) What do you think the value of each share might be in October? Give a reason for your answer.

3   This table shows the quarterly sales of cars at Autobuy Garages.

Year	1998				1999				2000			
Quarter	1	2	3	4	1	2	3	4	1	2	3	4
Sales	90	86	82	77	94	92	88	85	100	95	92	

(a) Draw a time series graph to represent this data.
(b) Comment on your graph.
(c) Make a prediction of sales for the last quarter of 2000. Give a reason for your answer.

> This is a frequency distribution. It shows the number of cars sold every quarter.

12.7 Histograms

You usually draw bar charts or bar-line graphs to represent frequency distributions. These diagrams use the heights of bars or lines to represent the frequency. If the data is continuous and is grouped you can use a **histogram**.

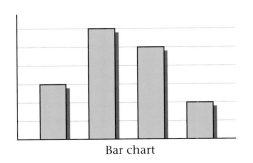

Bar chart

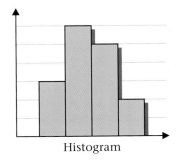

Histogram

> This histogram, with equal bar width and group size, is a special case. Most histograms do not have equal bar width.

You will notice that a histogram looks much like a bar chart except that there are no gaps between the bars in a histogram.

A **histogram** is used to display grouped data that is continuous.

> **Activity – Hand-spans**
>
> **(a)** Measure the hand-span of each person in your class.
> **(b)** Record the data in a frequency table using class intervals of equal width.
> **(c)** Draw a histogram to display your data.

12.8 Frequency polygons

Another useful way of displaying data is a **frequency polygon** in which the values at the midpoints of the class intervals are joined by straight lines.

The table shows the frequency distribution of the ages of members of a swimming club in 2001 and 2002.

Age	0–9	10–19	20–29	30–39	40–49	50–
2001	5	15	21	30	19	15
2002	10	24	28	22	10	6

You can draw histograms and join the midpoints to get a frequency polygon for each of the years.

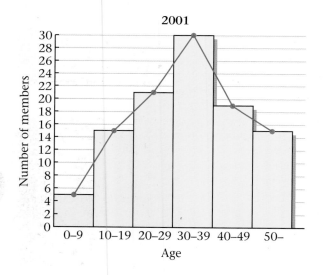

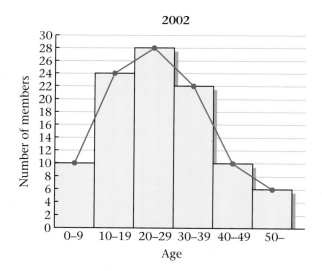

A **frequency polygon** can show the general pattern of data represented by a histogram.

It is often easier to compare data like this by placing one polygon on top of the other:

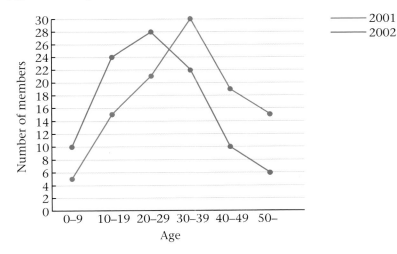

Exercise 12G

1   The numbers of students late for school in a two-week period are given in this table.

	Mon	Tue	Wed	Thu	Fri
Week 1	6	8	14	10	12
Week 2	9	13	8	6	10

(a)   Draw bar charts of this data.

(b)   Join the midpoints to make frequency polygons.

(c)   Use the frequency polygons to compare the two weeks and write down three observations.

> You can use a bar chart to help you draw a frequency polygon.

2   The table shows the results of 75 students in a fitness programme with assessments in September, January and May.

Mark	0–4	5–9	10–14	15–19	20–24
Sept	10	12	22	16	15
Jan	6	15	26	18	10
May	2	8	25	27	13

(a)   Draw frequency polygons for each set of results.

(b)   Make a tracing of the January polygon. Put it on the same axes as the May polygon.
Comment on the changes you find.

3 This table gives information on the sales of petrol and diesel in a garage during one week.

Day	Number of litres of petrol sold	Number of litres of diesel sold
Monday	400	400
Tuesday	600	200
Wednesday	700	300
Thursday	450	700
Friday	200	900
Saturday	700	800
Sunday	600	700

Draw two frequency polygons on the same axes to represent this data.

4 Mr North measured the times it took for his students to run around a track. Here are the results:

Time in seconds	Frequency
41–45	1
46–50	5
51–55	8
56–60	4
61–65	7
66–70	4

Draw a frequency polygon to show these results.

Mixed exercise 12

1 Helen collected 20 leaves and wrote down their lengths in centimetres. Here are her results:

4   8   4   3   4   2   6   7   5   4

7   6   4   3   5   7   6   4   8   5

(a) Copy and complete the following frequency table to show Helen's results.

Length of leaf in cm	Tally	Frequency
2		
3		
4		
5		
6		
7		
8		

(b) Draw a bar chart of Helen's results.

2 Martin weighed 20 bags of crisps in grams. Here are his results:

31 35 39 28 38 32 39 43 33 40
34 36 25 22 39 42 36 27 26 30

(a) Copy and complete the grouped frequency table for Martin's results.

Weight of crisps (grams)	Tally	Frequency
20–24		
25–29		
30–34		
35–39		
40–44		

(b) Write down the modal class.

(c) Copy and complete this graph to show these results.

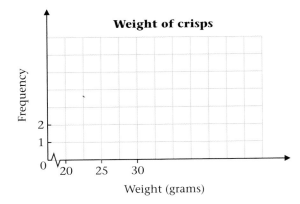

3 Here is a graph of the average temperatures last year in Manchester:

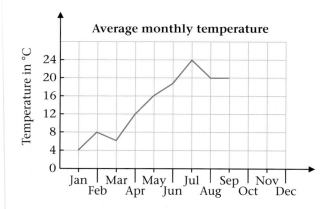

(a) Which month had the highest average temperature?

(b) Which month had the lowest average temperature?

The average temperatures in the remaining three months were:

    October   16 °C
    November 10 °C
    December 6 °C

(c) Copy and complete the line graph to show this information.

4 Here is a pictogram. It shows the number of boxes of chocolates sold last week from 'Chocs 4 U'.

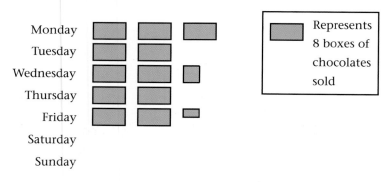

(a) Write down the number of boxes of chocolates sold on
    (i) Monday,   **(ii)** Tuesday,   **(iii)** Wednesday.

On Saturday, 32 boxes of chocolates were sold.

(b) Copy and complete the pictogram to show this information.

On Sunday, 11 boxes of chocolates were sold.

(c) Add this to the pictogram.

5   Mr North measured the times it took for his Year 7 class
    and his Year 10 class to run around a running track. Here
    are his results:

Time in seconds	Frequency Year 7	Frequency Year 10
41–45	1	2
46–50	3	7
51–55	5	8
56–60	8	4
61–65	5	3
66–70	2	1

(a) Draw two frequency polygons, on the same grid, to
     show the results for Mr North's two classes.

(b) What do your frequency polygons tell you about
     Mr North's classes?

6   The amount of petrol (in litres) in the storage tank at a
    garage was measured every hour between 7 am and 7 pm
    on one day. This is the shape of the line graph showing
    the results:

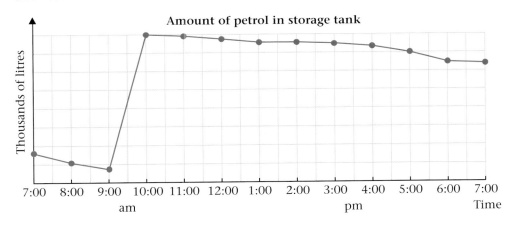

(a) When was the amount of petrol in the tank at its
     lowest?

(b) What do you think happened between 9 am and
     10 am?

(c) What were the sales like between 1 pm and 4 pm?

(d) Give a reason for your answer to part (c).

7 Muriel recorded the maximum and minimum
temperatures over a period of ten days. Her results are
given in this table.

April 2006	4th	5th	6th	7th	8th	9th	10th	11th	12th	13th
Max (°C)	12	9	10	10	13	17	15	19	16	18
Min (°C)	5	2	4	5	6	7	5	8	6	7

(a) Draw a graph to illustrate both sets of temperatures
   on the same axes.
(b) Write a comment about each set of data.

Summary of key points

1 **Tally charts** and **bar charts** are two ways of displaying data that can be counted.
   You must leave a gap between the bars when you draw bar charts of data that can
   be counted.

2 The **modal class** is the group which has the highest frequency.

3 A **dual bar chart** is used to compare two sets of data.

4 A **pictogram** is a quick, visual way of showing information by using a symbol to
   represent a quantity.

5 Data which can be counted is called **discrete data**.

6 Data which is measured is called **continuous data**.

7 **Line graphs** can be used to show continuous data.

8 A line graph used to illustrate data collected at intervals in time (e.g. hourly, daily,
   weekly, ...) is called a **time series** graph.

9 A **histogram** is used to display grouped data that is continuous.

10 A **frequency polygon** can show the general pattern of data represented by a
   histogram.

⓱ 3-D shapes

All the boxes and packets shown on the supermarket shelves
in the picture are 3-dimensional or 3-D. They have height,
width and depth. This chapter is all about 3-D shapes.

13.1 Horizontal and vertical surfaces

In the picture above the shelves are horizontal surfaces.
(The floor and ceiling would also be horizontal surfaces.)

The sides of the boxes are vertical surfaces.
(The walls would also be vertical surfaces.)

A flat surface is called a **plane**. The roof of this
block of flats is a horizontal plane. The end wall
is a vertical plane.

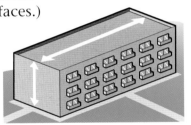

Exercise 13A

1   Identify and list 5 horizontal and 5 vertical surfaces in
    your classroom. You can include the floor and the walls
    as part of your answer.

2   Identify and list 5 horizontal and 5 vertical surfaces in
    this picture:

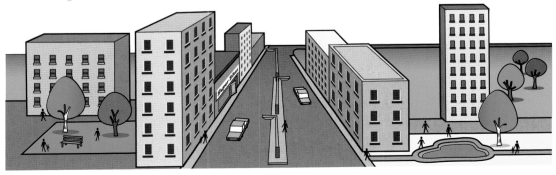

13.2 Faces, edges and vertices

Flat surfaces of 3-D shapes are called **faces**.

The shaded surface on the box is called a face.
The box has 6 faces.

The line where two faces meet is called an **edge**.

The box has 12 edges.

The point where three edges meet is called a **vertex**.

The box has 8 vertices.

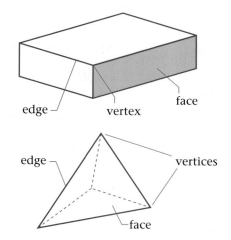

Broken lines show edges that you can't see.

Exercise 13B

1 Here are some 3-D shapes. Count the faces, edges and vertices of each shape and write them in a copy of the table below.

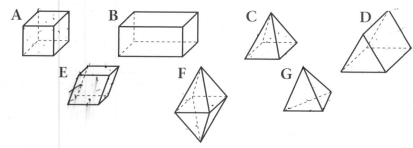

Shape	Number of faces	Number of vertices	Number of edges

2 There is a rule which connects the number of faces and the number of vertices with the number of edges. Use your results from question 1 to find this rule.

13.3 Looking at shapes

A **sketch** is a drawing which does not pretend to be exact.
But it should be good enough not to be misleading.

The chart below shows pictures, sketches, names and some of
the properties of some 3-D shapes.

In sketches parallel lines are drawn parallel. Vertical lines always look vertical. Horizontal lines may be drawn in any direction.

Name and properties	Picture	Sketch
Cube 6 square faces		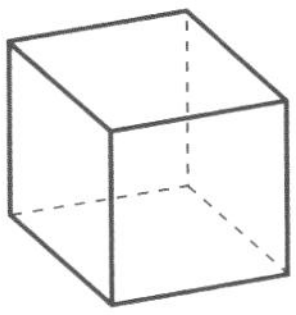
Cuboid 6 rectangular faces	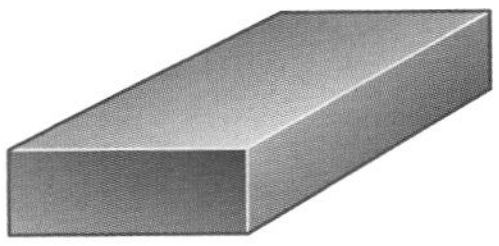	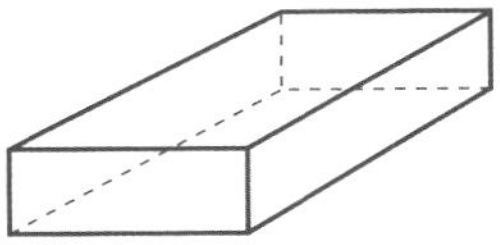
Sphere		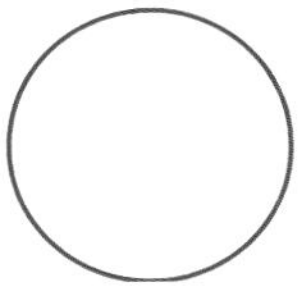
Square-based pyramid Square base, 4 triangular faces	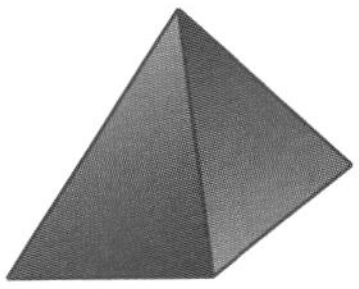	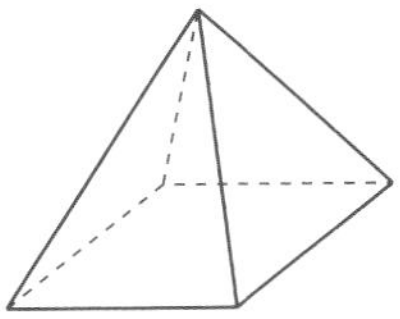
Triangular-based pyramid (tetrahedron) 4 triangular faces	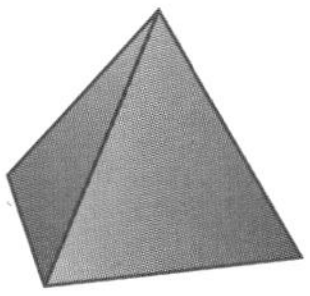	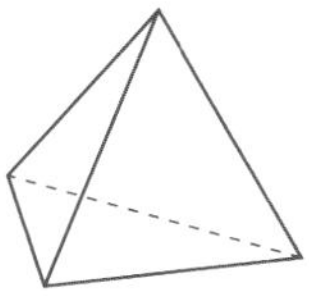
Cone A special pyramid with a circular base		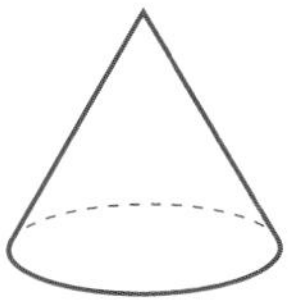
Cylinder 2 circular faces		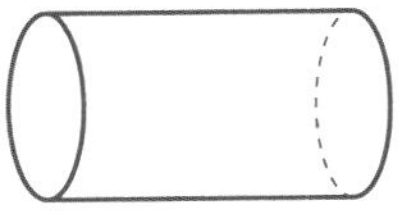

Example 1

Sketch a cube.

Step 1   Draw a square.

Step 2   Draw another square the same size, slightly to the right and slightly above the original square.

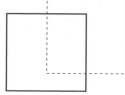

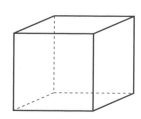

Step 3   Join the corners of the squares.

Example 2

Sketch a square-based pyramid:

Step 1   Draw the base.

Step 2   The top is above the middle of the base.

Step 3   Join the top to the other corners.

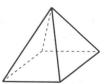

Exercise 13C

1   Look at the picture below and make a list of as many 3-D shapes as you can. For example, the football is a sphere.

> There are at least 12 3-D shapes.

2   Sketch
   (a)   a triangular-based pyramid
   (b)   a cuboid
   (c)   a cube
   (d)   a cylinder
   (e)   a square-based pyramid.

13.4 Prisms

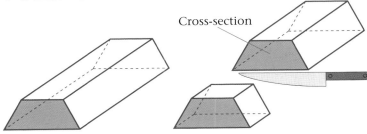

Cross-section

The faces at either end of this shape are identical and parallel. The cross-section is identical to the end faces. A shape that has a uniform cross-section like this is called a **prism**.

> Parallel means the faces are the same distance from each other at all points.

A **prism** is a shape which has a uniform cross-section.

A **cross-section** is a slice through the shape, parallel to the end faces.

Some other prisms are drawn below. Where the shape of the cross-section is a known 2-D shape then it is used to describe the type of prism.

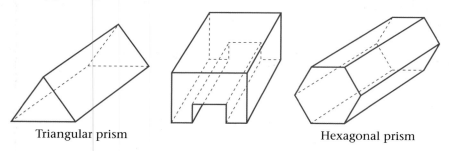

Triangular prism   Hexagonal prism

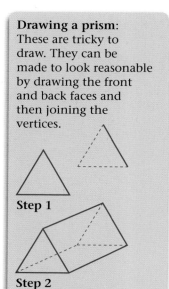
Exercise 13D

1 Which of the following shapes are prisms?

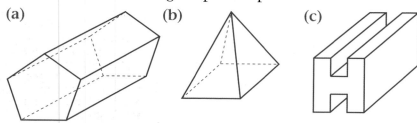

(a)   (b)   (c)

2 What name is usually given to a circular prism?

3 Write down the names of two other 3-D shapes that are also prisms.

4 Write down 5 things in your classroom which are prisms.

13.5 Nets

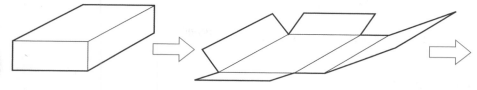

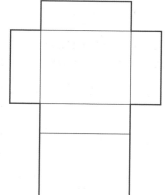

The box (cuboid) in the diagram has been opened out to make a 2-D shape. This 2-D shape is called the **net** of the box.

A **net** is a 2-D shape that can be folded into a 3-D shape.

Example 3

Draw the net of this triangular prism.

The prism has three rectangular faces measuring 6 cm by 3 cm which are joined along their long sides. These faces can be drawn as:

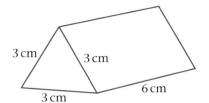

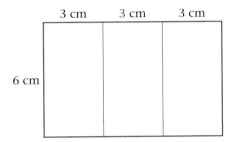

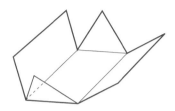

The faces at either end of the prism are equilateral triangles with 3 cm sides. These must join to the short side of one of the rectangles. This makes the complete net.

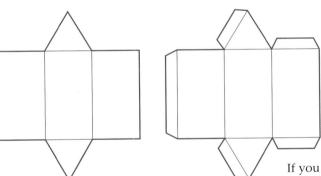

> You need to be able to construct accurate drawings of 2-D shapes if your nets are to fold together to make good solids. For more on accurate constructions see Chapter 7.

If you are going to make the shape put a tab on alternate sides. You can start with any side.

Exercise 13E

You need a ruler, pencil and pair of compasses for some of the questions in this exercise.

1 Sketch the nets of these solids:

(a)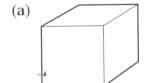

(b)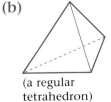
(a regular tetrahedron)

(c)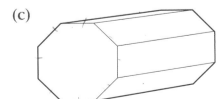

2 These nets will form a 3-D solid.
Draw a sketch of each solid.

(a)

(b)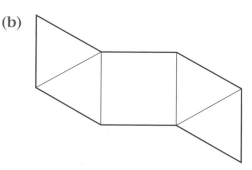

3 Which of the following are nets of a cube?

(a) 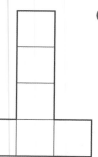   **(b)** 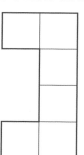   **(c)**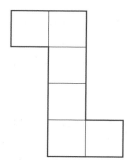

4 Which of the following are nets of a tetrahedron (triangular-based pyramid with base and all sides equilateral triangles)?

(a) 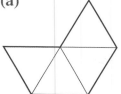   **(b)** 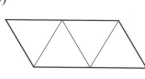   **(c)**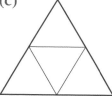

5 Draw accurate nets for these shapes:

(a)

5 cm 5 cm
4 cm 5 cm

(b)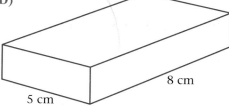

2 cm
8 cm
5 cm

(c)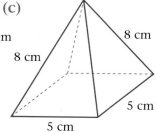

8 cm
8 cm
5 cm
5 cm

6 Draw an accurate net for each of the following shapes:

(a) a cube with sides of 5 cm

(b) a regular tetrahedron with sides of 4 cm.

> You could do this on card and make the shapes (remember to add tabs).

7 Here is a net of a cube:

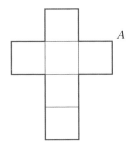

A

The net is folded to make the cube.
Copy the diagram.
Two other vertices of the net meet at *A*.
Mark each of them with the letter *A*.   [E]

8 Sketch the following solids and their nets:
   (a) cuboid   (b) cylinder
   (c) cone   (d) tetrahedron
   (e) hexagonal prism.

9 Sketch the solids that these nets form.
   Mark the measurements on your sketches.
   (a)   (b)

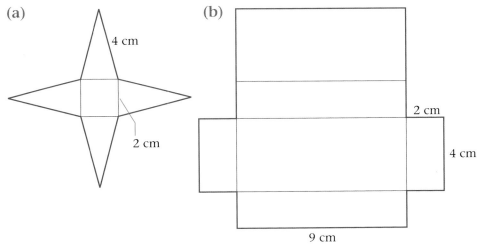

10 Draw an accurate net for each of these solids.
   (a)   (b)

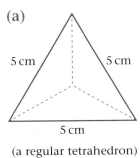

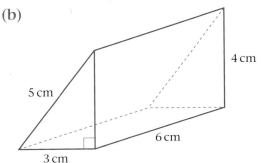

(a regular tetrahedron)

13.6 Plan and elevation

Architects and designers often represent
3-D objects with 2-D drawings.

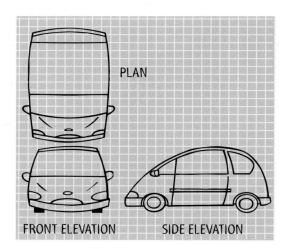

PLAN

FRONT ELEVATION   SIDE ELEVATION

The **plan** of a solid is the view when seen from above.

The **front elevation** is the view when seen from the front.

The **side elevation** is the view when seen from the side.

Example 4

Draw the plan and elevations of this shape.

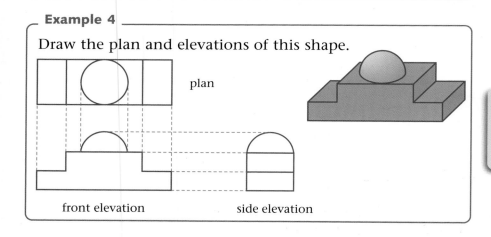

plan

front elevation   side elevation

> You should draw plans
> and elevations using
> dotted lines to show how
> the different drawings
> match up.

Exercise 13F

1 Sketch the plan and elevations of each of these shapes:

(a)

(b)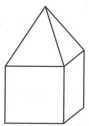

(c)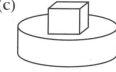

plan

side
elevation

front
elevation

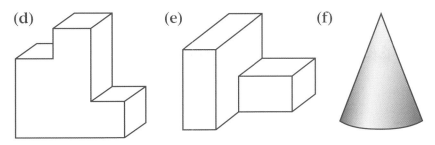

(d) **(e)** **(f)**

2   Use multilink cubes to construct these solids.
    Sketch each one.

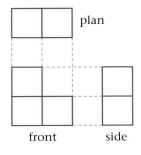

(a) plan / front / side

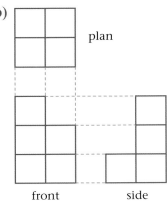

(b) plan / front / side

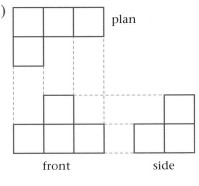

(c) plan / front / side

3   Describe the solids with these plans and elevations:

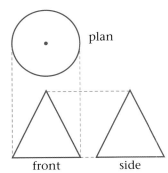

(a) plan / front / side

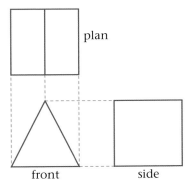

(b) plan / front / side

(c) Draw your own set of three shapes. Try to describe a
        solid which has your shapes as its plan, front
        elevation and side elevation.

4   Here are the plan and front
    elevation of a prism.
    The cross-section of the
    shape is represented by the
    front elevation.

    (a) On squared paper draw
        a side elevation.

    (b) Draw a 3-D sketch
        of the shape.

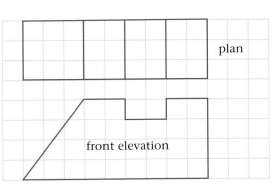

plan

front elevation

[E]

13.7 Symmetry in 3-D shapes

A 3-D shape has a **plane of symmetry** if the plane divides the shape into two halves and one half is the mirror image of the other half.

plane of symmetry

Example 5

Draw diagrams to show the planes of symmetry of a cuboid.

A cuboid has 3 planes of symmetry. To show the planes of symmetry clearly, draw a diagram for each plane:

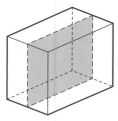 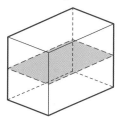 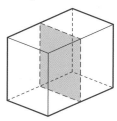

Exercise 13G

You may want to use tracing paper in this exercise.

1   Write down the number of planes of symmetry for each of the following shapes.

(a)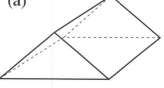

(b)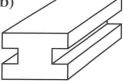

(c)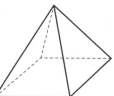

(d)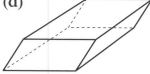

(e)

(f)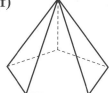

2 Copy or trace the following shapes and clearly mark any planes of symmetry on your drawings.

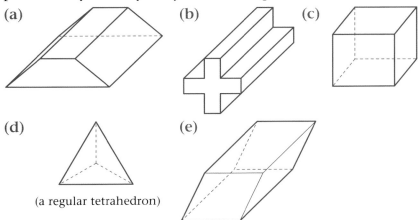

(a)

(b)

(c)

(d)

(a regular tetrahedron)

(e)

3 Copy these shapes that represent 3-D objects and draw all their planes of symmetry on separate diagrams.

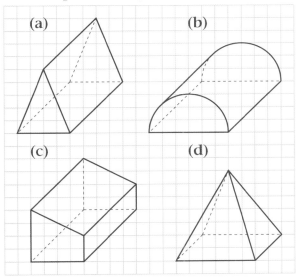

(a)

(b)

(c)

(d)

4 The drawings below each show half of a 3-D solid. Copy and complete each solid so that the shaded face forms a plane of symmetry.

(a)

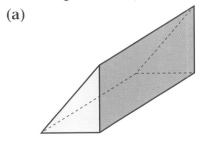

(b)

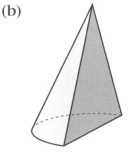

Mixed exercise 13

1 For each shape in this question write down
   (i) the name
   (ii) the number of edges
   (iii) the number of faces
   (iv) the number of vertices.

(a) 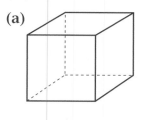 (b) 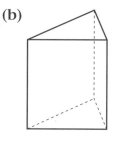 (c)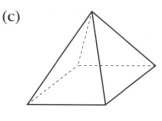

2 The base of each shape in question **1** is horizontal.
   (i) Write down the number of horizontal edges each shape has.
   (ii) Write down the number of vertical edges each shape has.

3 Which of these shapes are prisms?
   (a) 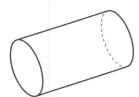 (b)  (c)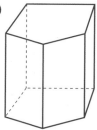

4 Here is the net of a 3-D shape.

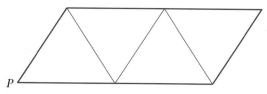

   (a) Write down the name of the 3-D shape.

   (b) Copy the net. When the net is folded to make the 3-D shape one vertex on the net meets vertex *P*. Mark that vertex with the letter *P*.

5 (a) For this shape write down the number of
   (i) edges
   (ii) vertices
   (iii) faces.

(b) Make a sketch of the solid.
   (i) Mark a vertical face.
   (ii) Mark a horizontal face.

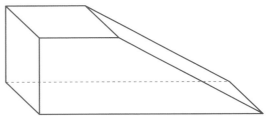

6 A, B, C, D and E are five 3-D shapes.
P, Q, R, S and T are five nets.
Match the shapes to the nets.

  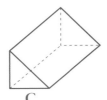 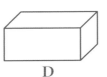

A   B   C   D   E

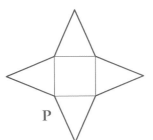 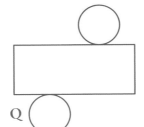 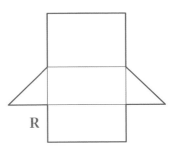

P   Q   R

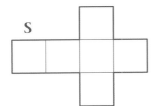 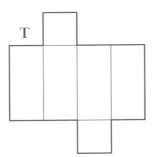

S   T

7 Write down the names of these shapes.

(a) 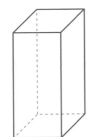   (b)

8 The diagram shows part of net for a cuboid.
One face of the cuboid is missing.
The cuboid is 2 cm by 3 cm by 4 cm.

(a) Write down the size of the missing face.

(b) Draw an accurate version of the net, including the missing face.

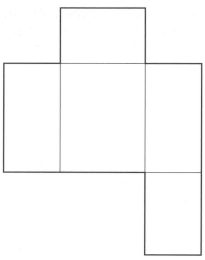

9 Draw an accurate net for each of the following shapes:

(a)

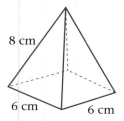

(b) a regular tetrahedron with sides of 4 cm.

10 Draw a sketch of a

(a) cube   (b) cuboid   (c) cylinder

(d) square-based pyramid   (e) triangular prism.

11 Here is a sketch of a 3-D shape.
Draw a sketch of the plan, front and side elevations of the shape.

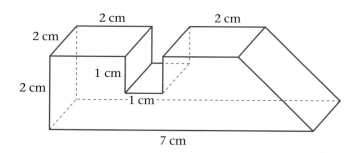

12 Make two copies of this 3-D shape.
Draw in one plane of symmetry of the shape on each copy.

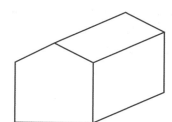

13 Here are the plan and front elevation of a prism.
The cross-section of the shape is represented by the front
elevation.

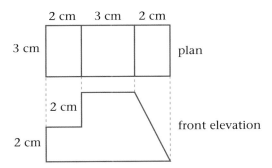

2 cm   3 cm   2 cm

3 cm   plan

2 cm

2 cm   front elevation

(a) Make an accurate drawing of the side elevation.

(b) Draw a sketch of the 3-D shape.

Summary of key points

1 A flat surface is called a **plane**.

2 Flat surfaces of 3-D shapes are called **faces**.

3 The line where two faces meet is called an **edge**.

4 The point where three edges meet is called a **vertex**.

5 A **prism** is a shape which has a uniform cross-section.
A **cross-section** is a slice through the shape, parallel to the end face

6 A **net** is a 2-D shape that can be folded into a 3-D shape.

7 The **plan** of a solid is the view when seen from
above.

8 The **front elevation** is the view when seen
from the front.

9 The **side elevation** is the view when seen
from the side.

10 A 3-D shape has a **plane of symmetry** if the plane
divides the shape into two halves and one half is
the mirror image of the other half.

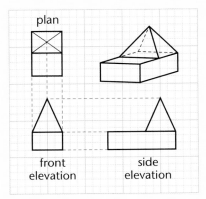

plan

front
elevation

side
elevation

14 Units of measure

14.1 Changing metric units

Before you tackle this section you will need to be able to multiply and divide whole numbers and decimals by 10, 100 and 1000.

> Check Chapters 1 and 5 if you need to remind yourself.

You need to know that:

Length	Weight	Capacity
10 mm = 1 cm	1000 mg = 1 g	100 cl = 1 litre
100 cm = 1 m	1000 g = 1 kg	1000 ml = 1 litre
1000 mm = 1 m	1000 kg = 1 tonne	1000 l = 1 cubic metre
1000 m = 1 km		

You need to remember:

When you change from small units to large units you divide.

When you change from large units to small units you multiply.

Example 1

(a) Change 2 kilometres to metres.
(b) Change 250 mm to cm.

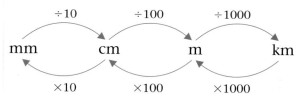

(a) Kilometres are larger units than metres so you multiply by the number of metres in a kilometre, which is 1000:

$$2 \times 1000 = 2000 \text{ m}$$

(b) Millimetres are smaller units than centimetres so you divide by the number of millimetres in a centimetre, which is 10:

$$250 \div 10 = 25 \text{ cm}$$

Exercise 14A

1 Change these lengths to centimetres.
  (a) 3 m   (b) 30 mm   (c) 6 m
  (d) 12 m   (e) 100 mm

2 Change these lengths to millimetres.
  (a) 2 cm   (b) 5 cm   (c) 12 cm
  (d) 20 cm (e) 100 cm

3 Change these lengths to metres.
  (a) 5 km   (b) 300 cm   (c) 10 km
  (d) 2000 cm (e) 60 km

4 Change these weights to grams.
  (a) 5 kg   (b) 40 kg   (c) 100 kg
  (d) 250 kg (e) 1000 kg

5 Change these capacities to litres.
  (a) 3000 ml (b) 8000 ml
  (c) 50 000 ml (d) 75 000 ml

6 Change these volumes to millilitres.
  (a) 6 l   (b) 40 l   (c) 100 l
  (d) 350 l (e) 25 l

7 Change these lengths to kilometres.
  (a) 3000 m (b) 7000 m
  (c) 40 000 m (d) 45 000 m

8 Change these weights to tonnes.
  (a) 4000 kg (b) 7000 kg
  (c) 30 000 kg (d) 55 000 kg

9 Change these weights to kilograms.
  (a) 2000 g (b) 3 tonnes (c) 50 000 g
  (d) 12 tonnes (e) 100 000 g

10 How many millimetres equal 1 metre?

11 Jeremy walks 10 kilometres. How many centimetres is this?

12 Jim's lorry weighs 8 tonnes. How many grams is this?

13 Work out the number of centimetres in 1 kilometre.

14 Pritti has an average pace length of 75 cm. When she walks 3 km how many paces does she take?

15 Work out the number of millimetres in 1 kilometre.

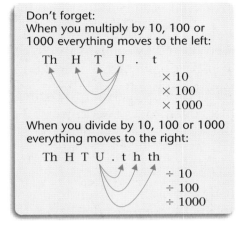

Don't forget:
When you multiply by 10, 100 or 1000 everything moves to the left:
Th H T U . t × 10 × 100 × 1000
When you divide by 10, 100 or 1000 everything moves to the right:
Th H T U . t h th ÷ 10 ÷ 100 ÷ 1000

75 cm

Exercise 14B

1 Put these weights in order, largest first.

250 g   25 g   2 kg   250 kg   3000 g

> Change them all into the same units.

2 Put these lengths in order, smallest first.

3 m   5 mm   20 cm   3 km   50 mm

3 Put these lengths in order, smallest first.

75 cm   3000 mm   2 m   4000 m   4 cm

4 Put these capacities in order, smallest first.

200 m*l*   5 *l*   600 m*l*   2000 m*l*   1 *l*

So far all of the answers in this section have been whole numbers. In the following exercises you will find it easier if you use your calculator *but* don't forget to **check if your answer is sensible.**

Example 2

(a) Change 450 g to kg.   (b) Change 2.4 *l* to m*l*.

(a) 450 ÷ 1000 = 0.45 kg

(b) 2.4 × 1000 = 2400 m*l*

> Changing small units to larger units so divide:
> 1000 g in 1 kg so ÷ 1000

> Changing large units to smaller units so multiply:
> 1000 m*l* in 1 *l* so × 1000

Exercise 14C

1 Change these lengths to metres.

  (a) 250 cm   (b) 50 cm   (c) 3.6 km

  (d) 75 cm   (e) 0.005 km   (f) 35 cm

  (g) 475 cm   (h) 0.6 km   (i) 0.04 km

  (j) 5 mm

2 Change these weights to grams.

  (a) 4.5 kg   (b) 0.4 kg   (c) 10.3 kg

  (d) 0.03 kg   (e) 0.005 kg

3 Change these lengths to centimetres.

  (a) 350 mm   (b) 2.5 m   (c) 5.4 m

  (d) 5 mm   (e) 0.08 m   (f) 0.8 m

  (g) 35 mm   (h) 50 mm   (i) 85 mm

  (j) 275 mm

125 cm or 1.25 m

4 Change these capacities to millilitres.

  (a) 3.5 *l*   (b) 0.5 *l*   (c) 15.4 *l*

  (d) 0.05 *l*   (e) 0.003 *l*

5 Change these lengths to millimetres.
   (a) 3.5 cm   (b) 0.7 cm   (c) 0.08 cm
   (d) 12.5 cm   (e) 0.005 m

6 Write these lengths in kilometres.
   (a) 300 m   (b) 50 m   (c) 1250 m
   (d) 75 m   (e) 375 m

7 Change these capacities to litres.
   (a) 250 m*l*   (b) 100 m*l*   (c) 50 m*l*
   (d) 3500 m*l*   (e) 1 m*l*

8 Change these weights to kilograms.
   (a) 500 g   (b) 0.3 tonnes   (c) 50 g
   (d) 5.5 tonnes   (e) 0.006 tonnes

9 Write these weights in tonnes.
   (a) 3500 kg   (b) 450 kg   (c) 50 kg
   (d) 3000 g   (e) 75 kg

10 How many 75 m*l* glasses can be filled from a bottle holding 1.5 *l* of cola?

11 How many 50 mm pieces of wood can be cut from a piece of wood of length 3 m, assuming there is no waste?

12 It takes 150 g of flour to make a batch of rock cakes. How many batches of rock cakes can be made from 1.2 kg of flour?

Exercise 14D

1 Write these lengths in order, smallest first.
   (a) 25 mm, 3 cm, 2.4 cm, 50 mm, 6 cm, 57 mm
   (b) 30 cm, 0.4 m, 270 mm, 1.2 m, 500 mm, 45 cm
   (c) 2 m, 340 cm, 4000 mm, 4 m, 370 cm, 3500 mm
   (d) 5 cm, 45 mm, 36 cm, 0.3 m, 55 mm, 0.2 cm, 4 mm
   (e) 50 cm, 0.4 m, 560 mm, 0.45 m, 34 cm

2 Write these weights in order, smallest first.
   (a) 250 g, 0.3 kg, 500 g, 0.05 kg
   (b) 500 g, 350 g, 0.4 kg, 0.52 kg
   (c) 5000 g, 3000 g, 4 kg, 4.5 kg, 0.5 tonnes, 400 kg

3 Write these capacities in order, smallest first.
   (a) 300 m*l*, 0.4 *l*, 500 m*l*, 250 m*l*, 0.3 *l*
   (b) 500 m*l*, 450 m*l*, 0.4 *l*, 360 m*l*, 0.05 *l*, 45 m*l*

14.2 Metric and imperial conversions

You may need to change from metric units to imperial units (the old style units) and vice versa. To do this it helps to memorise these facts:

Metric	Imperial
8 km	5 miles
1 kg	2.2 pounds
25 g	1 ounce
1 l	$1\frac{3}{4}$ pints
4.5 l	1 gallon
1 m	39 inches
30 cm	1 foot
2.5 cm	1 inch

These conversions are only approximate.

Some petrol pumps have a conversion table to show how many litres or gallons you are buying.

Example 3

Change 10 km to miles.

Using 8 km = 5 miles

First find 1 km.

$$1 \text{ km} = 5 \div 8 = 0.625 \text{ miles}$$

$$\text{So } 10 \text{ km} = 0.625 \times 10 = 6.25 \text{ miles}$$

Multiply by 10 to find 10 km.

 Exercise 14E

The Evans family are going on holiday to Scotland. The family consists of Mr and Mrs Evans and their three children, Glenys, Eira and Gareth.

1 Mr Evans works out the distance from their home in London to Scotland. He makes it 400 miles. Approximately what is this distance in kilometres?

2 Mrs Evans packs a 3 litre bottle of water for the trip. About how many pints is 3 litres?

3 The petrol tank of the family's car holds 15 gallons. About how many litres is this?

4 Glenys estimates the weight of all the luggage as 100 kg. About how many pounds is that?

5   Gareth puts 1 pint of water in the car's radiator.
    About how many litres is that?

6   Mr Evans puts 30 litres of petrol in the car.
    About how many gallons is that?

7   Mrs Evans puts 0.5 *l* of oil in the engine.
    About how many pints is that?

8   The family stop at a service station 150 km from home.
    About how many miles is that?

9   Eira buys 800 g of chocolate.
    About how many pounds is that?

10 When they get to Scotland there is half a bottle of water
    left. About how many pints is that?

Exercise 14F

Class 11E are taking part in their school's Inter Generation
Day. They invite local older people for a coffee morning.

1   Sybil brings ten 2 *l* cartons of milk to make hot
    chocolate. About how many gallons is this?

2   Henri brings 20 packets of biscuits.
    Each packet weighs 1 pound.
    About how many kilograms is this altogether?

3   Jonathan makes plates that are 6 inches across.
    About how many centimetres is this?

4   The trays the class use are 24 inches long and
    15 inches across.
    Change these measurements to centimetres.

5   The tables the class use are 48 inches long. Will
    tablecloths with a length of 1.2 m fit the tables?

6   Nilmini makes sandwiches and uses 5 kg of bread and
    500 g of spread.
    Change these weights to pounds.

7   At the end of the coffee morning there are 5 pints of
    milk left. About how many litres is this?

8   Claire cooks some rock cakes. She makes 72 cakes and
    uses 24 ounces of fat, 40 ounces of flour and 32 ounces
    of dried fruit. She only has a metric set of scales.
    Approximately how many grams of each ingredient
    should she use?

9 In the 'guess the weight of the cake' competition the correct answer was 5 pounds. Robin said the weight was 5.1 pounds and Hazel said 2.3 kilograms.
Which of these two answers was nearer the correct weight?

10 The visitors ate 3.5 kilograms of Claire's cakes.
About how many pounds is that?

14.3 Calculating time

You need to know that:

> 60 seconds = 1 minute
> 60 minutes = 1 hour
> 24 hours = 1 day
> 365 days = 1 year
> 366 days = 1 leap year
> 3 months = 1 quarter
> 12 months = 1 year

Many people make mistakes when they are calculating with time because they forget that there are 60 minutes in an hour and not 100.

> Why does 30 minutes and 45 minutes give 1 hour and 15 minutes?
>
> You can't use an ordinary calculator to add times.

___ **Example 4** _____

(a) How many minutes are there in 3 hours?

(b) How many hours are there in 135 minutes?

(a) $3 \times 60 = 180$ minutes

(b) $135 \div 60 = 2.25$ hours
Some people might write this as 2 hours 25 minutes but they would be *wrong*. To change the 0.25 hours to minutes you must multiply 0.25 by 60.

  $0.25 \times 60 = 15$

So 135 minutes is 2 hours 15 minutes.

___ **Example 5** _____

(a) Change 2.4 hours into hours and minutes.

(b) Change 5 hours 48 minutes into hours.

(a) **Step 1** Keep the 2 hours.
Step 2 Multiply the 0.4 hours by 60 (the number of minutes in an hour).
Step 3 Put the numbers together.

  2 hours and $0.4 \times 60 = 2$ hours and 24 minutes

(b) **Step 1** Keep the 5 hours.
Step 2 Divide the 48 minutes by 60 (the number of
minutes in an hour).
Step 3 Put the numbers together.

5 hours and $48 \div 60$ = 5 hours and 0.8 hours = 5.8 hours

Exercise 14G

1 Change these times into minutes.
(a) 2 hours
(b) 5 hours
(c) 2 hours 30 minutes
(d) $5\frac{1}{2}$ hours
(e) $6\frac{1}{4}$ hours
(f) 5 hours 15 minutes

2 Change these times into hours.
(a) 180 minutes
(b) 240 minutes
(c) 75 minutes
(d) 260 minutes
(e) 325 minutes
(f) 90 minutes
(g) 3 days
(h) $5\frac{1}{2}$ days
(i) 500 minutes

3 How many seconds are there in 1 hour?

4 How many minutes are there in 1 day?

5 How many seconds are there in
(a) a year
(b) a leap year?

6 Change these times into hours and minutes.
(a) 2.5 hours
(b) 3.6 hours
(c) $5\frac{1}{2}$ hours
(d) $3\frac{3}{4}$ hours
(e) 4.1 hours
(f) 3.25 hours
(g) 1.125 hours
(h) 2.7 hours

7 Change these times into decimals of an hour.
(a) 2 hours 30 minutes
(b) 5 hours 15 minutes
(c) 3 hours 36 minutes
(d) 4 hours 12 minutes
(e) 6 hours 20 minutes
(f) 3 hours 18 minutes
(g) 12 hours 45 minutes
(h) 8 hours 3 minutes

8 Sam worked out his time for a journey using the formula
$$\text{time} = \frac{\text{distance}}{\text{speed}}$$
Sam travelled a distance of 90 miles at a speed of
40 miles per hour. He said that the journey took 2 hours
and 25 minutes. Explain why Sam was wrong.

Time calculations

When you come to make calculations involving times you have to be careful when it comes to dealing with the carry digit.

Example 6

(a) Add $2\frac{1}{2}$ hours to the time of 10:40.

(b) Take 3 hours 15 minutes away from 11:10.

(a) 10:40
       2:30
     13:10   Not 70 because 70 minutes make 1 hour 10 minutes.
      1

(b) 11:10   You have to carry 60 minutes so 70 − 15 gives 55.
   − 3:15
      7:55

It might help to write 11:10 as 10:70:

11:10		10:70
− 3:15	is	− 3:15
7:55		7:55

Don't forget:
60 minutes make 1 hour

Exercise 14H

1 Add 15 minutes to each of these times.
(a) 10:30   (b) 09:45   (c) 11:40   (d) 09:55

2 Add 50 minutes to each of these times.
(a) 09:00   (b) 10:30   (c) 11:40   (d) 08:05

3 Add 2 hours 40 minutes to each of these times.
(a) 09:40   (b) 10:45   (c) 11:50   (d) 06:10

4 Add 12 hours 45 minutes to each of these times.
(a) 02:30   (b) 07:15   (c) 12:50   (d) 16:45

5 Subtract 15 minutes from each of these times.
(a) 09:55   (b) 11:40   (c) 08:10   (d) 09:05

6 Subtract 50 minutes from each of these times.
(a) 08:55   (b) 11:40   (c) 10:30   (d) 09:00

7 Subtract 2 hours 30 minutes from each of these times.
(a) 09:55   (b) 11:40   (c) 08:10   (d) 09:05

8 Subtract 12 hours 45 minutes from each of these times.
(a) 14:50   (b) 17:30   (c) 12:00   (d) 08:30

9 Jack's friend Dorota is taking the train from Oxford to Southampton. She is due to leave Oxford at 15:30 and arrive in Southampton 1 hours 25 minutes later. That day she phones Jack to tell him that the train is delayed by 45 minutes. What time will Dorota arrive in Southampton?

14.4 Dealing with dates

You will often need to add days onto dates.

This traditional rhyme can help:

> 30 days hath September, April, June and November. All the rest have 31 except for February alone which has just 28 days clear and 29 in each leap year.

Example 7

Jane agreed to go out with John in 10 days' time. Today is Tuesday 23rd April. When is their date?

It's a date then?   OK

	April					May				
Monday	1	8	15	22	29		6	13	20	27
Tuesday	2	9	16	23	30		7	14	21	28
Wednesday	3	10	17	24		1	8	15	22	29
Thursday	4	11	18	25		2	9	16	23	30
Friday	5	12	19	26		3	10	17	24	31
Saturday	6	13	20	27		4	11	18	25	
Sunday	7	14	21	28		5	12	19	26	

Start at 23rd April and count on 10 days.
You get to Friday 3rd May.

Remember that April has only 30 days.

Exercise 14I

1 Count on 10 days from the following dates.
   (a) 1st January   (b) 2nd March   (c) 3rd June
   (d) 5th July   (e) 10th September   (f) 20th May
   (g) 25th June   (h) 27th August

2 Count on 14 days from the following dates.
   (a) 2nd February   (b) 3rd March
   (c) 3rd April   (d) 7th December
   (e) 15th November   (f) 18th September
   (g) 23rd March   (h) 25th November

3   Count on 30 days from the following dates.
(a) 5th April   (b) 6th June   (c) 17th May
(d) 1st September   (e) 7th June   (f) 20th May
(g) 30th November   (h) 5th December

Use the calendar in Example 7 to answer the following questions.

4   What day of the week and date is 5 days after 5th April?

5   Which day and date is 5 days after 27th April?

6   Which day and date is 7 days before 20th May?

7   What is the day and date 10 days before 5th May?

8   Write down the day and date two weeks after 19th April.

14.5 Timetables

Bus and train timetables are often used to test your knowledge
of time in GCSE exams.

On the timetable in Example 8 each train's times start at the
top and then go down the page. The time it should leave a
stopping place can then be read off opposite the place name.

___ **Example 8** ___

Find how long it takes for the
08 15 train from Swindon to get to
London (Paddington).

07 10 train from Bristol
arrives in London at 08 40

You first have to find the 08 15
train from Swindon. It is in
the third column along. Follow
that column down to the
bottom to find the arrival
time in London, 09 10.

Bristol	07 10	07 25	07 40	07 55
Bath	07 30	07 45	08 00	08 10
Swindon	07 45	08 00	08 15	08 25
Didcot	08 05	08 20	08 35	08 45
Reading	08 15	08 30	08 45	08 55
London (Paddington)	08 40	08 55	09 10	09 20

08 15 train
from Swindon

Arrives in London at 09 10

You could subtract 08 15 from 09 10 by doing a subtraction and carrying a 60.
Here is another way of dealing with the problem that you may find easier:

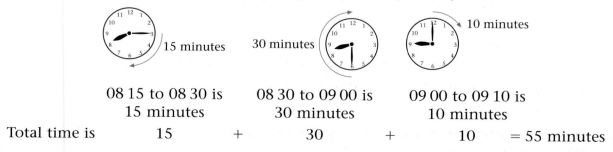

08 15 to 08 30 is   08 30 to 09 00 is   09 00 to 09 10 is
15 minutes   30 minutes   10 minutes

Total time is   15   +   30   +   10   = 55 minutes

Exercise 14J

Use these timetables to answer the following questions.

Bus timetable			
Coate	07 05	07 35	08 05
Piper's Way	07 10	07 40	08 10
Old Town	07 20	07 50	08 20
Drove Road	07 25	07 55	08 25
New Town	07 30	08 00	08 30
Bus Station	07 35	08 05	08 35

Train timetable			
Bristol	07 10	07 25	07 40	07 55
Bath	07 30	07 45	08 00	08 15
Swindon	07 45	08 00	08 15	08 30
Didcot	08 05	08 20	08 35	08 50
Reading	08 15	08 30	08 45	09 00
London (Paddington)	08 40	08 55	09 10	09 25

1 At what time should the 07 35 bus from Coate be at Drove Road?

2 At what time should the 07 40 train from Bristol be at Didcot?

3 At what time should the 08 30 train from Reading leave from Bristol?

4 At what time should the 08 00 bus from New Town be at Piper's Way?

5 Buses from Coate leave every half hour.
Continue the bus timetable for the next three buses. You can assume that each bus takes the same amount of time between stops as the previous ones.

6 Rashmi arrives at the train station in Bath at 07 35.
What time is the next train he could catch to London?

7 Claude arrives at the train station in Didcot at 08 25.
What time is the next train he could catch to London?

8 Trains from Bristol leave every quarter of an hour.
(a) Continue the train timetable for the next three trains. You can assume that each train takes the same amount of time between stations as the previous ones.
(b) Cecille arrives at the train station in Swindon at 09 10. What time is the next train she could catch to Reading?
(c) Sophia arrives at the train station in Bristol at 08 00. What time is the next train she could catch to Bath?

9 How long should it take to travel by bus from Coate to the Bus Station?

10 How long should it take to travel by bus from Piper's Way to New Town?

11 How long should it take to travel by train from Bristol to London (Paddington)?

12 How long should it take to travel by train from Swindon to Reading?

13 How long should it take to travel by train from Bath to Didcot?

14 The bus timetable is for a bus route in Swindon. It takes five minutes to walk from the bus station to the train platform. Use both timetables to work out which bus and train:

(a) Gareth catches at Piper's Way to be in London (Paddington) at 09:00

(b) Susan catches if she needs to be in Reading at 08:30 and she travels by bus from Coate

(c) Mario catches if he travels by bus from Old Town and needs to be in Didcot at 08:40

(d) Claudette catches at Drove Road to be in London (Paddington) by 10:00

(e) Bridgette catches if she needs to be in Reading at 09:30 and she travels by bus from Old Town

(f) Katrina caught if she travelled from Drove Road and arrived in Reading at 08:45.

Mixed exercise 14

1 Put these measurements in order, smallest first.
   (a) 12 cm, 15 mm, 5 m, 6.5 cm, 60 mm
   (b) 2.5 km, 3000 m, 1800 m, 3.6 km

2 Sarah and her boyfriend drove 50 miles to Bristol.
   About how many kilometres is 50 miles?

3 Siân bought 5 kg of potatoes.
   About how many pounds of potatoes was this?

4 Michelle filled her car's petrol tank with 50 l of petrol.
   About how many gallons of petrol was this?

5 Dick travelled from Manchester to London.
   He set off at 07:25. The journey took 3 hours 40 minutes.
   At what time did he arrive in London?

6 Here is part of a railway timetable.

A train leaves Manchester at 10 35.

Manchester	07 53	09 17	10 35	11 17	13 30	14 36	16 26
Stockport	08 01	09 26	10 43	11 25	13 38	14 46	16 39
Macclesfield	08 23	09 38	10 58	11 38	13 52	14 58	17 03
Congleton	08 31	–	–	11 49	–	15 07	17 10
Kidsgrove	08 37	–	–	–	–	–	17 16
Stoke-on-Trent	08 49	10 00	11 23	12 03	14 12	15 19	17 33

(a) At what time should this train arrive in Stoke-on-Trent?

Doris has to go to a meeting in Stoke-on-Trent.
She will catch the train in Stockport.
She needs to arrive in Stoke-on-Trent before 2 pm for her meeting.

(b) Write down the time of the latest train she can catch in Stockport.

(c) Work out how many minutes it should take the 14 36 train from Manchester to get to Stoke-on-Trent.

The 14 36 train from Manchester to Stoke-on-Trent takes less time than the 16 26 train from Manchester to Stoke-on-Trent.

(d) How many minutes less?   [E]

7

This signpost is on the road from Paris to Dijon.

(a) Work out the distance, in kilometres, from Paris to Dijon along this road.

(b) Work out the approximate distance, in miles, from the signpost to Paris.   [E]

8 Here is a timetable for Amina's school bus.
Amina catches the bus at Grange Drive.

Bus stop	Time
Bus Station	08 00
Station Road	08 15
Grange Drive	08 20
Holley Ave	08 30
King's Road	08 40
School Road	08 45

(a) At what time should the bus be at Grange Drive?

(b) How long should the bus take to get from Grange Drive to School Road?   [E]

9 Chippy the carpenter marks a 3 metre length of wood into three pieces.

One piece is 1.40 metres long.
Another piece is 84 centimetres long.
How long is the third piece of wood?

84 cm

1.40 m

Diagram NOT
accurately drawn

[E]

Summary of key points

1

Length	Weight	Capacity
10 mm = 1 cm 100 cm = 1 m 1000 mm = 1 m 1000 m = 1 km	1000 mg = 1 g 1000 g = 1 kg 1000 kg = 1 tonne	100 c*l* = 1 litre 1000 m*l* = 1 litre 1000 *l* = 1 cubic metre

2 When you change from small units to large units you divide.

3 When you change from large units to small units you multiply.

4

Metric	Imperial
8 km	5 miles
1 kg	2.2 pounds
25 g	1 ounce
1 *l*	$1\frac{3}{4}$ pints
4.5 *l*	1 gallon
1 m	39 inches
30 cm	1 foot
2.5 cm	1 inch

These conversions are only approximate.

5
60 seconds = 1 minute	60 minutes = 1 hour
24 hours = 1 day	365 days = 1 year
366 days = 1 leap year	3 months = 1 quarter
12 months = 1 year	

6 30 days hath September, April, June and November.
All the rest have 31 except for February alone
which has just 28 days clear and 29 in each leap year.

⑮ Percentages

15.1 Understanding percentages

Percentage
%
pc
} means 'number of parts per hundred'.

Look at the large square below. It has been divided into 100 equal small squares.

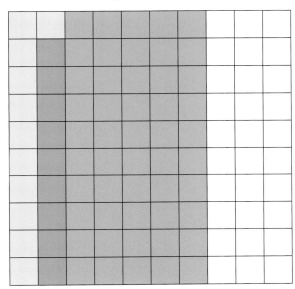

11 of the 100 small squares are shaded blue.
So 11% of the large square is shaded blue.

9 of the 100 small squares are shaded red.
So 9% of the large square is shaded red.

50 of the 100 small squares are shaded green.
So 50% of the large square is shaded green.

30 of the 100 small squares are unshaded.
So 30% of the large square is unshaded.

Exercise 15A

1 This large square is divided into 100 equal small squares.

  (a) What percentage of the large square is shaded

    (i) blue
    (ii) red
    (iii) green?

  (b) What percentage of the large square is unshaded?

  (c) What fraction of the large square is unshaded?

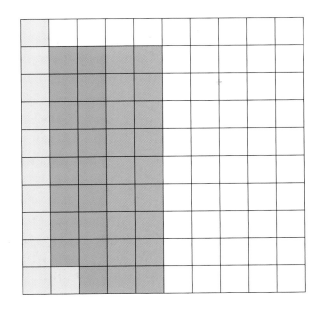

2   This large rectangle is divided into
    100 equal small rectangles.
    (a) What percentage of the large
        rectangle is shaded
            (i) yellow   (ii) blue
           (iii) red   (iv) green?
    (b) What percentage of the large
        rectangle is unshaded?
    (c) What fraction of the large rectangle is unshaded?

3   Draw a 10 by 10 square on squared paper. Shade in the
    following percentages:
    (a) 25% in grey   (b) 40% in red   (c) 28% in green
    (d) What percentage of the large square is not shaded?

4   Draw a large rectangle divided into 100 small rectangles
    as in question 2. Shade in the following percentages:
    (a) 30% in grey   (b) 22% in blue   (c) 36% in yellow
    (d) What percentage of the large rectangle is not shaded?

15.2 Percentages, fractions and decimals

In this large rectangle, 50% is shaded
blue and 50% is unshaded.

50% means 50 in a hundred, which
can be written as $\frac{50}{100}$

$\frac{50}{100}$ simplifies to $\frac{1}{2}$

So 50% is the same as $\frac{1}{2}$. You can write
$50\% = \frac{1}{2} = 0.5$

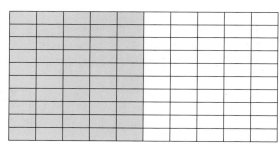

In this large square, 25% is shaded red
and 75% is unshaded.

25% means 25 in a hundred, which can
be written as $\frac{25}{100}$

$\frac{25}{100}$ simplifies to $\frac{1}{4}$

So 25% is the same as $\frac{1}{4}$. You can write
$25\% = \frac{1}{4} = 0.25$

Similarly, $75\% = \frac{75}{100} = \frac{3}{4} = 0.75$

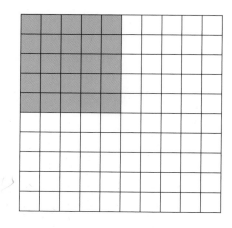

Remember these percentages and their equivalent fractions:
    $50\% = \frac{1}{2}$ $25\% = \frac{1}{4}$ $75\% = \frac{3}{4}$ $33\frac{1}{3}\% = \frac{1}{3}$ $66\frac{2}{3}\% = \frac{2}{3}$

Converting percentages to fractions and decimals

A percentage can be written as a fraction, with denominator (bottom) 100.

Example 1

Write 19% as a fraction.

$$19\% = \frac{19}{100}$$

> Notice that 5 is the highest common factor of 85 and 100

Example 2

Write 85% as a fraction.

$$85\% = \frac{85}{100}$$

Simplify $\frac{85}{100}$ $\overset{85 \div 5}{\curvearrowright}$ $\frac{17}{20}$

     $100 \div 5$

So $85\% = \frac{17}{20}$

Example 3

Write $3\frac{1}{2}\%$ as a fraction.

$$3\tfrac{1}{2}\% = \frac{3\frac{1}{2}}{100}$$

Simplify $\frac{3\frac{1}{2}}{100}$ $\overset{3\frac{1}{2} \times 2}{\curvearrowright}$ $\frac{7}{200}$

     100×2

So $3\tfrac{1}{2}\% = \frac{7}{200}$

To write a percentage as a decimal:
- write the percentage as a fraction
- convert the fraction to a decimal.

> Remember:
> Fractions can be changed into decimals by dividing the numerator by the denominator.

Example 4

Write 63% as a decimal.

$$63\% = \frac{63}{100} = 63 \div 100 = 0.63$$

Example 5

Write 15% as a decimal.

$$15\% = \frac{15}{100} = 15 \div 100 = 0.15$$

Exercise 15B

1 For this large rectangle, state
   (a)   (i)   what percentage is shaded blue
        (ii)   what fraction is shaded blue
   (b)   (i)   what percentage is shaded red
        (ii)   what fraction is shaded red
   (c)   (i)   what percentage is shaded green
        (ii)   what fraction is shaded green
   (d)   (i)   what percentage is unshaded
        (ii)   what fraction is unshaded.

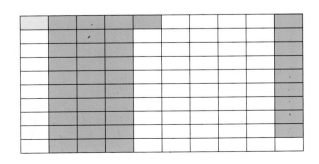

2 For this large rectangle, state
  - **(a)** **(i)** what percentage is shaded red
    (ii) what fraction is shaded red
  - **(b)** **(i)** what percentage is shaded green
    (ii) what fraction is shaded green
  - **(c)** **(i)** what percentage is shaded blue
    (ii) what fraction is shaded blue
  - **(d)** **(i)** what percentage is unshaded
    (ii) what fraction is unshaded.

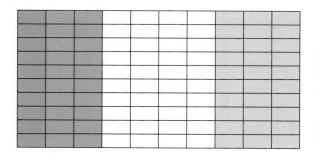

3 Write these percentages as fractions in their simplest form.
  - **(a)** 17%
  - **(b)** 99%
  - **(c)** 41%
  - **(d)** 3%
  - **(e)** 60%
  - **(f)** 80%
  - **(g)** 90%
  - **(h)** 30%
  - **(i)** 10%
  - **(j)** 70%
  - **(k)** 22%
  - **(l)** 6%
  - **(m)** 64%
  - **(n)** 96%
  - **(o)** 15%
  - **(p)** 65%

4 Write these percentages as decimals.
  - **(a)** 37%
  - **(b)** 49%
  - **(c)** 87%
  - **(d)** 7%
  - **(e)** 40%
  - **(f)** 15%
  - **(g)** 8%
  - **(h)** 28%
  - **(i)** 36%
  - **(j)** 95%
  - **(k)** 45%
  - **(l)** 3%
  - **(m)** $3\frac{1}{2}$%
  - **(n)** $6\frac{1}{2}$%
  - **(o)** $12\frac{1}{2}$%

5 Jack goes to the cinema with his little brother Joey. As they're both under 16, they're offered the special deal of the week. Jack decides to take the 12% discount off the price of a ticket, while Joey decides to take the $\frac{1}{12}$ off the price of a ticket. Who saves more money?

6 At the same cinema, 56% of people going at the weekend decide to see the latest blockbuster release.
  - **(a)** Express this as a fraction in its simplest form.
  - **(b)** Express this as a decimal.
  - **(c)** Express the percentage that saw another film as a fraction in its simplest form.

Converting decimals and fractions to percentages

To convert a decimal to a percentage, multiply the decimal by 100.

Example 6

Change to a percentage:
(a) 0.47   **(b)** 0.075

(a) $0.47 \times 100 = 47\%$ **(b)** $0.075 \times 100 = 7.5\%$

To write a fraction as a percentage:
- change the fraction to a decimal
- multiply the decimal by 100.

Example 7

Change to a percentage:

(a) $\frac{7}{10}$ (b) $\frac{17}{40}$

(a) $\frac{7}{10} = 7 \div 10 = 0.7$ (b) $\frac{17}{40} = 17 \div 40 = 0.425$

$\quad\quad 0.7 \times 100 = 70$ $\quad\quad 0.425 \times 100 = 42.5$

$\quad$ So $\quad \frac{7}{10} = 70\%$ So $\quad \frac{17}{40} = 42.5\%$

Exercise 15C

1 Change these decimals to percentages.

(a) 0.37 (b) 0.59 (c) 0.11 (d) 0.1 (e) 0.36

(f) 0.7 (g) 0.03 (h) 0.771 (i) 0.09 (j) 0.055

(k) 0.83 (l) 0.56 (m) 0.075 (n) 0.125 (o) 0.675

2 Write these fractions as percentages.

(a) $\frac{1}{2}$ (b) $\frac{3}{4}$ (c) $\frac{2}{5}$ (d) $\frac{4}{5}$ (e) $\frac{9}{10}$

(f) $\frac{7}{20}$ (g) $\frac{8}{25}$ (h) $\frac{19}{25}$ (i) $\frac{3}{20}$ (j) $\frac{3}{8}$

(k) $\frac{5}{8}$ (l) $\frac{3}{16}$ (m) $\frac{7}{50}$ (n) $\frac{9}{100}$ (o) $\frac{13}{1000}$

3 Copy and complete this table:

Percentage	Decimal	Fraction
	0.61	
		$\frac{7}{10}$
35%		
$8\frac{1}{2}\%$		
	0.15	
		$\frac{3}{25}$
	0.07	
$1\frac{1}{4}\%$		
		$\frac{2}{3}$

4 Out of 720 visitors to the Big Splash Water Sports complex, 90 decided to go windsurfing. Express this as a percentage, a decimal and a fraction in its simplest form.

15.3 Working out a percentage of an amount

There are a number of different methods of working out a percentage of an amount.

Example 8

Work out 15% of 40 kg.

Method 1

Change the percentage to a fraction:

$$15\% = \frac{15}{100}$$

Multiply the amount by the fraction:

Your calculator may have a short way of doing this with the **%** key.

$$\frac{15}{100} \times 40\,\text{kg} = \frac{15 \times 40\,\text{kg}}{100} = \frac{600\,\text{kg}}{100} = 6\,\text{kg}$$

So 15% of 40 kg = 6 kg.

Method 2

Change the percentage to a decimal:

$$15\% = \frac{15}{100} = 15 \div 100 = 0.15$$

Multiply the amount by the decimal:

$$0.15 \times 40\,\text{kg} = 6\,\text{kg}$$

So 15% of 40 kg = 6 kg.

Method 3

Work from 10%.

To find 10% of 40 kg means find one tenth of 40:

10% of 40 is 4

5% of 40 is 2 ———— half of 10%

15% of 40 is 6 kg.

Example 9

Work out 7.5% of £35.

Method 1

1% of £1 is 1p so 1% of £35 is 35p
7.5% is therefore $35 \times 7.5 = 262.5$p
To the nearest penny this is £2.63

Method 2

$$7.5\% = \frac{7.5}{100} = 0.075$$

$$0.075 \times £35 = £2.625$$

Method 3

Working from 10%:
10% of £35 is £3.50

5% of £35 is £1.75 ———— half of 10%

2.5% of £35 is 87.5p ———— half of 5%

7.5% is $10\% - 2.5\% = £3.50 - 87.5\text{p} = £2.625$ or £2.63

Exercise 15D

Work out these percentages.

1 60% of 165   2 45% of 920 kg   3 17% of £7000

4 90% of 80   5 6% of £420   6 10% of £16.80

7 17.5% of £164   8 30% of £264   9 5% of £31 240

10 0.3% of 250 tonnes   11 7.2% of £600

12 96% of 32 000 m   13 25% of 36 km

14 25% of 15.2 km   15 6.8% of £9840

16 4.8% of 3.6 litres

15.4 Increasing a number by a percentage

Prices and salaries often increase by a percentage. In this section you will be finding a percentage of an amount, and then adding it to the original amount.

When you invest money you get paid for lending other people your money.

The money you are paid is called **interest**. The interest is usually paid each year (often called per annum).

___Example 10___

Find the interest on £250 invested at 5% for one year.

> Find 10% first $\longrightarrow$ 10% of £250 = £25
>
> 5% is half of 10% $\rightarrow$ so 5% of £250 = £12.50

The interest is £12.50 for one year.

___Example 11___

Satinder earns £160 per week working at the supermarket. She is awarded a 5% pay rise.

(a) Work out the amount of the rise.   (b) Work out her new weekly wage.

(a) **Method 1** $5\% = \dfrac{5}{100}$

$\dfrac{5}{100} \times £160 = \dfrac{5 \times £160}{100} = \dfrac{£800}{100} = £8$

Rise = £8

Method 2   5% = 0.05   **Method 3**   Find 10% first:
                 0.05 × £160 = £8   10% of £160 = £16
                        Rise = £8   5% of £160 = £8 ———— half of 10%

(b) Either   £160 + £8 = £168
    or   New wage is 100% + 5% = 105% of old wage
          So new wage = 105% of £160

$$= \frac{105}{100} \times £160 \qquad \text{or } 105\% = 1.05$$
$$\qquad\qquad\qquad\qquad 1.05 \times £160 = £168$$
$$= \frac{105 \times £160}{100}$$
$$= \frac{£16\,800}{100}$$
$$= £168$$

To increase a number by a percentage, you find the percentage of that number and then add this to the starting number.

Exercise 15E

1 Increase
    (a) £50 by 10%   (b) 60 *l* by 5%
    (c) 400 m by 20%   (d) £150 by 15%
    (e) 35 g by 20%   (f) £450 by 12%
    (g) £85 by 8%   (h) 300 by 15%
    (i) 2 tonnes by 35%

2 Find the interest on £350 invested for one year at
    (a) 10%   (b) 11%   (c) 9%   (d) 15%
    (e) 1%   (f) 5%   (g) 8%   (h) 4%

3 Ray buys a bike for £200. He sells it for 15% more than he paid for it. How much does he sell the bike for?

4 Sandra buys an antique painting for £2000. Six months later she sells it, making a profit of 5%. How much does she sell the painting for?

5 Tommy invests £150 at an interest rate of $7\frac{1}{2}\%$.
How much interest will Tommy get after one year?

6 A market trader buys knitted jumpers for £8.60 each and sports shirts for £4.80 each. She sells them for 65% more than she bought them for.
Work out the selling price of each item.

7 Janice left £450 in her building society account for one year. The building society paid interest of $6\frac{1}{2}\%$ per annum.
How much interest did Janice's money earn in the year?

8 Last year, a skiing holiday in Italy cost £276. The price was made up of fares £80, hotel £120, skiing instruction £30 and hire of equipment £46.
This year, the cost of fares had risen by 12%, hotel costs had risen by 8%, the cost of instruction had increased by 50% and hire of equipment by 10%.
Work out the total cost of the holiday this year.

15.5 Decreasing a number by a percentage

Reductions in numbers or prices are often described using percentages. There are several ways you can work out the actual numbers involved.

A 12% discount means that the price is reduced by 12%.

Example 12

At the beginning of a year the number of unemployed people in a city was 5500. This number fell by 1% during the year.

(a) Work out the fall in the number of unemployed people.

(b) Work out the number of people remaining.

(a) Fall in the number of unemployed people:

Either $1\% = \dfrac{1}{100}$ 　　　　　 **or** 　 $1\% = 0.01$

$\dfrac{1}{100} \times 5500 = \dfrac{1 \times 5500}{100} = \dfrac{5500}{100} = 55$ 　　　　$0.01 \times 5500 = 55$

(b) Number of people remaining:

Either $5500 - 55 = 5445$
or 　New number is $100\% - 1\% = 99\%$ of old number

So the number remaining = 99% of 5500

$$= \dfrac{99}{100} \times 5500$$ 　**or** 　 $99\% = 0.99$

$$= \dfrac{99 \times 5500}{100}$$ 　　　 $0.99 \times 5500 = 5445$

$$\doteqdot \dfrac{544\,500}{100} = 5445$$

To decrease a number by a percentage, you find the percentage of that number and then take it away from the starting number.

Exercise 15F

1 Work out the sale price of a TV that normally costs £120 if the discount is

    (a) 10%   **(b)** 20%

    (c) 5%   **(d)** 15%

2 Gareth is offered a discount of 10% for paying cash for a car that has an original price of £3000. How much does Gareth pay for the car?

3 Rob gets a discount of 5% off his ticket to Paris. The original price was £150. How much does Rob have to pay for his ticket?

4 In their spring sale, Sonic Sound reduced the price of all CDs and DVDs by 30%.

Calculate

    (a) the reduction in price

    (b) the new price of a CD usually costing £12.

5 A furniture store reduced all normal prices by 15% for the spring sale.

Work out

    (i) the reduction in price   **(ii)** the spring sale price of

    (a) a table normally priced at £80

    (b) a settee normally priced at £740

    (c) a TV table normally priced at £40.60

6 Fun In The Sun Holidays advertises a discount of 18% off all holiday prices.

How much would it cost for

    (a) a fly drive holiday originally priced at £360

    (b) an activity holiday originally priced at £168?

15.6 VAT

VAT or value added tax is a tax imposed by the government on sales of some goods and services.

In 2005, VAT was set at $17\frac{1}{2}$%.

> To apply VAT you add $17\frac{1}{2}$% extra onto the original cost.

Example 13

$17\frac{1}{2}$% VAT is added to Harry's bill of £24.
What is the total bill?

To work this out you have to find $17\frac{1}{2}$% of £24 and then add it on to the £24.

There is an easy non-calculator method for working out VAT at $17\frac{1}{2}$%.

First find 10% of £24	£2.40	10%
Then halve it to find 5%	£1.20	5%
Then halve this to find $2\frac{1}{2}$%	£0.60	$2\frac{1}{2}$%
	£4.20	$17\frac{1}{2}$%

£24 + £4.20 = £28.20

VAT can be worked out by finding 10%
then 5%
then $2\frac{1}{2}$% +
$17\frac{1}{2}$%

Exercise 15G

1 Find $17\frac{1}{2}$% of these amounts:
  (a) £10 (b) £30 (c) £32 (d) £40
  (e) £16 (f) £120 (g) £250 (h) £360

2 Work out the total bill in each of these cases when VAT is added at $17\frac{1}{2}$%.
  (a) £100 (b) £300 (c) £320 (d) £40
  (e) £160 (f) £120 (g) £2500 (h) £3600

3 Value added tax (VAT) is charged at the rate of $17\frac{1}{2}$%. How much VAT is there to pay on
  (a) a telephone bill of £52.40 before VAT
  (b) a restaurant bill of £28 before VAT
  (c) a wedding reception costing £1980 before VAT
  (d) a builder's bill for repairs of £158.80 before VAT?

15.7 Index numbers

An **index number** shows how a quantity changes over time.

A **price index** shows how the price of something changes over time.

Index numbers are often used to mark changes in retail prices. The amount an average family spends on food, fuel etc. is worked out for a particular year, known as the **base year**. Any changes in prices are collected and the overall rise or fall in the amount of money spent by an average family is given as a percentage of the base year price.

The index always starts at 100.

If the price (or quantity) rises over time, the index rises above 100.

If the price (or quantity) falls over time, the index falls below 100.

This table shows an index of retail prices for January to April last year.

January	February	March	April
100	104.5	103.0	106.8

This means that prices rose by 4.5% from January to February. Although in March they fell by 1.5 percentage points compared with February, prices were still 3% above the January figure. April shows a rise of 6.8% on the January figure.

Example 14

The table shows the index numbers for the sales of ice cream each month.

Month	August	September	October	November
Index	100	95	87	76

(a) What was the percentage change from August to November?
(b) In which period was there the greatest fall in sales?
(c) What is the overall trend in sales figures?

(a) From August to November: $100 - 76 = 24$; a fall of 24%.
(b) August to September: 5
   September to October: 8
   October to November: 11
   The greatest fall was in the period October to November.
(c) The sales fell each month:

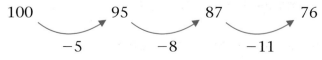

Exercise 15H

1   The table shows an index for the number of winter coats sold
    by a shop.

Month	Jan	Feb	Mar	Apr
Index	100	110	102	98

(a)   What happened to the sale of winter coats between
      March and April?

(b)   In which period was there the greatest decrease in sales?

(c)   What is the difference in sales between January and
      April?

2   The table shows an index for the service costs of a car, over a
    period of time.

Year	2001	2002	2003	2004
Index	100	120	135	130

(a)   Write down the base year for the index table.

(b)   In which period was there the greatest increase in costs?

(c)   What was the percentage change from 2001 to 2004?

3   The table shows an index for the value of a computer over
    time.

Year	2000	2001	2002	2003	2004
Index	100	80	62	44	28

(a)   In which period was there the greatest change in value?

(b)   There was an 80% reduction from 2000 to 2005. What is
      the index for 2005?

4   The table shows an index for the number of newspapers sold
    by a shop in a week.

Day	Mon	Tue	Wed	Thu	Fri
Index	100	105	92	96	110

(a)   Write down the base day for the table.

(b)   What was the percentage change from Monday to
      Wednesday?

(c)   Between which two days was there the greatest change in
      newspaper sales?

15.8 Writing one quantity as a percentage of another quantity

Example 15

The top mark in a test is 34 out of 40.
What is this as a percentage?

To find one quantity as a percentage of another follow these steps:

Step 1 Write the two amounts as a fraction: $\frac{34}{40}$

Step 2 Convert the fraction to a decimal:

$$\frac{34}{40} = 34 \div 40 = 0.85$$

Step 3 Multiply the decimal by 100:

$$0.85 \times 100 = 85$$

The top mark is 85%.

Example 16

A jacket is reduced in price from £80 to £62.
What is the percentage reduction?

The actual reduction is £80 − £62 = £18

Step 1 Write this as a fraction of the original price: $\frac{18}{80}$

Step 2 Convert to a decimal:

$$18 \div 80 = 0.225$$

Step 3 Multiply by 100:

$$0.225 \times 100 = 22.5\%$$

The percentage reduction is 22.5%.

To write one amount as a percentage of another:
- write the amounts as a fraction
- convert the fraction to a decimal
- multiply the decimal by 100.

$$\text{Percentage change} = \frac{\text{actual change}}{\text{original amount}} \times 100$$

Exercise 15I

1   (a)   What percentage of £100 is £5?
    (b)   What percentage of 5 kg is 600 g?
    (c)   What percentage of £160 is £24?
    (d)   What percentage of 2*l* is 150 m*l*?
    (e)   What percentage of 3 hours is 1 hour 15 mins?
    (f)   What percentage of £4.20 is 35p?
    (g)   What percentage of £16 000 is £480?
    (h)   What percentage of 20 tonnes is 200 kg?
    (i)   What percentage of 3.6 m is 180 cm?

2   (a)   Write £15 as a percentage of £200.
    (b)   Write £600 as a percentage of £3000.
    (c)   Write 15 minutes as a percentage of 1 hour 15 mins.
    (d)   Write 6.3 m as a percentage of 157.5 m.
    (e)   Write £5.60 as a percentage of £140.
    (f)   Write 36 kg as a percentage of 900 kg.
    (g)   Write 20 tonnes as a percentage of 320 tonnes.
    (h)   Write 4.5 mm as a percentage of 90 cm.
    (i)   Write £850 as a percentage of £4000.
    (j)   Write £1575 as a percentage of £63 000.

3   Shoes in a sale are reduced in price from £60 to £42.
    What is the percentage reduction?

4   A factory employing 300 people made 18 people
    redundant.
    What percentage of the employees were made
    redundant?

5   Peter bought a new motor bike for £840 and sold it two
    years later for £378.
    By what percentage had its value fallen compared with
    the two years?

6   A games console, normally sold for £215, is offered for
    sale at £180.60.
    Calculate the percentage reduction.

7   A shopworker received a wage increase from £160 per
    week to £165 per week.
    What was the percentage increase?

8 Shona deposited £450 in a bank savings account.
Interest paid after a year increased the amount in her
account to £478.80.
What percentage rate of interest did the bank pay?

9 Ali paid a deposit of £108 on a secondhand car costing
£1350.
What percentage of the price was the deposit?

10 Last year the number of students in a school grew from
1050 to 1500.
What was the percentage increase in the number of
students?

15.9 Comparing different proportions using percentages

Example 17

Write in order of size, smallest first:

$65\%, \frac{3}{5}, 0.66, \frac{5}{8}$

First, change them to percentages:

$$\frac{3}{5} = 3 \div 5 = 0.6 = 60\%$$
$$0.66 = 66\%$$
$$\frac{5}{8} = 5 \div 8 = 0.625 = 62.5\%$$

Then write in order: $\frac{3}{5}, \frac{5}{8}, 65\%, 0.66$

60%	62.5%	65%	66%
$\frac{3}{5}$	$\frac{5}{8}$	65%	0.66

Example 18

In three class tests, Robin scored 8 out of 10 in English,
17 out of 20 in science and 42 out of 50 in history. Which
was his best result?

First, change the marks to percentages:

English: 8 out of 10 $= \frac{8}{10} = 8 \div 10 = 0.8 = 80\%$

Science: 17 out of 20 $= \frac{17}{20} = 17 \div 20 = 0.85 = 85\%$

History: 42 out of 50 $= \frac{42}{50} = 42 \div 50 = 0.84 = 84\%$

So Robin's best result was for science.

To compare percentages, fractions and decimals, you can first
change them all to percentages.

Exercise 15J

1 Rearrange in order of size, smallest first:
   (a) 52%, 0.53, $\frac{9}{15}$
   (b) 72%, $\frac{7}{10}$, 0.71
   (c) 0.07, $\frac{1}{10}$, 8%
   (d) $\frac{3}{8}$, 30%, 0.36

2 In end of term tests, Sheila's results were:

English:	16 out of 24	Geography:	58 out of 100
Maths:	27 out of 40	Science:	11 out of 20
History:	31 out of 50	Technology:	33 out of 60

   (a) Which was her best result?   (b) Which was her worst result?

3 Top Cooks Catering offered two different courses to its students. 45 out of 50 recommended Cake Baking, whilst 37 out of 40 recommended Pizza Making. Which scored the higher percentage of recommendations from students?

15.10 Interest and depreciation

When you invest money in a bank or building society, you receive interest on the amount you invest.

> Example 10 in Section 15.4 showed you how to calculate simple interest.

Simple interest is when the same interest is added each year. You find the interest for one year and multiply it by the number of years.

Zebra Investments
Great rates for savers

Example 19

Find the simple interest on £1000 invested for two years at 5% per annum.

Year 1:   10% of £1000 is £100   so   5% of £1000 is £50

Year 2:   5% of £1000 is £50

Total interest is £50 + £50 = £100

However, you can choose to add the interest for one year to the amount already in your account. In that case, interest for the next year is based on the combined amounts.

Example 20

Tanvi invests £1000 at 5% per annum. She adds the interest for Year 1 to the money already in her account. Find the total interest at the end of Year 2.

Year 1:   10% of £1000 is £100   so   5% of £1000 is £50

The interest is added on, so there is £1050 in the account at the end of Year 1.

Year 2:   10% of £1050 is £105   so   5% of £1050 is £52.50

The interest is added on, so there is £1102.50 in the account at the end of Year 2.

Total interest is £50 + £52.50 = £102.50

When you buy a car the value of the car gets smaller and smaller as time goes by. This is called **depreciation**.

Example 21

Find the value of a car that was bought for £10 000 after depreciation at 10% per annum for two years.

Year 1:   10% of £10 000 is £1000

The car has a value of £10 000 − £1000 = £9000 at the end of Year 1.

Year 2:   10% of £9000 is £900

The car has a value of £9000 − £900 = £8100 at the end of Year 2.

Exercise 15K

1 Find the simple interest when
   (a) £100 is invested for two years at 10% per annum.
   (b) £500 is invested for three years at 10% per annum
   (c) £200 is invested for two years at 5% per annum
   (d) £1000 is invested for two years at 4% per annum
   (e) £50 is invested for four years at 5% per annum.

2 Find the total interest after two years when the interest for the first year is added to the amount already in the account.
   (a) £100 invested at 10% per annum
   (b) £500 invested at 10% per annum
   (c) £200 invested at 5% per annum
   (d) £1000 invested at 4% per annum
   (e) £50 invested at 5% per annum.

3 Jasmine invested £1000 for two years at 8%. She left the interest for the first year in her account.
   How much money was in Jasmine's account at the end of the two years?

4 James invested £100 for two years at 4%. He left the interest for the first year in his account.
   How much money was in James's account at the end of the two years?

5 Ben bought a car for £12 000. The value of the car depreciated at 10% a year. What was the value of Ben's car after two years?

6 Jane bought a car for £8000. The value of the car depreciated at 20% a year. What was the value of Jane's car after two years?

7   Susan bought a flute for £200. The value of the flute
    depreciated at 10% a year.
    What was the value of the flute after two years?

8   Joe buys a new truck for £100 000. The value of the truck
    depreciates at 20% a year.
    What is the value of Joe's truck after two years?

Mixed exercise 15

1   Copy and complete this table of equivalent fractions,
    decimals and percentages.

Fraction	Decimal	Percentage
$\frac{1}{2}$		
	0.6	
		20%
	0.35	
$\frac{1}{20}$		

2   James bought a new boat for £10 000.
    It had lost 60% of its value after three years.

    (a) Work out the loss in value.

    (b) What is the value of the boat after three years?

3   The same sort of bike is for sale in two shops.
    Work out the price you would have to pay in each shop.

WHEELIE'S
Mountain bikes $\frac{1}{4}$ OFF
Price was £198
Price now

CHEAPER BIKES
Mountain bikes
30% OFF
BIGGEST REDUCTION
Last week's price was £239
This week's price is

4   Find the percentage reduction
    on the Mega Games System
    in the sale.

    Mega Games System
    Normal Price   £300
    Sale Price   £225

5   Janet invests £50 in a building society for one year.
    The interest rate is 4% per year.

    (a) How much interest, in pounds, does Janet get?

Nisha invests £20 in a different building society. She gets £3 interest after one year.

(b) Work out the percentage interest rate that Nisha gets.

6 Nigel works in a service station and earns £12 500 per year. He is given a pay rise of 15%.
Ryan is a football player earning £17 500 per year. He is given a pay rise of 1.5%.
Who has the bigger rise in pay?

7 Work out the cost of each item after VAT at 17.5% is added.

(a) Kevin's TV, cost £80 plus VAT.

(b) Julie's microwave, cost £64 plus VAT.

(c) Sophie's saxophone, cost £240 plus VAT.

(d) Roger's boat, cost £720 plus VAT.

(e) Terri's motorbike, cost £360 plus VAT.

8 Rearrange the following in order of size, starting with the smallest:

(a) 36%, $\frac{7}{19}$, 0.37

(b) 0.09, 19%, $\frac{1}{6}$

(c) $\frac{17}{27}$, 60%, $\frac{5}{8}$, 0.62

9 The table shows an index for the price of vintage comics.

Year	2001	2002	2003	2004
Index	100	104	109	117

(a) What was the percentage price rise from 2001 to 2002?

(b) What was the percentage price rise from 2001 to 2004?

(c) Jim paid £50 for a comic in 2001. What would the price be in 2004?

10 A shopkeeper increases the prices of goods in the shop in line with the rate of inflation.
The rate of inflation is 2.1%.
Calculate

(a) the increase in the price of a table marked at £160

(b) the new price of a chair marked at £85

(c) the increase in the price of a bed marked at £249

(d) the new price of a settee marked at £1350.

11 In an election, 6600 people were eligible to vote. 45% voted for Edwards, 28% voted for Philips and 6% voted for Fortescue. The remainder did not vote.

(a) What percentage of voters did not vote?

(b) How many votes did each candidate receive?

12 House prices in a town increased on average by 8% during the year 2000. Calculate

(a) the price increase of a house previously valued at £84 000

(b) the new price of a house previously valued at £102 250.

13 An insurance agent is paid 2% commission on the value of any policies she sells. How much commission is she paid when she sells a policy worth

(a) £4500 (b) £6550?

14 A new chainsaw costs £240. With depreciation its value is expected to fall each year by 15% of its value at the beginning of the year.
What will be the value of the chainsaw in 2 years' time?

15 £900 is invested for two years at $4\frac{1}{2}\%$. The interest at the end of the first year is left in the account.
What is the total interest earned?
Give your answer to the nearest penny.

Summary of key points

1 Percentage
%
pc
} means 'number of parts per hundred'.

2 Remember these percentages and their equivalent fractions:

$50\% = \frac{1}{2}$ $25\% = \frac{1}{4}$ $75\% = \frac{3}{4}$ $33\frac{1}{3}\% = \frac{1}{3}$ $66\frac{2}{3}\% = \frac{2}{3}$

3 A percentage can be written as a fraction with denominator (bottom) 100.

4 To write a percentage as a decimal:
- write the percentage as a fraction
- convert the fraction to a decimal

5 To convert a decimal to a percentage, multiply the decimal by 100.

6 To write a fraction as a percentage:
   - change the fraction to a decimal
   - multiply the decimal by 100.

7 To increase a number by a percentage, find the percentage of that number and then add this to the starting number.

8 To decrease a number by a percentage, you find the percentage of that number and then take it away from the starting number.

9 VAT can be worked out by finding   10%

$$
\begin{array}{rl}
\text{then} & 5\% \\
\text{then} & 2\frac{1}{2}\% \; + \\
\hline
& 17\frac{1}{2}\%
\end{array}
$$

10 An **index number** shows how a quantity changes over time.

   A **price index** shows how the price of something changes over time.

   The index always starts at 100.

   If the price (or quantity) rises over time, the index rises above 100.

   If the price (or quantity) falls over time, the index falls below 100.

11 To write one amount as a percentage of another:
   - write the amounts as a fraction
   - convert the fraction to a decimal
   - multiply the decimal by 100.

12 Percentage change $= \dfrac{\text{actual change}}{\text{original amount}} \times 100$

13 To compare percentages, fractions and decimals, you can first change them all to percentages.

14 **Simple interest** is when the same interest is added each year. You find the interest for one year and multiply it by the number of years.

16 Coordinates and graphs

16.1 Coordinates in the first quadrant

You can describe the position of a place on a grid by using two numbers.

You write the number of units across first and the number of units up second.

On this map 6 across, 3 up gives the position of the Water Hole. You can write this as the point (6, 3). The numbers 6 and 3 are the **coordinates**.

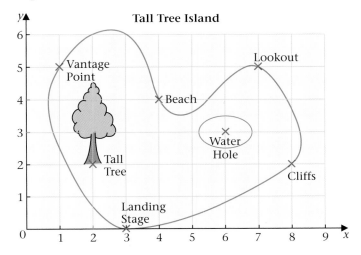

Exercise 16A

1   Write down the names of the places on the map above with these coordinates:

   (a) (8, 2)   (b) (7, 5)   (c) (1, 5)

2   Write down the coordinates of these places on the map of Tall Tree Island above:

   (a) Tall Tree   (b) Landing Stage   (c) Beach

3   On squared paper draw a coordinate grid and number it from 0 to 12 across the page and 0 to 6 up the page. Join these points in the order given:

   (2, 3) (3, 1) (10, 1) (11, 3) (7, 3) (9, 5) (6, 5) (4, 3) (2, 3)

4   Write down the coordinates of all the points marked red in the diagram below.

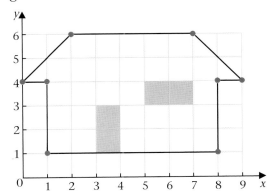

5 Write down the coordinates of all the corner points that make up this ship.

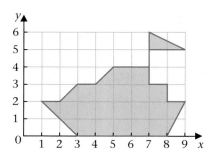

6 Draw a coordinate grid from 0 to 10 in both directions. On your grid plot each of these sets of points and join them in the order given.
 (a) (1, 1) (4, 1) (4, 4) (1, 4) (1, 1)
 (b) (6, 1) (9, 1) (9, 6) (6, 6) (6, 1)
 (c) (0, 6) (5, 6) (0, 10) (0, 6)
 (d) (5, 7) (5, 10) (8, 10) (5, 7)

7 Draw a coordinate grid from 0 to 10 in both directions. On your grid draw a shape of your own and label the coordinates of each point.

8 Invent an island of your own and mark positions on it using a coordinate grid. List all the places with their coordinates.

Coordinates of the mid-point of a line segment

Here is a straight line through points A and B.
The section of line between A and B is called a **line segment** AB.

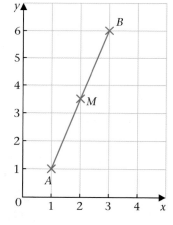

A has coordinates (1, 1) B has coordinates (3, 6)
Halfway along line segment AB is M.
M is called the **mid-point of the line segment** AB.
You can find the coordinates of the mid-point.

1 Add the x-coordinates and divide by 2:
$$\frac{1+3}{2} = \frac{4}{2} = 2$$

2 Add the y-coordinates and divide by 2:
$$\frac{1+6}{2} = \frac{7}{2} = 3\frac{1}{2}$$

So the coordinates of the mid-point are $(2, 3\frac{1}{2})$.

Example 1

Work out the coordinates of the mid-point of the line segment AB where A is (2, 3) and B is (7, 11).

Mid-point x-coordinate is $\dfrac{2+7}{2} = \dfrac{9}{2} = 4\frac{1}{2}$

Mid-point y-coordinate is $\dfrac{3+11}{2} = \dfrac{14}{2} = 7$ So the mid-point is $(4\frac{1}{2}, 7)$.

Exercise 16B

1 Work out the coordinates of the mid-point of each of these line segments on the grid below.

(a) *AB*   (b) *CD*   (c) *EF*   (d) *GH*

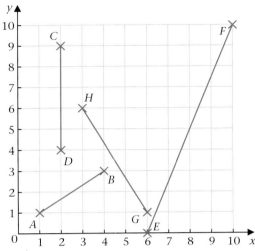

2 Work out the coordinates of the mid-point of each of these line segments:

(a) *AB* where *A*(0, 0) and *B* is (4, 5)

(b) *CD* where *C*(3, 1) and *D* is (4, 9)

(c) *EF* where *E*(5, 7) and *F* is (1, 6)

(d) *GH* where *G*(1, 0) and *H* is (5, 8)

(e) *IJ* where *I*(9, 10) and *J* is (3, 7)

16.2 Linear graphs

You can use graphs to show relationships. For example, if you buy several packets of crisps the price you pay is related to the number of packets you buy.

___ Example 2 ___

Stan sells packets of crisps at 30p each. He wants a quick way of remembering how much different numbers of packets cost.

He makes a table:

Number of packets	1	2	3	4	5	6
Cost in pence	30	60	90	120	150	180

Notice that the cost goes up by 30p for each extra packet.

A pattern like the one in the table is known as a **linear relationship**. Linear relationships can be spotted very easily by drawing a graph.

Plot the points (1, 30), (2, 60), (3, 90), (4, 120), (5, 150) and (6, 180) to draw a graph of Stan's table.

When the points are they plotted make a straight line.

If the line of Stan's graph is made longer, the cost of 7 and 8 packets can be read off. Check the broken lines to see that the costs of 7 and 8 packets are 210p and 240p.

0 packets cost 0p, so extend the graph back to (0, 0).

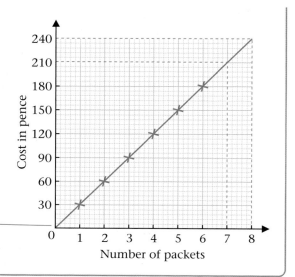

A graph representing a **linear relationship** always has a straight line.

Example 3

Sharon charges £2 for the use of her taxi and £1.50 per mile after that.

(a) Use this information to draw up a table

(b) Plot the points on a graph.

Work out the cost for these journeys

(c) 7 miles   (d) 1 mile.

(a) The table gives the charges for some journeys up to 6 miles long.

Distance in miles	0	2	4	6
Cost in £	2	5	8	11

(b) Plot the points (0, 2), (2, 5), (4, 8), (6, 11). The graph gives a straight line.

(c) The cost of a 7 mile journey is £12.50

(d) The cost of a 1 mile journey is £3.50

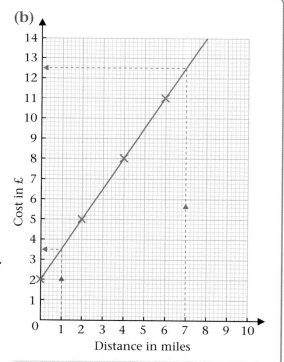

Because the relationship is linear, you can use the graph to find the cost of a journey of more than 6 miles and for journeys between the values that you have worked out.

Exercise 16C

1   The table shows the cost of potatoes per kg.

Weight in kg	1	2	3	4	5
Cost in pence	30	60	90	120	150

   (a) Draw a graph for this table.
   (b) Work out how much 2.5 kg of potatoes would cost.
   (c) Extend the graph to work out the cost of 6 kg of
        potatoes.

2   The table shows the cost of ice lollies.

Number of ice lollies	1	2	3	4	5
Cost in pence	25	50	75	100	125

   (a) Draw a graph for the cost of ice lollies from the table.
   (b) Extend the graph and then use it to work out the
        cost of
        (i) 8 ice lollies   (ii) 6 ice lollies.

3   The table shows the number of litres of petrol left in a
    car's petrol tank on a journey.

Travelling time in hours	1	2	3	4	5	6	7	8
Number of litres left	55	50	45	40	35	30	25	20

   (a) Draw a graph from the information given in the table.
   (b) How many litres were in the tank at the start of the
        journey (after 0 hours)?
   (c) How many litres were in the tank after $5\frac{1}{2}$ hours?

4   A car uses 2 litres of petrol for every 5 km it travels.
   (a) Copy and complete the table showing how much
        petrol the car uses.

Distance travelled in km	0	5	10	15	20	25
Petrol used in litres	0	2	4			

   (b) Draw a graph from the information in your table.
   (c) Work out how much petrol is used to travel 4 km.
   (d) Work out how many kilometres had been travelled
        by the time 15 litres of petrol had been used.

5   The water in a reservoir is 144 m deep. During a dry period the water level falls by 4 m each week.

(a) Copy and complete this table showing the expected depth of water in the reservoir.

Weeks	0	1	2	3	4	5	6	7	8
Expected depth of water in m	144	140							

(b) Draw a graph from the information in your table.

(c) How deep would you expect the reservoir to be after 10 weeks?

If the water level falls to 96 m the water company will divert water from another reservoir.

(d) After how long will the water company divert water?

16.3 Conversion graphs

A **conversion graph** is used to convert a measurement into different units.

This conversion graph relates temperatures in degrees Fahrenheit (°F) to temperatures in degrees Celsius (°C).

To draw a conversion graph you need to know two pairs of values linking the two sets of units.

In this case use the facts that

$0\,°C = 32\,°F$ (the freezing point of water)

and $100\,°C = 212\,°F$ (the boiling point of water).

To make the conversion graph you draw a horizontal axis from 0 to 100 for °C and a vertical axis from 0 to 212 for °F. Then plot the two points and join them with a straight line.

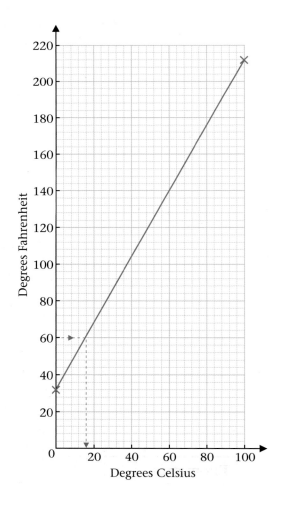

Example 4

Change 60° Fahrenheit to degrees Celsius.

- Draw a horizontal line from 60 °F across to the straight line on the graph.
- From the line draw a vertical line down to the °C axis.
- Read off the scale.

The answer is 16 °C.

Exercise 16D

1   Copy the table and use the temperature conversion graph on page 304 to complete it.

°C	5	20		28			35	80		40
°F			80		50	100			200	

2   (a)   Draw a conversion graph from pounds to kilograms.
        Use the fact that 0 pounds is 0 kilograms and
        50 kilograms is approximately 110 pounds.
        On your graph draw axes for kilograms and pounds
        using scales of 1 cm = 10 pounds and 1 cm = 10 kg.
        Plot the points (0, 0) and (50, 110) and join them
        with a straight line.

   (b)   Copy and complete this table using your conversion
        chart to help you.

Kilograms	0			45	30	15			35	50
Pounds	0	10	20				50	14		110

3   Copy this table and then use the information in the table
    to draw a conversion graph from inches into centimetres.
    Use your graph to help you fill in the missing values.

Inches	0	1	2				9	8		12
Centimetres	0			10	15	20			25	30

4   Copy this table and then use the information in the table
    to draw a conversion graph from miles into kilometres.
    Use your graph to help you fill in the missing values.

Miles	0	5		40		30			24	50
Kilometres	0		16		36		72	20		80

5 Copy this table and then use the information in the table to draw a conversion graph from acres into hectares. Use your graph to help you fill in the missing values.

Hectares	0			12	15	17			3	20
Acres	0	20	30				24	45		50

16.4 Distance–time graphs

Distance–time graphs give information about journeys.
You always use the horizontal axis for time and the vertical axis for distance.

___ **Example 5** _____

Mary travels to work by bus.

She walks the first 750 metres in 10 minutes, waits at the bus stop for 5 minutes, then travels the remaining 3000 metres by bus. She arrives at the work bus stop 21 minutes after she set off from home.

> Use squared paper.
> Distance is the vertical axis.
> Time is the horizontal axis.

(a) Draw a distance–time graph of her journey.

(b) Work out the average speed of the bus in kilometres per hour.

(a)

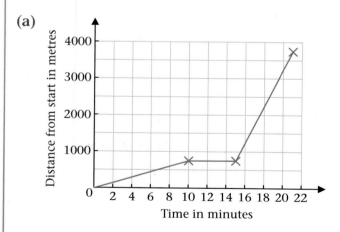

(b) From the graph, the bus travels
$\qquad$ 3000 m (3 km) in 6 minutes.
So in 1 hour (= 6 minutes × 10)
it travels 3 km × 10 = 30 km
The speed is 30 km per hour.

Example 6

This is a graph showing the journey made by an ambulance.

On the graph from O to A the ambulance travels 10 km in 10 minutes. From A to B the ambulance travels 20 km in 10 minutes. From B to C the ambulance does not go anywhere for 5 minutes. The 30 km journey back to base takes 15 minutes.

Work out the speed of the ambulance for each part of the journey.

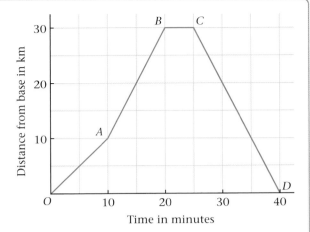

Between O and A:
  speed = 10 km in 10 minutes
    = 1 km per minute
    = 60 km per hour

> There are 60 minutes in 1 hour, so speed = 1 × 60 km per hour (km/h).

Between A and B:
  speed = 20 km in 10 minutes
    = 2 km per minute
    = 120 km per hour

Between B and C: speed = 0 km per hour

Between C and D:
  speed = 30 km in 15 minutes
    = 2 km per minute
    = 120 km per hour

Distance–time graphs are used to relate the distance travelled to the time taken, and to calculate speeds.

Exercise 16E

1 Jane walks to the shops, does some shopping then walks home again.
  (a) How many minutes did it take Jane to walk to the shops?
  (b) How far away were the shops?
  (c) How many minutes did Jane spend shopping?
  (d) How many minutes did it take Jane to walk home?
  (e) Work out the speed at which Jane walked to the shops. First give your answer in metres per minute, then change it to km per hour.
  (f) Work out the speed at which Jane walked back from the shops. First give your answer in metres per minute, then change it to km per hour.

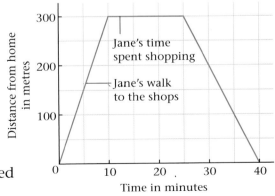

> Remember:
> 1000 m = 1 km

2 Here is a graph of David's car journey to see his aunt.

(a) Write a story of the journey explaining what happened during each part of it.

(b) Work out David's speed during each part of the journey.
Give your answers in km per hour.

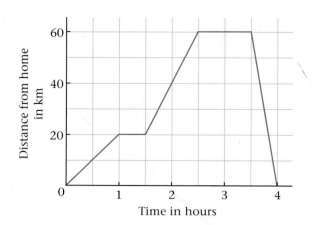

3

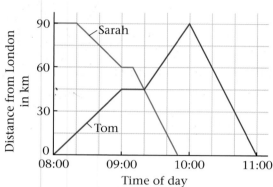

This graph shows Tom's and Sarah's journeys. Tom sets off from London at 08:00 and travels to a town 90 km away to meet his girlfriend Sarah. He stops for a rest on the way. Once he gets to Sarah's he turns around and drives straight home because he discovers that she set off for London some time ago to see him.

(a) Describe Tom's journey in detail explaining after what distance he stopped on the way and for how long.

(b) Describe Sarah's journey in detail explaining after what distance she stopped on the way and for how long.

(c) At what time did Sarah and Tom pass each other and what distance were they from London when it happened?

4 Imran has a bath. The graph shows the depth of the bath water.

He starts at *O* by turning the hot and cold water taps on.

Between *O* and point *A* on the graph the depth of water goes up to 20 cm in 5 minutes.

Explain what happens between points *A* and *B*, *B* and *C*, *C* and *D*, *D* and *E*, and *E* and *F* on the graph and how long each part of the process takes.

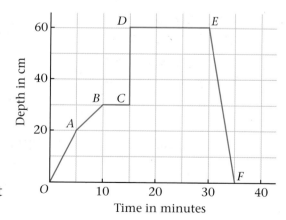

5 Gerald walked to the post box near his house to post a letter. It took him 4 minutes to walk to the post box, which was 400 m away. Gerald chatted to a friend for 2 minutes and he walked home in 3 minutes. Use graph paper to draw a distance–time graph for this journey.

6   Kirsti took a trip in a hot-air balloon. The balloon rose 400
    metres in the air in one hour and stayed at this height for
    two and a half hours. The balloon then came back to the
    ground in half an hour. Use graph paper to draw a
    distance–time graph for this balloon flight.

7   Annabel travels to school. She walks the 250 metres to the bus
    stop in 4 minutes, waits at the bus stop for 5 minutes and then
    travels the remaining 1000 metres by bus. She arrives at the bus
    stop outside the school 15 minutes after she sets off from home.
    (a) Draw a distance–time graph of the journey.
    (b) Work out the speed of the bus, first in metres per minute,
         then in km per hour.

8   Mae went shopping by car. She drove the 10 miles to the shops
    in 30 minutes. She stayed at the shops for 30 minutes and then
    started to drive home. The car then broke down after 5 minutes
    when she had travelled 4 miles from the shops. It took
    10 minutes to repair the car and another 5 minutes to get
    home. Draw a distance–time graph for Mae's journey.

16.5 Curved graphs

Sometimes you will come across a distance–time graph where
the line is curved.

Example 7

The distance fallen by a stone
when it is dropped from a cliff
is shown on this graph.

(a) What distance did the
     stone fall in 2 seconds?

(b) How long did the stone
     take to fall 32 metres?

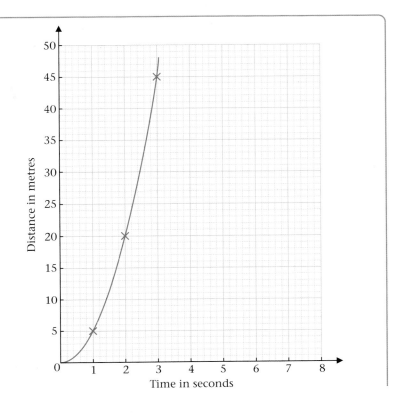

(a) Draw a line up from 2 seconds to meet the curve. Then draw across to the distance axis. It cuts it at 20 metres. The stone fell 20 metres in 2 seconds.

(b) Draw a line across from 32 metres to the curve. Then draw down to the time axis. It cuts it at about 2.6 seconds. The stone took 2.6 seconds to fall 32 metres.

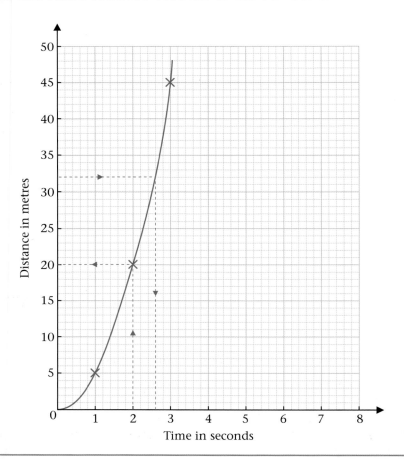

Exercise 16F

1 Use the graph in Example 7 to find

(a) the distance fallen by the stone in

(i) 1.5 seconds

(ii) 3 seconds

(b) the time taken for the stone to fall

(i) 40 metres

(ii) 25 metres.

2 Karen skis down a mountain. This graph shows her run.

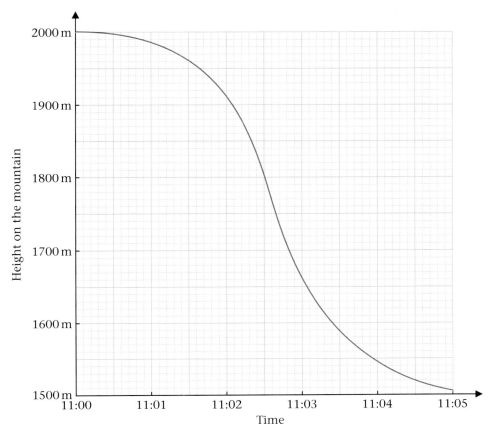

(a) From the graph write down the height Karen was at after
    (i) 1 minute
    (ii) 2 minutes 30 seconds
    (iii) 4 minutes 15 seconds.
(b) Use the graph to write down the time at which Karen
    was at the following heights:
    (i) 1900 m   (ii) 1750 m   (iii) 1625 m

3 The speed of a ball when it is dropped is shown in the
following table of values.

Distance in metres	0	5	10	15	20	25
Speed in metres per second	0	10	14	17	20	22

(a) Draw a graph using the information given in the table.
(b) Use the graph to work out the speed when the
    distance fallen is 12 metres.
(c) Use the graph to work out the distance fallen when
    the speed is 18 metres per second.

Join up your points with a
smooth curve.

16.6 Coordinates in four quadrants

In Section 16.1 you learned how to plot points on a grid with positive coordinates only. You also need to be able to plot coordinates that include negative numbers.

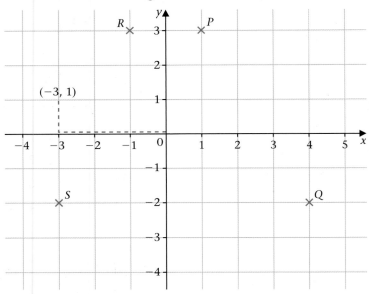

The horizontal axis is called the **x-axis**.

The vertical axis is called the **y-axis**.

The point (0, 0) is called the **origin** and is labelled 0.

Point P is (1, 3).

Point R is at −1 along the x-axis and 3 up the y-axis, so R is (−1, 3).

Point Q is (4, −2) and point S is (−3, −2).

To plot the point (−3, 1), move to −3 on the x-axis, then up 1.

Exercise 16G

1 Write down the coordinates of all the points A to L marked on the coordinate grid.

2 Draw a coordinate grid with the horizontal axis (the x-axis) marked from −4 to +4 and the vertical axis (the y-axis) marked from −10 to +10.

Plot the following points and join them in the order given:

(−1, 6) (−2, 6) (−4, 5) (−4, 6) (−2, 7) (0, 8)
(1, 7) (1, −2) (2, −6) (1, −8) (0, −9) (−1, −9)
(−2, −8) (−3, −6) (−2, −5) (−1, −5) (0, −6) (−2, −6)
(−1, −8) (0, −8) (1, −6) (−1, −2) (−3, 0) (−3, 2) (−1, 6)

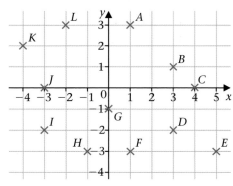

16.7 Using algebra to describe lines

This graph shows a linear (straight line) relationship between the numbers on the horizontal and vertical axes. You can use algebra to describe the relationship and the line.

> Remember:
> The horizontal axis is called the x-axis and the vertical axis is called the y-axis.

In a pair of numbers the x-coordinate is given first; the y-coordinate is given second:

(x, y)

For example, in the point $(3, 2)$ the x-coordinate is 3 and the y-coordinate is 2.

Look for a number pattern connecting the coordinates to give the line a name. On the grid above all the x-coordinates are 2 so the line is called $x = 2$

The **equation** of the line is $x = 2$

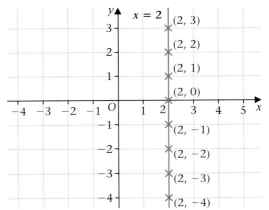

In the graph on the right, all the y-coordinates are -2 so the line is called $y = -2$

The **equation** of the line is $y = -2$

The **equation of a line** uses algebra to show a relationship between the x- and y-coordinates of points on the line.

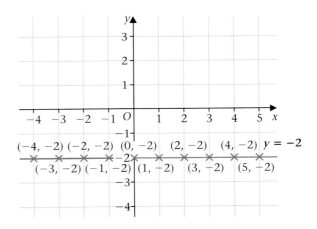

Exercise 16H

1   Write down the equations of the lines marked (a) to (d) in this diagram.

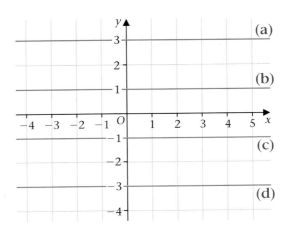

2 Write down the equations of the lines labelled (a) to (d) in this diagram.

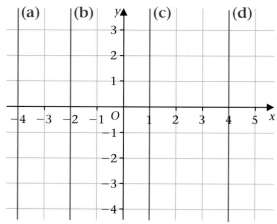

3 Draw a coordinate grid with x- and y-axes labelled from -5 to 5. On the grid draw and label the graphs of

(a) $x = 4$ (b) $x = -2$ (c) $x = -4$ (d) $x = 1$

4 Draw a coordinate grid with axes labelled from -5 to 5. On the grid draw and label the graphs of

(a) $y = 4$ (b) $y = -2$ (c) $y = -4$ (d) $y = 1$

5 Draw a coordinate grid with axes labelled from -5 to 5. On the grid draw and label the graphs of

(a) $y = 3$ (b) $x = -1$

(c) Write down the coordinates of the point where the two lines cross.

Example 8

Draw the graph of $y = x - 1$

Step 1 Choose some values for x, for example let $x = -2$, 0 and $+2$

Step 2 Put these values of x into the equation $y = x - 1$:

When $x = -2$: $y = -2 - 1 = -3$

When $x = 0$: $y = 0 - 1 = -1$

When $x = 2$: $y = 2 - 1 = 1$

Step 3 Write these pairs of values in a table.

x	-2	0	2
y	-3	-1	1

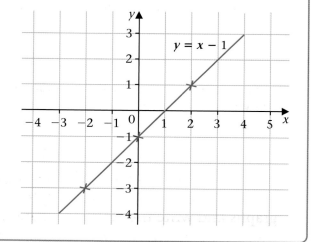

Step 4 Plot the points $(-2, -3)$, $(0, -1)$ and $(2, 1)$ and join them. Extend the line to the edges of the grid.

Step 5 Label the line.

Worked examination question

Draw and complete a table of values for the graphs of $y = 2x - 1$ and $y = -x + 1$.

Draw the graphs and write down the coordinates of the point where they cross.

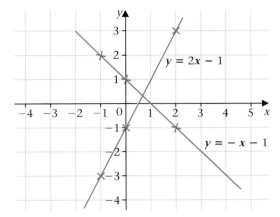

Step 1
Choose three values for x.
For example $x = -1, 0, 2$

Step 2
Put these values of x into each equation:

$y = 2x - 1$ $x = -1$ $y = -2 - 1 = -3$
              $x = 0$ $y = 0 - 1 = -1$
              $x = 2$ $y = 4 - 1 = 3$

$y = -x + 1$ $x = -1$ $y = 1 + 1 = 2$
              $x = 0$ $y = 0 + 1 = 1$
              $x = 2$ $y = -2 + 1 = -1$

These pairs of values make $y = 2x - 1$ true:

x	-1	0	2
y	-3	-1	3

These pairs of values make $y = -x + 1$ true:

x	-1	0	2
y	2	1	-1

Step 3
Plot the points $(-1, -3)$, $(0, -1)$ and $(2, 3)$ and join them with a straight line.

Plot the points $(-1, 2)$, $(0, 1)$ and $(2, -1)$. and join them with a straight line.

> Make sure you read the coordinates accurately from your graph.

The lines cross at about $(\frac{2}{3}, \frac{1}{3})$.

$y = mx + c$ is the general equation of a straight line.
m is the gradient and c is where the line crosses the y-axis.

Exercise 16I

1 On a coordinate grid with axes labelled from -5 to 5 draw the following graphs:

> Choose three values from -5 to 5

  (a) $y = x + 2$ **(b)** $y = x + 4$ **(c)** $y = x + 1$

  (d) $y = x - 2$ **(e)** $y = x - 4$ **(f)** $y = x - 1$

2 On a coordinate grid with the x-axis labelled from -4 to 4 and the y-axis labelled from -10 to 10 draw the following graphs and write the values of m and c.

> Hint for (a):
> Compare with $y = mx + c$.
> ($m = 1$ and $c = 2$)

  (a) $y = x + 2$ **(b)** $y = 2x + 3$ **(c)** $y = 3x - 2$ **(d)** $y = \frac{1}{2}x + 3$

3 On a coordinate grid with the *x*-axis labelled from −3 to 6 and the *y*-axis labelled from −2 to 6 draw the graph of $x + y = 4$.

> Hint: The coordinates of the points on the line $x + y = 4$ always add up to 4.

4 On a coordinate grid with the *x*-axis labelled from −4 to 4 and the *y*-axis labelled from −6 to 6 draw the following graphs.

    (a) $y = -2x - 1$ **(b)** $y = x + 2$

    (c) Write down the coordinates of the point where they cross.

5 **(a)** Copy and complete this table of values for $y = 3x + 1$.

x	−2	−1	0	1	2	3
y	−5			4		10

    (b) On a coordinate grid with the *x*-axis labelled from −2 to 3 and the *y*-axis labelled from −5 to 10 draw the graph of $y = 3x + 1$.

    (c) Use your graph to find the value of *x* when $y = 6$. [E]

16.8 1-D, 2-D or 3-D?

The number line goes in one direction (either horizontally or vertically).

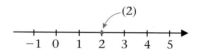

> The number line is **1-dimensional** or **1-D**.
> You can describe position on the number line using one number or coordinate, for example (2).

Coordinate grids and flat shapes go in two directions.

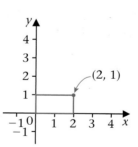

> Flat shapes are **2-dimensional** or **2-D**.
> You can describe position on a flat shape using two numbers or coordinates, for example (2, 1).

Solid shapes go in three directions.

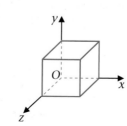

> Solid shapes are **3-dimensional** or **3-D**.
> You can describe position in a solid shape using three numbers or coordinates, for example (4, 1, 2).

This diagram shows a 3-D grid. The *x*-, *y*- and *z*-axes are all at right angles to each other. The lengths of the edges of the cuboid are 2, 2 and 1 units.

To get to point *P* from *O*, you go 4 units along the *x*-axis, then 1 unit parallel to the *y*-axis, then 2 units parallel to the *z*-axis.

The coordinates of point *P* are (4, 1, 2).

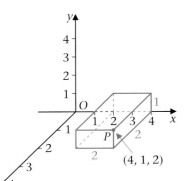

___ **Example 9** ___

Say whether each shape is 1-D, 2-D or 3-D.

(a)   (b) 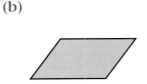 (c)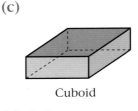

Cone   Parallelogram   Cuboid

(a) 3-D   (b) 2-D   (c) 3-D

___ **Example 10** ___

The diagram represents a cuboid on a 3-D grid.
OR = 2 units, *OP* = 5 units and *OS* = 4 units.
Find the coordinates of
(a) *S* (b) *P* (c) *R* (d) *V* (e) *U* (f) *O*

(a) To get to *S* from *O* you go 0 along the *x*-axis,
    4 units up the *y*-axis and 0 units parallel to the *z*-axis.
    So *S* = (0, 4, 0)
(b) Similarly *P* = (0, 0, 5)
(c) *R* = (−2, 0, 0)
(d) *V* = (−2, 4, 0)
(e) To get to *U* from *O* you go −2 units along the *x*-axis,
    4 units parallel to the *y*-axis and 5 units parallel to the *z*-axis.
    So *U* = (−2, 4, 5)
(f) *O* = (0, 0, 0)

Exercise 16J

1 Say whether each shape is 1-D, 2-D or 3-D.

(a)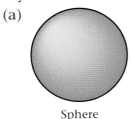
Sphere

(b)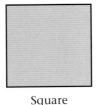
Square

(c)
Line

(d)
Pyramid

2 Say whether each shape is 1-D, 2-D or 3-D.

(a) Hexagon   (b) Cylinder

(c) Circle   (d) Cube

3 Write down all the 3-dimensional coordinates from this list:

(6)   (3, 1, 1)   (4, 2)   (6, 6, 9)   (3)

(12, 8)   (4, 1, 16)   (9, 3)   (28, 1, 8)   (126)

4 Write down the coordinates of each vertex of this cuboid:

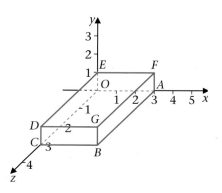

5 Write down the coordinates of each vertex of this cuboid:

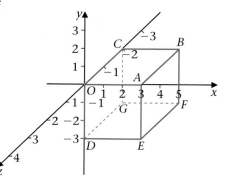

Mixed exercise 16

1 (a) Write down the coordinates of the point
    (i) P
    (ii) Q

(b) Draw a pair of coordinate axes.
    (i) Plot the point (4, −3).
        Label the point A.
    (ii) Plot the point (0, 3).
        Label the point B.

(c) Work out the mid-point of the line PQ.

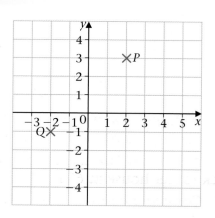

2 This table gives information about the cost of ice creams.

Number of ice creams	1	2	3	4	5
Cost of ice creams in pence	60	120	180	240	300

   (a) Draw a graph for the cost of ice creams.

   (b) Extend the graph to find the cost of
   (i) 9 ice creams   **(ii)** 6 ice creams.

   (c) How many ice creams can be bought for £4.20?

   (d) How much would you have to pay for 25 ice creams?

3 This table gives some approximate conversion between inches and centimetres.

Centimetres	2.5	5	10	30	50
Inches	1	2	4	12	20

   (a) Draw a conversion graph from inches to centimetres.

   (b) Use your graph to find the number of centimetres in
   (i) 6 inches   **(ii)** 10 inches

   (c) Use your graph to find out the number of inches in
   (i) 25 cm   **(ii)** 40 cm

4 Here is part of a travel graph of Siân's journey from her house to the shops and back.

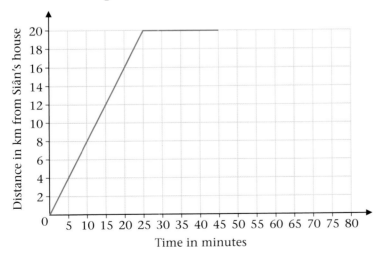

   (a) Work out Siân's speed for the first 20 minutes of her journey. Give your answer in km/h.

   Siân spends 20 minutes at the shops. She then travels back to her house at 60 km/h.

   (b) Copy and complete the travel graph.   [E]

5 Draw a coordinate grid with x values from -4 to $+4$ and y values from -6 to $+6$. On the grid draw the graphs of the following straight lines:

(a) $x = 3$ (b) $y = -2$

(c) $x = -1$ (d) $y = 4$

(e) $y = x$ (f) $y = -x$

(g) $y = 2x - 1$ (h) $y = -2x + 1$

6 This cuboid has sides of 3, 3 and 2 units. Write down the coordinates of each vertex.

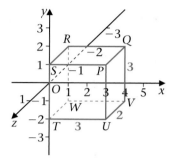

7 On a coordinate grid with the x-axis labelled from -4 to 4 and the y-axis labelled from -10 to 10 draw the following graphs:

(a) $y = x + 1$ (b) $y = 2x - 2$ (c) $y = 2x - 3$

(d) Write down the coordinates of the points where they cross as accurately as you can.

8 (a) Copy and complete the table of values for the following graphs:

(i) $y = 3x - 2$

x	-1	0	1	2
y				

(ii) $y = 5 - x$

x	-1	0	1	2
y				

(b) Draw the graphs on graph paper and write down the coordinates of the point where they cross.

9 List the coordinates of all the vertices of the cuboid.

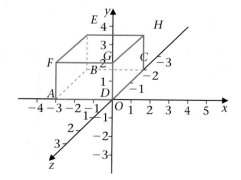

10 Jon went to Spain.
He changed £300 into euros (€).
The exchange rate was £1 = €1.50
(a) How many euros did he get?

When he came home he changed €14.70 back into pounds.
The exchange rate was now £1 = €1.40
(b) How many pounds did he get?

11 Prendeep bought a necklace in the United States of America.
Prendeep paid $108.

Arthur bought an identical necklace in Germany.
Arthur paid €117.

The exchange rates are

| £1 = $1.44 |
| £1 = €1.6 |

Calculate, in pounds, the difference between the prices paid for the two necklaces.
Explain how you worked out your answer.   [E]

Summary of key points

1 A graph representing a **linear relationship** always has a straight line.

2 A **conversion graph** is used to convert a measurement into different units.

3 **Distance–time graphs** are used to relate the distance travelled to the time taken, and to calculate speeds.

4 The **equation of a line** uses algebra to show a relationship between the x- and y-coordinates of points on the line.

5 The number line is **1-dimensional** or **1-D**. You can describe position on the number line using one number or coordinate, for example (2).

6 Flat shapes are **2-dimensional** or **2-D**. You can describe position on a flat shape using two numbers or coordinates, for example (2, 1).

7 Solid shapes are **3-dimensional** or **3-D**. You can describe position in a solid shape using three numbers or coordinates, for example (4, 1, 2).

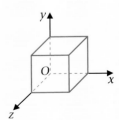

17 Ratio and proportion

17.1 What is a ratio?

A **ratio** is a way of comparing two numbers or quantities.

Ratios can be used to compare costs, weights and sizes ...

On the deck there are 2 women and 1 man.
So $\frac{2}{3}$ of the people on deck are women and $\frac{1}{3}$ of the people are men.
You can also say that:

> the ratio of men to women is 1 to 2. This is written as $1:2$
> the ratio of women to men is 2 to 1, written $2:1$

Sharing in the ratio $2:1$ is the same as dividing into thirds:

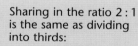

On the deck there are also 5 cars and 2 bicycles. So you can say that:

> the ratio of cars to bicycles is 5 to 2, or $5:2$
> the ratio of bicycles to cars is 2 to 5, or $2:5$

Ratios are used to work out the exact quantities needed in mixtures. Pharmacists making up medicines, manufacturers making biscuits, cooks baking cakes and builders mixing concrete all need to be able to make exact mixtures.

Example 1

Frank is making fruit smoothies for 5 of his friends.
How much of each ingredient does he need?

> oranges $4 \times 5 = 20$ oranges
> apples $2 \times 5 = 10$ apples

I use 4 oranges and 2 apples to make a smoothie for one person.

In Example 1 the ratio of oranges to apples is $4:2$.

Example 2

To make a mixer full of concrete you need 15 shovels of sand, 9 shovels of gravel and 6 shovels of cement. Vijay needs 4 mixers full of concrete.

(a) How much sand, gravel and cement will he need?

(b) Write the ratio of sand to gravel to cement.

15 shovels of sand
9 shovels of gravel and
6 shovels of cement

(a) sand $15 \times 4 = 60$ shovels
    gravel $9 \times 4 = 36$ shovels
    cement $6 \times 4 = 24$ shovels

(b) The ratio of sand to gravel to cement is $15:9:6$

Example 3

For the tile pattern below find

(a) the fraction of the pattern that is blue

(a) the ratio of white tiles to blue tiles.

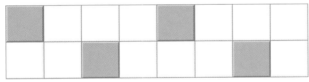

(a) $\frac{4}{16}$ or $\frac{1}{4}$ is blue

(b) white : blue

    $12:4$ which can be simplified to

    $3:1$

Divide both sides of the ratio by 3.

Exercise 17A

1 Here are some tile patterns. For each one write down
   (i) the fraction of the pattern that is red
   (ii) the ratio of red tiles to blue tiles in the pattern.

(a)

(b)

(c)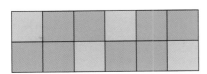

(d)

2 A recipe for 6 rock cakes needs 40 g of margarine and 100 g of flour. How much margarine and flour are needed to make
(a) 12 rock cakes (b) 18 rock cakes (c) 30 rock cakes
(d) 3 rock cakes (e) 15 rock cakes?

3 A recipe for a rice cake weighing 1200 g is:

 200 g of butter 400 g of ground rice
 400 g of sugar 4 eggs (eggs weigh 50 g each)

How much of each ingredient would you use to make a rice cake weighing
(a) 2400 g (b) 600 g (c) 1800 g (d) 3000 g?

4 42 strawberries, 6 bananas and 12 apples are used to make 6 glasses of fruit smoothie. How much of each ingredient is needed to make
(a) 3 glasses (b) 4 glasses (c) 1 glass?

5 A builder prepares 120 kg of mortar by mixing 20 kg of cement with 10 kg of lime and 90 kg of sand. How much cement, lime and sand does he use to prepare
(a) 60 kg of mortar (b) 180 kg of mortar
(c) 12 kg of mortar?

6 To make 25 kg of bronze you mix 6 kg of tin with 19 kg of copper.
How much tin and copper do you need to make
(a) 50 kg of bronze (b) 250 kg of bronze
(c) 100 kg of bronze?

7 Brass is an alloy (mixture) of zinc and copper in the ratio 3 : 17
How much copper would you expect to be in a brass cross which contains 120 g of zinc?

17.2 Simplifying ratios

You need to be able to solve problems using ratios. It is often easier if you simplify the ratios first.

These ratios below are **equivalent** – the relationship between each pair of numbers is the same:

 10 : 20
 3 : 6
 2 : 4
 1 : 2 This ratio is the **simplest form** of the ratio 10 : 20

To **simplify** a ratio you divide both its numbers by a common factor.

Example 4

Simplify the ratio $30 : 100$

10 is a common factor of 30 and 100. Dividing both numbers by 10 gives:

$$\div 10 \Big(\overset{30 : 100}{\underset{3 : 10}{}} \Big) \div 10$$

When a ratio cannot be simplified it is said to be in its **lowest terms**. Ratios are usually written in their lowest terms.

Example 5

Write 40p to £1 as a ratio.

First, you make the units the same so you are comparing pennies with pennies: 40p to 100p

The ratio is:

$40 : 100$

$4 : 10$ ——— Divide by 10.

$2 : 5$ ——— Divide by 2.

The ratio of 40p to £1 is $2 : 5$ in its lowest terms.

> Always write the ratio in its lowest terms.

Exercise 17B

1 Write these ratios in their lowest terms.
   (a) $2 : 4$ (b) $3 : 9$ (c) $3 : 18$ (d) $6 : 24$
   (e) $8 : 24$ (f) $16 : 24$ (g) $10 : 2$ (h) $28 : 4$
   (i) $32 : 48$ (j) $15 : 9$

2 Write these ratios in their lowest terms.
   (a) $20 \text{ cm} : 100 \text{ cm}$ (b) $20 \text{ cm} : 1 \text{ m}$
   (c) $25\text{p} : £2$ (d) $£3 : 60\text{p}$

> Remember that the units must be the same before you write a ratio without units.

3 Write these ratios in their simplest form.
   (a) $2 \text{ cm} : 1 \text{ m}$ (b) $350 \text{ mg} : 1 \text{ g}$
   (c) $10 \text{ m}l : 2\,l$ (d) $64 \text{ g} : 4 \text{ kg}$
   (e) $£3 : 40\text{p} : £1.20$ (f) $150 \text{ mm} : 40 \text{ cm}$
   (g) $340 \text{ m} : 1.2 \text{ km}$ (h) $40 \text{ min} : 2 \text{ h} : \frac{1}{2} \text{ h}$
   (i) $45 \text{ g} : 1 \text{ kg}$ (j) $42\text{p} : £1.05$
   (k) $45 \text{ cm} : 0.1 \text{ m}$ (l) $2.4 \text{ tonnes} : 132 \text{ kg}$

4 Write the ratios of these comparisons in their lowest terms.

    (a) A small loaf cost 49p and a large loaf cost 63p.

    (b) Jeanette weighs 40 kg and Pauline weighs 44 kg.

    (c) Spey School has 660 boys and Tree School has 750 boys.

    (d) Mr Johnson takes 1 hour to get to work by train but 2 hours by car.

    (e) A salesman made 27 successful calls and 21 unsuccessful calls.

    (f) A factory employs 66 craft workers, 18 clerical staff and 12 sales staff.

5 Abi buys a bracelet for £120, whilst Hayley buys some beads for 72p.

    Write these prices as a ratio in its lowest terms.

17.3 Equivalent ratios

In Section 17.2 you learned how to simplify a ratio. Sometimes it is useful to find other equivalent ratios.

For example, if the ratio of teachers to students is $1:30$ (or one per class of 30) then three classes will need a ratio of $3:90$ since $1:30$ and $3:90$ are **equivalent ratios**.

> Two ratios are **equivalent** when one simplifies to the other.

Example 6

A hotel used to employ 2 cooks and 7 waiters.

The hotel then expanded and the number of cooks was increased to 10.

If the number of waiters is kept in proportion to the number of cooks, how many waiters should there be?

                       cooks : waiters

ratio before increase: 2 : 7

ratio after increase: 10 : ?

You need to find the number that makes these ratios **equivalent**.

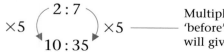

$\times 5 \overset{\curvearrowright}{\underset{\curvearrowright}{\begin{matrix} 2:7 \\ 10:35 \end{matrix}}} \times 5$ Multiplying both numbers in the 'before' ratio by the same number will give an equivalent ratio. Try 5.

$2:7$ and $10:35$ are equivalent ratios.

The number of waiters after the increase is 35.

Exercise 17C

1   Calculate the missing numbers in these ratios:
    (a) $3:5 = 12:?$ (b) $4:7 = 16:?$
    (c) $6:5 = 3:?$ (d) $4:5 = ?:35$
    (e) $8:3 = ?:15$ (f) $7:? = 49:63$

2   The numbers of mugs made in a pottery in the morning
    and in the afternoon are in the ratio $4:9$. They are
    always completed in this ratio.
    (a) How many mugs are made in the afternoon when 60
         are made in the morning?
    (b) How many are made in the morning when 189 are
         made in the afternoon?

3   The ratio of students going home for lunch to students
    staying at school for lunch is $3:5$. When 273 students go
    home for lunch how many stay at school?

4   The ratio of the length of a room to its width is $5:4$.
    The length of the room is 6 metres. What is the width?

5   An alloy contains iron and tungsten in the ratio $5:1$.
    If there is 15 kg of iron in a quantity of the alloy, how
    much tungsten is there?

6   A mortar mix is made by adding sand and cement in the
    ratio $4:1$. Five buckets of cement are used.
    How much sand is needed?

7   The ratio of males to female in the crowd at a rock
    concert is $5:4$. There are 120 males in the crowd.
    How many females are there?

8   The ratio of the lengths of two rectangles is $5:6$.
    The length of the first rectangle is 12.5 cm.
    What is the length of the second rectangle?

17.4 Writing ratios in unitary form

Ratios can be written in the form $1:n$ or $n:1$.
The number n is written as a decimal (unless it is a whole
number). When one of the numbers in a ratio is 1, the ratio is
in **unitary form**.

Example 7

(a) Write these ratios in the form $1 : n$.
   (i) $8 : 10$ (ii) $5\,cm : 1\,km$ (iii) $20 : 1$
(b) Write these ratios in the form $n : 1$.
   (i) $21 : 5$ (ii) $1\,kg : 4\,g$

(a) (i) $8 : 10$
            $1 : \frac{10}{8}$ —————— Divide both numbers by 8.
            $1 : 1.25$

   (ii) $5\,cm : 1\,km$
            $5 : 100\,000$ —— Write both numbers in cm.
            $1 : 20\,000$ —— Divide by 5.

   (iii) $20 : 1$
            $1 : \frac{1}{20}$ —————— Divide by 20.
            $1 : 0.05$

(b) (i) $21 : 5$
            $4.2 : 1$ —————— Divide by 5.

   (ii) $1\,kg : 4\,g$
            $1000\,g : 4\,g$ ——————— Write both quantities in g.
            $250 : 1$ ——————— Divide by 4.

> $10 \div 8 = \frac{10}{8}$

Exercise 17D

1 Write these ratios in the form $1 : n$.

(a) $2 : 5$ (b) $32\,g : 8\,g$
(c) $10\,cm : 10\,m$ (d) $4 : 10$
(e) $32p : £2$ (f) $2 : 15$
(g) $5 : 11$ (h) $25\,g : 1\,kg$

2 Write these ratios in the form $n : 1$.

(a) $6 : 8$ (b) $1\,km : 2\,cm$
(c) $3\,h : \frac{1}{2}h$ (d) $£3 : 40p$
(e) $5\,l : 10\,ml$ (f) $2\,m : 2\,mm$
(g) $1000 : 30$ (h) $5p : 25p$

17.5 Dividing quantities in a given ratio

Ratios can be used to share or divide quantities.

Example 8

Patrick and Colleen share £35 in the ratio $3 : 4$
How much does each person get?

The total number of shares is $3 + 4 = 7$

Each share is worth $\dfrac{£35}{7} = £5$

$$3 : 4$$

Patrick gets $\quad 3 \times £5 = £15$

Colleen gets $\; 4 \times £5 = £20$

£15 $\qquad\qquad$ £20

> You could also write that Patrick gets $\frac{3}{7}$ of the total amount of money: $\frac{3}{7} \times £35 = £15$

Exercise 17E

1 £360 is divided between Sally and Nadir in the ratio $5:4$. How much should each person receive?

2 Nick, Mark and Gavin share £480 in the ratio $4:5:3$. How much should each person receive?

3 Share 40 sweets in the ratio $2:5:1$.

4 Henry, Sue and Rebecca agree to look after the cake stall in the ratio $2:4:3$. Rebecca looked after it for 1 hour. How long did
(a) Henry $\qquad$ (b) Sue
spend looking after the stall?

5 Copy and complete this table. The first one is done for you.

Quantity	Divided in the ratio		
	4 :	3 :	2
£27	£12	£9	£6
9 lb			
36 km			
63 miles			
81 tonnes			
£144			

In questions **6**, **7** and **8** divide the quantities in the ratios given.

6 (a) £14.91 in the ratio $2:5$ (b) £45 in the ratio $4:5$
(c) £51.92 in the ratio $2:9$ (d) £170.52 in the ratio $1:4:7$

7 (a) 600 g in the ratio $3:2$ (b) 32 cm in the ratio $3:5$
(c) 23.4 l in the ratio $1:5$ (d) 34.65 m in the ratio $2:4:5$

8 **(a)** 30.78 m in the ratio 4 : 5
   (b) 75 cm in the ratio 3 : 2
   (c) 48 kg in the ratio 3 : 5
   (d) £357 in the ratio 1 : 2 : 4

9 The ratio of girls to boys in a class is 4 : 3.
   There are 28 students in the class.
   How many are **(a)** girls **(b)** boys?

10 The angles of a triangle are in the ratio 6 : 5 : 7.

   Find the sizes of the three angles.

> Remember:
> the angles of a triangle
> add up to 180°.

11 Shortcrust pastry is made from flour and fat in the ratio 2 : 1.
   How much flour do you need to make 600 g of pastry?

12 A business makes a profit of £660. The directors divide it
   in the ratio 3 : 4 : 8.
   How much do they each receive?

13 An alloy is made from iron, copper, nickel and
   phosphorus in the ratio 6 : 4 : 3 : 1.
   Find the weight of **(a)** copper **(b)** nickel
   in 714 g of the alloy.

14

   Mortar is made by mixing 5 parts by weight of sand
   with 1 part by weight of cement. How much sand is
   needed to make 8400 kg of mortar?   [E]

17.6 Solving ratio and proportion problems by the unitary method

A useful way of solving ratio problems is to first find the value
of one unit of the quantity. This is called the **unitary method**.

Example 9

If 6 similar CDs cost £30, how much will 8 CDs cost?

   6 CDs cost £30

   1 CD costs $\dfrac{£30}{6}$ ———— **Find the cost of one CD.** It costs less.

   8 CDs cost $\dfrac{£30}{6} \times 8 = £40$ ———— Eight CDs cost 8 × the cost of one CD.

Example 10

If 6 men can build a shed in 3 days, how long will it take
4 men working at the same rate?

6 men take   3 days

1 man takes 3×6 days

4 men take $\dfrac{3 \times 6}{4} = 4\frac{1}{2}$

**Find how long it would
take one man.**
It takes longer.

Four men take $\frac{1}{4}$ the time
taken by one man.

$\dfrac{3 \times 6}{4}$ is the same as
$3 \times 6 \times \frac{1}{4}$

Example 11

Zoe paid £3.20 for 8 mince pies. How much would
12 mince pies cost?

8 mince pies cost   320 pence

1 mince pie costs $\dfrac{320}{8}$

**Find how much one
mince pie costs.**

12 mince pies cost $\dfrac{320}{8} \times 12$

12 pies cost $12 \times$ the
cost of one mince pie.

12 mince pies cost 480 pence or £4.80

Exercise 17F

1 Ten leisure centre tickets cost £48.
   What would 25 tickets cost?

2 Twenty daffodil bulbs cost £2.50.
   What would 36 bulbs cost?

3 Paul paid £7.20 for 24 Christmas cards.
   How much would he have to pay for 36 similar cards?

4 Camilla paid £40 for 15 CDs.
   How much would she have to pay for 24 similar CDs?

5 Vijay buys 18 postcards for £2.16.
   How much would he pay if he buys 27?

6 Bronwen bought 15 roses for £9.
   How many roses could she have bought for £12.60?

7 A train travels at 80 miles per hour.
   How long will it take to travel
   (a) 140 miles   (b) 440 miles   (c) 640 miles?

8 A cyclist travels at an average speed of 16 km per hour.
At the same rate
  (a) how far would she travel in 4 hours
  (b) how long would it take her to cycle 100 km?

9 A wall took 6 hours for 4 men to build. At the same rate
  (a) how long would it have taken 10 men
  (b) how many men would have been needed to build it
     in 12 hours?

10 Eight men can build a chalet in 18 days. Working at the
same rate how long would it take
  (a) 12 men   (b) 5 men?
  (c) How many men would be needed to build it in 3 days?

17.7 Direct proportion

Two quantities are in **direct proportion** if their ratio stays the
same as the quantities increase or decrease.

Example 12

A car uses 8 litres of petrol to travel 124 km. If the amount
of petrol used is in direct proportion to the distance
travelled, how far can the car travel on 1 litre?

8 litres is used for 124 km, a ratio of 8 : 124.

Dividing both numbers by 8 gives

$$1 : \frac{124}{8}$$

So on 1 litre the car can travel $\frac{124}{8} = 15.5$ km.

Example 13

Method 1
Seven pencils cost 63p. The cost is directly proportional to
the number of pencils. How much will 12 pencils cost?

First find out what one pencil costs:

  7 pencils cost 63p

So   1 pencil costs $\frac{63p}{7} = 9p$

12 pencils cost 9p × 12 = £1.08

You used this method to
solve problems in Section
17.6

Method 2

The ratio of the number of pencils to the cost is $7 : 63$.

If the cost of 12 pencils is x, the ratio of the number of pencils to the cost is $12 : x$.

To get from 7 to 12 you multiply 7 by $\frac{12}{7}$:

To get from the cost of 7 pencils to the cost x of 12 pencils you multiply 63p by $\frac{12}{7}$.

$$\frac{12}{7} \diagdown \begin{array}{c} 7 \;\; : 63 \\ 12 \;\; : \;\; x \end{array} \diagup \frac{12}{7}$$

So the cost of 12 pencils $x = 63 \times \frac{12}{7}$ pence
$$= 108 \text{ pence} = £1.08$$

> You saw this method in Section 17.3

Worked examination question

Here is a list of ingredients for making some Greek food. These amounts make enough for six people:

> 2 cloves of garlic
> 4 ounces of chick peas
> 4 tablespoons of olive oil
> 5 fluid ounces of Tahina paste

Change the amounts so that there will be enough for nine people.   [E]

Nine people is one and a half times as much as six (six has been multiplied by 1.5 to give nine).

> The 2 cloves of garlic become 3.
> The 4 ounces of chick peas become 6.
> The 4 tablespoons of olive oil become 6.
> The 5 fluid ounces of Tahina paste become $7\frac{1}{2}$.

> Using the unitary method
> $9 : 6$
> $1.5 : 1$

> $2 : 4 : 4 : 5$
> is equivalent to
> $3 : 6 : 6 : 7\frac{1}{2}$

Exercise 17G

1 Dress material costs £23.40 for 4 metres.
   How much does 1 metre cost?

2 $14 \, \text{cm}^3$ of copper weighs 126 g.
   What is the weight of $1 \, \text{cm}^3$?

3 Betty is paid £38.50 for seven hours' work at a nursing home.
   How much should she receive for five hours' work?

4 Six stamps cost £2.52.
   How much will ten stamps cost?

5 A machine makes 490 engine parts in 35 minutes.
How many engine parts will the machine make in one hour?

6 Four packets of tea cost £1.28.
How much will three packets cost?

7 Six tickets to the theatre cost £19.80.
How much would eight tickets cost?

8 Seven tubes of toothpaste have a total weight of 854 g.
Work out the weight of eight tubes of toothpaste.

9 Anisha buys 12 bananas for £1.80.
How much would 15 bananas cost?

10 Five bottles of detergent have a capacity of 1560 cm³.
Work out the total capacity of nine similar bottles.

11 The recipe for eight small cakes includes the following:
 480 g flour, 720 g fat, 2 eggs.
Change the amounts so there will be enough to make
12 small cakes.

12 A telegraph pole 60 feet high casts a shadow 12 feet long.
At the same time of day, how long is a shadow cast by
(a) a 90 foot pole **(b)** a 40 foot pole **(c)** a 25 foot pole?

13 A machine can produce 1120 plastic mugs in 8 hours.
At that rate
(a) how many plastic mugs will it produce in 10 hours
(b) how long will it take to produce 840 plastic mugs?

14 A car travels 126 miles on 18 litres of petrol.
(a) How far will it travel on 40 litres?
(b) How many litres will be needed to travel 540 miles?

15 Mario is paid £31.50 for working 6 hours in the
supermarket. At that rate
(a) how much will he be paid for working 8 hours
(b) how long would it take him to earn £63?

17.8 Scales in maps and diagrams

Ratios called **scales** are used to show the relationship between
distances on a map and distances on the ground.

A common scale is 1 : 50 000; this means that 1 cm on the map
represents 50 000 cm on the ground.
$$50\,000\text{ cm} = 500\text{ m} = 0.5\text{ km}$$
So 1 cm on the map represents 0.5 km on the ground.

Remember:
10 mm = 1 cm
100 cm = 1 m
1000 m = 1 km

Example 14

Two towns are 5.2 cm apart on a map whose scale is
1 : 50 000. How far apart are the towns in real life?

    1 cm   represents 0.5 km
   5.2 cm represents $0.5 \text{ km} \times 5.2 = 2.6 \text{ km}$

The towns are 2.6 kilometres apart.

> To convert from cm
> to m, divide by 100:
> 260 000 cm ÷ 100
> = 2600 m
>
> To convert from m to km,
> divide by 1000:
> 2600 m ÷ 1000 = 2.6 km

Exercise 17H

1 A map has a scale of 1 : 50 000. What is the distance on
the ground if the distance on the map is
  (a) 2.5 cm   **(b)** 3.6 cm
  (c) 5.2 cm   **(d)** 6.2 cm?

2 What is the distance on the map from question **1** if the
distance on the ground is
  (a) 6 km   **(b)** 5.2 km
  (c) 8.4 km   **(d)** 25.6 km?

3 A town map has a scale of 1 : 6000.
  (a) The town hall is 1500 metres from the station.
       How far is this on the map?
  (b) On the map the hotel is 4.6 cm from the harbour.
       How far is this on the ground?
  (c) Adrian plans a walk round the town. He measures it
       on the map to be 36.5 cm.
       How far is he planning to walk?

4 A model radio-controlled aircraft is built to scale,
using 1 cm to represent 1.4 metres.
  (a) Write this scale as a ratio.
  (b) What is the length of the model if the length
       of the real aircraft is 42 metres?

5 A model of a van is made to a scale of 1 : 20.
The height of the model is 10 cm.
Work out the height, in metres, of the full-size van.

6 A map is drawn on a scale of 3 cm to 1 km.
  (a) Work out the real length of a lake which is 4.2 cm
       long on the map.
  (b) The distance between the church in Canwick and
       the town hall in Barnton is 5.8 km. Work out the
       distance between them on the map.

> 'A scale of 3 cm to 1 km'
> This means that a real
> length of 1 km is
> represented on the map
> by a length of 3 cm.

Mixed exercise 17

1 Robert used these ingredients to make 24 buns:

   100 g of sugar   90 g of flour
   80 g of butter   30 ml of milk
   2 eggs

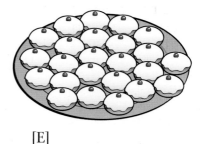

   Robert wants to make 36 similar buns.

   Write down how much of each ingredient he
   needs for 36 buns.   [E]

2 Jack shares £180 between his two children Ruth and Ben.
   The ratio of Ruth's share to Ben's share is 5 : 4.
   Work out how much each child is given.   [E]

3 7200 people took part in a survey, with a ratio of 5 : 4
   people preferring the taste of Ice Cool's new lemonade
   drink to the old drink. How many people liked each drink?

4 Anna, Beth and Cheryl share the total cost of a holiday
   in the ratio 6 : 5 : 4. Anna pays £294.
   (a) Work out the total cost of the holiday.
   (b) Work out how much Cheryl pays.   [E]

5 Kelly bought 4 identical computer disks for £3.60.
   Work out the cost of 9 of these computer disks.

6 A city map has a scale of 1 : 14 000.
   (a) Cornhill Street is 18 mm long on the map.
        Work out the real distance in metres.
   (b) Commercial Street is 840 metres long.
        What is the length of the street on the map, in
        millimetres?

7 In Year 11 at Tree Valley High School there were 108 boys
   and 132 girls. Write this as a ratio in its simplest form.

8 The ratio of hurdlers to long jumpers at the local athletics
   club is 3 : 5. If there are 15 hurdlers, how many long
   jumpers are there?

9 Seven tickets to the cricket match cost £86.10. If the cost
   of tickets is directly proportional to the number of
   tickets, how much will three tickets cost?

10 A map is drawn on a scale of 2 cm to 1 km.
   (a) Work out the real length of a bridge which is 1.5 cm
        long on the map.
   (b) The distance between Clifton and Hitchin is 6.5 km.
        Work out the distance between them on the map.

11 Bill gave his three daughters a total of £32.40.
The money was shared in the ratio $4:3:2$.
Jane had the largest share.
Work out how much money Bill gave to Jane.   [E]

Summary of key points

1 A **ratio** is a way of comparing two numbers or quantities. For example $3:2$.

2 To **simplify** a ratio you divide both its numbers by a common factor.
For example:

$$\div 2 \overset{\curvearrowright}{\left(\begin{array}{c} 2:6 \\ 1:3 \end{array} \right)} \div 2 \qquad \text{Divide by the common factor 2.}$$

$2:6$ simplifies to $1:3$

3 When a ratio cannot be simplified it is said to be in its **lowest terms**. Ratios are usually written in their lowest terms.

4 Two ratios are **equivalent** when one simplifies to the other.

5 Ratios can be written in the form $1:n$ or $n:1$. The number n is written as a decimal (unless it is a whole number).
When one of the numbers in a ratio is 1, the ratio is in **unitary form**. For example, $2:3$ can be written as $1:1.5$ in unitary form.

6 Ratios can be used to share or divide quantities.

7 A useful way of solving ratio and proportion problems is to first find the value of one unit of the quantity. This is called the **unitary method**. For example, to find the cost of 12 pies when you know the cost of 8 pies:

8 pies cost	320 pence
1 pie costs	$\dfrac{320}{8}$ — Find the cost of one pie.
So 12 pies cost	$\dfrac{320}{8} \times 12$ — $12 \times$ the cost of one pie

8 Two quantities are in **direct proportion** if their ratio stays the same as the quantities increase or decrease.

9 Ratios called **scales** are used to show the relationship between distances on a map and distances on the ground.
On a $1:50\,000$ scale map, 1 cm represents $50\,000$ cm (or 0.5 km) on the ground.

18 Symmetry

18.1 Reflective symmetry in 2-D shapes

The two-dimensional (2-D) picture of a butterfly on the right is **symmetrical**. If you could fold it in half along the dotted line each half would fit exactly on top of the other.

The dotted line is called a **line of symmetry**. One half of the shape is a mirror image of the other half.

Some shapes have more than one line of symmetry. The flags below have more than one line of symmetry.

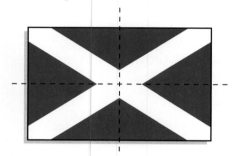

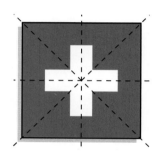

A good way to find the lines of symmetry of a shape is to draw it on tracing paper. Then you can actually fold the shape and check that each half fits exactly on top of the other. Another method is to use a mirror.

> A 2-D shape has a **line of symmetry** if the line divides the shape into two halves and one half is the mirror image of the other half.

> A line of symmetry is sometimes called a **mirror line**.

___ **Example 1** ___

Half of a symmetrical shape is shown here. The dotted line is a line of symmetry. Copy and complete the shape.

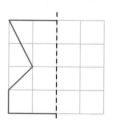

Method 1

Mark the mirror images of the points (or vertices) in first...

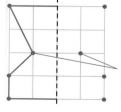

Each point has a mirror image the same distance away from the line of symmetry, but on the other side.

... then join the dots.

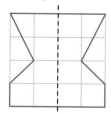

Method 2

You could copy the shape onto tracing paper, flip it over and use the reflected image to draw the reflected shape.

Copy...   ... then draw

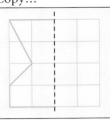 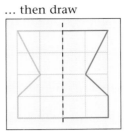

Exercise 18A

1 This question is about the following tiles.

A   B    C    D

E   F   G   H

Which shape(s) have

(a) only one line of symmetry

(b) no lines of symmetry

(c) exactly three lines of symmetry

(d) exactly four lines of symmetry

(e) exactly two lines of symmetry?

2 Copy these shapes and draw all the lines of symmetry on each.

(a) 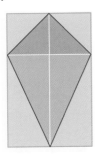   (b)   (c)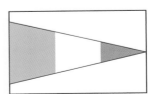

3 In each of these shapes the dotted line is a line of symmetry. Copy and complete each shape.

> In questions 3 and 4 you need a larger grid than is shown.

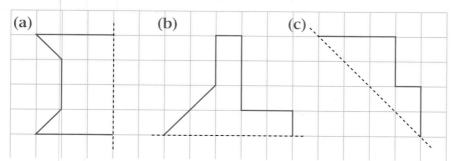

(a) (b) (c)

4 Use the two lines of symmetry to copy and complete each of these shapes.

> Hint:
> Use just one line of symmetry at a time.

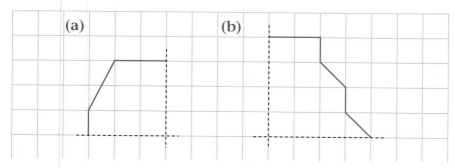

(a) (b)

5 Write out the capital letters of the alphabet which have
  (a) one line of symmetry
  (b) more than one line of symmetry
  (c) no lines of symmetry.

18.2 Reflective symmetry in pictures and patterns

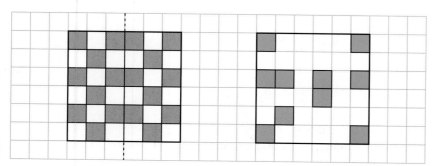

This pattern is **symmetrical**. It can be divided into two halves that are mirror images of each other.

This pattern is **asymmetrical** (not symmetrical). One half is **not** a mirror image of the other.

Exercise 18B

You may want to use a mirror or tracing paper in this exercise.

1   Look at these patterns.

A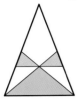

B

C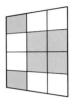

D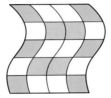

E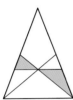

F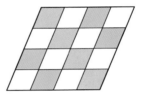

(a)   Which patterns have only one line of symmetry?

(b)   Which of these patterns are asymmetrical?

(c)   Which of these patterns have two lines of symmetry?

> **Remember:**
> Asymmetrical shapes have no lines of symmetry.

2   Copy these patterns. Draw in all the lines of symmetry on each one.

(a)

(b)

(c)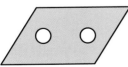

(d)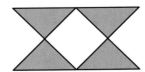

(e)

(f)

3 In how many different ways can you arrange six squares (which must touch) to form a symmetrical pattern?

Draw your patterns. Two are done for you.

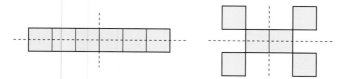

18.3 Rotational symmetry

When a square is rotated or turned through 360° it looks exactly as it did at the start on four different occasions during the rotation.

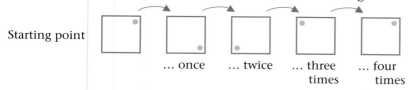

Starting point ... once ... twice ... three times ... four times

A 2-D shape with **rotational symmetry** repeats the appearance of its starting position two or more times during a full turn.

The **order** of rotational symmetry is the number of times the original appearance is repeated in a full turn.

A square has order of rotational symmetry 4 as it looks the same four times during one complete turn.

Looking for rotational symmetry

Sometimes rotational symmetry can be hard to spot, so you may want to try one of the following ideas.

Either actually turn the book or paper the shape is drawn on, **or** trace the shape onto tracing paper and turn it on top of the shape in the book. Then you will be able to see when the shapes match.

This image of a zebra does not have rotational symmetry.

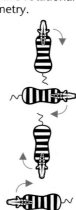

Example 2

Does a kite have rotational symmetry?

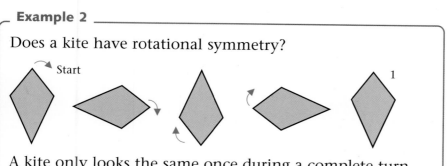

A kite only looks the same once during a complete turn, so it does not have rotational symmetry.

Example 3

Write down the order of rotational symmetry of this flag:

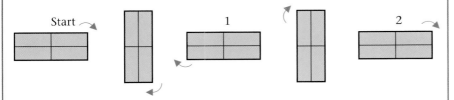

As the flag is turned through 360° it looks the same twice.
The order of rotational symmetry is 2.

Exercise 18C

You may want to use tracing paper in this exercise.

1 Write down whether or not each of these shapes has
rotational symmetry.

(a)    (b) 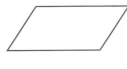   (c)

(d)    (e)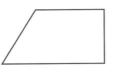

2 State the order of rotational symmetry of each of these
shapes.

(a)   (b) 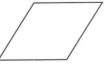   (c)

(d)   (e)

18.4 The symmetry of regular polygons

A regular hexagon has
  6 sides
  6 lines of symmetry
  order of rotational symmetry 6.

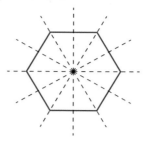

Regular polygons have the same number of lines of symmetry as they have sides.

The order of rotational symmetry of a regular polygon is the same as the number of sides.

Exercise 18D

For each of these regular polygons, find:
(a) the number of lines of symmetry
(b) the order of rotational symmetry.

1 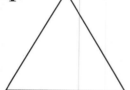   2    3    4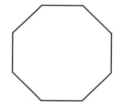

Mixed exercise 18

1 How many lines of symmetry does a kite have?

2 Draw a rectangle showing all the lines of symmetry.

3 Which regular polygon has five lines of symmetry?

4 Sketch a regular octagon showing its lines of symmetry.

5 What is the order of rotational symmetry of a regular octagon?

6 Which special triangle has rotational symmetry of order 3?

7 Copy or trace the shapes below. Draw all the lines of symmetry and write down the order of rotational symmetry for each shape.

(a)

(b)

(c)

(d)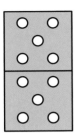

(e)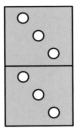

8 Copy and complete the shapes below using the lines of symmetry given.

> In questions 8 and 9 you need a larger grid than is shown.

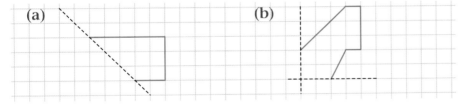

(a)

(b)

9 Using the lines of symmetry shown, copy and complete the missing parts of the patterns.

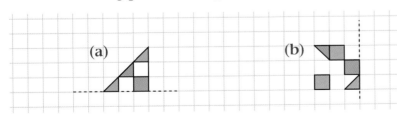

(a)

(b)

10 On a copy of each of these shapes, draw all of its lines of symmetry, if it has any.

(a)

(b)

(c)

[E]

11 These shapes each have at least one line of symmetry.

- (a) Copy these shapes and show all the lines of symmetry.
- (b) Explain how you could check whether or not a line of symmetry was correct.

12 *ABCDE* is a regular pentagon. *O* is the centre of the pentagon.

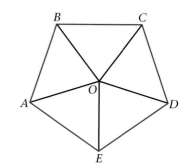

- (a) Write down the order of rotational symmetry of the regular pentagon.
- (b) Write down the number of lines of symmetry of triangle *OCD*.

13 Which of the designs below have line symmetry?

A

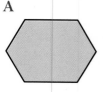

Floor tile

B

Asian carpet design

C

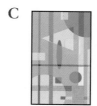

Contemporary art

D

Wallpaper pattern

E

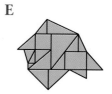

Tile design

Summary of key points

1 A 2-D shape has a **line of symmetry** if the line divides the shape into two halves and one half is the mirror image of the other half.

2 A line of symmetry is sometimes called a **mirror line**.

3 A 2-D shape with **rotational symmetry** repeats the appearance of its starting position two or more times in a full turn.

4 The **order** of rotational symmetry is the number of times the original appearance is repeated in a full turn.

5 Regular polygons have the same number of lines of symmetry as they have sides.

6 The order of rotational symmetry of a regular polygon is the same as the number of sides.

19 Simple perimeter, area and volume

19.1 Perimeter

The **perimeter** of a 2-D shape is the distance around the edge of the shape.

Example 1

Find the perimeter of this rectangle.

The rectangle has two sides of length 5 cm and two sides of length 3 cm. The perimeter is

$$5 + 3 + 5 + 3 = 16 \text{ cm}$$

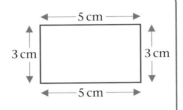

Exercise 19A

1 Work out the perimeters of these shapes:

(a)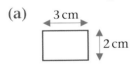

(b)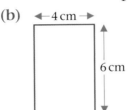

(c)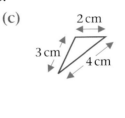

(d)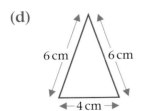

(e)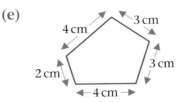

2 Work out the perimeters of these shapes:
(a) a square with side 5 cm
(b) a rectangle with sides 4 cm and 2 cm
(c) an equilateral triangle with all sides 6 cm
(d) an isosceles triangle with two sides of 5 cm and one of 6 cm.

Perimeter of composite shapes

Example 2

Find the perimeter of this shape.

The shape is made up from a rectangle and a triangle. The rectangle is 9 cm by 6 cm and the triangle has sides 8 cm, 6 cm and 10 cm.

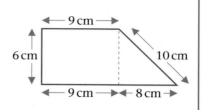

The perimeter is

$$6 + 9 + 10 + 8 + 9 = 42\,\text{cm}$$

Remember that the perimeter is the distance around the outside edge of the shape. It does not include any lines inside the shape.

Exercise 19B

Find the perimeters of these shapes.

1

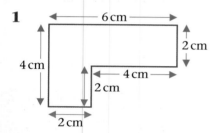

2

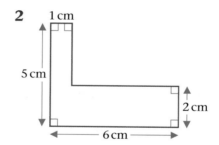

3

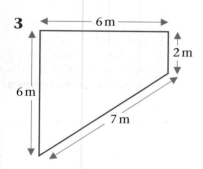

4

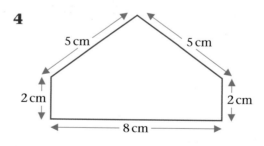

5

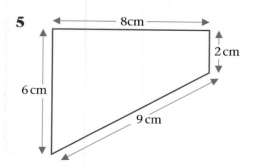

6

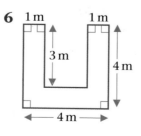

Measure these shapes and then find their perimeters.

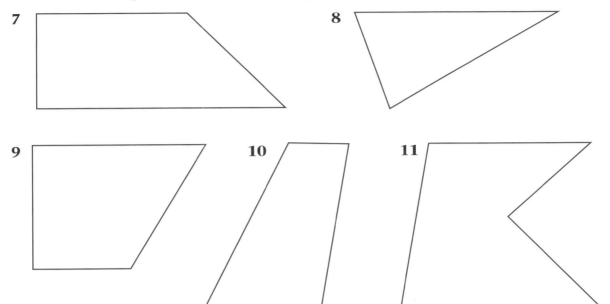

19.2 Area

The **area** of a 2-D shape is a measure of the amount of space it covers. Typical units of area are square centimetres (cm²), square metres (m²) and square kilometres (km²).

You can use a cm² grid to work out the area of a shape.

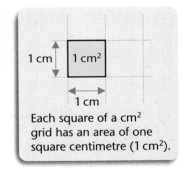

Each square of a cm² grid has an area of one square centimetre (1 cm²).

Example 3

Find the area of this rectangle.

This rectangle covers up 6 squares.

Each square is 1 cm by 1 cm and has an area of 1 square centimetre or 1 cm².

The rectangle has an area of 6 cm².

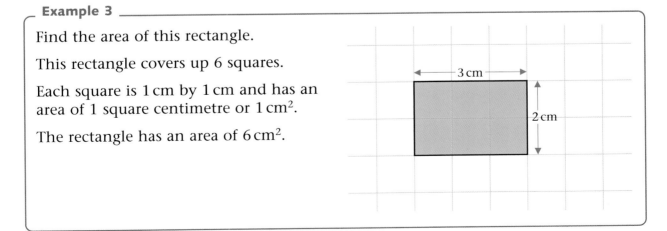

Exercise 19C

Find the areas of these shapes in cm² by counting squares.

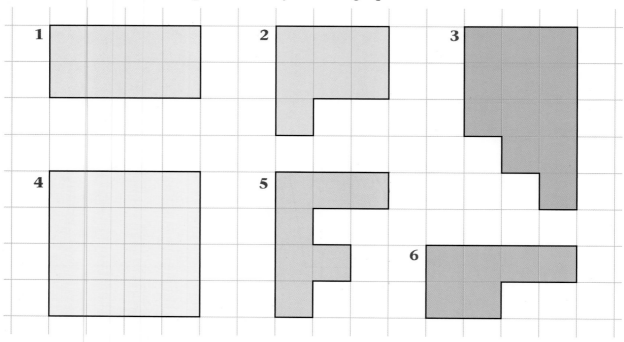

Estimating the areas of irregular shapes

You can use a cm² grid to help you estimate the area of an irregular shape.

Sometimes shapes do not fit exactly into whole squares. In these cases try and match up part squares to make whole ones.

Example 4

Estimate the area of this shape in cm² by counting squares.

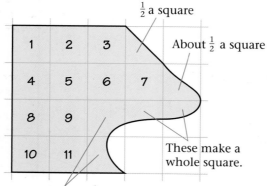

$\frac{1}{2}$ a square

About $\frac{1}{2}$ a square

These make a whole square.

These make about $1\frac{1}{2}$ squares.

This shape has a total area of about
$11 + 1\frac{1}{2} + 1 + \frac{1}{2} + \frac{1}{2} = 14\frac{1}{2}$ cm².

It is a good idea to number the squares as you count to make sure that you don't miss a square or part of a square.

Exercise 19D

Estimate the areas of these shapes in cm² by counting squares.

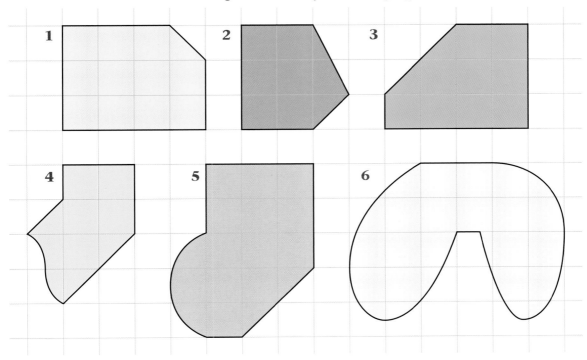

19.3 Volume

The **volume** of a 3-D shape is a measure of the amount of space it occupies. Typical units of volume are cubic centimetres (cm³) and cubic metres (m³).

In Section 19.2 you estimated an area using a grid of squares with area 1 cm². To estimate a volume you can use cubes of volume 1 cm³.

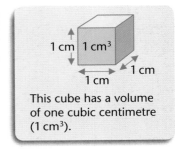

This cube has a volume of one cubic centimetre (1 cm³).

Example 5

This cuboid is made from cubes with sides all 1 cm long. Find the volume of the cuboid.

There are 8 (= 4 × 2) cubes in the top layer.
There are 3 layers of cubes so the total number of cubes is 8 × 3 = 24.

This can be worked out from 4 × 2 × 3 which is length × width × height for the cuboid.

The volume of the cuboid is 24 cm³.

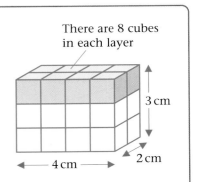

There are 8 cubes in each layer

3 cm

4 cm

2 cm

Exercise 19E

Find the volumes of these shapes in cm³ by counting cubes.

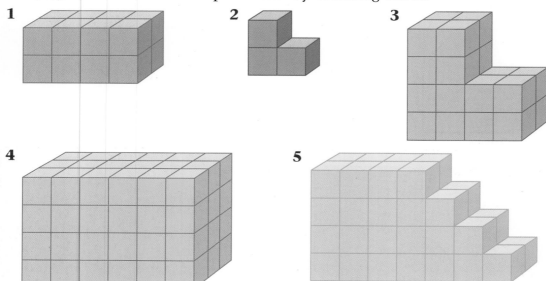

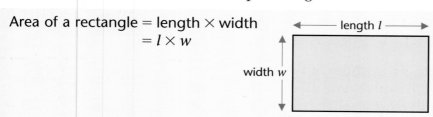

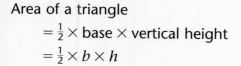
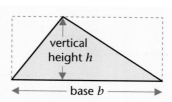

19.4 Finding areas using formulae

You can find the areas of some shapes using formulae:

> Area of a rectangle = length × width
> $= l \times w$

length l

width w

> A **formula** is a relationship between quantities, written using either letters or words. There is more about formulae in Chapter 21.

Since a square is a special type of rectangle then:

> Area of a square = length × length
> $= l \times l$
> $= l^2$

length l

length l

The area of a triangle is half the area of a rectangle that encloses it so:

> Area of a triangle
> $= \frac{1}{2} \times$ base × vertical height
> $= \frac{1}{2} \times b \times h$

vertical height h

base b

You can cut a corner off a rectangle and replace it on the other side to make a parallelogram so:

Area of a parallelogram = base × vertical height
= $b \times h$

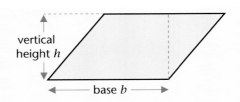

You will need to learn these formulae for your exam.

Example 6

Find the areas of these shapes.

(a)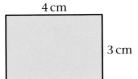

(b)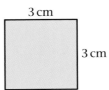

(c)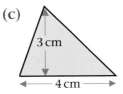

(a) Area of rectangle = $l \times w$
$= 4 \times 3 = 12\,\text{cm}^2$

(b) Area of square = $l \times l$
$= 3 \times 3 = 9\,\text{cm}^2$

(c) Area of triangle = $\frac{1}{2} \times b \times h$
$= \frac{1}{2} \times 4 \times 3$
$= \frac{1}{2} \times 12 = 6\,\text{cm}^2$

Exercise 19F

Find the areas of these shapes.

1 (a)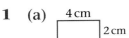

(b)

(c)

(d)

2 (a)

(b)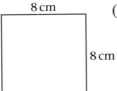

(c)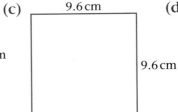

(d)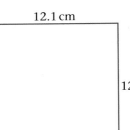

3 (a)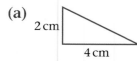

(b)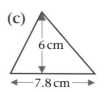

(c)

(d)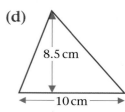

4 (a)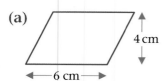

(b)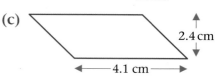

(c)

5 Copy this table and complete the columns.

	Shape	Length	Width	Area
(a)	Rectangle	5 cm	6 cm	
(b)	Rectangle	4 cm		20 cm²
(c)	Rectangle	2 cm		20 cm²
(d)	Rectangle		5 cm	40 cm²
(e)	Rectangle		12 cm	60 cm²

6 Copy this table and complete the columns.

	Shape	Base	Vertical height	Area
(a)	Triangle	10 cm	5 cm	
(b)	Triangle		12 cm	60 cm²
(c)	Triangle		5 cm	40 cm²
(d)	Triangle	4 cm		32 cm²
(e)	Triangle	16 cm		64 cm²

Area of a composite shape

You can find the area of a more complicated shape by splitting it up into simple shapes.

Example 7

Find the area of this shape.

Area of rectangle $= l \times w$
$= 8 \times 6$
$= 48 \text{ cm}^2$

Area of triangle $= \frac{1}{2} \times b \times h$
$= \frac{1}{2} \times 5 \times 8$
$= 20 \text{ cm}^2$

Total area $= 48 + 20 = 68 \text{ cm}^2$

You can split this shape into a rectangle and a triangle.

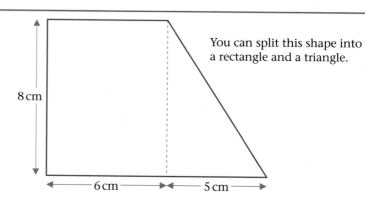

Exercise 19G

Find the areas of these shapes.

1 (a) 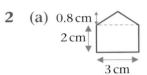 (b) 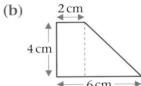 (c) (d)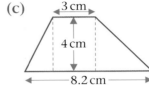

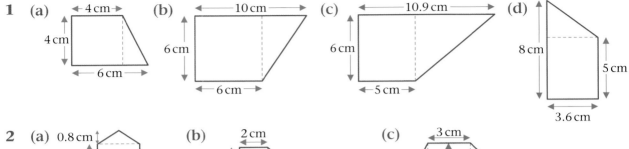

2 (a) (b) (c)

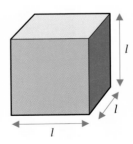

19.5 Finding volumes of cuboids using formulae

In Section 19.3 you found the volumes of cuboids by counting cubes. There is also a formula for finding the volume of such shapes:

> Volume of a cuboid = length × width × height
> $= l \times w \times h$

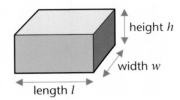

In a cube the length, width and height are all the same size so the formula is:

> Volume of a cube = length × length × length
> $= l \times l \times l$
> $= l^3$

Example 8

Find the volume of a cuboid with length 8 cm, width 6 cm and height 4 cm.

> Volume $= l \times w \times h$
> $= 8 \times 6 \times 4 = 192 \text{ cm}^3$

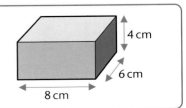

Example 9

This solid shape is made from 2 cm cubes.
Find its volume.

For each cube:

$$\text{volume} = l \times l \times l$$
$$= 2 \times 2 \times 2 = 8 \text{ cm}^3$$

There are 7 cubes in the shape so the total volume is

$$7 \times 8 = 56 \text{ cm}^3$$

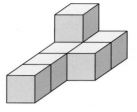

You cannot see one
of the base cubes.

Exercise 19H

Find the volumes of these shapes.

1
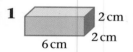
6 cm   2 cm   2 cm

2
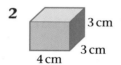
4 cm   3 cm   3 cm

3
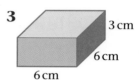
6 cm   3 cm   6 cm

4
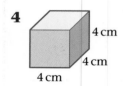
4 cm   4 cm   4 cm

5
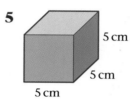
5 cm   5 cm   5 cm

6
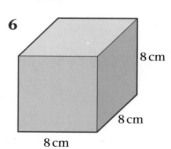
8 cm   8 cm   8 cm

7
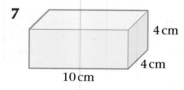
10 cm   4 cm   4 cm

8
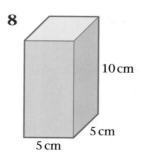
5 cm   5 cm   10 cm

9
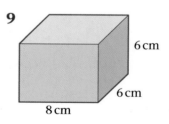
8 cm   6 cm   6 cm

10
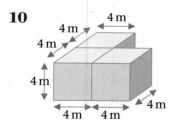
4 m   4 m   4 m   4 m   4 m   4 m   4 m

11
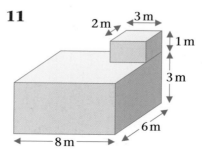
2 m   3 m   1 m   3 m   8 m   6 m

19.6 Surface area

You also need to be able to work out the surface area of simple solid shapes.

The **surface area** is the total area of all the faces of a solid shape.

Example 10

Work out the surface area of this cuboid.

The top and bottom faces are 5 m × 8 m rectangles.
They each have area 40 m².
The sides are 2 m × 5 m rectangles. They each have area 10 m².

The front and back faces are 2 m × 8 m rectangles.
They each have area 16 m².

The total surface area of the cuboid is

top + bottom + right side + left side + front + back = 40 + 40 + 10 + 10 + 16 + 16
= 132 m²

Example 11

Work out the surface area of this prism.

Area of sloping face = 5 × 9 = 45 cm²
Area of back face = 3 × 9 = 27 cm²
Area of base = 4 × 9 = 36 cm²
Area of side = $\frac{1}{2}$ × 4 × 3 = 6 cm²
Area of side = $\frac{1}{2}$ × 4 × 3 = 6 cm²

Total = 120 cm²

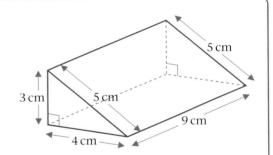

Remember: A prism is a shape with uniform cross-section.

Exercise 19I

Work out the surface areas of these shapes.

1

2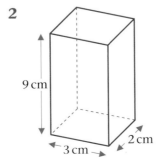

3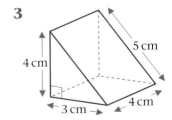

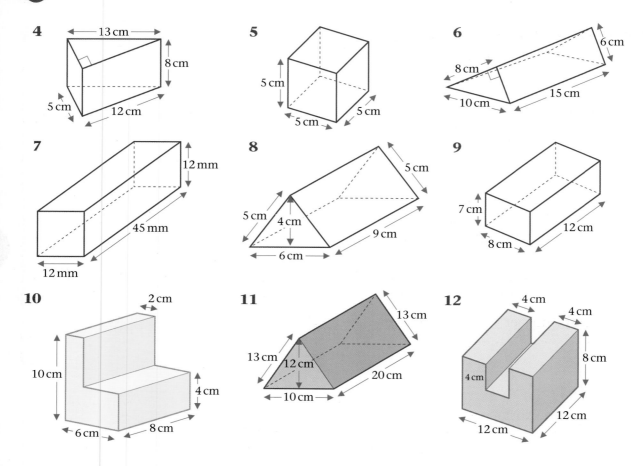

4 13 cm, 8 cm, 5 cm, 12 cm

5 5 cm, 5 cm, 5 cm

6 6 cm, 8 cm, 10 cm, 15 cm

7 12 mm, 45 mm, 12 mm

8 5 cm, 5 cm, 4 cm, 9 cm, 6 cm

9 7 cm, 8 cm, 12 cm

10 2 cm, 10 cm, 4 cm, 6 cm, 8 cm

11 13 cm, 13 cm, 12 cm, 20 cm, 10 cm

12 4 cm, 4 cm, 8 cm, 4 cm, 12 cm, 12 cm

19.7 Fitting boxes into larger boxes

Sometimes we have to calculate how many times small boxes
will fit into a larger box.

Example 12

The diagram shows a packet for a sharpener $4\,\text{cm} \times 2\,\text{cm} \times 2\,\text{cm}$, and a box for
packets of sharpeners $40\,\text{cm} \times 20\,\text{cm} \times 20\,\text{cm}$.

How many packets will completely fill the box?

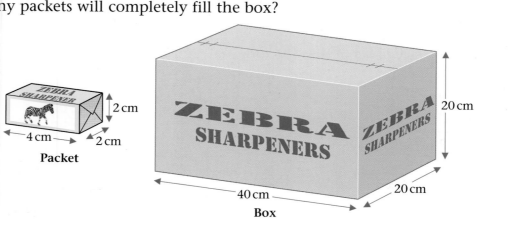

2 cm
4 cm
2 cm
Packet

20 cm
40 cm
20 cm
Box

Compare each of the corresponding sides of the packet and the box.

The length of the packet (4 cm) will fit into the length of the box (40 cm) 10 times. That is, 10 packets can fit along the length of the box.

The width of the packet (2 cm) will fit into the width of the box (20 cm) 10 times. That is, 10 packets can fit across the width of the box.

The height of the packet (2 cm) will fit into the height of the box (20 cm) 10 times. That is, 10 packets can fit up the height of the box.

The total number of packets that will fit in the box is

$$10 \times 10 \times 10 = 1000$$

Exercise 19J

In each question the diagrams show a packet and a box.
Find out how many packets will completely fill the box.

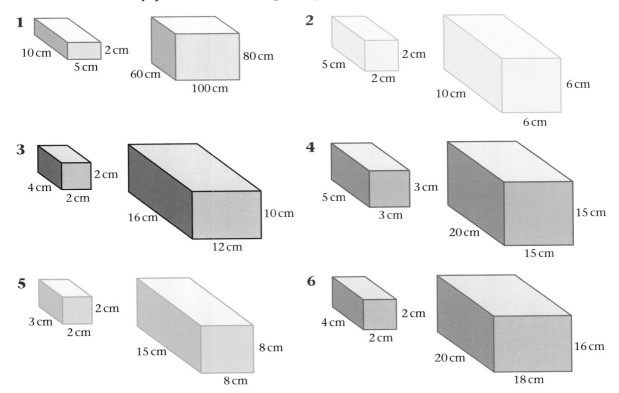

19.8 Area and volume problems

In real-life problems you sometimes need to round answers.

Example 13

A wall is 10 m long and 4 m high.
A tin of paint covers 12 m².
How many tins of paint are needed to paint the wall?

Area of wall = 10 × 4 = 40 m²

40 ÷ 12 = 3.33...

You cannot buy 0.33... tins of paint. Round the answer up.

4 tins of paint are needed.

Exercise 19K

Keith and Mary have bought an old house and are having some work done on it.

1   The lounge is a rectangle 4 m by 3 m and the carpet they buy covers it completely. The carpet costs £7.95 per square metre. How much does the carpet cost them?

2   The kitchen is rectangular and measures 3.4 m by 2.7 m. They have to buy a whole number of square metres of vinyl to cover the floor. The vinyl costs £12.50 per square metre. How much will it cost to cover the floor?

3   The bathroom walls need to be tiled to a height of 1.5 m. The tiles are all 15 cm square. The bathroom measures 3 m by 3 m. The tiles cost 65p each.
   (a)   How many tiles are needed for the height?
   (b)   How many tiles are needed for the length of one wall?
   (c)   How many tiles are needed for all 4 walls? You can ignore the space taken up by the door.
   (d)   Work out the cost of all the tiles.

4   The small bedroom measures 3 m by 2 m and the walls are 2.5 m high. The walls of this room are going to be painted with emulsion paint. Each tin of paint will cover 15 m². How many tins will they need?

5   The central heating system runs on oil. The oil tank is a cuboid with length 2.5 m, width 1 m and height 1.5 m. How many litres of oil will the tank contain?

Remember that
1*l* = 1000 m*l* or 1000 cm³.

6   All the tiles on the roof need to be replaced. Each tile measures 30 cm by 30 cm. Each of the two sides of the roof measures 10 m by 8 m. There needs to be an allowance of an extra 50% for overlaps.
   How many tiles are needed for the roof?

7 The lawn needs replacing and they decide to replace the worn-out grass with strips of turf that measure 2 m by 0.3 m. The new lawn is to measure 20 m by 12 m. Work out how many strips they need to buy.

8 Keith wants to replace the surface of the drive, which measures 12 m by 8 m. He needs to dig out the old surface to a depth of 30 cm.

   (a) Work out the volume of rubble that Keith needs to dig out.

   (b) How many 4 m³ skips will be needed to carry away the rubble?

19.9 Converting units of area and volume

You may be asked in the examination to convert square centimetres (cm²) to square metres (m²) or m² to cm².

Here are two pictures of the same square. The only difference is that one is measured in metres and the other in centimetres.

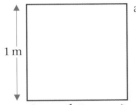

area = 1 m × 1 m
= 1 m²

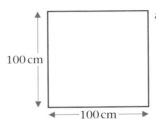

area = 100 cm × 100 cm
= 10 000 cm²

1 m² = 100 × 100 cm² = 10 000 cm²

Similarly you may be asked to convert cubic centimetres (cm³) to cubic metres (m³).

Here are two pictures of the same cube. The only difference is that one is measured in metres and the other in centimetres.

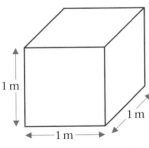

volume = 1 m × 1 m × 1 m
= 1 m³

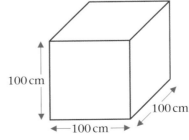

volume = 100 cm × 100 cm × 100 cm
= 1 000 000 cm³

1 m³ = 100 × 100 × 100 cm³ = 1 000 000 cm³

Example 14 _____

A square has an area of 1.2 m².
What is its area in cm².

$$1\,m^2 = 10\,000\,cm^2$$
$$\text{So } 1.2\,m^2 = 1.2 \times 10\,000\,cm^2$$
$$= 12\,000\,cm^2$$

Example 15 _____

The volume of an oil drum is 2 340 000 cm³.
Write down the volume of the oil drum in m³.

$$1\,m^3 = 1\,000\,000\,cm^3$$
$$\text{So } 2\,340\,000\,cm^3 = \frac{2\,340\,000}{1\,000\,000}\,m^3$$
$$= 2.34\,m^3$$

Exercise 19L

1 Work out the number of
  (a) cm² in 2 m²
  (b) cm² in 13 m²
  (c) cm² in 2.4 m²
  (d) cm² in 15.2 m²
  (e) m² in 120 000 cm²
  (f) m² in 23 000 cm²
  (g) m² in 164 300 cm²
  (h) cm² in 0.42 m²
  (i) cm² in 0.03 m²
  (j) m² in 3000 cm²
  (k) m² in 100 cm²

2 Work out the number of
  (a) cm³ in 7 m³
  (b) cm³ in 15 m³
  (c) cm³ in 3.5 m³
  (d) cm³ in 4.78 m³
  (e) m³ in 4 000 000 cm³
  (f) m³ in 3 780 000 cm³
  (g) m³ in 14 789 000 cm³
  (h) cm³ in 0.8 m³
  (i) cm³ in 0.002 m³
  (j) cm³ in 0.000 024 m³
  (k) m³ in 37 800 cm³
  (l) m³ in 142 000 cm³
  (m) m³ in 3000 cm³

3 The area of a pane of glass is 12 000 cm².
  Write down the area of the pane of glass in m².

4 The diagram shows a door.
  (a) Work out the area of the surface of the door in m².
  (b) Write down your answer to part **(a)** in cm².

5 The volume of a large packing case is 2.3 m³.
  Write down the volume of the packing case in cm³.

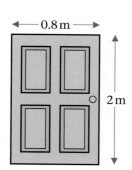

6 The dimensions of a washing machine are shown in the diagram.

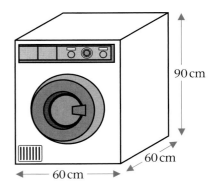

  (a) Work out the volume of the washing machine in cm³.

  (b) Write down your answer to part (a) in m³.

19.10 Compound measures: speed

Sometimes you need to work with two units at the same time. For example, the speed of a car can be measured in miles per hour – a measurement involving a unit of length and a unit of time.

For an object moving at a constant speed:

$$\text{speed} = \frac{\text{distance}}{\text{time}} \qquad \text{time} = \frac{\text{distance}}{\text{speed}}$$

$$\text{distance} = \text{speed} \times \text{time}$$

Typical units are miles per hour, and metres per second.

Usually the speed of a car is not constant for the whole journey so you use the average speed:

$$\text{average speed} = \frac{\text{total distance travelled}}{\text{total time taken}}$$

You can use this triangle to help you remember the formulae.

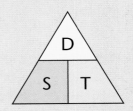

Cover the value you wish to find with your thumb: e.g. to find speed, cover S. You are left with D over T, that is $\frac{\text{distance}}{\text{time}}$.

Example 16

What speed does my car average if I travel 90 miles in 3 hours?

$$\text{average speed} = \frac{\text{total distance travelled}}{\text{total time taken}}$$

$$= 90 \div 3 = 30 \text{ miles per hour}$$

Example 17

How long does it take to travel 400 miles at a constant speed of 50 miles per hour?

$$\text{time} = \frac{\text{distance}}{\text{speed}}$$

$$= 400 \div 50 = 8 \text{ hours}$$

Example 18

How far can you go if you travel for 3 hours at 10 miles per hour?

distance = speed × time
= 10 × 3
= 30 miles

Exercise 19M

1 Elizabeth walked for 3 hours at 4 miles per hour.
   How far did she walk?

2 Andrew drove 100 miles in 4 hours.
   At what average speed did he travel?

3 Karen drove 300 miles at an average speed of 60 miles per hour.
   How long did her journey take her?

4 David was travelling by canal boat and went 30 miles in 8 hours.
   At what average speed was he travelling?

5 Amanda rode her bike for 3 hours and travelled 21 miles.
   At what average speed was she travelling?

6 Gerry ran for 2 hours and covered 16 miles.
   At what average speed was he running?

7 Brigit swam for 3 hours and travelled 4 miles.
   At what average speed was she swimming?

8 Alfred set off from home at 8 am. He travelled 200 miles by car and arrived at 11 am.
   At what average speed was he travelling?

9 Jason set off for work at 07:55. He arrived at work at 08:10.
   If he lives 5 miles from work, at what average speed did he travel?

10 Frances was using a keep fit treadmill. She ran for 40 minutes and 'travelled' 10 kilometres.
    At what average speed was she running?

19.11 Problem solving with a spreadsheet

Look at this problem:

A farmer has 200 metres of fencing. He wants to use all the fencing to enclose a rectangular area of his field for his animals to graze. Find the length and width of the rectangle which gives his animals the maximum grazing area.

You can solve problems like this on a computer by using a spreadsheet.

Exercise 19N

1 Think of all the rectangles you can draw whose perimeters are 200 metres. For example, some could be long and thin; others short and wide.

Use a spreadsheet to record the length L and width W of each rectangle.

Then multiply the values of L and W to get the area of each rectangle.

Formula
A3 = A2 + 10

(W = 100 − L)
Formula
B2 = 100 − A2

(A = L × W)
Formula
C2 = A2 × B2

	A	B	C	D
1	L	W	LW	
2	0	100	0	
3	10			
4	20			
5				
6				

> The perimeter of each rectangle is 200 metres, so
> $$2L + 2W = 200$$
> You can divide by 2 to make this equation simpler:
> $$L + W = 100$$
> Use your spreadsheet to try lots of values for L from $L = 0$ to $L = 100$ metres.
> Increase L by 10 metres each time. For each value of L calculate a value for W using
> $$W = 100 − L$$

> Make sure your spreadsheet has at least 12 rows and 3 columns. Use column A for the length, column B for the width and column C for the area of each rectangle.

What is the maximum value for the area?

2 Draw a graph of the data in your spreadsheet.

> Drawing a graph of the data can give you a better understanding of how the area changes as the lengths and widths of the rectangles change.

Mixed exercise 19

1 **(a)** Work out the perimeter of this shape:

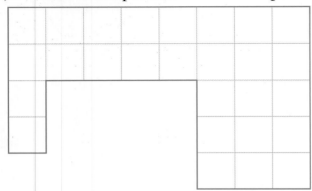

(b) Work out the area of the shape.

2 Measure and write down the perimeter of this shape.

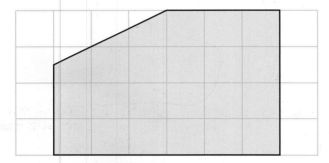

3 Work out the perimeter of the shape on the right.

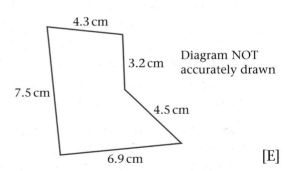

Diagram NOT accurately drawn

[E]

4 The diagram represents an L-shaped room whose corners are all right angles.

(a) **(i)** Work out the value of x.
  (ii) Work out the value of y.
(b) Work out the perimeter of the shape.
(c) Work out the area of the shape.

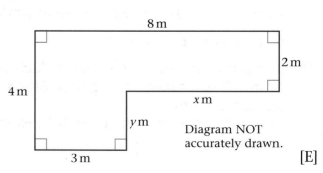

Diagram NOT accurately drawn.

[E]

5   The diagram represents the babies'
    pool, with paving around, at a leisure
    centre. The pool is rectangular, 8 m
    long by 5 m wide, and has a depth of
    0.6 m throughout.

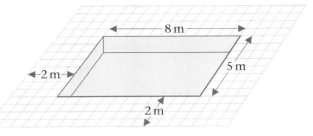

   (a) Work out the volume of the
        pool in m³.

    The paving around the pool is 2 m wide.

   (b) Work out the area of the paving.

6   The diagram shows a paved
    surface.
    All the corners are right angles.
    Work out the area of the paved
    surface.   [E]

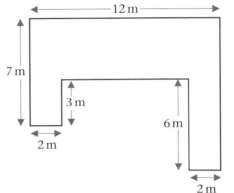

Diagram NOT
accurately drawn

7   The diagram represents a large tank in the
    shape of a cuboid.
    The tank has a base. It does not have a top.
    The width of the tank is 2.8 metres.
    The length of the tank is 3.2 metres.
    The height of the tank is 4.5 metres.

    The outside of the tank is going to be painted.
    1 litre of paint will cover 2.5 m² of the tank.
    The cost of the paint is £2.99 for each litre tin.

    Calculate the cost of the paint needed to
    paint the outside of the tank.

4.5 m   Diagram NOT
         accurately drawn

2.8 m

3.2 m

8   Daniel leaves his house at 07:00.
    He drives 87 miles to work.
    He drives at an average speed of 36 miles per hour.
    At what time does Daniel arrive at work?   [E]

9   Change 8 m³ to cm³.   [E]

10 Ben fills a container with boxes. Each box is a cube of side
    0.5 m. The container is a cuboid of length 9 m, width 4 m
    and height 3 m.
    Work out how many boxes will fit exactly into the
    container.   [E]

Summary of key points

1 The **perimeter** of a 2-D shape is the distance around the edge of the shape.

2 The **area** of a 2-D shape is a measure of the amount of space it covers. Typical units of area are square centimetres (cm^2), square metres (m^2) and square kilometres (km^2).

3 **Area formulae** for 2-D shapes:

Area of a rectangle   = length × width
                                   = $l \times w$

Area of a square   = length × length
                                   = $l \times l = l^2$

Area of a triangle   = $\frac{1}{2}$ × base × vertical height
                                   = $\frac{1}{2} \times b \times h$

Area of a parallelogram = base × vertical height
                                   = $b \times h$

4 The **volume** of a 3-D shape is a measure of the amount of space it occupies. Typical units of volume are cubic centimetres (cm^3) and cubic metres (m^3).

5 **Volume formulae** for cuboids (3-D):

Volume of a cuboid = length × width × height
                            = $l \times w \times h$

Volume of a cube   = length × length × length = $l \times l \times l = l^3$

6 The **surface area** is the total area of all the faces of a solid shape.

7 $1\ m^2 = 100 \times 100\ cm^2 = 10\,000\ cm^2$
$1\ m^3 = 100 \times 100 \times 100\ cm^3 = 1\,000\,000\ cm^3$

8 For an object moving at a constant speed:

$$\text{speed} = \frac{\text{distance}}{\text{time}} \qquad \text{time} = \frac{\text{distance}}{\text{speed}} \qquad \text{distance} = \text{speed} \times \text{time}$$

Typical units are miles per hour, and metres per second.

9 When an object's speed varies as it travels:

$$\text{average speed} = \frac{\text{total distance travelled}}{\text{time taken}}$$

20 Presenting and analysing data 1

The word average is often used. Think about these statements:

'Jenny is of average height.'

'A centre forward averages one goal a game.'

'Teenagers in Britain spend an average of £5 a week on hair care products.'

Here the word average means that something is typical, or describes something that typically happens.

In mathematics an **average** is usually a single value which is used to represent a set of data. It is in some way typical of the data and gives an idea of what the data is like.

Three different averages are commonly used:

- the **mode**   • the **median**   • the **mean**.

This chapter shows you how each one is found and why it is useful.

On average this family size box contains 500 g of cereal. The weight of cereal in the box is only allowed to vary within a very small range.

20.1 The mode

The **mode** of a set of data is the value which occurs most often.

___ Example 1 ___

The numbers of goals scored by a team in ten matches were:

1, 5, 2, 0, 4, 2, 1, 2, 2, 3

Find the mode of this data.

The score that occurred most often was 2 goals, so the mode is 2.

___ Example 2 ___

Find the mode of this team's scores:

3, 1, 0, 1, 4, 3, 6, 2, 1, 3

There are two modes: 1 and 3.

___ Example 3 ___

Find the mode of this team's scores:

2, 5, 3, 4, 0, 1, 6

There is no mode since each score occurred only once.

Exercise 20A

1 Four students recorded the number of text messages they got on each day in a week. Here are their results:

John: 8, 8, 7, 6, 8, 5, 8
Kit: 6, 7, 5, 4, 6, 5, 8
Mary: 6, 5, 4, 8, 7, 3, 9
Tina: 3, 4, 4, 7, 3, 6, 6

(a) For each student, write down the mode(s) of the numbers of text messages.

(b) What is the overall mode for all the numbers of text messages?

2 Here are the CPU speeds, in GHz, of 18 computers in an office:

1.6	1.8	2.2	1.8	2.2	1.8
1.6	1.5	1.8	1.6	2.0	2.0
1.4	2.0	2.1	2.3	1.6	1.7

(a) Write down (i) the fastest speed, (ii) the slowest speed.

(b) Write down the modal speed.

3 Here are some sets of numbers. Add a number, or numbers, to each set so that the new set has the mode shown on the right.

(a) 8, 5, 9, 6, 3, 7, 4   : mode 6
(b) 3, 7, 5, 8, 4, 3, 6, 9   : mode 5
(c) 2, 6, 7, 8, 5, 3, 2   : mode 4
(d) 11, 7, 15, 12, 15, 8, 9 : modes 11 and 15
(e) 6, 3, 8, 9, 4, 6, 5   : mode 7
(f) 8, 3, 6, 2, 7, 9, 7, 5   : modes 5 and 6

4 The table shows the numbers of goals scored by the teams in a hockey competition.

Number of goals	0	1	2	3	4	5
Number of teams	3	3	6	4	3	1

(a) Make a list of all the numbers of goals scored by all the teams.

(b) Write down the modal number of goals.

(c) How many teams were in the competition?

20.2 The median

The **median** is the middle value when the data is arranged in order of size.

Example 4

Find the median of Brian's homework marks for
(a) English: 5, 7, 9, 4, 1, 3, 7, 4, 6
(b) history: 6, 8, 3, 7, 5, 3, 7, 2

(a) Arrange the English marks in order of size:

$\qquad$ 1, 3, 4, 4, 5, 6, 7, 7, 9

The middle mark is 5. Brian has four marks higher and four marks lower than this.

The median is 5.

(b) Arrange the history marks in order of size:

$\qquad$ 2, 3, 3, 5, 6, 7, 7, 8

The 'middle mark' lies between the 5 and 6 so the

median is $5\frac{1}{2}$.

> Notice that the median history mark is not a mark Brian has actually scored.
>
> Because there is an even number of marks there is no 'middle mark' in the data.
>
> Instead the value of a middle mark has been calculated.

Example 5

The table shows the shoe sizes of a group of students. Find the median shoe size.

Shoe size	7	$7\frac{1}{2}$	8	$8\frac{1}{2}$	9	$9\frac{1}{2}$
Number of students	2	2	5	4	3	3

To find the median you could list all the shoe sizes:

$\quad$ 7, 7, $7\frac{1}{2}$, $7\frac{1}{2}$, 8, 8, 8, 8, 8, $8\frac{1}{2}$, $8\frac{1}{2}$, $8\frac{1}{2}$, $8\frac{1}{2}$, 9, 9, 9, $9\frac{1}{2}$, $9\frac{1}{2}$, $9\frac{1}{2}$

You can see that the middle value or median is $8\frac{1}{2}$.

An easier way of finding the middle value is to add up the numbers of students. There are 19 students altogether so the middle student is the 10th.

Starting at the left of the data table, the 10th student is in the '$8\frac{1}{2}$' column, so the median shoe size is $8\frac{1}{2}$.

Exercise 20B

1 Rearrange the following marks in order and write down the median in each case.

   (a) 5, 8, 3, 2, 7, 9, 6   **(b)** 15, 18, 9, 11, 17, 8, 12, 10, 9

   (c) 9, 4, 7, 3, 1, 6, 3, 8   **(d)** 8, 12, 18, 9, 14, 7, 10, 6

2 Give examples of

   (a) seven different numbers with a median of 12

   (b) nine different numbers with a median of 8

   (c) eight different numbers with a median of 10

   (d) six different numbers with a median of 4.5

3 Here are some sets of numbers. Add a number to each set to obtain the median given on the right.

   (a) 1, 8, 5, 2   : median 5

   (b) 8, 4, 5, 3, 8, 4, 2, 9   : median 4

   (c) 7, 5, 3, 6, 8, 2, 7   : median $6\frac{1}{2}$

   (d) 7, 4, 3, 6, 2, 6, 8, 4   : median 5

> Hint: you need to make 5 the middle number.

4 The table shows some students' results from a quiz.

Marks	0	1	2	3	4	5	6	7	8	9	10
Number of students	0	0	2	3	1	1	2	5	4	6	4

   (a) Write down the median mark.

   (b) Write two statements making use of the median.

5 The chart below shows the numbers of parking tickets issued by a traffic officer on seven days of a week.

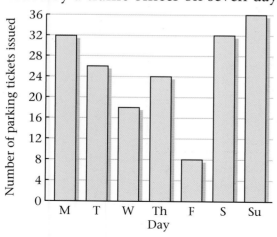

   (a) Work out the median number of tickets issued per day.

   (b) Write down the modal number.

20.3 The mean

The **mean** of a set of data is the sum of the values divided by the number of values:

$$\text{mean} = \frac{\text{sum of the values}}{\text{number of values}}$$

Example 6

Find the mean of 3, 8, 4, 7, 7, 6, 4, 1

The sum of the values is:

$$3 + 8 + 4 + 7 + 7 + 6 + 4 + 1 = 40$$

There are 8 values, so divide 40 by 8:

$$40 \div 8 = 5$$

The mean is 5.

Example 7

The mean of three numbers is 5, and the mean of four other numbers is 8. What is the mean of all seven numbers?

The sum of the three numbers is 15 ——— $\frac{15}{3} = 5$

The sum of the four numbers is 32 ——— $\frac{32}{4} = 8$

$$\text{Mean of all seven numbers} = \frac{\text{Total sum}}{7} = \frac{15 + 32}{7} = \frac{47}{7} = 6.7$$

Example 8

The mean of four numbers is 6. Three of the numbers are 4, 8 and 3. Find the value of the other number.

The sum of the four numbers is 24 ——— $\frac{24}{4} = 6$

If x is the missing number, $4 + 8 + 3 + x = 24$

$$15 + x = 24$$
$$x = 9$$

The other number is 9.

Exercise 20C

1 Calculate the mean for each set of data.

   (a) 12, 18, 9, 14, 8, 17   (b) 23, 15, 37, 26, 16, 21, 33, 23

   (c) 15, 25, 22, 34, 19, 20   (d) 25, 12, 31, 26, 31, 19, 30, 16

2 The heights of a group of students, in centimetres, are:

158, 162, 172, 157, 161

(a) Calculate the mean height.

(b) Another student joins the group. His height is
159 cm.
Calculate the new mean height.

> You can use your calculator to work out the mean. Either add the numbers then divide, or use the data entry key then press the MEAN key.

3 The weights of four parcels, in grams, are:

515, 620, 542, 563

(a) Calculate the mean weight.

(b) A fifth parcel is added. The new mean is 710 g.
Calculate the weight of the parcel.

4 The mean of four numbers is 94, and the mean of another nine different numbers is 17. What is the mean of all thirteen numbers?

5 Here are some sets of numbers. Find one more number for each set to obtain the mean given on the right.

(a) 8, 3, 6, 7, 8, 4   : mean 7
(b) 17, 14, 8, 11, 15, 17   : mean 14
(c) 6, 3, 9, 7, 2, 6, 5   : mean 5.5
(d) 23, 31, 20, 27, 32, 24   : mean 26

20.4 The range

The mean of a set of data is an average value. It does not tell you how spread out the data is.

One way of measuring the spread of a set of data is to find its **range**:

> The **range** of a set of data is the difference between the highest value and the lowest value:
>
> the range = highest value − lowest value

Two sets of data may have the same mean but different ranges. Compare these two batsmen's scores after four innings:

Peter: 0, 96, 100, 0   Mean 49   Range 100 − 0 = 100
Hanif: 49, 51, 46, 50   Mean 49   Range 51 − 46 = 5

Both have the same mean or average score but Hanif has a much smaller range. His scores are less spread out which shows he is a more consistent player.

Exercise 20D

1   Here are the distances thrown by two athletes in a javelin competition:

Fiona Yass: 18, 17, 14, 18, 16, 22, 17, 16
Ulga Perez: 17, 15, 15, 18, 18, 15, 18, 20

(a) Work out the range for each athlete.

(b) Which athlete was (i) better (ii) more consistent? Give reasons for your answers.

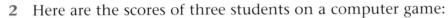

2   Here are the scores of three students on a computer game:

Tim: 47, 51, 36, 78, 43, 20, 39, 27
Franz: 35, 38, 42, 55, 28, 43, 61, 54
Pani: 45, 51, 57, 44, 50, 48, 43, 49

(a) Which student was least consistent? Give a reason for your answer.

(b) One of the students scored 75 in his next game. His range is now 32. Who was it?

3   Copy and complete the table below. The first one is done for you.

Make	Basic model	Top model	Price range
Audi 2.0	£21 025	£26 265	£5240
Citroën C4 2.0	£16 695	£20 495	
Ford Focus 2.0		£16 680	£2180
Mazda 2.0	£15 200		£4000
Nissan Almera 2.0		£15 650	£3000
Peugeot 407 2.0	£16 950		£4000
Renault Mégane 2.0	£13 900	£18 600	
Toyota Corolla 2.0		£15 895	£1700
Volkswagen Golf 2.0	£12 990	£18 250	

4   The table shows the maximum and minimum temperatures one day last year in degrees Fahrenheit.

(a) Calculate the range in each city.

(b) List the cities in order, highest range first.

(c) Give a reason why someone might want to know these ranges.

City	Maximum	Minimum
London	64	42
Paris	69	47
Moscow	38	9
New York	72	59
Luxor	101	88

20.5 Using appropriate averages

The different types of averages are useful in different situations.

The **mode** is useful when you need to know, for example:

- which shoe size is most common
- which brand of cat food is most popular.

The **mean** is useful for finding a 'typical' value when most of the data is closely grouped, for example the height of a typical student in your class.

The mean may not give a very typical value if the data is very spread out, or if it includes a few values that are very different from the rest. For example:

> A company chairwoman earns £200 000 a year and her nine employees each earn £15 000.
> Their mean pay is £33 500.

The mean height of the students in your class will be 'typical' unless some people are very much taller or shorter than the rest.

In situations like this, the **median** or middle value may be more typical. Median earnings in this company are £15 000.

___
Example 9
___

Shah records the number of hits on his web page every day.
Here are his results:

> 1, 3, 17, 18, 19, 20, 21, 21, 24

Find the mode, median and mean of these numbers.

The mode is 21.   Two days had 21 hits.

The mean is $\frac{144}{9} = 16$.   Notice that only two days had fewer hits than this.

The median is 19.   There were four days with more hits and four days with fewer hits.

You can see that the two days with low numbers of hits lowered the result for the mean. If the days with 1 and 3 hits had 15 and 16 hits, the mean would have been 19, but the mode and median would have remained the same.

___
Example 10
___

Here are the numbers of rooks in each of 10 rookeries in Yorkshire:

> 38, 35, 35, 35, 30, 29, 28, 28, 11, 5

Find the mode, median and mean of the numbers of rooks and the range. Comment on your results.

The mode is 35, the median is 29.5, the mean is 27.4 and the range is 33.

Here the median gives the best idea of a 'typical' number of rooks – half the rookeries have more and half have fewer.

The mean has been distorted by the two very low numbers of rooks, and only two rookeries have fewer rooks.

The mode is not representative as only one rookery has more rooks.

The range just tells you that there is a wide spread of the numbers of rooks.

Advantages and disadvantages of the three averages

	Advantages	Disadvantages
Mode	Easy to see or pick out Not influenced by extreme values	There can be more than one mode Cannot be used for further calculations
Median	Not influenced by extreme values	Actual value may not exist (see Example 4)
Mean	Can easily be calculated Uses all the data Can be used for further calculations	Extreme values can distort the result

Activity – Bicycles

How many bicycles are there in your home?
● Collect data for the whole class.
● Work out the mode, median and mean of your data.
● Comment on your findings.

Exercise 20E

1 Find the mode, median and mean in each of the following and make a comment about each.

(a) The numbers of cars left in the station car-park overnight during one week were:

12, 6, 14, 9, 13, 6, 10

(b) The numbers of passengers boarding the train between 9 am and 12 noon were:

24, 17, 32, 24, 35, 32, 28

(c) The costs of the first five tickets sold were:

£1.15, £12.40, £3.60, £3.60, £2.95

2 The weekly wages for the station staff were:

1 station manager	£400
2 ticket office clerks	£280 each
2 train dispatch officials	£240 each
3 cleaners	£200 each
2 trainees	£185 each

(a) Calculate the total weekly wages bill.

(b) What is
    (i) the modal wage
    (ii) the median wage
    (iii) the mean wage
    (iv) the range?

(c) Comment on your answers to part (b).

3 Find six numbers which have a mean of 5, a mode of 2 and a median of $4\frac{1}{2}$.

20.6 Stem and leaf diagrams

A stem and leaf diagram is another way of presenting data. It has the advantage that the shape of the way the data is distributed can be seen without losing the detail of the original data.

0	5, 8
1	2, 5, ⑦ ——————— This leaf represents 17
2	4, 4, 5, 8
3	0, 3, 9
4	1, 5, 6

Key
4|1 means 41

Remember:
You must always add a key to the diagram to show how the stem and leaf combine.

The data represented is

5, 8, 12, 15, 17, 24, 24, 25, 28, 30, 33, 39, 41, 45, 46

Example 11

Here are the total numbers of medals won by Great Britain in the Olympic Games since 1896.

7, 30, 2, 145, 41, 44, 34, 20, 16, 14, 23, 11
24, 20, 18, 13, 18, 13, 21, 37, 24, 20, 15, 28, 30

(a) Show this data in a frequency chart.

(b) Represent the data in a stem and leaf diagram.

(c) Find the median.

(a)

Class interval	Tally	Frequency
0–9	||	2
10–19	ⅢⅡ |||	8
20–29	ⅢⅡ |||	8
30–39	||||	4
40–49	||	2
140–149	|	1

(b) Write the data as stem and leaves.

0	2, 7
1	5, 3, 8, 3, 8, 1, 4, ⑥ — This leaf represents 16
2	8, 0, 4, 1, 0, 4, 3, 0
3	0, 7, 4, 0
4	4, 1
14	5

Key
2 | 8 means 28

Now write the leaves in order:

0	2, 7
1	1, 3, 3, 4, 5, 6, 8, 8
2	0, 0, 0, 1, 3, 4, 4, 8
3	0, 0, 4, 7
4	1, 4
14	5

Key
2 | 8 means 28

(c) There are 25 data values, so the median (the middle number) is the 13th data value.

If you had only drawn a frequency chart you would not have been able to find the median value. You can count across your ordered stem and leaf diagram to find the 13th data value. The median is 20.

A **stem and leaf** diagram shows the shape of the distribution and keeps the original data values.

Always include a **key** with a stem and leaf diagram to show how the stem and leaf are combined.

Activity – World temperatures

(a) From a newspaper, collect one day's temperatures for cities around the world.
(b) Represent the data in a stem and leaf diagram.
(c) Find the mode, median, mean and range of your data.
(d) Comment on your findings.

Exercise 20F

1 Forty people were asked 'What are the last two digits of your telephone number?' The results were:

45	15	55	26	43	27	22	36	98	81
17	36	24	36	55	30	43	08	24	26
25	08	23	45	72	29	57	17	67	69
44	53	68	14	90	26	36	49	52	37

(a) Copy and complete this stem and leaf diagram. The 10–19 class interval is done for you.

0	
1	4, 5, 7, 7
2	
3	
4	
5	
6	
7	
8	
9	

Key
$1|4$ means 14

(b) What is the median?

2 Forty-one pupils recorded the time taken in seconds to solve a puzzle at the school fête. The times were:

```
25  38  50   9  35  48   9  12  47  34
52  11  32  41  36  29   7  44  18  23
39  22  17   4  49  38  57  15  33  58
14   8  35  27  17  43  20  37   6  26  24
```

(a) Represent this data using a stem and leaf diagram, including a key.
(b) What is the median time?

3 Marks (out of 60) in a mock examination were:

```
25  42  54  37  18  35  29  53  47  53
44  56  35  26  34  43  37  15  55  34
52  35   9  43  58  27  52  45  50  20
24  43  55  46  35  14  38  27  44  32
35  19  36  28  46  34  45  34  40  59
```

(a) Using class intervals 0–9, 10–19, etc. draw a frequency chart to represent this data.
(b) Draw a stem and leaf diagram to represent this data, including a key.
(c) In which class interval is (i) the mode (ii) the median?
(d) Calculate the mean of the marks in the class interval 30–39. Give your answer to 1 decimal place.
(e) If the pass mark was 2 above the median, what percentage passed?

20.7 Pie charts

A **pie chart** is a good way of displaying data when you want to show how something is shared or divided.

How Wayne spent the last 24 hours

Land use in the UK

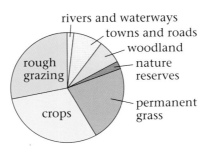

The market share for different cat food brands

Drawing a pie chart

Each slice of a pie chart is called a **sector**.

When you know the angle of each sector at the centre of a pie chart, here is how to draw it.

Example 12

Draw a pie chart whose angles at the centre are: 108°, 90°, 72°, 60° and 30°.

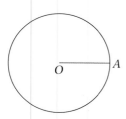 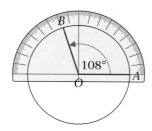 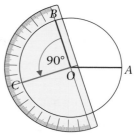

Draw a circle. Draw a line *OA* from its centre to its circumference.

Use your protractor to measure the angle 108°. Mark it and draw the line *OB*.

Place your protractor along *OB*. Measure the angle 90°, mark it and draw the line *OC*.

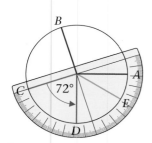 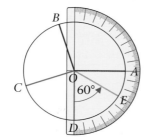 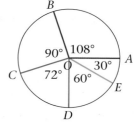

Place your protractor along *OC*. Measure the angle 72°, mark it and draw *OD*.

Place your protractor along *OD*. Measure the angle 60°, mark it and draw *OE*.

Check that the angle remaining is 30° and mark it.

The angles at the centre of a pie chart add up to 360°.

Exercise 20G

1 Clive wants to draw a pie chart to show the result of his traffic survey. He calculates these angles:

Speed (mph)	Under 70	70–80	More than 80
Angle	210°	90°	60°

Draw a pie chart for Clive's traffic survey.

2 Tarina wants to draw a pie chart to show the votes in the General Election in 2005. Here are some of the angles she calculates:

(a) Copy and complete the table.

(b) Draw the pie chart.

	Angle
Labour	127°
Conservative	116°
Liberal Democrat	
Other	38°

Activity – The General Election

(a) From the internet, find the number of Parliamentary seats won by
  (i) the Labour party
  (ii) the Conservative party
  (iii) the Liberal Democrat party
  (iv) all the other parties,
     in the General Election in 2005.

(b) Draw a pie chart to display your findings.

(c) Compare your pie chart to the one you drew in question **2**.

Calculating the angles

Twenty students were asked on which day they would help paint the scenery for the school play. The replies were: Monday 5, Tuesday 4, Wednesday 8 and Thursday 3. Here is the data shown on a pie chart.

The circle represents all 20 students and each section represents one of the days.

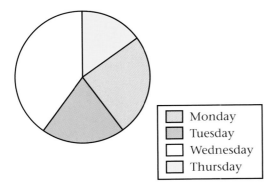

▨	Monday
▨	Tuesday
☐	Wednesday
☐	Thursday

Separating the sections shows that to fit together again the shaded angles must add up to 360°: the total sum of the angles at the centre of the circle.

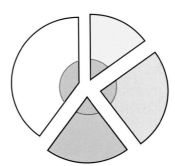

The angles at the centre of a pie chart add up to 360°.

Here is how to calculate the angles of each sector:

20 students are represented by 360°

1 student is represented by $\dfrac{360}{20} = 18°$

Monday: 5 students so the angle is $5 \times 18° = 90°$
Tuesday: 4 students so the angle is $4 \times 18° = 72°$
Wednesday: 8 students so the angle is $8 \times 18° = 144°$
Thursday: 3 students so the angle is $3 \times 18° = 54°$

Check: 20 students so the angle is $20 \times 18° = 360°$

Another way of calculating the angles is to find what fraction of 360° the students represent:

Monday: $\dfrac{5}{20} \times 360° = 90°$

Tuesday: $\dfrac{4}{20} \times 360° = 72°$

Wednesday: $\dfrac{8}{20} \times 360° = 144°$

Thursday: $\dfrac{3}{20} \times 360° = 54°$

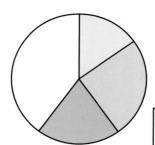

☐ Monday
☐ Tuesday
☐ Wednesday
☐ Thursday

Interpreting pie charts

___ **Example 13** ___

This pie chart shows the proportions of gold, silver and bronze medals won by Great Britain in the Olympic Games in Athens in 2004.

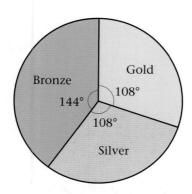

The total number of medals won by the UK was 30.
Find the numbers of gold, silver and bronze medals.

Method 1

30 medals are represented by 360°

1 medal is represented by $\dfrac{360°}{30} = 12°$

Gold: The angle is 108° so the number of medals is $\dfrac{108°}{12°} = 9$ medals

Silver: The angle is 108° so the number of medals is $\dfrac{108°}{12°} = 9$ medals

Bronze: The angle is 144° so the number of medals is $\dfrac{144°}{12°} = 12$ medals

Method 2

Find what fraction of the 30 medals each angle represents.

Gold: Silver: Bronze:

$\dfrac{108°}{360°} \times 30 = 9$ medals $\dfrac{108°}{360°} \times 30 = 9$ medals $\dfrac{144°}{360°} \times 30 = 12$ medals

---

Worked examination question

720 students were asked how they travelled to school.

The pie chart shows the results of this survey.

Work out
(a) how many of the students travelled to school by bus
(b) how many students walked to school.

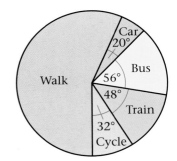

(a) **Method 1**

360° represents 720 students

1° represents $\dfrac{720}{360} = 2$ students

The angle of the bus sector of the pie chart is 56°, so the number of students is:

$56 \times 2 = 112$

Method 2

The bus sector is 56° and the whole pie chart is 360°,

so the fraction travelling by bus is $\dfrac{56}{360}$

There are 720 students so the number of students travelling by bus is

$\dfrac{56}{360} \times 720 = 112$

(b) First, find the angle of the 'walk' sector:

$$360 - (20 + 56 + 48 + 32) = 360 - 156$$
$$= 204°$$

Either each 1° represents 2 students   **or** $\dfrac{204}{360} \times 720 = 408$ students

$204 \times 2 = 408$ students

Exercise 20H

1   In a survey 300 people were asked 'Do you believe in God?' The results are summarised in the pie chart.

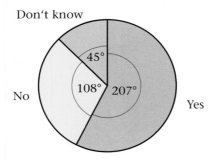

Use the information in the pie chart to work out the number of people who said 'No'.

2   The pie chart gives information about the medals won by Great Britain in the Olympic Games at Seoul in 1988.

Copy and complete the table.

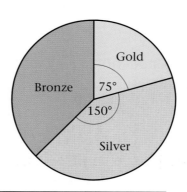

	Degrees	Number of medals
Gold	75°	
Silver	150°	
Bronze		9
Total	360°	24

3 Thirty students were asked to name their favourite ice cream. The results are shown in this pie chart.

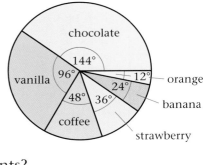

(a) What does the whole circle represent?

(b) Which ice cream does the largest sector represent?

(c) What does the smallest sector represent?

(d) Use the given angles to calculate the number of students who liked strawberry ice cream.

(e) How could you select a randon sample of 30 students?

4 (a) Kasha takes home £240 per week. He allocates his money like this:

Rent £60   Travel £18   Clothes £28

Food £80   Savings £40   Spare £14

Draw a pie chart to show how he allocates his money.

(b) Kasha has a £60 rise. He now allocates his money as shown in the pie chart.

   (i) Calculate how much he now spends on rent, travel, clothes, food, savings and how much he has spare.

   (ii) Which items have not changed?

5 The numbers of pens and pencils in five students pencil cases are shown in the table.

Name	Number	Angle needed
Gwyneth	3	45°
Peter	8	
Wes	4	
Mario	2	
Nesta	7	

(a) Copy and complete the table by calculating the angles needed to draw a pie chart.

(b) Draw the pie chart.

6 The table shows the numbers and types of tickets sold at a cinema box office.

Type of ticket	Standard	Student	Senior
Number sold	38	24	10

Draw a pie chart to illustrate this data.

Mixed exercise 20

1 A rugby team played 10 games.
Here are the numbers of points the team scored.

     12   22   14   11   7   18   22   14   36   14

   (a) Write down the mode.

   (b) Work out the range.

   (c) Work out the mean.

   (d) Work out the median.

2 Here are the times, in minutes, to do the washing up:

     6   11   16   13   8   9   21   36   25   16

     21   34   16   26   10   9   10   20   17   11

   (a) Draw a stem and leaf diagram to show these times.

   (b) Work out the median.

   (c) Calculate the mean.

3 Jan measures the heights, in millimetres, of 20 plants in her greenhouse. Here are her results:

     178   189   147   147   166

     167   153   171   164   158

     189   166   165   155   152

     147   158   148   151   172

   (a) Copy and complete the stem and leaf diagram to show this information.

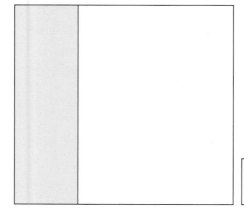

Key

   (b) Work out the median.   [E]

4   A fire service put out 90 fires last year.
The table shows information about the months when
the fires were put out.
Sam is going to draw a pie chart to show this
information.

  (a) Complete the table to show the sizes of the angles
       Sam needs to draw the pie chart.

Months	Number of fires put out	Angle
January to March	15	
April to June	26	
July to September	35	
October to December	14	

  (b) Draw an accurate pie chart to show this information.

5   40 passengers at Gatwick Airport were asked which
country they were flying to. Here is a frequency table
which shows that information:

Country	Number of passengers
USA	14
France	10
Spain	11
Greece	5

Draw an accurate pie chart to show this information.   [E]

6   The table shows the maximum and minimum
temperatures, in degrees Celsius, for one day last year.

City	Maximum	Minimum
Vienna	12	1
Rome	13	4
Madrid	19	3
Cape Town	35	16
Melbourne	26	14

  (a) Calculate the range in each city.
  (b) List the cities in order, highest range first.
  (c) Which city has the smallest range?

7 Sita spent £90 as in the table.

(a) Calculate the angle of each sector.

(b) Draw a pie chart to show her spending.

Items	Amount spent	Angle of sector
Bus fares	£12	
Going out	£25	
Clothes	£30	
Records	£15	
Other	£8	
Total spending	**£90**	**Total angles 360°**

[E]

Summary of key points

1 The **mode** of a set of data is the value which occurs most often.

2 The **median** is the middle value when the data is arranged in order of size.

3 The **mean** of a set of data is the sum of the values divided by the number of values:

$$\text{mean} = \frac{\text{sum of values}}{\text{number of values}}$$

4 The **range** of a set of data is the difference between the highest value and the lowest value:

range = highest value − lowest value

5 A **stem and leaf diagram** shows the shape of the distribution and keeps all the data values.

Always include a **key** with a stem and leaf diagram to show how the stem and leaf are combined.

6 A **pie chart** is a good way of displaying data when you want to show how something is shared or divided.

7 The angles at the centre of a pie chart add up to 360°.

21 Formulae and inequalities

You learned about equations in Chapter 11. This chapter shows you how to use word and algebraic formulae and equations to help solve problems.

21.1 Using word formulae

Example 1

David works in a factory. He is paid by the hour and is given an extra bonus at the end of the week. His pay can be calculated using this **word formula**:

pay = rate of pay × hours worked + bonus

Work out his pay when he works for 40 hours at a rate of pay of £7 an hour and earns a bonus of £20.

pay = £7 × 40 + £20
    = £280 + £20 = £300

He earns £300.

Exercise 21A

1   To work out his pay Keith uses the word formula:

pay = rate of pay × hours worked + bonus

   (a) Work out his pay when he works for 30 hours at a rate of pay of £6 an hour and earns a bonus of £30.

   (b) Work out his pay when he works for 35 hours at a rate of pay of £5.50 an hour and earns a bonus of £15.

2   To work out the distance around her bicycle wheel Davina uses the formula:

distance = 3 × diameter

   (a) Work out the distance around the wheel if the diameter is 60 cm.

   (b) Work out the distance around the wheel if the diameter is 50 cm.

3 Use the formula

cost of pens = cost of one pen × number of pens

to work out the cost of 17 pens if one pen costs 25p.

Writing word formulae

Sometimes you will need to write a word formula from information you are given.

Example 2

Jill worked for 30 hours at a rate of pay of £8 an hour. How much should she get paid?

You can write a word formula to find her pay for any number of hours she works:

pay = hours worked × rate of pay

    = 30 × £8

    = £240

Example 3

Rashmi buys 24 pens at 65 pence each.
Work out the total cost of the pens.

Here is a suitable word formula:

cost = number of pens × cost of one pen

    = 24 × 65p

    = 1560p = £15.60

A **word formula** uses words to represent a relationship between quantities.

Exercise 21B

For each of the following questions, first write down a word formula, then use it to help you find the answers.

1 Daniel works for 30 hours at a rate of pay of £9 an hour. How much should he get paid?

2 Helen works for 20 hours at a rate of pay of £7.50 an hour. How much should she get paid?

3 Abdul works for 30 hours at a rate of pay of £5.75 an hour. How much should he get paid?

4 Susan buys 12 pens at £1.20 each. Work out the total cost of the pens.

5 Roger buys 24 pens at 50p each. Work out the total cost of the pens.

6 Rachel buys 12 books at 28p each. Work out the total cost of the books.

7 Keith buys 15 stamps at 30p each. Work out the total cost of the stamps.

8 Andy buys 20 stamps at 42p each. Work out the total cost of the stamps.

9 Karen sells 50 cakes at 40p each. How much money does she collect?

10 Louise sells 45 loaves of bread at 92p each. How much money does she collect?

11 Mark adds together his age and the age of his sister Pauline. He gets a total of 28. If Mark is 16 how old is Pauline?

12 James loses some £1 coins from his money bag. He had £12 to start with and now only has £7. How many coins has he lost?

13 A chocolate bar machine holds 48 bars of chocolate. After 23 are sold how many are left?

14 At Anne's birthday party there were 48 cans of drink. Everybody at the party had 4 cans. How many people were at the party?

15 Naomi shared a bag of sweets equally between herself and her 6 friends. There were 56 sweets in the bag. How many sweets did the 7 people have each?

16 Evan and his 9 friends were playing football and smashed a window. The cost of repairing the window was £126. The 10 friends decided to split the cost equally between them. How much did they each have to pay?

21.2 Writing algebraic formulae

It is usual in algebra to write a word formula using letters.

For example:
Area of a rectangle $= l \times w$

$$A = lw$$

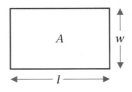

Example 4

Write the word formula used in Example 2 as an algebraic formula.

pay = hours worked × rate of pay

Use the letters P for pay, H for hours worked, and R for rate of pay. The algebraic formula is:

$$P = H \times R \quad \text{or} \quad P = HR$$

Example 5

Write the word formula used in Example 3 as an algebraic formula.

cost = number of pens × cost of one pen

Use the letters C for cost, N for number of pens, and P for cost of one pen. The algebraic formula is:

$$C = N \times P \quad \text{or} \quad C = NP$$

An **algebraic formula** uses letters to repressent a relationship between quantities.

Exercise 21C

Write an algebraic formula for questions 10–16 in Exercise 21B. Remember to explain what each letter stands for.

21.3 Using algebraic formulae

Section 21.2 showed you how to write **algebraic formulae**. You also need to know how to use algebraic formulae, by substituting number values for the letters.

The next two exercises provide practice in substituting numbers into algebraic expressions.

Example 6

Let $a = 3$, $b = 2$ and $c = 5$

Work out the value of **(a)** $a + b$ **(b)** ab **(c)** $3c - 2a$

(a) $a + b = 3 + 2 = 5$

(b) $ab = a \times b = 3 \times 2 = 6$

(c) $3c - 2a = 3 \times c - 2 \times a$
$\qquad\qquad = 3 \times 5 - 2 \times 3$
$\qquad\qquad = 15 - 6 = 9$

Exercise 21D

In this exercise $a = 3$, $b = 2$, $c = 5$ and $d = 0$

Work out the value of these expressions.

1 $a + c$	**2** $b + c$	**3** $a + b + c$
4 $2a$	**5** $3c$	**6** $5d$
7 ac	**8** ad	**9** $5b + 2a$
10 $4c - 2b$	**11** $5a + 2b$	**12** $2a + 3b + 4c$
13 $c - a$	**14** $c - 2d$	**15** $ab - c$
16 $4b + 2d$	**17** $3c - 2b$	**18** $5a - 3c$
19 $ac - ab$	**20** abc	**21** $2c - ad$

Exercise 21E

In this exercise $p = 2$, $q = 4$, $r = 3$ and $s = 0$

Work out the value of these expressions.

1 $3p$	**2** $4q$	**3** $5r$
4 $10s$	**5** $p + q$	**6** $q + r$
7 $r + s$	**8** $p + q + r$	**9** $2p + 4q$
10 $3s + 3p$	**11** $5r - 2q$	**12** $4r - 3q$
13 pq	**14** qr	**15** rs
16 pqr	**17** $5q - 8p$	**18** $3p - 2r + 3pq$
19 $4p - 2s$	**20** $3q - pr$	**21** $2pq + 3qr - 2pqr$

Using numbers in algebraic formulae

Example 7

Write

(a) a word formula

(b) an algebraic formula

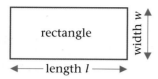

for the perimeter of a rectangle.

(c) Use your formula to find the perimeter of a rectangle with length 10 and width 2.

> **Remember:**
> Perimeter is the distance around the boundary of a shape.

(a) perimeter = 2 × length + 2 × width

(b) $P = 2l + 2w$ where P is the perimeter, l is length and w is width

(c) When $l = 12$ and $w = 10$:

$$P = 2 \times 12 + 2 \times 10 = 24 + 20 = 44$$

Exercise 21F

1 The formula for the perimeter of an equilateral triangle is $P = 3l$. Work out the value of P when

(a) $l = 5$ (b) $l = 7$

(c) $l = 4$ (d) $l = 12.4$

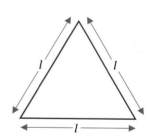

2 The formula for the area of a rectangle is $A = lw$. Find the value of A when

(a) $l = 6$ and $w = 4$ (b) $l = 5$ and $w = 3$

(c) $l = 10$ and $w = 5.6$ (d) $l = 7.5$ and $w = 3.4$

3 James uses the formula $d = st$ to work out the distance travelled, where the time taken is t and the speed is s. Find the value of d when

(a) $s = 40$ and $t = 4$ (b) $s = 50$ and $t = 2.5$

(c) $s = 70$ and $t = 3$ (d) $s = 15.8$ and $t = 5$

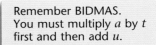

4 Ayesha uses the formula $v = u + at$ to work out velocity.
Find the value of v when

    (a) $u = 3$, $a = 2$ and $t = 5$
    (b) $u = 5$, $a = 10$ and $t = 3$
    (c) $u = 0$, $a = 10$ and $t = 6$
    (d) $u = 2.5$, $a = 3$ and $t = 1.5$

> Remember BIDMAS.
> You must multiply a by t
> first and then add u.

5 Alex uses the formula $P = rh + b$ to work out
his pay, where r is his rate of pay per hour,
h is the number of hours worked, and b is
his bonus.
Work out the value of P when

    (a) $r = 4$, $h = 12$ and $b = 5$
    (b) $r = 5$, $h = 40$ and $b = 10$
    (c) $r = 1.5$, $h = 4$ and $b = 1$
    (d) $r = 2.5$, $h = 6$ and $b = 2.5$

21.4 Using negative numbers

Sometimes you will need to substitute negative numbers into
algebraic formulae.

The next four exercises provide practice in using negative
numbers in expressions.

Exercise 21G

Work out these additions and subtractions.

1 $2 - 5$	**2** $-2 + 4$	**3** $-2 - 4$
4 $3 + (-7)$	**5** $-3 + 5$	**6** $-5 - 3$
7 $2 - (-3)$	**8** $6 - (-5)$	**9** $10 + (-10)$
10 $-1 - 8$	**11** $1 - (-7)$	**12** $-4 - (-2)$

> Remember:
> Two like signs next to
> each other are replaced
> by a +
> Two unlike signs next to
> each other are replaced
> by a −
> So
> | | | | |
> |---|---|---|---|
> | + | + | = | + |
> | + | − | = | − |
> | − | + | = | − |
> | − | − | = | + |

___ Example 8 ___

Find **(a)** $a - b$ **(b)** $c + b$ **(c)** $a + c$ **(d)** $a - c$
when $a = 4$, $b = 6$ and $c = -3$

(a) $a - b = 4 - 6 = -2$
(b) $c + b = -3 + 6 = 3$
(c) $a + c = 4 + (-3) = 4 - 3 = 1$
(d) $a - c = 4 - (-3) = 4 + 3 = 7$

Exercise 21H

In this exercise let $a = 3$, $b = -2$, $c = -5$ and $d = 0$
Work out the value of these expressions.

1 $a + b$	**2** $a + c$	**3** $b + c$
4 $c + d$	**5** $a - b$	**6** $c - a$
7 $b - c$	**8** $c - d$	**9** $b - a$
10 $a - c$	**11** $c - b$	**12** $d - c$
13 $a + b + c$	**14** $a + b - c$	**15** $a + b - d$
16 $d - a$	**17** $a - b + c$	**18** $a - b - c$
19 $d - a + b$	**20** $d - b + a - c$	**21** $c - b - a$

Exercise 21I

Work out these multiplications.

1 4×-3	**2** -2×6	**3** 10×-1	**4** -2×-2
5 3×-7	**6** -8×4	**7** -6×-5	**8** -3×-9

Remember:
When you multiply two numbers:

$+$	$\times$	$+$	$=$	$+$
$+$	$\times$	$-$	$=$	$-$
$-$	$\times$	$+$	$=$	$-$
$-$	$\times$	$-$	$=$	$+$

Example 9

If $a = -5$, $b = 3$ and $c = -3$, find   **(a)** $2a$ **(b)** ab **(c)** ac

(a) $2a = 2 \times a = 2 \times -5 = -10$
(b) $ab = a \times b = -5 \times 3 = -15$
(c) $ac = a \times c = -5 \times -3 = 15$

Exercise 21J

Let $a = -3$, $b = 2$, $c = -5$ and $d = 0$
Work out the value of these expressions.

1 $a + c$	**2** $b + c$	**3** $a + b + c$
4 $2a$	**5** $3c$	**6** $5d$
7 ac	**8** ad	**9** $5b + 2a$
10 $4c - 2b$	**11** $5a + 2b$	**12** $2a + 3b + 4c$
13 $c - a$	**14** $c - 2d$	**15** $ab - c$
16 $4b + 2d$	**17** $3c - 2b$	**18** $5a - 3c$
19 $ac - ab$	**20** $abc - 2ad$	**21** $3c - 2ab + 4b$

Negative numbers in algebraic formulae

Example 10

The formula $v = u + at$ is used in maths and science to work out velocities.

Work out the value of v when $u = 5$, $a = -2$ and $t = 10$.

$v = u + at$

$v = 5 + -2 \times 10$

$v = 5 + -20$

$v = -15$

Exercise 21K

1 Using the formula $v = u + at$, find the value of v when

(a) $u = 3$, $a = -2$, $t = 5$ (b) $u = -5$, $a = 10$, $t = 3$

(c) $u = 0$, $a = -10$, $t = 6$ (d) $u = -2.5$, $a = -3$, $t = 1.5$

2 Using the formula $P = a(b - c)$, find the value of P when

(a) $a = 2$, $b = 3$, $c = 3$ (b) $a = 2$, $b = 3$, $c = -3$

(c) $a = 3$, $b = -2$, $c = 3$ (d) $a = 3$, $b = -2$, $c = -3$

3 Using the formula $r = st + (t - s)$, find the value of r when

(a) $s = 2$, $t = -3$ (b) $s = 3$, $t = -2$

(c) $s = -2$, $t = 3$ (d) $s = -2$, $t = -3$

(e) $s = 4$, $t = 2$ (f) $s = 5$, $t = -4$

21.5 Substituting into more complicated formulae

Sometimes you have to use formulae containing powers.

Example 11

Use the formula $s = \frac{1}{2}at^2$ to find s when $t = 4$ and $a = 10$.

$s = \frac{1}{2} \times 10 \times 4^2$

$s = \frac{1}{2} \times 10 \times 16$

$s = 5 \times 16 = 80$

> Remember BIDMAS.
> Work out Indices before
> Multiplication.

Exercise 21L

1 The formula for working out how far a ball has fallen when dropped off a cliff is:

$$s = 5t^2$$

Find the value of s when t is:

(a) 1   (b) 2   (c) 5   (d) 10   (e) 3.5

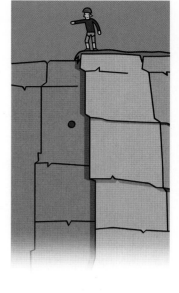

2 Copy this table of values.

x	-3	-2	-1	0	1	2	3
$y = 3x^2 + 4$							

Complete the table by substituting the values of x into the formula to find the values of y.

3 If $a = 2$, $b = 8$ and $c = -4$ work out the value of:

(a) $a^2 + b$ (b) $c^2 - b$

(c) $b^3 - a^2$ (d) $b^2 - c^2$

(e) $b - (a^2 + c)$ (f) $c^2 + (a - c^2)$

(g) $2(a + b)^2$ (h) $c(a + b)^3$

(i) $(a + b)^2 + (a + c)^2$ (j) $2(b + c)^2 - 3(b - c)^2$

4 The speed of a car is given by the formula:

$$v = \sqrt{(u^2 + 2as)}$$

By substituting in values, find v when

(a) $u = 10$, $a = 2$, $s = 5$ (b) $u = 5$, $a = 5$, $s = 10$

(c) $u = 5$, $a = 0$, $s = 10$ (d) $u = -5$, $a = 2$, $s = 5$

(e) $u = -10$, $a = -5$, $s = 10$ (f) $u = 0$, $a = 10$, $s = 10$

More substitution

Example 12

Evaluate the expression $\dfrac{2a + b}{c}$ when $a = 3$, $b = 4$ and $c = 2$.

Evaluate means 'Find the value of'.

$$2a = 2 \times 3 = 6$$

so $2a + b = 6 + 4 = 10$

and $\dfrac{2a + b}{c} = \dfrac{10}{2} = 5$

Exercise 21M

Work out the value of these algebraic expressions using the values given.

1   (a) $4a + 1$ if $a = 3$
    (b) $3b + c$ if $b = 5$, $c = 2$
    (c) $2f - g$ if $f = 1.5$, $g = 4$
    (d) $hg - 2$ if $h = 1.5$, $g = 3$
    (e) $10 + 3x$ if $x = -2$
    (f) $2x - 3y$ if $x = 4$, $y = -2$
    (g) $2x + 3$ if $x = \frac{1}{5}$
    (h) $3ab$ if $a = \frac{1}{4}$, $b = 2$

2   (a) $2(a + 3)$ if $a = 5$
    (b) $3(s - 2)$ if $s = 7$
    (c) $4(p + q)$ if $p = 5$, $q = 3$
    (d) $r(8 - s)$ if $r = 3$, $s = 5$
    (e) $3(b + 7)$ if $b = -2$
    (f) $2(3 - c)$ if $c = -4$

> Remember BIDMAS.
> Brackets first.

3   (a) $5(a + b)$ if $a = 3$, $b = 4$
    (b) $4(x + y)$ if $x = 5$, $y = -3$
    (c) $\dfrac{a}{4} + 3$ if $a = 12$
    (d) $\dfrac{a}{b} + 5$ if $a = 20$, $b = 4$
    (e) $\dfrac{m - 4}{2}$ if $m = 12$
    (f) $\dfrac{7 - x}{y}$ if $x = -3$, $y = -2$

4   (a) $\dfrac{m + n}{r}$ if $m = 8$, $n = 7$, $r = 5$

    (b) $\dfrac{4q + r}{6}$ if $q = 5$, $r = 4$

    (c) $\dfrac{3s - r}{t}$ if $s = 8$, $r = 6$, $t = 3$

    (d) $\dfrac{3s}{4} - r$ if $s = 8$, $r = 3$

    (e) $x - \dfrac{3y}{6}$ if $x = 3$, $y = -4$

Activity – Number patterns

(a) (i)   Copy and complete this table by putting values for r and t into the algebraic expression $2r + t$.
     (ii) Look for number patterns in the table.
     (iii) Try to explain the number patterns.
     (iv) Do the number patterns still hold for negative values of r and t?

$2r + t$		t			
	0	1	2	3	4
0	0	1	2	3	4
1	2	3	4	5	6
r 2	4	5	6		
3	6	7			
4					

(b) Repeat part **(a)** for other algebraic expressions involving two letters.
For example, use
$r + 2t, 2r + 3t, r + t, 2(r + t), rt + 1.$

?	0	1	2	3	4
0	0	1	2	3	4
1	4	5	6	7	8
2	8	9	10	11	12
3	12	13	14	15	16
4					

(c) Find the algebraic expression used to make the table on the right.

(d) Set some problems like part **(c)** for your friends.

21.6 Using algebraic equations

You can solve some problems using **algebraic equations**. Though they can look similar, an equation is different from a formula:

- **Formulae** can be used to calculate a result. For example:

  pay = rate of pay × hours worked

  You could put **any** values into these parts of the formula and get a result for the amount of pay.

- **Equations** may be true for one value or several values, but are not generally true for any value. For example:

  $3x = 6$

  This equation is **only** true when $x = 2$.
  $x = 2$ is called a **solution** of the equation.

An **algebraic equation** can be solved to find an unknown quantity.

Example 13

The perimeter of this rectangle is 30 cm.
The length is x cm and the width is 4 cm.

Work out the value of the length.

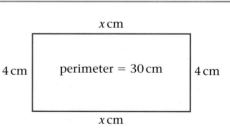

$$x + x + 4 + 4 = 30$$
$$2x + 8 = 30$$
$$2x + 8 - 8 = 30 - 8 \quad \text{Subtract 8 from each side.}$$
$$2x = 22$$
$$x = 11 \quad \text{Divide each side by 2.}$$

The length x is 11 cm.

Example 14

Suzanne thought of a number, multiplied it by 4 and then subtracted 3. The answer was 13.
What was the number she thought of?

$$4 \times n - 3 = 13 \qquad\qquad n \text{ represents the number.}$$
$$4n - 3 = 13$$
$$4n - 3 + 3 = 13 + 3 \quad\text{——— Add 3 to each side.}$$
$$4n = 16$$
$$n = 4 \quad\text{——— Divide each side by 4.}$$

Exercise 21N

1 Use the information in these diagrams to find the values of the letters.

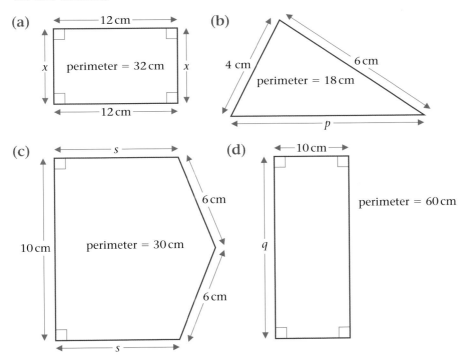

(a) 12 cm, x, perimeter = 32 cm, x, 12 cm

(b) 4 cm, 6 cm, perimeter = 18 cm, p

(c) s, 6 cm, 10 cm, perimeter = 30 cm, 6 cm, s

(d) 10 cm, perimeter = 60 cm, q

2 The perimeter of this isosceles triangle is 30 cm. Work out the lengths of the sides marked y.

y cm y cm   12 cm

3 Gail thought of a number. She multiplied it by 5 and then added 4. The answer was 14. What number did she first think of?

4 Andrew thought of a number. He multiplied it by 6 and then subtracted 15. The answer was 27. What number did Andrew first think of?

5 Darren started a new book and read x pages of the book for each of the first four days. On the fifth day he read 12 pages and finished the book. The book had 100 pages. Work out the value of x.

6 Julia thought of a number, subtracted 5 from it and then multiplied the answer by 6 to get a final answer of 30. What number did Julia first think of?

7 There were 25 chocolates in a box. Four friends had an equal number of chocolates and this left 9 chocolates in the box.
How many chocolates did each of the friends have?

8 Trevor thought of a number, added 7 to it and then multiplied the answer by 5. This gave an answer of 55. What number did Trevor first think of?

9 Sigourney thought of a number, subtracted 12 from it and then divided her answer by 3 to get a final answer of 4. What number did Sigourney first think of?

More algebraic equations

Example 15

Use the diagram to write down an equation in terms of x. Solve your equation.

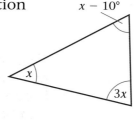

$$x + x - 10 + 3x = 180$$
$$5x - 10 = 180$$
$$5x = 190$$
$$x = 38$$
$$x = 38°$$

> Remember:
> The angles of a triangle add up to 180°.

Exercise 210

In each question
(a) use the diagram to write down an equation in terms of x
(b) solve your equation.

1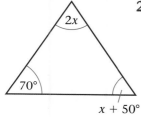

2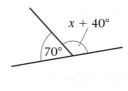

3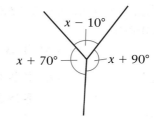

4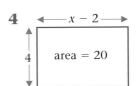

5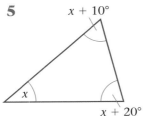

6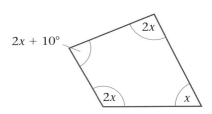

7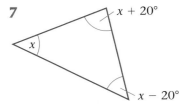

8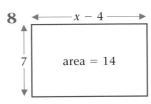

9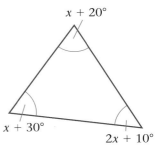

10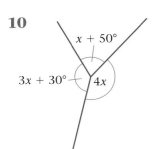

11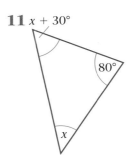

12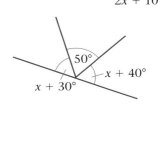

21.7 Inequalities

There are lots of apples, but there are only a few bananas. If a is the number of apples and b is the number of bananas, then a is greater than b. You can write this as $a > b$.

> The smaller end of the symbol always points towards the smaller number.
>
> The larger end points towards the larger number.

$>$ means **greater than** $<$ means **less than**
$\geqslant$ means **greater than or equal to** $\leqslant$ means **less than or equal to**

Example 16

Put the correct sign between each pair of numbers to make a true statement.

(a) 6, 7

(b) 8, 5

(a) 6 is less than 7

$6 < 7$

(b) 8 is greater than 5

$8 > 5$

406 Chapter 21 Formulae and inequalities

Example 17

Write down the values of x that are integers and satisfy these inequalities:

(a) $2 < x < 7$

(b) $-2 < x \leqslant 3$

> Integers are the negative and positive whole numbers including zero.

(a) $2 < x$ means the same as $x > 2$ so the numbers must be greater than 2: 3, 4, 5, 6, 7, 8 ... $x < 7$ so the numbers must stop before 7. The answer is 3, 4, 5, 6.

(b) $x > -2$ so the numbers must be greater than -2: $-1, 0, 1, 2, 3, 4, 5...$ $x \leqslant 3$ so the numbers must stop at 3. The answer is $-1, 0, 1, 2, 3$.

> A number **satisfies** an inequality if it makes that inequality true.
> $x = 3$ **satisfies** the inequality $x < 7$ because $3 < 7$.

Exercise 21P

1 Put the correct sign between each pair of numbers to make a true statement.

(a) 4, 6   (b) 5, 2   (c) 12, 8   (d) 6, 6

(e) 15, 8   (f) 3, 24   (g) 10, 3   (h) 0, 0.1

(i) 6, 0.7   (j) 4.5, 4.5   (k) 0.2, 0.5   (l) 4.8, 4.79

2 Write down whether each statement is true or false. If it is false, write down the pair of numbers with the correct sign.

(a) $6 > 4$ (b) $2 > 6$ (c) $6 > 6$ (d) $6 > 8$

(e) $6 < 5$ (f) $8 = 14$ (g) $7 < 6.99$ (h) $6 > 6.01$

(i) $7 < 0$ (j) $4 < 4$ (k) $6 = 4$ (l) $6 > 0.84$

3 Write down the values of x that are whole numbers and satisfy these inequalities:

(a) $4 < x < 6$ (b) $3 < x < 8$

(c) $0 \leqslant x < 4$ (d) $3 < x < 6$

(e) $1 < x \leqslant 4$ (f) $2 < x < 6$

(g) $4 \leqslant x < 7$ (h) $-2 \leqslant x < 4$

(i) $-1 < x < 5$ (j) $-2 < x \leqslant 6$

(k) $-3 \leqslant x < 3$ (l) $-4 \leqslant x \leqslant 2$

(m) $0 < x < 5$ (n) $-1 < x \leqslant 4$

(o) $-5 \leqslant x < 0$ (p) $-3 \leqslant x \leqslant 3$

Inequalities on a number line

You can show inequalities on a number line.

Example 18

Draw a number line from 0 to 10. Show the inequality

$x > 4$

x is greater than 4. You shade all the numbers to the right of 4:

Draw an empty circle at 4 since the number 4 is *not* included.

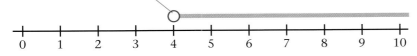

Example 19

Draw a number line from 0 to 10. Show the inequality

$3 \leqslant x < 8$

x is greater than or equal to 3 and less than 8. You shade in the numbers between 3 and 8:

Draw a solid circle at 3 since the number 3 *is* included ($x \geqslant 3$).

Draw an empty circle at 8 since the number 8 is *not* included.

Example 20

Draw a number line from -5 to 5. Show the inequality

$-3 < x \leqslant 4$

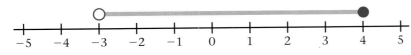

Exercise 21Q

1   Draw six number lines from 0 to 10.
    Show these inequalities:

(a) $x > 6$ (b) $x > 5$

(c) $x < 4$ (d) $x > 8$

(e) $x < 6$ (f) $x > 9$

2 Draw ten number lines from 0 to 10.
Show these inequalities:

(a) $3 < x < 7$ (b) $5 < x < 8$

(c) $5 \leqslant x < 8$ (d) $7 < x \leqslant 9$

(e) $4 \leqslant x \leqslant 6$ (f) $2 < x \leqslant 8$

(g) $3 \leqslant x < 5$ (h) $4 < x < 7$

(i) $5 \leqslant x < 6$ (j) $2 < x \leqslant 5$

3 Draw ten number lines from -5 to 5.
Show these inequalities:

(a) $-3 \leqslant x < 4$ (b) $-2 < x < 5$

(c) $-1 < x \leqslant 3$ (d) $-4 \leqslant x \leqslant 0$

(e) $0 < x < 4$ (f) $-3 < x \leqslant 2$

(g) $-4 \leqslant x < 1$ (h) $0 \leqslant x \leqslant 3$

(i) $-5 \leqslant x < -2$ (j) $-2 \leqslant x < 1$

4 Write down the inequalities represented by the shading
on these number lines:

(a)
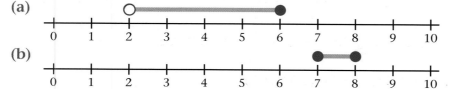

(b)

(c)
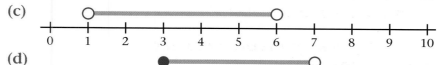

(d)
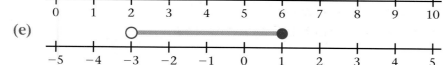

(e)
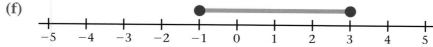

(f)

(g)
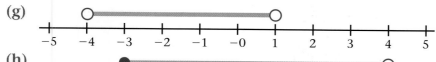

(h)
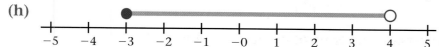

Mixed exercise 21

1 (a) Write in symbols the rule 'To find y, double x and add 1'.

(b) Use your rule from part (a) to calculate the value
of x when $y = 9$.   [E]

2 Here is the formula for working out the perimeter of a rectangle:

$$P = 2(l + w)$$

Use the formula to work out the value of P when $l = 6$ and $w = 4$. [E]

3 A quarterly gas bill is given by the formula

$$C = S + nx$$

where C is the total cost of the bill in pence

   S is the standing charge in pence

   n is the number of units used

   x pence is the cost per unit.

Calculate the value of C when $S = 860$, $n = 152$ and $x = 7$.

4 Find the value of $x(x + y)$ when $x = -2$ and $y = 1$. [E]

5 If $a = 1$, $b = 2$ and $c = -3$, find the value of

(a) $\dfrac{c - ab}{c + ab}$ (b) $3(a + b)^2 - 2(b - c)^2$

6 To work out the cost of his mobile phone calls Derek uses this formula:

   cost of calls = total time (minutes) $\times$ 10p

Work out, in pounds, the cost of a 25 minute call.

7 This word formula is used to work out the cost of placing an advertisement in a newspaper:

   cost of advertisement = area (cm^2) $\times$ £15

Work out the cost of an advert which is 3 cm wide and 10 cm tall.

8 $a = 4$, $b = \frac{1}{4}$, $c = -3$

Work out

(a) $\dfrac{5a}{b} + 7$ (b) $\dfrac{6a + 2c}{3}$

(c) $3a - 6b + c$ (d) $a(a - 8b)$

9 Write down an expression in terms of n and g for the total cost, in pence, of n buns at 18 pence each and 5 bread rolls at g pence each. [E]

10 Choc bars cost 27 pence each.
Write down a formula for the cost, C pence, of n choc bars. [E]

11 The air temperature, $T°C$, outside an aircraft flying at a height of h feet is given by the formula $T = 26 - \dfrac{h}{500}$.

An aircraft is flying at a height of 27 000 feet.

(a) Use the formula to calculate the air temperature outside the aircraft.

The temperature outside an aircraft is $-52°C$.

(b) Calculate the height of the aircraft.   [E]

12 Mary thought of a number and multiplied it by 5 and subtracted 4. The answer was 31. What is the number she thought of?

13 (a) Use each diagram to write down an equation in terms of x.

(i)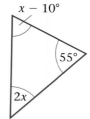

(ii)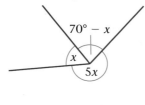

(b) Solve your equations from part (a).

14 Draw a number line from -6 to $+6$.

(a) Show in these inequalities:

(i) $-3 < x \leqslant 5$ (ii) $-2 \leqslant x < 3$ (iii) $-5 < x < 0$

(b) List the integer values that satisfy each inequality.

15 Write down the inequalities represented by these number lines:

(a)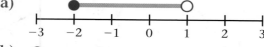

(b)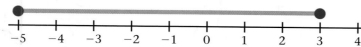

Summary of key points

1 A **word formula** uses words to represent a relationship between quantities.

For example: pay = rate of pay × hours worked

2 An **algebraic formula** uses letters to represent a relationship between quantities.

For example, the perimeter of a rectangle is related to its length l and width w by:

$P = 2l + 2w$

3 An **algebraic equation** can be solved to find an unknown quantity.

4 $>$ means **greater than** $<$ means **less than**

$\geqslant$ means **greater than or equal to** $\leqslant$ means **less than or equal to**

22 Transformations

Karen decided to rearrange the furniture in her bedroom.

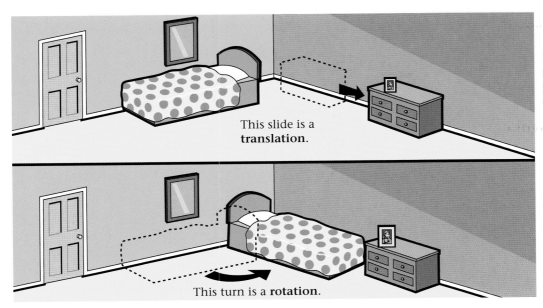

This slide is a **translation**.

This turn is a **rotation**.

First she moved her storage unit further along the wall by sliding it.

Then she turned her bed a quarter turn.

The mirror was now in a position where she could see her own **reflection** close up without the bed being in the way.

The photograph on the storage unit was rather small, so she had an **enlargement** made of it.

Reflections, rotations, translations and enlargements are all **transformations**. To help distinguish between the 'before' and 'after' positions of a shape they have special names: the starting shape is called the **object** and the finishing position of the shape is called the **image**.

22.1 Translation

The rook in these pictures has moved 4 squares forwards.

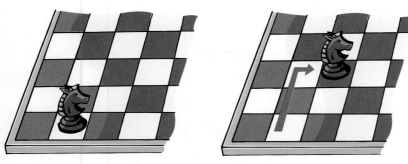

The knight has moved 2 squares forwards and 1 square to the right.

A sliding movement is called a **translation**.

Here are some examples:

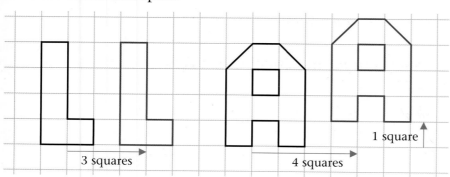

3 squares

4 squares

1 square

Object and image are congruent.

In a translation all the points of the shape move exactly the same amount.

Example 1

Draw the image of *ABCD* after a translation of 3 squares to the right and 1 square up.

The vertices are all going to be displaced 3 squares to the right and 1 square up.

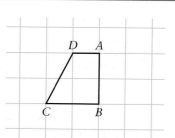

Translate each vertex.

Join up the vertices.

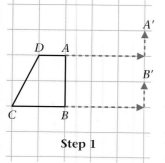

Step 1

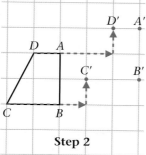

Step 2

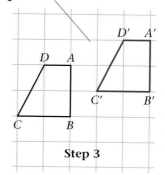

Step 3

You could check that this is right by making the shape out of card or paper and sliding it from object to image.

Exercise 22A

1 Copy each shape onto squared paper and translate it by the amount shown.

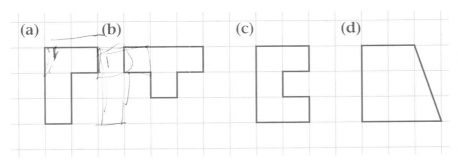

(a)   (b)   (c)   (d)

    2 squares right   3 squares up   4 squares down   1 square left

2 Copy each shape onto squared paper and draw their images after translating by the amount shown.

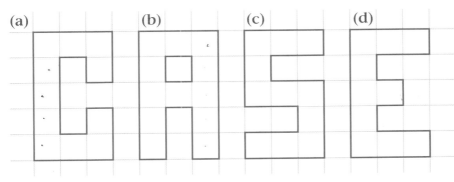

(a)   (b)   (c)   (d)

| 2 squares right and 3 squares up | 2 squares left and 4 squares down | 4 squares right and 1 square down | 3 squares left and 4 squares up |

3 Perform the four translations in question **2** on this shape. Draw a separate diagram for each transformation.

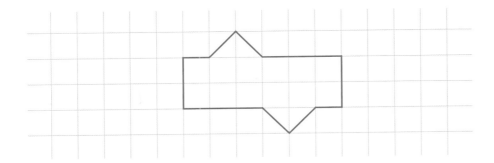

4 Describe the translation for each object–image pair.

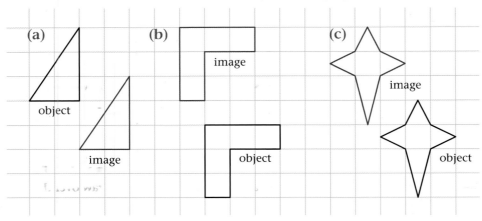

22.2 Rotation

Images of a shape which are formed by turning are called **rotations** of the shape.

The rotation can be described as a fraction of a full turn or as an angle. If no direction is given the turn is in an anticlockwise direction.

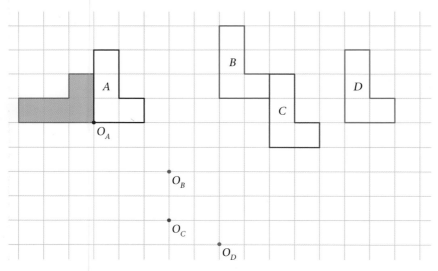

> The shaded shape rotated around point O_A becomes A.
>
> The shaded shape rotated around point O_B becomes B.

> Object and image are congruent.

> You might find it useful to use tracing paper.

The shaded shape is the object. All the others are images and they are all $\frac{3}{4}$ turns anticlockwise but they are not the same rotation.

The point about which the turning occurs is important.

The point about which the turning occurs is called the **centre of rotation**.

How to rotate a shape on paper

To rotate this shape half a turn about the point marked with a dot:

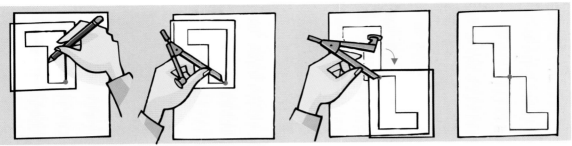

Trace the shape and the fixed point. Turn the tracing over and draw the outline on the back in pencil.

Place the tracing exactly over the original shape. Keep the point fixed using the point of a pair of compasses.

Rotate the tracing through half a turn (180°). Scribble over it to transfer the image.

Draw over the image to make it clear.

You could also do this using a card cut-out of the shape.
This pattern has been made by repeated rotations.
A is rotated to **B**, **B** is rotated to **C**, **C** is rotated to **D**.

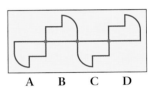

A   B   C   D

Example 2

Draw the image of each shape after it has been rotated $\frac{1}{4}$ turn clockwise using the point O as centre.

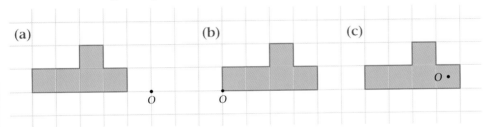

(a)   (b)   (c)

Using tracing paper:

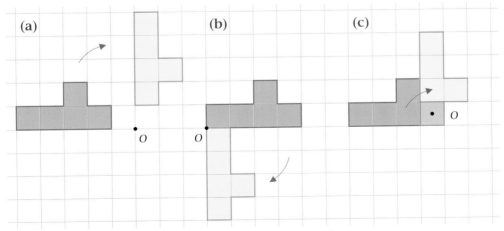

(a)   (b)   (c)

Notice that each line of the object has turned $\frac{1}{4}$ turn clockwise. This is obvious on this shape which is drawn on grid lines but would be true for diagonal lines as well.

Exercise 22B

1   Draw separate images for each shape after a rotation of 90° clockwise about each of the centres marked.

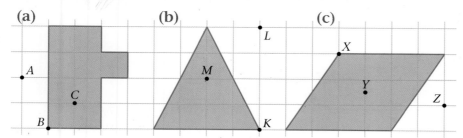

(a)   (b)   (c)

2   Copy these shapes and rotate them through a $\frac{1}{2}$ turn using the centres marked.

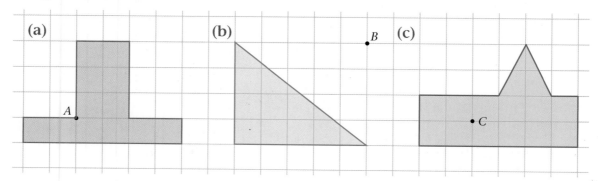

(a)   (b)   (c)

3   Each diagram shows an object and its image. Copy each diagram and write down how much the object has been rotated and the direction of the rotation. Try to identify the centre of the rotation and mark it on your diagram.

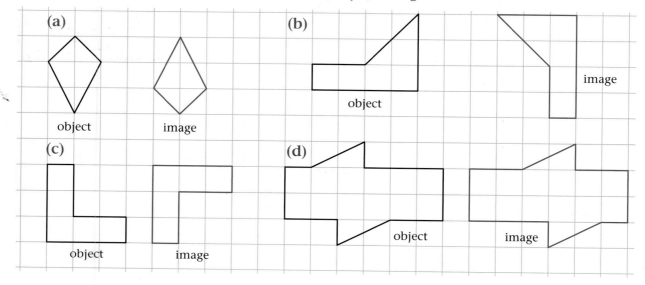

(a)   (b)   (c)   (d)

22.3 Reflection

When you next look in a mirror check to see that your image appears to be as far behind the mirror as you are in front. You can test this by moving nearer and further away from the mirror.

In a mathematical **reflection** the image is the same distance behind the mirror line as the object is in front.

Example 3

Reflect the shape in the mirror line.

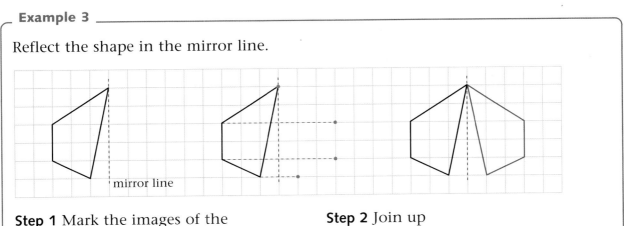

mirror line

Step 1 Mark the images of the vertices. These are the same distance on the other side measured at right angles.

Step 2 Join up the vertices.

Mirror lines are **two-way**. The mirror line may go through the object, requiring reflections to go both ways.

> Object and image are congruent.

Here is a reflection which is two-way:

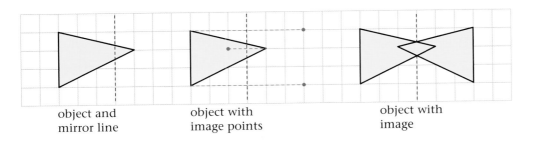

object and   object with   object with
mirror line   image points   image

Example 4

Reflect the shape in the sloping mirror line.

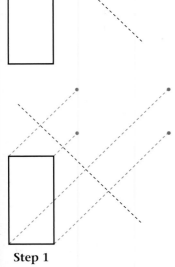

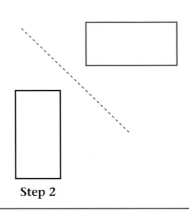

Step 1

Step 2

When the mirror line is sloping it is a good idea to turn the paper until the mirror line is vertical.

This way it is easier to find the images of the vertices.

Exercise 22C

1 Copy each shape onto squared paper and draw the image after reflection using the dotted line as the mirror line.

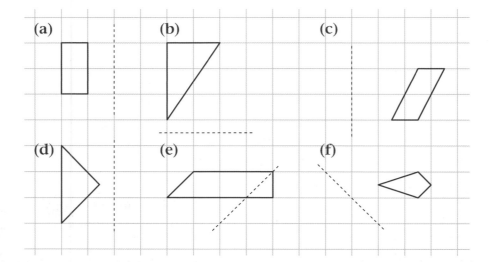

(a)

(b)

(c)

(d)

(e)

(f)

2 Each diagram shows an object with its image. Copy the diagrams onto squared paper and draw in the mirror line.

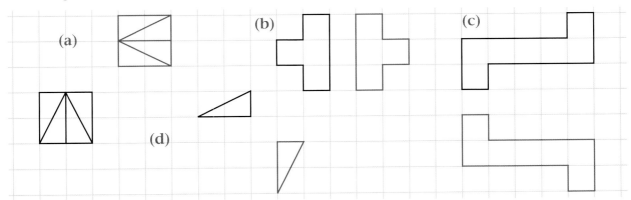

22.4 Enlargement

In an **enlargement**, all angles stay the same and all lengths are changed in the same proportion.

The **scale factor** of the enlargement is the value that the lengths of the original object are multiplied by.

This photograph has been enlarged by scale factor 2.
new length = 2 × old length
new width = 2 × old width

_____ Example 5 _____

Enlarge the shape $ABCD$ by a scale factor of 2 using A as the centre of enlargement.

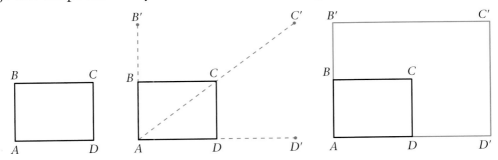

Point A is the centre of enlargement and is fixed. A' is at A.

All other points move 2 times as far away.

$A'D' = 2AD$ $A'C' = 2AC$ $A'B' = 2AB$

> $A'D'$ is the image of AD.

The **centre of enlargement** determines the final position of the enlarged image.

> When one shape is an enlargement of another the shapes are called **similar shapes**.

Example 6

Enlarge shape *EFGHJ* by a scale factor of 2 using the centre of enlargement *C* marked inside the shape.

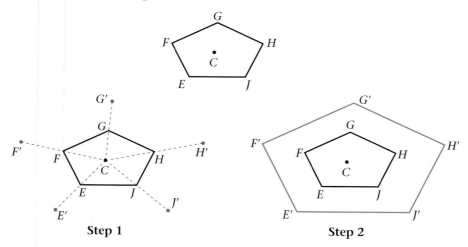

Again, all points move to image positions which are 2 times as far away from the fixed centre.

Example 7

Enlarge the shape *PQRS* by a scale factor of 2 using the centre of enlargement *O* marked outside the shape.

The scale factor is 2, so all the image points are twice as far away from the fixed centre as the object points.

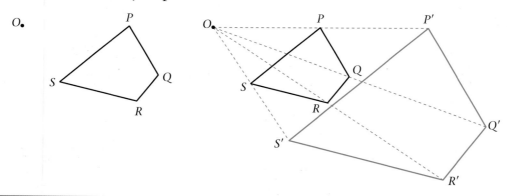

In an enlargement, image lines are **parallel** to their corresponding object lines.

You can check that sloping lines are parallel by regarding them as a combination of a sideways movement and an up/down movement.

If the shape is drawn on a grid you can see if the lines which go along the grid lines are the right length by counting.

Example 8

Enlarge shape *KLMN* by a scale factor of 2 and with the centre of enlargement at the origin.

K is 5 across and 2 up, so *K'* will be 10 across and 4 up. *K'L'* will be twice the length of *KL*.

LM is 2 across and 3 up.

The image *L'M'* will be 4 across and 6 up.

MN is 4 left and 1 down.

The image *M'N'* will be 8 left and 2 down.

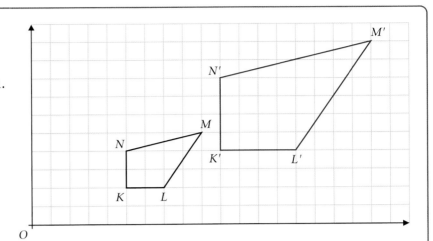

Exercise 22D

In this exercise each question has a scale factor (SF) and three possible centres of enlargement. Copy each diagram and draw the three enlargements either on the same diagram or on separate diagrams.

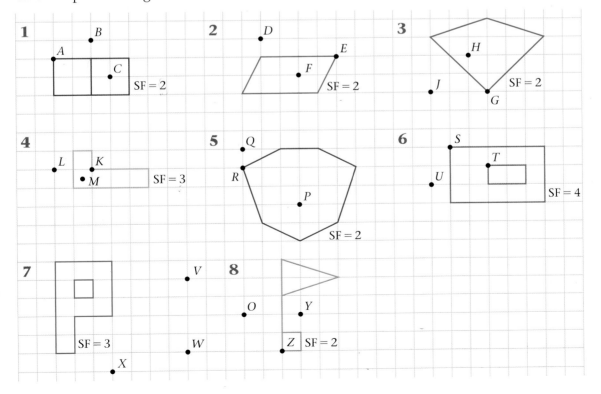

Mixed exercise 22

1 Copy this shape onto squared paper. Enlarge it by a scale factor of 3 using P as the centre of enlargement.

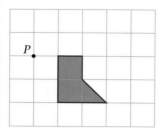

[E]

2 Copy and reflect each of the shapes in the mirror line given.

(a)

(b)

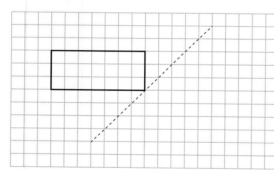

[E]

3 Copy this shape and translate it 8 squares to the right and 2 squares up.

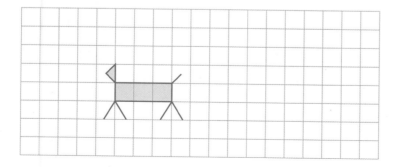

4 **(a)** Make a copy of the diagram. Reflect the shape A in the mirror line.

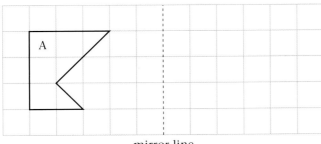

mirror line

Label the reflection B.

(b) Describe the transformation which maps the triangle C onto the triangle D.

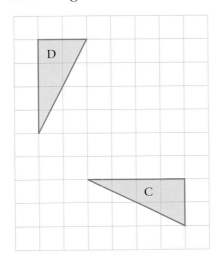

[E]

5 Copy the diagram onto squared paper, and reflect the shape in the mirror line.

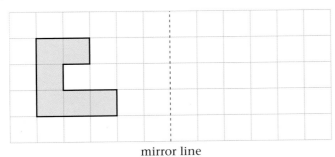

mirror line

Summary of key points

1 A sliding movement is called a **translation**.

2 Images of a shape which are formed by turning are called **rotations** of the shape.

3 The point about which the turning occurs is called the **centre of rotation**.

4 In a mathematical **reflection** the image is the same distance behind the mirror line as the object is in front.

5 Mirror lines are **two-way**. The mirror line may go through the object, requiring reflections to go both ways.

6 In an **enlargement**, all angles stay the same and all lengths are changed in the same proportion.

7 The **scale factor** of the enlargement is the value the lengths of the original object are multiplied by.

8 The **centre of enlargement** determines the final position of the enlarged image.

9 In an enlargement, image lines are **parallel** to their corresponding object lines.

23 Probability

This morning there is a chance of heavy rain with the possibility of thunder. In the afternoon the rain will die away and it is likely that the sun will break through the clouds, probably towards evening.

Weather forecasts are made by studying weather data and using a branch of mathematics called probability.

Probability uses numbers to represent how likely or unlikely it is that an event such as 'a thunderstorm' will happen.

Probability is used by governments, scientists, economists, medical researchers and many other people to **predict** what is likely to happen in the future by studying what has already happened.

23.1 The probability scale

An event which is **certain to happen** has a **probability of 1**.

For example, the probability that night will follow day is 1.

An event which **cannot happen** has a **probability of 0**.

For example, the probability that you will grow to be 5 metres tall is 0.

All probabilities must have a value greater than or equal to 0 and less than or equal to 1.

This can be shown on a **probability scale**:

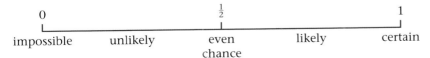

Exercise 23A

1   Draw a 0 to 1 probability scale and mark on it the probability that
  (a)   it will rain tomorrow
  (b)   the sea will disappear
  (c)   Boxing Day will follow Christmas Day this year
  (d)   you will buy a new pair of shoes soon
  (e)   you will have homework tonight
  (f)   the sun will not rise next week
  (g)   a member of the class will be late tomorrow
  (h)   if you toss a coin it will land tail up
  (i)   you will see a TV star on your way home.

2   Give two examples of events that you think
  (a)   are impossible   **(b)**   are unlikely
  (c)   have about an even chance
  (d)   are likely   **(e)**   are certain.

23.2 Using numbers to represent probabilities

In Exercise 23A you may have found it difficult to know where to put some of the statements on the probability scale in question **1**. It becomes easier if the probability is given a value.

In a tennis match, a coin is tossed to decide which player will serve first.

When you toss a coin there are two possible outcomes: either a head or tail. One of these outcomes is tossing a head.

The probability P of tossing a head can be written:

$$\text{probability of a head} = \frac{\text{number of successful outcomes}}{\text{total number of possible outcomes}}$$

$$= \frac{1 \text{ outcome (head)}}{2 \text{ possible outcomes (head or tail)}} = \frac{1}{2}$$

Another way of writing this is:

  $P(\text{head}) = \frac{1}{2}$

Probabilities can be written as fractions, decimals or percentages:

  $P(\text{head}) = \frac{1}{2}$
      $= 0.5$
      $= 50\%$

The probability that an event will happen is:

$$\text{probability} = \frac{\text{number of successful outcomes}}{\text{total number of possible outcomes}}$$

assuming that the outcomes are all equally likely.

Probability is a measure of *how likely* it is that something will happen on a scale from 0 to 1. If you toss a coin 10 times that does not mean you will get *exactly* 5 heads, but if you toss a coin 500 times it is *likely* that you will get about 250 heads.

If getting a head is a *success* then getting a tail is a *failure*.

Example 1

Find the probability of getting a 5 or a 6 when a fair dice is rolled.

$$P(5 \text{ or } 6) = \frac{\text{number of successful outcomes}}{\text{total number of possible outcomes}}$$

$$= \frac{2}{6} = \frac{1}{3}$$

These are two successful outcomes: 5, 6.

There are six possible outcomes: 1, 2, 3, 4, 5, 6.

> The word **fair** means that each number has an equal chance of turning up: the outcomes are *equally likely*.

Exercise 23B

1 A fair six-sided dice is rolled.
What is the probability of getting:

(a) a 4
(b) a 1 or 2
(c) an odd number
(d) an even number
(e) a multiple of 3
(f) 3 or more
(g) less than 5
(h) a prime number
(i) more than 6
(j) $2\frac{1}{2}$?

2 A card is selected from a pack of 52 cards.
What is the probability it will be:

(a) an ace
(b) the ace of spades
(c) a black card
(d) a 5 or 6
(e) smaller than a 4
(f) a picture card
(g) a 3, 4 or 5
(h) a diamond
(i) a club or spade
(j) any card other than a club?

3   A token is taken from a bag containing 6 red and 5 blue tokens. What is the probability that the token will be

(a) blue   (b) red

(c) yellow   (d) red or blue?

4   A bag contains 1 white, 3 black and 5 blue beads. Omar selects a bead at random. What is the probability that the bead he chooses is

(a) white   (b) black   (c) blue

(d) not white   (e) white or black?

5   In a game at a fete a pointer is spun. You win the amount of money written in the sector where the pointer stops. Each sector is equally likely.
Work out the probability that you win

(a) no money   (b) 25p   (c) 50p

(d) 74p   (e) £1

6   In a raffle 5000 tickets are sold. Jasmir buys 20, Karen buys 100, Lucy buys 50 and Winston buys 25 tickets. There is one winning ticket. Work out the probability that

(a) Jasmir wins   (b) Karen wins

(c) Lucy wins   (d) Winston wins.

7   A box of sweets contains 4 toffees, 3 mints, 5 bonbons, 6 eclairs, 2 wine gums and 10 sherbet lemons. One sweet is chosen at random. Work out the probability that it will be

(a) a toffee   (b) a sherbet lemon

(c) a bonbon   (d) a wine gum

(e) an eclair or a mint   (f) not a sherbet lemon.

'not a sherbet lemon' means any other type of sweet.

8   A set of coloured pencils contains 1 black, 1 white, 2 red, 3 green, 3 blue, 4 brown, 2 yellow, 1 pink and 1 purple pencil. If one pencil is selected at random, find the probability that it will be

(a) white   (b) red   (c) green

(d) blue   (e) brown   (f) yellow

(g) pink   (h) purple   (i) not yellow

(j) not brown   (k) red or green   (l) mauve.

9   A letter is chosen at random from the word PROBABILITY. Work out the probability that it will be

(a) R   (b) Y   (c) B

(d) I or A   (e) B or I

23.3 Certain and impossible events

In question 3 of Exercise 23B it is *impossible* to pick a yellow token. It is *certain* that you will pick either a red or a blue token because they are the only colours available.
If you write these probabilities as fractions you find:

P(yellow) which is *impossible* is $\dfrac{0}{11}$ which is 0.

P(red or blue) which is *certain* is $\dfrac{11}{11}$ which is 1.

The probability of an event happening is always greater than or equal to 0 (impossible) and less than or equal to 1 (certain). This can be written:

$0 \leqslant \text{probability} \leqslant 1$

> **Remember:**
> $a < 5$ a is less than 5
> $a \leqslant 5$ a is less than or equal to 5
> $5 > a$ 5 is greater than a
> $5 \geqslant a$ 5 is greater than or equal to a

Exercise 23C

1 Write down the probability of the following:
  (a) you will grow to be 5 centimetres tall
  (b) Christmas Day will be on 25th December this year
  (c) if you toss a coin it will be a tail
  (d) you will live to be 150 years old
  (e) you will die
  (f) if you roll a dice it will be an odd number.

2 Write three statements for each of the following.
  The first one is started for you.
  (a) a probability of 0
    'A baby will be born with false teeth' has a probability of 0.
  (b) a probability of 1
  (c) a probability of about $\frac{1}{2}$
  (d) a probability of about $\frac{3}{4}$

3 On the right are the nets of two differently numbered dice.

  If one dice is rolled what is the probability using
  (i) Dice A (ii) Dice B
  that you will get
  (a) a 6
  (c) a score of 4 or more
  (e) an even number
  (g) a prime number
  (b) a 5
  (d) a 2
  (f) an odd number
  (h) a square number?

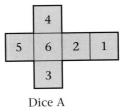

Dice A

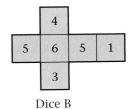

Dice B

4 A bowl of fruit contains 3 apples, 4 bananas, 2 pears and 1 orange. Norma takes one piece of fruit without looking. What is the probability that she takes

    (a) an apple   **(b)** a banana

    (c) a pear   **(d)** an orange?

Write each answer in three ways **(i)** as a fraction **(ii)** as a decimal and **(iii)** as a percentage.

The first one is done for you.

    (a) P(apple) is   **(i)** $\frac{3}{10}$ **(ii)** 0.3   **(iii)** 30%

5 A hundred raffle tickets are sold. Raman buys 8 tickets, Susan 5 tickets and Gary 12 tickets. What is the probability that the first prize will be won by

    (a) one of these three

    (b) Raman

    (c) Susan

    (d) somebody other than Gary?

Write each answer in three ways: **(i)** as a fraction, **(ii)** as a decimal and **(iii)** as a percentage.

Surely one of us will win something?

With my 12 tickets I hope so.

6 Meryl, James and Gita are playing Monopoly. The probability that Meryl will win is $\frac{1}{3}$. The probability that James will win is $\frac{1}{4}$.

What is the probability that Gita will win?

23.4 The probability that something will *not* happen

The probability of rolling a 6 on a fair dice is $P(6) = \frac{1}{6}$.

The probability of *not* getting a 6 is:

$$P(\text{not a 6}) = \frac{5}{6}$$

There are five ways of not getting 6: 1, 2, 3, 4, 5

The six possible outcomes are still: 1, 2, 3, 4, 5, 6

Notice that $P(6) = \frac{1}{6}$

$$P(\text{not a 6}) = \tfrac{5}{6} = 1 - \tfrac{1}{6} = 1 - P(6)$$

Notice also that
$P(6) + P(\text{not a 6}) = \frac{1}{6} + \frac{5}{6}$
$= 1$

If the probability of an event happening is p then the probability of it *not* happening is $1 - p$.

Exercise 23D

1 **(a)** The probability that it will rain tomorrow is $\frac{1}{3}$.
What is the probability that it will not rain?

(b) The probability that it will snow on Christmas Day is 0.2.
What is the probability that it will not snow on Christmas Day?

(c) The probability that Rovers will get to the next round of a competition is 30%.
What is the probability that they will not get to the next round?

2 This spinner is spun.
What is the probability of getting:

(a) a 1
(b) not a 1
(c) an odd number
(d) not an odd number?

The 3-sided spinner has landed on 2.

3 The probability of Ahmed winning his game of chess is 0.62. The probability of him drawing is 0.24
What is the probability of him losing?

4 Susan rolls a fair six-sided dice.
What is the probability that she will:

(a) get a 2
(b) *not* get a 2
(c) get 3 or more
(d) *not* get 3 or more
(e) *not* get an even number?

5 Nine counters numbered 2 to 10 are put in a bag.
One counter is selected at random.
What is the probability of getting a counter with

(a) a number 5
(b) an odd number
(c) not an odd number
(d) a prime number
(e) a square number
(f) a multiple of 3?

6 A bag contains 20 coloured balls. 8 are red, 6 are blue, 3 are green, 2 are white and 1 is brown. A ball is chosen at random from the bag.
What is the probability that the ball chosen is

(a) blue
(b) not blue
(c) brown
(d) not brown
(e) blue or red
(f) red or green
(g) green or white or brown?

7 The probability of Jane scoring a 20 on this special darts board is $\frac{1}{5}$.

What is the probability of Jane not scoring 20?

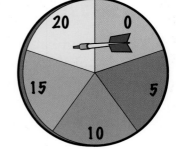

8 A bag contains 20 balls. There are three different colours: green, red and blue. A ball is chosen at random from the bag. The probability of a green ball is $\frac{1}{4}$.

The probability of a red ball is $\frac{2}{5}$.

(a) What is the probability of a blue ball?

(b) How many balls are red?

(c) How many balls are green?

(d) How many balls are blue?

23.5 Finding an estimated probability by experimenting

Sometimes you will need to estimate the probability that an event will happen.

For example, you can estimate the probability of getting a head when you toss a coin by carrying out a trial.

Toss it several times and keep a record of:
- the number of successful trials (heads)
- the total number of trials (how many tosses altogether).

> The **estimated probability** that an event will happen in a game or experiment is:
>
> $$\text{estimated probability} = \frac{\text{number of successful trials}}{\text{total number of trials}}$$

The estimated probability may be different from the theoretical probability.

> The **estimated probability** is given by the **relative frequency** with which the event occurs in a trial or experiment.

Relative frequency is dealt with in more detail in Section 23.8

Example 2

If you toss a coin 20 times and get 12 heads and 8 tails the **estimated probability** of getting a head is: $\frac{12}{20} = \frac{3}{5}$

The **theoretical probability** is: $\frac{10}{20} = \frac{1}{2}$

From the experiment it would seem that you are more likely to get a head than a tail. Next time you do the same experiment you may well get a different result but the theoretical probability is *always* $\frac{1}{2}$.

You can use estimated probability to predict results. If the estimated probability of Adrian winning a tennis match is $\frac{3}{4}$ then if he plays 24 matches he would expect to win 18 times. ———————— $\frac{3}{4} \times 24 = 18$

Exercise 23E

1 (a) Roll a dice 36 times and record your results in a frequency table like the one below. Work out the probability of rolling each number from your results.

Number	Tally	Frequency	Probability
1			$\overline{36}$
2			$\overline{36}$
3			$\overline{36}$
4			$\overline{36}$
5			$\overline{36}$
6			$\overline{36}$
		Total	$\overline{36}$

Use your table to answer these questions.
   (b) What is the probability of rolling
         (i) a 3   (ii) a 5?
   (c) What is the probability of rolling an even number?
   (d) What is the total of all the probabilities?
   (e) Explain your result to part (d).

2 Roll a dice another 36 times and complete a table as in question **1**.
   Compare the results with those from question **1** and make comments.

3 Combine your results for questions **1** and **2** in a table and comment on the probabilities you obtain.

4 Roll two dice 36 times, add the total spots on the uppermost faces and record your results in a table like this:

Number	Tally	Frequency	Probability
2			
3			
4			
12			

Total 8

(a) What is the probability of a score being
    (i) 12   (ii) 7   (iii) 3
    (iv) 11   (v) 1   (vi) even
    (vii) greater than 8   (viii) a square number

(b) What is the total of the probabilities?

(c) What is the probability that you will not score 12?

5 Roll two dice a further 36 times and complete a table as in question **4**.
Compare the results with those from question **4**.

6 Combine your results for questions **4** and **5** in a table and make comments on your results.

7 (a) Draw a bar chart to show your results from rolling two dice. Use the data in the frequency column from question **6**.

(b) Which number occurred the most times?

(c) Which number occurred the fewest times?

(d) Write two sentences about the shape of your bar chart.

(e) Which of these numbers is most likely to occur:
    (i) 12   (ii) 6   (iii) 2?

(f) Why did the number 1 not occur?

23.6 Using a sample space diagram to find theoretical probabilities

If you roll a red dice and a blue dice what are all the outcomes?
If the red dice shows 1 the blue dice could show 1, 2, 3, 4, 5 or
6. You can record these outcomes as ordered pairs, putting the
red result first and then the blue result, like this:

$$(1, 1)\ \ (1, 2)\ \ (1, 3)\ \ (1, 4)\ \ (1, 5)\ \ (1, 6)$$

red dice 1

blue dice 6

If the red dice showed 2, the outcomes could be:

$$(2, 1)\ \ (2, 2)\ \ (2, 3)\ \ (2, 4)\ \ (2, 5)\ \ (2, 6)$$

You can represent all the outcomes on a **sample space diagram**:

```
6 ┤ (1,6)  (2,6)  (3,6)  (4,6)  (5,6)  (6,6)

5 ┤ (1,5)  (2,5)  (3,5)  (4,5)  (5,5)  (6,5)

4 ┤ (1,4)  (2,4)  (3,4)  (4,4)  (5,4)  (6,4)
Blue dice
3 ┤ (1,3)  (2,3)  (3,3)  (4,3)  (5,3)  (6,3)

2 ┤ (1,2)  (2,2)  (3,2)  (4,2)  (5,2)  (6,2)

1 ┤ (1,1)  (2,1)  (3,1)  (4,1)  (5,1)  (6,1)
    └────────────────────────────────────
      1     2      3      4      5      6
                 Red dice
```

The sample space diagram shows that there are 36 possible
outcomes.

A **sample space diagram** represents all possible outcomes.

Example 3

Use a sample space diagram to find the
probability of getting a total score of
7 when two dice are rolled.

There are 6 ways of scoring 7:

$$(1, 6)\ \ (2, 5)\ \ (3, 4)\ \ (4, 5)\ \ (5, 2)\ \ (6, 1)$$

There are 36 possible outcomes so:

$$P(\text{scoring } 7) = \tfrac{6}{36} \text{ or } \tfrac{1}{6}$$

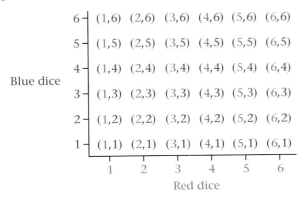

Exercise 23F

1 Use the sample space diagram in Example 3 to find the probability of

   (a) rolling a total score of **(i)** 5   **(ii)** 9   **(iii)** 12

   (b) rolling a score that is **(i) not** more than 4
                               (ii) not less than 10

   (c) rolling a 2 on either one or both of the dice

   (d) rolling a double

   (e) rolling a double 6.

2 This sample space diagram shows the outcomes when the ace, king, queen, jack, and ten from both the spades and hearts suits are placed in two separate piles and one card is taken from each pile.

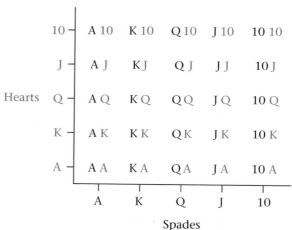

	A	K	Q	J	10
10	A 10	K 10	Q 10	J 10	10 10
J	A J	K J	Q J	J J	10 J
Q	A Q	K Q	Q Q	J Q	10 Q
K	A K	K K	Q K	J K	10 K
A	A A	K A	Q A	J A	10 A

Hearts (vertical axis), Spades (horizontal axis)

Find the probability that

   (a) both cards will be kings

   (b) both of the cards will be either an ace or a king

   (c) both cards will be a pair

   (d) at least one card will be an ace

   (e) neither card will be a 10

   (f) neither card will be a king or a jack

   (g) one card will be a spade

   (h) both cards will be hearts.

3 Write out all the possible outcomes for each of the following pairs of events:

   (a) tossing a coin twice

   (b) obtaining an odd number followed by an odd number when a dice is rolled twice

   (c) tossing a coin and rolling a dice.

4 Work out the number of possible outcomes:
   (a) when a fair six-sided dice is thrown twice
   (b) when two discs are taken, one at a time, from a bag
       containing red, blue, and yellow discs (the first disc is
       put back in the bag before the second is taken out).

5 Four discs are placed in a bag: red, green, yellow and blue.
   One disc is taken at random, its colour is recorded and
   then it is replaced. A second disc is then taken. Draw a
   sample space diagram to show all the possible outcomes.

6 (a) Copy and complete this table to show the possible
        outcomes when a red dice and a blue dice are rolled.

Total score	Ordered pairs	Theoretical probability
2	(1,1)	$\frac{1}{36}$
3	(1,2) (2,1)	$\frac{2}{36}$
4	(1,3) (2,2) (3,1)	$\frac{3}{36}$
5		
6		
7		
11		
12		

   (b) Which was the most likely score?
   (c) What is the sum of all the probabilities? Explain
       your answer.

7 Nicola can turn left or right at a T-junction. List all the
   possible outcomes after she has passed two junctions.

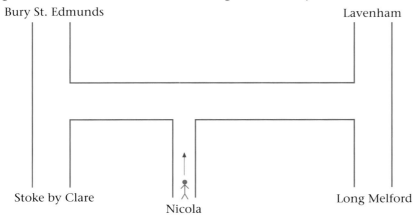

Bury St. Edmunds   Lavenham

Stoke by Clare   Long Melford
              Nicola

23.7 Using two-way tables to find probabilities

Another way to show possible outcomes is to use a two-way table.
You can do this even if you do not know all the outcomes.

Example 4

This table shows some information about how students in Mr Graham's maths set travel to school.
None of them come by car.

	Walk	Bus	Cycle	Total
Girls	4	p	3	12
Boys	7	q	u	t
Total	r	9	s	25

(a) Copy and complete the table.

(b) Mr Graham chooses a student at random.

    What is the probability they are:
    (i) a girl who walks to school
  (ii) a boy who cycles to school
 (iii) a student who comes by bus?

(a) Girls: $4 + p + 3 = 12$ so the number who travelled by bus p is 5.

    Boys: The total who travelled by bus is 9, where $5 + q = 9$
          so the number of boys who travelled by bus, q, is 4.
          The total r who walked is $4 + 7 = 11$.
          The total number of students is 25, where $11 + 9 + s = 25$
          so the total s who cycle is 5.
          The total t of boys is $25 - 12 = 13$
          The number u of boys who cycle is $5 - 3 = 2$

The completed table is:

	Walk	Bus	Cycle	Total
Girls	4	5	3	12
Boys	7	4	2	13
Total	11	9	5	25

(b) (i) 4 out of 25 walked so the probability is $\frac{4}{25}$.
   (ii) 2 out of 25 cycled the probability is $\frac{2}{25}$.
 (iii) 9 out of 25 travel by bus so the probability is $\frac{9}{25}$.

Two-way tables can be used to help solve probability problems.

Exercise 23G

1 The numbers of clients interviewed by Jackie and Sam about their holidays are shown in this table:

	Monday	Tuesday	Total
Jackie	25	35	
Sam			
Total	55		100

(a) Copy and complete the table.

(b) How many people did Jackie interview altogether?

(c) How many people did Sam interview on Monday?

(d) How many people were interviewed on Tuesday?

(e) If one of these clients is chosen at random what is the probability that they were interviewed by

> A **random** selection is one in which each person has the same chance of being chosen.

    (i) Jackie on Monday

   (ii) Sam on Tuesday

  (iii) Jackie

  (iv) Sam on Monday or Jackie on Tuesday?

2 Jackie and Sam asked the 100 clients how they travelled to France and in which month they travelled.
Some of the information is recorded in this table:

	Air	Eurotunnel	Boat	Total
July	8		10	20
August	15	5		50
September		8		
Total	30			100

(a) Copy and complete the table.

(b) What is the probability that a client selected at random travelled:

    (i) in July   (ii) in August or September

  (iii) by air   (iv) by boat

    (v) by Eurotunnel in August

  (vi) by boat in August

 (vii) not by air   (viii) in July, but not by boat?

3 The same 100 people were asked if they had their holiday in France, went on to Italy or went elsewhere.
Some details are given in this table:

	France	Italy	Elsewhere	Total
July		10	4	20
August	18		8	
September		16		30
Total	28	50		

(a) Copy and complete the table.

(b) What is the probability that a randomly picked holidaymaker

   (i)   went to Italy

  (ii)   went to France

 (iii)   went in July

 (iv)   did not go to Italy

  (v)   went elsewhere in August

 (vi)   went to France in September

(vii)   went to Italy in September?

4 The same 100 people were also asked what type of accommodation they stayed in.
Part of the information is given in this table:

	Hotel	Caravan	Camping	Other	Total
July	11	4	3		
August		14		6	
September		7	4	3	30
Total	49		15	11	100

(a) Copy and complete the table.

(b) What is the probability a person selected at random

   (i)   stayed in a hotel in August

  (ii)   stayed in a caravan in July

 (iii)   stayed in a hotel

 (iv)   did not stay in a hotel

  (v)   stayed in a caravan

 (vi)   used other accommodation

(vii)   went camping in August?

23.8 Relative frequency

In Section 23.5 you learned that you can estimate the probability that an event will occur by carrying out an experiment or game and using the rule:

$$\text{estimated probability} = \frac{\text{number of successful trials}}{\text{total number of trials}}$$

This is also called the **relative frequency**.

$$\text{relative frequency} = \frac{\text{number of successful trials}}{\text{total number of trials}}$$

The relative frequency of an event occurring is used when the outcomes are not equally likely.

It can also be used to test whether a game of chance is fair, for example to test whether a dice is fair.

Example 5

Describe how you might undertake an experiment and set out the results to test whether a coin is fair or not.

Step 1   The number of trials (times the coin is tossed) must be large (about 500).

Step 2   Record in a table the numbers of heads (successful trials) after 50 throws, 100 throws, 150 throws and so on.

Step 3   Work out the relative frequency (estimated probability) correct to 2 d.p. and record it in the table.

Number of trials	Number of successful trials	Relative frequency
50	20	$\frac{20}{50} = 0.40$
100	45	$\frac{45}{100} = 0.45$
150	71	$\frac{71}{150} = 0.47$
200	104	$\frac{104}{200} = 0.52$
250	119	$\frac{119}{250} = 0.48$
300	146	$\frac{146}{300} = 0.49$
350	172	$\frac{172}{350} = 0.49$
400	203	$\frac{203}{400} = 0.51$
450	222	$\frac{222}{450} = 0.49$
500	245	$\frac{245}{500} = 0.49$

Step 4 Illustrate your results using a line graph.

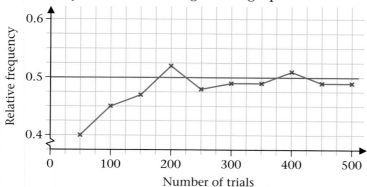

The red line shows the theoretical probability of getting a head, assuming that both outcomes are equally likely.

As the number of trials increases, the relative frequency of throwing a head (the estimated probability that you throw a head) settles down at about 0.49. This is very close to the theoretical probability of 0.5, so it is reasonable to assume that the coin is fair.

Exercise 23H

You need a dice, blue beads, red beads, a bag, card and scissors.

1 Test a dice of your own to see whether or not it is fair.

2 Ask a friend to place some of the blue beads and red beads in the bag. You must not look in the bag or ask how many there are of each colour. You need to use relative frequency to estimate the ratio of red to blue beads.

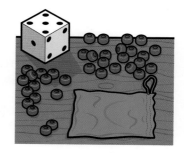

(a) Carry out an experiment to work out the relative frequency of red beads.

Record your results in a table and work out the relative frequency after different numbers of trials.

(b) Record the relative frequencies on a line graph.

(c) Read off the relative frequency where the graph 'settles down'.

(d) Use the relative frequency to work out the ratio of red to blue beads in the bag.

3 Make a dice of your own out of card.
Test the dice to see whether it is fair or not.

4 A dice is thrown and the score is recorded. After many trials the relative frequency of throwing a 5 is found to be 0.09. Compare this with the theoretical probability based on equally likely outcomes for a fair dice.
Do you think the dice is fair?

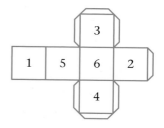

Net of dice

Mixed exercise 23

1   A box contains only blue pencils and red pencils.
    6 of the pencils are blue and 5 are red.
    A pencil is to be taken at random from the box.
    Write down the probability that
    (a) a blue pencil will be taken
    (b) a blue pencil will **not** be taken.   [E]

2   Some pupils have thought of a game to use at a school
    fair.
    A tennis ball is rolled down a slope into one of eight
    holes. It can score a number from 1 to 8.
    The pupils try out their game **200 times**.
    The frequencies of the scores are shown on the diagram.

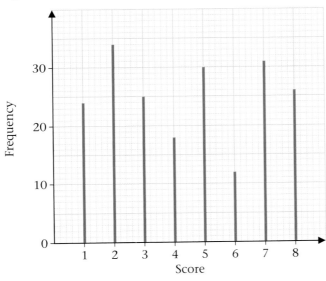

    According to the diagram, which number is
    (a)   (i) the hardest to score
          (ii) the easiest to score?
    (b) Estimate the probability that the next ball rolled will
        score 3.   [E]

3   A bag contains a red bead, a black bead, a yellow bead
    and a white bead.
    One single bead is to be picked out at random.
    What is the probability that the bead picked will be
    (a) red
    (b) pink
    (c) not white?   [E]

4   Anil is conducting a series of tests on a biased coin.

He does 5 tests.

In each test he throws the coin 10 times and counts the number of heads.

The table shows the results of the 5 tests.

1st 10 throws	2nd 10 throws	3rd 10 throws	4th 10 throws	5th 10 throws
7 heads	6 heads	8 heads	6 heads	9 Heads

Anil then calculates the proportion of heads throughout his tests.

He sets out his calculations as shown below.

	Number of heads	Proportion of heads
1st 10 throws	7	$\frac{7}{10} = 0.7$
1st 20 throws	$7 + 6 = 13$	$\frac{13}{20} = 0.65$
1st 30 throws	$7 + 6 + 8 = 21$	
1st 40 throws		
1st 50 throws		

(a) Copy and complete the table.

(b) Explain what happens to the proportion of heads as the number of throws increases.   [E]

5   80 students each visited one attraction last week.

The two-way table shows some information about these students.

	Theme Park	Aquarium	Circus	Total
Male			14	46
Female	21			
Total		29	24	80

(a) Copy and complete the two-way table.

One of the students is picked at random.

(b) Write down the probability that the student

    (i)   visited the aquarium

    (ii) visited the theme park

   (iii) is female and visited the aquarium.

6 A game is played with two spinners.
You multiply the two numbers on which the spinners
land to get the score.

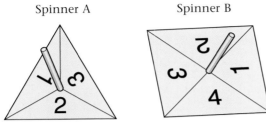

Spinner A   Spinner B

This score is 2 × 4 = 8

(a) Copy and complete the table to show all the possible
scores.
One score has been done for you.

Spinner B

×	1	2	3	4
1				
2				8
3				

Spinner A

(b) Work out the probability of getting a score of 6.

(c) Work out the probability of getting a score that is an
odd number.   [E]

7 60 British students each visited one foreign country last
week.
The two-way table shows some information about these
students.

	France	Germany	Spain	Total
Female			9	34
Male	15			
Total		25	18	60

(a) Copy and complete the two-way table.

One of the students is picked at random.

(b) Write down the probability that the student visited
Germany last week.   [E]

Summary of key points

1 An event which is **certain to happen** has a **probability of 1**.

2 An event which **cannot happen** has a **probability of 0**.

3 The probability that an event will happen is:

$$\text{probability} = \frac{\text{number of successful outcomes}}{\text{total number of possible outcomes}}$$

assuming that the outcomes are all equally likely.

4 The probability of an event happening is always greater than or equal to 0 (impossible) and less than or equal to 1 (certain). This can be written:

$$0 \leqslant \text{probability} \leqslant 1$$

5 If the probability of an event happening is p then the probability of it *not* happening is $1 - p$.

6 The **estimated probability** that an event will happen in a game or experiment is:

$$\text{estimated probability} = \frac{\text{number of successful trials}}{\text{total number of trials}}$$

The **estimated probability** is given by the **relative frequency** with which the event occurs in a trial or experiment.

7 A **sample space diagram** represents all possible outcomes.

8 **Two-way tables** can be used to help solve probability problems.

9 The **relative frequency** of an outcome in an experiment is:

$$\text{relative frequency} = \frac{\text{number of successful trials}}{\text{total number of trials}}$$

24 Presenting and analysing data 2

24.1 Scatter diagrams

Statements such as 'Smoking can cause lung cancer' and 'Drink driving causes accidents' are often made in the media. Sometimes they are supported by data showing, for example, whether there is a relationship between a smoking habit and the chance of getting lung cancer.

This section shows you how to compare two sets of data to see whether there is a relationship between them. For example, is there a relationship between the number of ice-creams sold at a kiosk and the average daytime temperature? James collected data to find out.

Average temperature (°C)	12	13	10	20	21	16	17	13	19	20	19	15	16	14
No. of ice-creams sold	5	9	1	51	48	20	30	15	32	42	37	23	25	14

He plotted each pair of values, (12, 5), (13, 9) and so on, on a graph. This is called a **scatter diagram** or **scatter graph**.

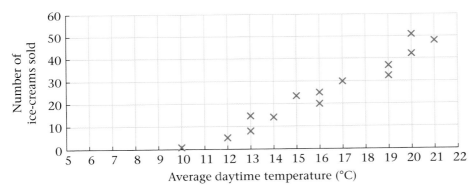

There does appear to be a relationship between the average daytime temperature and the number of ice-creams sold: the hotter it is, the more ice-creams are sold.

Here is another example. On a journey Chandra noted down how many miles there were still to go. She did this every ten minutes:

Time (mins)	10	20	30	40	50	60	70	80	90	100
Miles to go	72	60	50	42	40	32	25	18	10	0

Here is a scatter diagram showing this data:

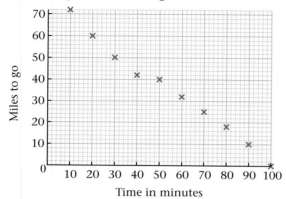

There is a relationship between the time she has been travelling and the number of miles still to go: the greater the time travelling, the fewer miles there are to go.

Sometimes there is no relationship between two sets of data Every Monday Trish recorded the temperature in °F and the rainfall in mm. Her results were:

Temperature (°F)	74	70	63	68	65	64	60	51	54	56	50
Rainfall (mm)	1	0	2	7	5	1	8	2	11	4	6

A scatter graph of this data looks like this:

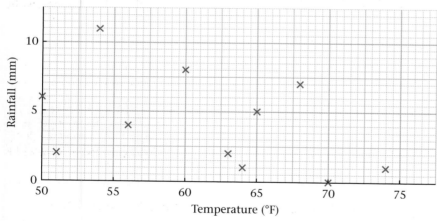

There does not appear to be any relationship.

Activity – Height and arm-span

Is there a relationship between your height and your arm-span?

(a) Collect data for your class.
(b) Draw a scatter graph to represent your data.
(c) Describe the relationship.

Correlation

A relationship between two sets of data is called
a correlation.

You need to be able to recognise different types of
relationships between two sets of data. Look at these three
scatter graphs:

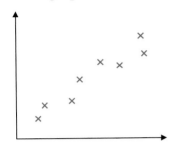

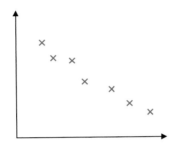

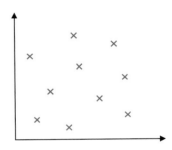

As one value increases the
other one also increases.
There is a **positive correlation**.

As one value increases the
other decreases. There is a
negative correlation.

The points are randomly and
widely spaced out. There is
no correlation.

Line of best fit

When there is positive or negative correlation on a
scatter diagram you can draw a line of best fit to
describe the relationship between the two sets of data.

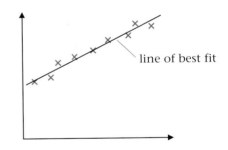

The **line of best fit** is a straight line that passes
through or is as close to as many of the plotted points
as possible.

For your GCSE exam you should use a ruler and draw
your line of best fit by eye.

> There are usually roughly
> equal numbers of points
> above and below the line.

Example 1

The table shows the acidity of seven lakes near to an industrial plant and their
distance from it.

Distance (km)	4	34	17	60	6	52	42
Acidity (pH)	3.0	4.4	3.5	7.0	3.2	6.8	5.2

(a) Draw a scatter graph to illustrate this data.
(b) Draw and label the line of best fit on your scatter graph.
(c) Work out the equation of the line of best fit.
(d) Use your line of best fit to predict the acidity of a lake at a distance of 25 km.

(a), (b)

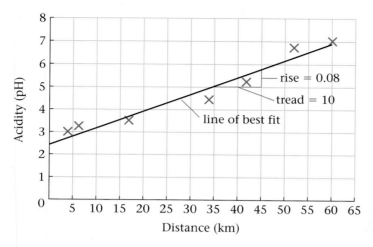

(c) The equation of the line of best fit is of the form $y = mx + c$.
m is the gradient and c is the intercept with the y-axis.
To find m, draw a right-angled triangle:

$$m = \frac{\text{rise}}{\text{tread}} = \frac{0.8}{10} = 0.08$$

From the graph: $c = 2.4$
The equation is $y = 0.08x + 2.4$

(d) Read up from 25 on the distance axis to the line of best fit, and across to the acidity axis. Using your line of best fit you can predict that the pH will be 4.3

Exercise 24A

1 The table shows the engine sizes of various cars and the distances they travel on one litre of petrol.

Engine size (litres)	0.8	1.6	2.6	1	2.1	1.3	1.8
Distances travelled (km)	13	10	5	12	7	11	9

   (a) Draw a scatter diagram to represent this data.
   (b) What type of correlation do you find?

2 What type of correlation would you expect if you compared the following data:
   (a) heights of people and shoe sizes
   (b) ages of cars and their selling prices
   (c) time taken to get to school and marks in French
   (d) sizes of gardens and the numbers of birds in them
   (e) marks in science and marks in maths?

3　Write down an example which you might expect would give each of the following correlations:

（a）negative　　　（b）none　　　（c）positive.

4　A group of students went to a fitness centre. Their heights and weights were recorded and they were rated 0–40 on a number of activities.
The results are recorded in this table:

Weight	65	60	72	66	61	56	68	61	62	58	57	64
Height	175	172	182	179	174	165	176	168	172	170	162	175
Agility	24	19	32	26	23	18	34	12	35	28	16	21
Strength	29	22	32	35	26	18	25	14	30	26	20	33
Reactions	35	17	28	33	15	27	19	22	29	37	31	25
Skipping	26	34	20	18	36	28	22	36	32	28	38	16

（a）Draw scatter graphs for each of the following:
　　（i）weight and height　　（ii）weight and agility
　（iii）height and skipping　（iv）strength and reactions
　　（v）agility and reactions　（vi）strength and skipping.

（b）For each of your scatter graphs state what type of correlation is shown, if any.

（c）If possible, draw and label a line of best fit on each of your scatter graphs.

> Remember:
> You can't draw a line of best fit if there is no correlation.

5　Here are sketches of six scatter diagrams:

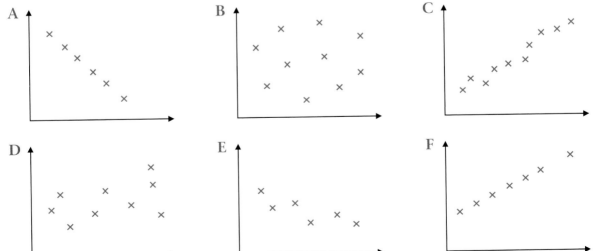

Which diagram(s) show

（a）positive correlation　　　（b）negative correlation　　　（c）no correlation?

6 This is a scatter diagram showing students' percentage scores in Paper 1 and Paper 2 of a mathematics examination:

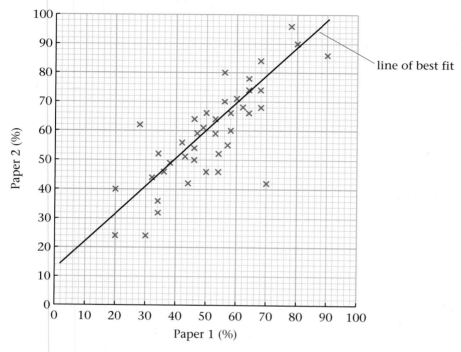

line of best fit

(a) What type of correlation does this diagram show?

Student A scored 43% on Paper 1, but did not take Paper 2.

(b) Use the line of best fit to estimate the percentage the student might have scored on Paper 2. [E]

24.2 Finding averages

In Chapter 20 you learned about different averages for a set of data. You should remember that:

The **mode** of a set of data is the value which occurs most often.

The **mean** of a set of data is the sum of the values divided by the number of values:

$$\text{mean} = \frac{\text{sum of values}}{\text{number of values}}$$

The **median** is the middle value when the data is arranged in order of size.

How to find the position of the median

An easy way to find the position of the median value in a set of data is to add 1 to the number of values, then divide the result by 2.

Suppose you needed to find the median value for a set of 30 data values.

$$\frac{30 + 1}{2} = 15.5$$

so the median is between the 15th and 16th values when data is arranged in order. It is the mean of the 15th and 16th values.

This method works whether there is an odd or an even number of items of data.

Exercise 24B

1   Find the mean of
(a) 5, 11, 23, 16 and 20   (b) 114, 107, 134, 96 and 49

2   The mean of six numbers is 12. Five of the numbers are 11, 7, 21, 14 and 9. Calculate the sixth.

3   In training Fritz ran the 100 m in 10.8, 11.1, 10.7, 10.9 and 10.8 seconds.
(a) What was his average (mean) time?
(b) How fast must he run in the next race to bring his average down to 10.8 seconds?

4   Use the information given to find the value of n in each of the following sets of numbers.
(a) 5, 7, 4, 1, n, 5   : the mean is 6
(b) 3, 1, 4, 5, 4, n : the mode is 4
(c) 1, 7, 2, 1, n, 4, 3 : the modes are 1 and 2
(d) 2, n, 5, 7, 1, 3   : the median is $3\frac{1}{2}$
(e) 2.6, 3.5, n, 6.2   : the mean is 4
(f) 4, 7, 2, n, 2, 9, 6 : the median is 5

5   A stallholder bought 5 boxes of fruit at £12.40 a box and 3 boxes at £16.20.
What was the mean cost of the boxes?

6 The bar chart shows the number of cans of cola bought by Class 10C during a two-week period.

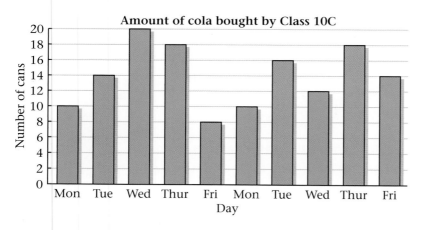

Amount of cola bought by Class 10C

Find

(a) the mode

(b) the median

(c) the mean number of cans bought.

24.3 Averages from frequency distributions

In Chapter 12 you learned that it is convenient to collect large amounts of data in a tally chart or a frequency distribution table.

This section shows you how to find the mean, mode and median when the information is given in a frequency table.

> A set of data which shows the number of times each value occurs is called a frequency distribution.

Example 2

In a survey, the number of eggs in seagulls' nests in June was counted.

The table shows the results.

Find

(a) the mode

(b) the median

(c) the mean number of eggs.

Number of eggs x	Frequency f
0	17
1	12
2	23
3	37
4	18
Total	107

(a) The mode is the value which occurs most often. In a frequency table this is the item of data which has the highest frequency. For this data the mode is 3 eggs. There are more nests with 3 eggs than any other number of eggs.

(b) The median is the middle value of the data. There are 107 nests altogether. The data in the table is in order.

So the median value is the $\dfrac{n + 1}{2}$th value.

The middle nest is nest $(107 + 1) \div 2 = $ nest 54.

  Nests 1–17 have 0 eggs
  Nests 18–29 have 1 egg
  Nests 30–52 have 2 eggs
  Nests 53–89 have 3 eggs

So nest 54 is a 3-egg nest. The median is 3 eggs.

(c) The mean is the total number of eggs divided by the total number of nests (the total frequency):

Number of eggs x	Frequency f	Frequency × number of eggs $f \times x$
0	17	0
1	12	12
2	23	46
3	37	111
4	18	72
Totals	107	241

The number of eggs in 2-egg nests is $23 \times 2 = 46$.

The total number of eggs is the sum of all the $f \times x$ values.

The mean = total number of eggs ÷ total frequency

$$= \frac{241}{107} = 2.25 \text{ eggs}$$

The mean of a frequency distribution

A short way of writing the mean uses the Greek letter sigma Σ to represent the sum of a set of values:

For a frequency distribution:

$$\text{mean} = \frac{\Sigma fx}{\Sigma f}$$

the sum of all the $(f \times x)$ values in the distribution

the sum of the frequencies

Exercise 24C

1 Copy and complete the table. Use your table to calculate the mean, mode and median numbers of cars per household.

> Don't forget you can use your calculator to work out the mean.

Cars per household x	Frequency f	$f \times x$
0	6	
1	20	
2	13	
3	4	
4	2	
Totals		

The frequency tables in questions **2–4** are written sideways in rows. You might find it easier to rewrite them in columns.

> Start your table off like this.

2

Dice score	1	2	3	4	5	6
Frequency	23	17	24	22	19	15

Dice score x	Frequency f	$f \times x$
1	23	23

Work out the mode, median and mean dice scores.

3 A factory takes random samples of 102 items and tests them for faults. (This is their method of maintaining standards. It is called quality control.)
Here are their results for last week:

Number of faults per sample	0	1	2	3	4	5
Number of samples	76	13	6	3	3	1

> 'Per sample' tells you that you need to divide the total number of faults by the total number of samples. So the 'number of samples' is the frequency.

Work out the mode, median and mean numbers of faults per sample.

4 Samir asked 24 people how many packets of crisps they ate last week. The results are shown in the table.

Number of packets of crisps	0	1	2	3	4	5	6	7	8
Number of people (frequency)	4	0	6	5	3	2	1	3	0

(a) Write down the modal number of packets eaten.

(b) Work out the median number of packets eaten.

(c) Calculate the mean number of packets eaten, correct to 1 d.p.

5 Some teachers were asked how many National Lottery tickets they bought last week.

The results are shown in the table.

(a) Which number of tickets is the mode?

(b) Work out the mean number of tickets.

(c) Find the median number of tickets.

Number of tickets	Number of teachers
0	2
1	7
2	5
3	2
4	0
5	3
6	1

[E]

24.4 Spread from frequency distributions

The median is the middle value, with half the data on one side and half the data on the other.

The **quartiles** are found when you divide the data up into four parts.

$$0 \quad 1 \quad 1 \quad \boxed{2} \quad 3 \quad 5 \quad 5 \quad \boxed{5} \quad 7 \quad 9 \quad 9 \quad \boxed{10} \quad 10 \quad 11 \quad 12$$

Lower quartile
($\frac{1}{4}$ way along)
$\frac{1}{4}(n + 1)$th value

The median or
middle value
$\frac{n + 1}{2}$ th value

Upper quartile
($\frac{3}{4}$ way along)
$\frac{3}{4}(n + 1)$th value

← Interquartile range →

The interquartile range is the difference between the upper quartile and the lower quartile.

Interquartile range $= 10 - 2 = 8$ for this data.

> Quartiles and the interquartile range will not be tested in your exam, but may be useful for your coursework.

When the data is arranged in ascending order:
- the **lower quartile** is the value one quarter of the way into the data
- the **upper quartile** is the value three quarters of the way into the data
- the **interquartile range** = upper quartile − lower quartile.

Example 3

In a school, stars are awarded for very good work. The number of stars awarded to each of 95 students is shown in this frequency table.

Number of stars	3	4	5	6	7	8	9	10	11	Total
Number of students	1	2	4	7	17	23	24	16	1	95

Work out (a) the range (b) the interquartile range.

(a) Range = highest value − lowest value = 11 − 3 = 8 stars

(b) The lower quartile is the $\frac{1}{4}(95 + 1) = $ 24th value.

Adding up the number of students in order:

$$1 + 2 + 4 + 7 = 14 \quad \text{and} \quad 1 + 2 + 4 + 7 + 17 = 31$$

As the 24th value is between the 14th and 31st values, it is one of the 17 values recorded as 7 stars. So the lower quartile is 7 stars.

Using the same method, the upper quartile is the $\dfrac{3(95 + 1)}{4} = $ 72nd value.

Adding up the frequencies in order:

$$1 + 2 + 4 + 7 + 17 + 23 = 54 \quad \text{and} \quad 1 + 2 + 4 + 7 + 17 + 23 + 24 = 78$$

As the 72nd value is between the 54th and 78th values, it is one of the 24 values recorded as 9 stars. So the upper quartile is 9 stars.

The interquartile range is:

$$\text{upper quartile} - \text{lower quartile} = 9 - 7 = 2 \text{ stars}$$

Exercise 24D

Work out **(a)** the range **(b)** the interquartile range
for the data shown in the frequency table in each question.

1 The number of letters delivered to each house in a road
of 39 houses:

Number of letters	0	1	2	3	4	5	6	7
Frequency (number of houses)	8	13	9	7	1	0	0	1

2 The marks gained by 63 pupils in an examination:

Mark	10	20	30	35	40	45	50	65
Frequency	0	4	8	13	16	10	7	5

3 The number of whole months over the age of 15 years of
29 pupils in a class:

Number of months over 15 years	0	1	2	3	4	5	6	7	8	9	10	11
Frequency	1	0	1	2	3	3	3	1	2	4	5	4

4 The amounts spent by 100 people on newspapers in one week:

Amount (£)	0	1	2	3	4	5	6	7	8
Frequency	5	17	25	19	13	12	5	2	2

24.5 Averages from grouped data

In Chapter 12 you also learned how to group large amounts of data in class intervals. What averages can be found from grouped data?

The manager of a hotel checks the cost of phone calls made by each guest by looking at the number of units used per call. She summarises the data from the phone calls in a frequency table, grouping it in class intervals.

Number of units	Frequency
1–5	73
6–10	161
11–15	294
16–20	186
21–25	65
over 25	11
Total	790

The median: There were 790 phone calls so the position of the median data value is the $(790 + 1) \div 2 = 395\frac{1}{2}$th value. It is in the class interval 11–15.
You cannot give an exact value for the median.

The $395\frac{1}{2}$th value is in this class interval.

> For grouped data, you can state the class interval that contains the median.

The modal class: The class interval 11–15 units per call has the highest frequency.

> For grouped data, the class interval with the highest frequency is called the **modal class**.

The modal class only makes sense as a measure of the average if the class intervals are the same.

The mean: Each class interval contains calls using different numbers of units, so you have not got the exact data you need to calculate the mean, but you can calculate an **estimate of the mean**. This is *not* a guess, but a calculation. Here is how to do it.

Assume each call in a class interval uses the middle number of units in that class interval.

Number of units used per call	Frequency f	Middle value x	$f \times x$
1–5	73	3	219
6–10	161	8	1288
11–15	294	13	3822
16–20	186	18	3348
21–25	65	23	1495
over 25	11	28	308
Totals	790		10 480

The middle value of the class interval 1–5 is 3. The middle value of class interval 6–10 is 8 and so on.
The 161 calls did not all use 8 units each. The errors made by overestimating approximately balance those made by underestimating.
A middle value must be chosen for calls over 25 units. This is a matter of judgement. Here 28 is used.

Now you can calculate an estimate of the mean in a similar way to that for ungrouped data:

For more on calculating the mean see Section 24.3.

$$\text{estimate of mean} = \frac{\text{sum of (middle values} \times \text{frequencies)}}{\text{sum of frequencies}}$$

$$= \frac{\Sigma fx}{\Sigma f} = \frac{10\,480}{790} = 13.3$$

For grouped data, you can calculate an estimate of the mean using the middle value of each class interval.

In the phone calls example the data is discrete. You can use exactly the same method to find an estimate of the mean of continuous data. The method works even if the class intervals are not the same size and the middle values are not whole numbers.

Remember:
Discrete data can be counted. It takes a fixed number of values.
Continuous data is measured. It can take any value in a range.

Exercise 24E

1 The students at Loovilla College decided to have a biscuit eating competition. A random sample of 25 students was taken. The table shows the numbers of students eating different numbers of biscuits in 4 minutes

Number of biscuits eaten in 4 minutes	Frequency f	Middle value x	$f \times x$
1–5	2		
6–10	8		
11–15	7		
16–20	5		
21–25	2		
26–30	1		
Totals	25		

   (a) Calculate an estimate of the mean number of biscuits eaten in 4 minutes.
   (b) Write down the modal class interval.
   (c) 250 students entered the competition.
        Estimate how many of them will eat more than 20 biscuits in the 4 minutes.   [E]

2 In a five-leg darts match a record is kept of the scores for each throw of three darts.

Score	1–20	21–40	41–60	61–100	101–140	141–180
Frequency	3	17	25	56	8	3

   (a) What is the modal class?
   (b) Calculate an estimate of the mean score.

3   The heights of students in a class are measured. The table shows the results.

Height interval (h cm)	Number of students
$150 \leqslant h < 155$	4
$155 \leqslant h < 160$	4
$160 \leqslant h < 165$	8
$165 \leqslant h < 170$	7
$170 \leqslant h < 175$	5
$175 \leqslant h < 180$	2

(a) What is the modal class?

(b) Work out an estimate of the mean height.

4   Ian looked at a passage from a book. He recorded the number of words in each sentence in a frequency table using class intervals of 1–5, 6–10, 11–15, etc.

Class interval	Frequency f	Middle value x	$f \times x$
1–5	16		48
6–10	28		
11–15	26	13	
16–20	14		
21–25	10		230
26–30	3		
31–35	1		
36–40	0		
41–45	2		86
Total		Total	

(a) Copy and complete the table.

(b) Write down the modal class interval.

(c) Write down the class interval in which the median lies.

(d) Work out an estimate for the mean number of words in a sentence.   [E]

5   The table shows how long couples had been married whose marriages ended in divorce in 2005.

Length of marriage in completed years	0–2	3–4	5–9	10–14	15–19	20–24	25–29	30–40
Frequency as a %	9	14	27	18	13	10	5	4

Work out an estimate for the mean length of a marriage that ended in a divorce.

Mixed exercise 24

You will need graph paper.

1 The table contains information about the returns of postal surveys sent out by a market research organisation.

Issued	2000	2500	3000	2800	1400	2100	2000	1800	2400	2600
Returned	480	605	712	683	308	515	492	421	592	624

(a) Construct a scatter graph of the postal surveys issued and returned.

(b) Draw in a line of best fit.

(c) Describe the correlation between the postal surveys issued and returned.

2 The ages of 12 cross-channel swimmers and their swimming times are recorded as:

17 yrs in 15 hrs 26 min   23 yrs in 14 hrs 32 min
36 yrs in 18 hrs 5 min   25 yrs in 11 hrs 12 min
18 yrs in 21 hrs 21 min   28 yrs in 13 hrs 43 min
26 yrs in 17 hrs 50 min   31 yrs in 12 hrs 7 min
21 yrs in 15 hrs 12 min   30 yrs in 16 hrs 10 min
42 yrs in 14 hrs 28 min   21 yrs in 11 hrs 42 min

(a) Draw a scatter graph of the ages and swimming times of the swimmers.

(b) Comment on the correlation between the ages of the swimmers and their swimming times.

3 This table shows the number of certificates gained by students for outstanding sporting achievement during the year.

Number of certificates	Tally	Frequency
1	||||	4
2	|||| ||||	9
3	|||| |||	8
4	|||| ||||	10
5	|||| |	6
6	|||	3

(a) Calculate (i) the mean
            (ii) the mode
            (iii) the median.

(b) Which one of these averages could be used to encourage students to take part?
Explain the reasons for your choice.

4 A goal shooter has scores of 14, 18, 10, 24, 32, 26, 32 in seven games.
How many must she score in the 8th game to bring her mean score up to 24?

5 The mean content of 11 boxes of matches is 46.
How many matches are there altogether?
The next box checked contains 49 matches.
What is the mean content when this box is included?

6 Four boys have a mean height of 160 cm.
Seven girls have a mean height of 154 cm.
What is the mean height of the eleven young people?

7 The mean of 15, 17, x, 28 and 19 is 16.
What is the value of x?

8 What mark should Leo get in his next test to get the
median stated?
(a) marks so far: 1, 8, 5, 2   : median 5
(b) marks so far: 8, 2, 4, 5, 3, 8, 4, 2, 9 : median 4

9 Eleanor conducted a survey in which she recorded the
shoe sizes of 40 girls. Her results are shown in the
frequency table.

Shoe size	3	$3\frac{1}{2}$	4	$4\frac{1}{2}$	5	$5\frac{1}{2}$	6	$6\frac{1}{2}$	7	$7\frac{1}{2}$	8
Number of girls	1	2	2	5	5	6	7	5	4	1	2

(a) Write down the modal shoe size.
(b) Work out the median shoe size.
(c) Work out the range of the shoe sizes.
(d) Calculate the mean shoe size, giving your answer
correct to 1 d.p.

10 Cole's sells furniture and will deliver up to a distance of
20 miles. The diagram shows the delivery charges made
by Cole's. The table shows the information in the
diagram and also the numbers of deliveries made in the
first week of May 2005.

Distance (d) from Cole's in miles	Delivery charge in pounds	Number of deliveries			
$0 < d \leqslant 5$	15	27			
$5 < d \leqslant 10$	20	11			
$10 < d \leqslant 15$	25	8			
$15 < d \leqslant 20$	30	4			

(a) Copy the table and calculate the mean charge per
delivery for these deliveries.
(b) Calculate an estimate for the mean distance of the
customers' homes from Cole's.

11 This table gives the marks scored by pupils in a French test and in a German test.

French	15	35	34	23	35	27	36	34	23	24	30	40	25	35	20
German	20	37	35	25	33	30	39	36	27	20	33	35	27	32	28

(a) Draw a scatter graph of the marks scored in the French and German tests on a grid like this:

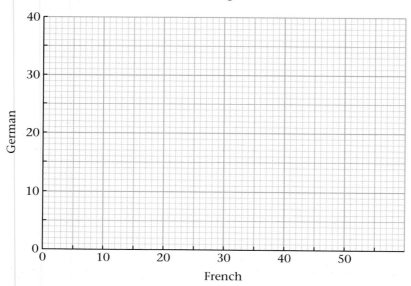

(b) Describe the correlation between the marks scored in the two tests.

(c) Draw and label the line of best fit on your scatter graph.

(d) Use your line of best fit to predict the German mark of a pupil who scored 28 in their French test. [E]

12 For each pair of variables below, state whether you think there would be:

   positive correlation
   or **negative** correlation
   or **no** correlation.

Give a brief reason for your choice.

(a) *the amount of rain falling* and *the number of people outdoors.*

(b) *the number of apples a person ate* and *the person's results in mathematics tests.* [E]

13 Jez chews bubble gum until the taste has gone. He cannot decide between two different brands. He measures his chewing times on six occasions for each brand. This table shows his chewing times in minutes.

Brand A	11	10	13	9	17	12
Brand B	11	13	12	12	14	10

The mean and range of the chewing times for Brand A are given in the next table. Calculate the mean and range of the chewing times for Brand B.
Which brand should Jez decide to use, assuming they cost the same?
Give a clear explanation.

	Mean	Range
Brand A	12	8
Brand B		

[E]

Summary of key points

1 A relationship between two sets of data is called a **correlation**.

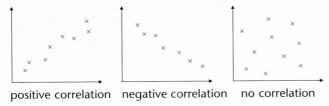

positive correlation   negative correlation   no correlation

2 The **line of best fit** is a straight line that passes through or is as close to as many of the plotted points as possible.

3 For a frequency distribution:

$$\text{mean} = \frac{\Sigma fx}{\Sigma f}$$

the sum of all the ($f \times x$) values in the distribution
the sum of all the frequencies

4 When the data is arranged in ascending order:
- the **lower quartile** is the value one quarter of the way into the data
- the **upper quartile** is the value three quarters of the way into the data
- the **interquartile range** = upper quartile − lower quartile.

5 For grouped data:
- you can state the class interval that contains the median
- the class interval with the highest frequency is called the **modal class**
- you can calculate an estimate of the mean using the middle value of each class interval.

25 Pythagoras' theorem

This chapter shows you how to calculate the lengths of sides of right-angled triangles. This topic is regularly included in GCSE exams.

25.1 Using Pythagoras' theorem to find the hypotenuse

The longest side of a right-angled triangle is the one opposite the right angle. It is called the **hypotenuse**.

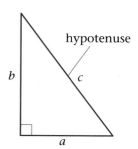

Exercise 25A

1 The right-angled triangle *ABC* has sides 3 cm, 4 cm and 5 cm. Squares have been drawn on each of its sides.

(a) Find the number of cm squares in
   (i) the square *CBFG*
   (ii) the square *ACHI*
   (iii) the square *BADE*.

(b) Add your answers for (a) (i) and (a) (ii).

(c) Write down what you notice.

2 The right-angled triangle *PQR* has sides 2.5, 6 and 6.5.
Squares have been drawn on each side of the triangle.

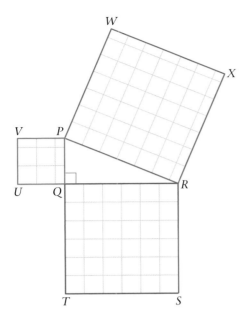

(a) Count the number of small squares in
   (i) the square *PQUV*
   (ii) the square *QRST*
   (iii) the square *RPWX*.
(b) Add your answers for (a) (i) and (a) (ii).
(c) Write down what you notice.

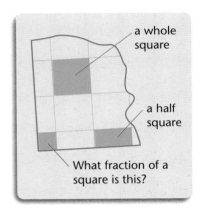

a whole square

a half square

What fraction of a square is this?

A relationship between areas

Exercise 25A shows that there is a relationship between squares drawn on the sides of a right-angled triangle.

Another way to see the relationship is to calculate the areas of the squares.

Example 1

In triangle *ABC* the square on the hypotenuse is:

$$AC^2 = 5^2 = 25$$

The sum of the squares on the other two sides is:

$$AB^2 + BC^2 = 3^2 + 4^2 = 9 + 16 = 25$$

so $\quad\quad\quad 5^2 = 3^2 + 4^2$

and $\quad\quad AC^2 = AB^2 + BC^2$

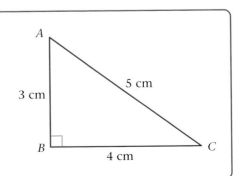

Example 2

In triangle PQR the square on the hypotenuse is:

$$PR^2 = 6.5^2 = 42.25$$

The sum of the squares on the other two sides is:

$$PQ^2 + QR^2 = 2.5^2 + 6^2 = 6.25 + 36 = 42.25$$

so $\qquad 6.5^2 = 2.5^2 + 6^2$

and $\qquad PR^2 = PQ^2 + QR^2$

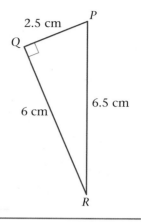

These are examples of a result, called a **theorem**, that was proved by **Pythagoras**, a Greek philosopher and mathematician who lived around 500BC.

> **Pythagoras' theorem** states that in a right-angled triangle the square on the hypotenuse is equal to the sum of the squares on the other two sides.
>
> $$c^2 = a^2 + b^2 \quad \text{or} \quad a^2 + b^2 = c^2$$

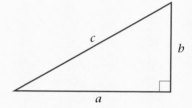

Example 3

In this right-angled triangle calculate the length of the side marked z.

Use
$$c^2 = a^2 + b^2$$
$$z^2 = 12^2 + 5^2$$
$$= 144 + 25$$
$$= 169$$
so $\qquad z = \sqrt{169} = 13$ cm

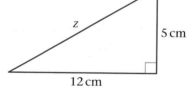

Example 4

In triangle ABC calculate the length of AC using a calculator. Give your answer correct to 3 significant figures.

$AC^2 = 5^2 + 6^2$ so $AC = \sqrt{5^2 + 6^2}$.

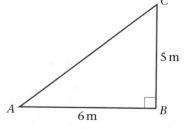

The display shows ⁊.8102497 so the answer is 7.81 m (to 3 significant figures).

Example 5

In triangle LMN, angle $N = 90°$,
$LN = 18.3$ cm and $MN = 7$ cm.
Calculate LM correct to one decimal place.

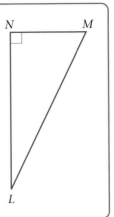

Use $\quad c^2 = a^2 + b^2$
$$LM^2 = MN^2 + LN^2$$
$$= 7^2 + 18.3^2$$
$$= 49 + 334.89$$
$$= 383.89$$
so $\quad LM = \sqrt{383.89} = 19.59... $ cm
$$= 19.6 \text{ cm (to 1 d.p.)}$$

Exercise 25B

1 Calculate the lengths marked with letters in these triangles.
For **(e)** and **(f)** give your answers correct to one decimal place.

(a)

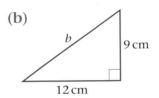

5 cm, a, 12 cm

(b)

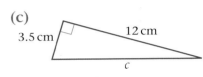

b, 9 cm, 12 cm

(c)

3.5 cm, 12 cm, c

(d)

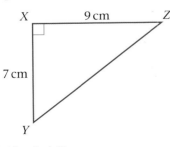

6 cm, 4.5 cm, d

(e)

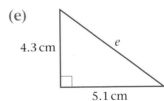

4.3 cm, e, 5.1 cm

(f)

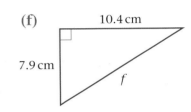

10.4 cm, 7.9 cm, f

2 Give your answers correct to one decimal place.

(a) Find YZ.

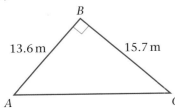

X, 9 cm, Z, 7 cm, Y

(b) Find SU.

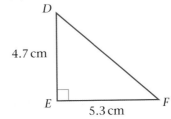

S, 23 cm, T, 27 cm, U

(c) Find JL.

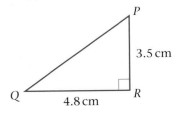

J, 5.3 m, K, 4.8 m, L

(d) Find AC.

B, 13.6 m, 15.7 m, A, C

(e) Find DF.

D, 4.7 cm, E, 5.3 cm, F

(f) Find PQ.

P, 3.5 cm, Q, 4.8 cm, R

3 A rectangle is 13 cm long and 7 cm wide.
Work out the length of a diagonal of the rectangle.

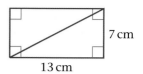

4 A boat leaves Broadstairs and sails due East for 5 km. The boat then changes course and sails due South for 3 km. Calculate the final distance of the boat from Broadstairs, giving your answer correct to one decimal place.

5 A railway at a seaside resort goes from the promenade to the top of the cliffs. The cliff top is 42 m above the promenade and the bottom of the railway is 35 m from the base of the cliff. Work out the length of the railway track.

25.2 Using Pythagoras' theorem to find one of the shorter sides of a triangle

With the formula $c^2 = a^2 + b^2$ you can calculate the longest side c of a right-angled triangle. If you need to find one of the shorter sides (a, for example) it is easier to change the formula so that a^2 is on its own on one side.

Pythagoras' theorem states:

$$c^2 = a^2 + b^2$$

> To calculate either of the shorter sides a or b use Pythagoras' theorem
>
> $a^2 = c^2 - b^2$ or $b^2 = c^2 - a^2$

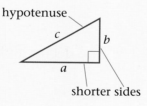

Example 6

In triangle DEF, angle F is a right angle, $DF = 5$ cm and $DE = 7$ cm. Calculate the length of EF.

Use $a^2 = c^2 - b^2$

$\quad EF^2 = 7^2 - 5^2$

$\quad\quad\quad = 49 - 25$

$\quad\quad\quad = 24$

so $EF = \sqrt{24}$

$\quad\quad\quad = 4.898 \ldots = 4.9$ cm (correct to 1 d.p.)

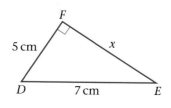

Hint: always check that the hypotenuse is still the longest side. If not, look for your mistake.

24 is not a square number, so $\sqrt{24}$ cannot be worked out exactly as an ordinary number. It is a non-terminating decimal number.

However $\sqrt{24}$ is an exact value. A number written like this (the square root of an integer) is called a **surd**. A surd is always the positive square root.

> If you were not allowed to use a calculator, you could leave your answer to Example 6 in surd notation as $\sqrt{24}$ cm.

Example 7

In triangle *STU* calculate the length of *ST* using a calculator. Give your answer correct to 3 significant figures.

$$ST^2 = 10^2 - 4^2 \text{ so } ST = \sqrt{10^2 - 4^2}$$

The display shows 9.16515139 so the answer is 9.17 m (to 3 significant figures).

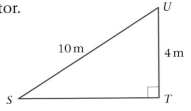

Example 8

An isosceles triangle *PQR* has *PQ* = 14.3 cm, *PR* = 14.3 cm and *QR* = 9.8 cm.

Calculate the height of the triangle correct to 1 d.p.

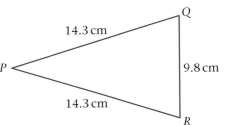

In this diagram *PN* is the height of the triangle. *PN* is a line of symmetry so *QN* = *NR*.

$$NR = \tfrac{1}{2} \times 9.8 = 4.9 \text{ cm}$$

Triangle *PNR* has a right angle at *N* so you can use Pythagoras' theorem.

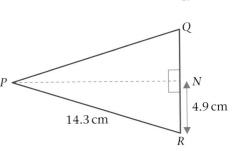

Use $\quad a^2 = c^2 - b^2$

$$PN^2 = 14.3^2 - 4.9^2$$
$$= 204.49 - 24.01$$
$$= 180.48$$

so $\quad PN = \sqrt{180.48}$
$$= 13.43...$$

The height of the triangle is 13.4 cm (correct to 1 d.p.)

Exercise 25C

1   Calculate the lengths marked with letters in these
    triangles. For parts (c) to (f) give your answers correct to one
    decimal place.

(a)

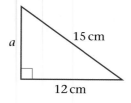

(b)

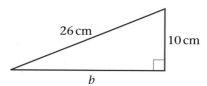

(c)

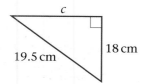

(d)

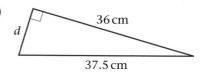

(e)

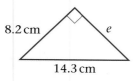

(f)

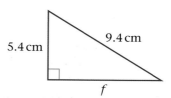

2   Give your answers correct to one decimal place.

(a) Find ON.

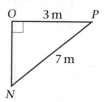

(b) Find RS.

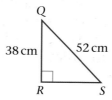

(c) Find TV.

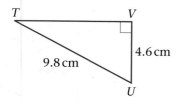

(d) Find XY.

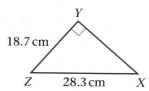

(e) Find AB.

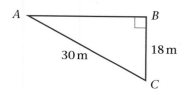

(f) Find EF.

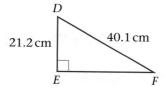

Mixed exercise 25

1 Calculate the lengths marked with letters.

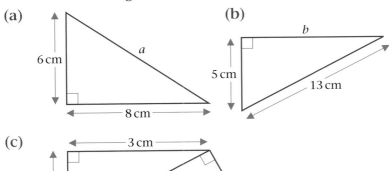

(a)

6 cm

a

8 cm

(b)

b

5 cm

13 cm

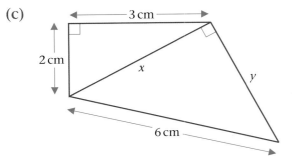

(c)

3 cm

2 cm

x

y

6 cm

> In part **(c)** leave your answers for *x* and *y* in surd notation.

2 A ladder is 5 metres long. It leans against a wall with one end on the ground 1 metre from the wall. The other end of the ladder just reaches a windowsill.
Calculate the height of the windowsill above the ground.

3 Rowena is in her helicopter above the Canary Wharf tower. She flies due West for 4.6 miles and then due North for 1 mile. She is then above Senate House.
Calculate the direct distance, in miles, of the Canary Wharf tower from Senate House.

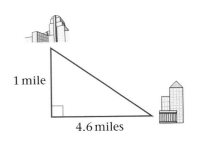

1 mile

4.6 miles

4 An isosceles triangle *ABC* has *AB* = 9.5 cm and *BC* = 9.5 cm. The height of the triangle is *BD* and *BD* = 7.2 cm.
Work out the length of *AC*.

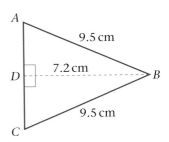

A

9.5 cm

D   7.2 cm   *B*

9.5 cm

C

5 An isosceles triangle *XYZ* has *XY* = 26 cm, *ZX* = 26 cm and *ZY* = 18 cm.
Calculate the height of triangle *XYZ*.

6 A mother zebra leaves the rest of the herd to go in search of water. She travels due South for 0.9 km and then due East for 1.2 km. How far is she from the rest of the herd?

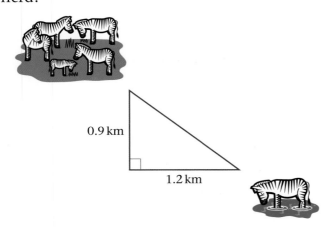

0.9 km

1.2 km

7 *ABC* is a right-angled triangle. *AB* is of length 4 m and *BC* is of length 13 m. Calculate the length of *AC*.

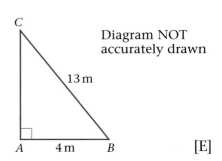

Diagram NOT accurately drawn

C

13 m

A   4 m   *B*

[E]

8 Work out the length, in metres, of side *AB* of the triangle.

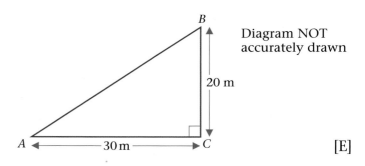

Diagram NOT accurately drawn

B

20 m

A ◄——— 30 m ———► *C*

[E]

Summary of key points

1 **Pythagoras' theorem** states that in a right-angled triangle the square on the hypotenuse is equal to the sum of the squares on the other two sides.

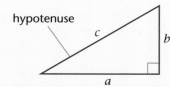

hypotenuse

c

b

a

2 Use $c^2 = a^2 + b^2$ to calculate the hypotenuse.
Use $a^2 = c^2 - b^2$ or $b^2 = c^2 - a^2$ to calculate one of the shorter sides.

26 Advanced perimeter, area and volume

This chapter shows you how to find perimeters, areas and volumes for a variety of 2-D and 3-D shapes.

26.1 Perimeters and areas of 2-D shapes

You should remember these facts from Chapter 19:

The **perimeter** of a shape is the total length of its boundary:

$$\text{perimeter of a rectangle} = l + l + w + w$$
$$= 2(l + w)$$

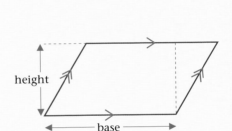

The area of a shape is a measure of the amount of space it covers:

$$\text{area of a rectangle} = \text{length} \times \text{width}$$
$$= l \times w$$

$$\text{area of a parallelogram} = \text{base} \times \text{height}$$
$$= b \times h$$

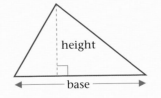

$$\text{area of a triangle} = \tfrac{1}{2} \times \text{base} \times \text{height}$$
$$= \tfrac{1}{2} \times b \times h$$

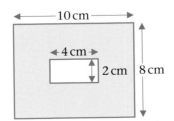

Example 1

Find the shaded area.

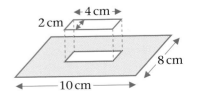

It is easiest to find the area of both the rectangles and then take away the area of the small rectangle from the area of the larger rectangle.

Area of large rectangle $10 \times 8 = 80$
Area of small rectangle $4 \times 2 = 8$
So the shaded area is $80 - 8 = 72 \text{ cm}^2$

Area of a trapezium

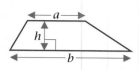

area of a trapezium $= \frac{1}{2}(a + b)h$ •

$\frac{1}{2}(a + b)h$ is $\frac{1}{2}$ the sum of the parallel sides × the perpendicular distance between them.

Example 2

Use the formula to calculate the area of this trapezium.

Area of trapezium $= \frac{1}{2}(a + b)h = \frac{1}{2}(3 + 10) \times 4$

$\qquad\qquad = \frac{1}{2} \times 13 \times 4 = \frac{1}{2} \times 52$

$\qquad\qquad = 26 \text{ cm}^2$

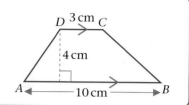

Example 3

Work out the area of this shape.

Method 1

Divide the shape into parts whose areas you can find.
This can be done in several ways. One way is:

Area of rectangle **A** $= l \times w = 7 \times 4 = 28 \text{ cm}^2$

Area of trapezium **B** $= \frac{1}{2}(a + b)h = \frac{1}{2}(7 + 2) \times 4 = \frac{1}{2} \times 9 \times 4$

$\qquad\qquad = 18 \text{ cm}^2$

So the shaded area is $28 + 18 = 46 \text{ cm}^2$

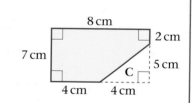

Method 2

Add on a small triangle to make a larger rectangle.

Area of large rectangle $= l \times w = 7 \times 8 = 56 \text{ cm}^2$

Area of small triangle **C** $= \frac{1}{2} \times \text{base} \times \text{height}$

$\qquad\qquad = \frac{1}{2} \times 4 \times 5 = 10 \text{ cm}^2$

So the shaded area is $56 - 10 = 46 \text{ cm}^2$

Exercise 26A

1 Calculate the areas of these shapes:

(a)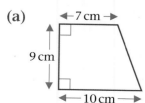

(b)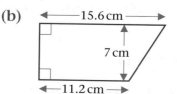

(c)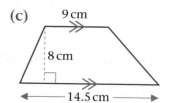

2 Work out the area of the shape *ABCDEF*.

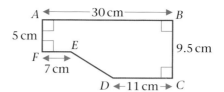

3 Find the shaded areas.

(a)

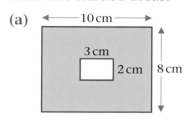

(b)

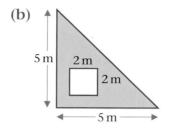

(c)

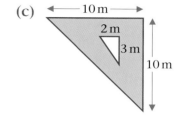

26.2 Circumference of a circle

The perimeter of a circle is called its **circumference**. The circumference of a circle is related to its diameter; Exercise 26B will help you see how.

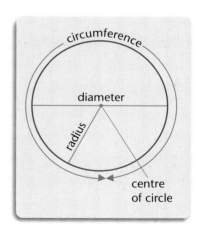

Exercise 26B

You will need a ruler, compasses and some string or thread.

1 **(a)** Mark a point on your paper. Use compasses to draw a circle with the marked point as its centre.

(b) Use a piece of string or thread and place it round your circle. Cut the string to fit exactly round the circumference once and measure its length. The length of the string is the same as the circumference of the circle.

(c) Measure the diameter of the circle.

(d) Work out: $\dfrac{\text{circumference of circle}}{\text{diameter of circle}}$

2 Repeat question **1** for two more circles with a different radius each time.

3 What do you notice about the ratio

$\dfrac{\text{circumference of circle}}{\text{diameter of circle}}$ for each of your circles?

Introducing π (pi)

If you compare answers to Exercise 26B with your friends you should find that the circumference of a circle divided by its diameter is approximately equal to 3 each time. The actual value is a special number called π.

You cannot write down the value of π exactly. The number π is an **irrational number** (a non-recurring, non-terminating decimal) somewhere between 3.141 592 and 3.141 593.

3.141 592   3.141 593

π = 3.141 592 65... is somewhere here but you cannot pinpoint its position exactly

If you press the π key on a calculator the value 3.141592654... appears.

In calculations you often use the value correct to 2 d.p. (3.14) or correct to 3 d.p. (3.142).

Finding a formula for the circumference

You can rearrange the relationship

$$\frac{\text{circumference}}{\text{diameter}} = \pi \quad \text{or} \quad \frac{C}{d} = \pi$$

to give a formula to find the circumference of a circle from its diameter.

Multiply both sides by d:

$$\frac{C}{d} \times d = \pi \times d$$

so $C = \pi \times d$

or $C = \pi d$

You can also find a formula to find the circumference from the radius.

The diameter is twice the radius:

$$d = 2r$$

so $C = \pi \times 2r$

or $C = 2\pi r$

The perimeter of a circle is called the **circumference**:

$C = \pi d$ where C is the circumference,

or d is the diameter and

$C = 2\pi r$ r is the radius.

Example 4

Find the circumference of a circle
with diameter 5 cm.

$C = \pi d$

$C = 3.14 \times 5 = 15.7$ cm

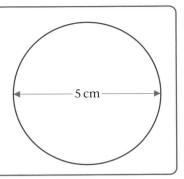

5 cm

Exercise 26C

Use the π key or
$\pi = 3.14$

In these questions give your answers to 3 significant figures.

1 Work out the circumferences of the circles with these diameters:

(a) 2 cm   (b) 3 cm   (c) 4 cm

(d) 10 cm   (e) 8 cm   (f) 12 cm

2 Calculate the circumferences of the circles with these diameters:

(a) 20 cm   (b) 5 m   (c) 50 cm

(d) 2.5 cm   (e) 3.6 cm   (f) 8.25 cm

Finding the circumference given the radius

Example 5

Find the circumference of a circle
with radius 4 cm.

$C = 2\pi r$

$C = 2 \times 3.14 \times 4 = 25.1$ cm

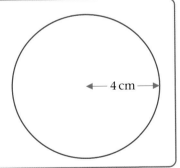

4 cm

Exercise 26D

In these questions give your answers to 3 significant figures.

Find the circumferences of the circles with these radii:

Radii is the plural of
radius.

1	2 cm	2	3 cm	3	5 cm	4	10 cm
5	8 cm	6	12 cm	7	20 cm	8	5 m
9	50 cm	10	2.5 cm	11	3.6 cm	12	8.25 cm

Use the π key or
$\pi = 3.14$

Exercise 26E

In these questions give your answers to 3 significant figures.

Work out the circumference of each of the following.

Use the π key or $\pi = 3.14$

1 a circle with a radius of 9 cm

2 a circle with a diameter of 9 cm

3 a circular table with a diameter of 90 cm

4 a circular fish pond whose radius is 60 cm

5 a circular paving slab of radius 15 cm

6 a circular flower bed of diameter 2.5 m

7 a circular candle of diameter 1.5 cm

8 a circular flower pot of diameter 6 inches

9 a pencil whose radius is 0.3 cm

10 a pen whose radius is 0.5 cm

Finding the diameter when you know the circumference

Sometimes you know the circumference of the circle and you have to calculate the radius or diameter.

Example 6

Susie's bike wheel has a circumference of 62.8 cm.
Work out the diameter and the radius of the wheel.

$$C = \pi d$$

so $62.8 = 3.14 \times d$

Dividing both sides by 3.14 gives:

$d = 62.8 \div 3.14$

$d = 20$ cm

To find the radius divide the diameter by 2.
The radius is 10 cm.

Exercise 26F

In these questions give your answers to 3 significant figures.
Copy this table and work out the diameter and radius of each
circular shape.

Use the **π** key or
π = 3.14

	Shape	Circumference	Diameter	Radius
1	Circle	9.42 cm		
2	Circle	12.56 cm		
3	Circular table	3.14 m		
4	Circular fish pond	10 m		
5	Circular paving slab	90 cm		
6	Circular flower bed	7.5 m		
7	Circular candle	5 cm		
8	Circular flower pot	6 inches		
9	Pencil	1 cm		
10	Pen	2.5 cm		

26.3 Area of a circle

Example 7

Here is a circle with radius 4 units drawn on a square grid.
Estimate the area of the circle.

There are 44 whole or nearly whole squares.
The area of these is about 44 square units.

The shaded shapes are each about $\frac{3}{4}$ square plus
$\frac{1}{4}$ square which makes about a whole square.

So the 8 shaded shapes make about 8 whole squares,
with area 8 square units.

Each of these shapes is
about $\frac{1}{4}$ square + $\frac{3}{4}$ square.

The total area of the circle is about 44 + 8 = 52 square units.

Exercise 26G

 You will need a ruler, compasses, a protractor, squared paper and glue.

1 (a) Draw a circle with a radius of 9 units on squared paper.

   (b) Estimate the area of the circle in square units, by counting the squares.

   (c) Divide your answer to (b) by 81 (which is 9 × 9, the square of the radius).

2 (a) Draw a circle with radius 3 cm.

   (b) Draw diameters at angles of 20° to each other to divide the circle into 18 parts.
       Carefully cut out the 18 parts.

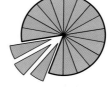

   (c) Draw a straight line.
       Place the cut-out pieces alternately corner and curved edge against the line.
       Stick them close together.

3 Repeat question 2, but draw diameters at 10° to each other to divide the circle into 36 equal parts.

Finding a formula for the area of a circle

The shape you made with the 18 pieces in question 2 of Exercise 26G should be approximately a rectangle.

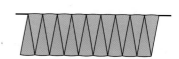

The shape from question 3 should be closer to a rectangle.

It would be very difficult to cut out the parts of the circle if you used 1° between the diameters, but the final shape would be almost an exact rectangle.

The two longer sides of the rectangle make up the whole circumference πd or $2\pi r$, so one length is πr. The width is the same as the radius of the circle, r.

half the circumference
πr

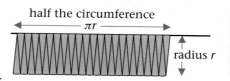

radius r

> The more parts the circle is divided into, the closer to a rectangle the shape becomes.

So the area of the rectangle is length × width = $\pi r \times r = \pi r^2$.
This is the same as the area of the circle, so

area of a circle = $A = \pi r^2$

Example 8

Find the area of a circle with a
radius of 5 cm.

$$A = \pi r^2$$
$$A = 3.14 \times 5 \times 5 = 78.5 \text{ cm}^2$$

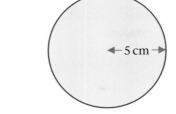

← 5 cm →

Remember:
The value of pi (π) is
approximately 3.14. You
may have a more accurate
value on your calculator.

Example 9

Find the area of a circle with diameter 4 cm.

If the diameter is 4 cm then the radius is $4 \div 2 = 2$ cm and
the area is

$$A = \pi r^2$$
$$A = 3.14 \times 2 \times 2 = 12.56 \text{ cm}^2$$

Exercise 26H

 Round your answers to 3 s.f.

Use the π key or
$\pi = 3.14$

1 Find the areas of the circles with these radii:

(a) 2 cm   (b) 3 cm

(c) 4 cm   (d) 10 cm

(e) 8 cm   (f) 12 cm

2 Work out the areas of the circles with these radii:

(a) 20 cm   (b) 5 m

(c) 50 cm   (d) 2.5 cm

(e) 3.6 cm   (f) 8.25 cm

3 Find the areas of the circles with these diameters:

(a) 2 cm   (b) 3 cm

(c) 5 cm   (d) 10 cm

(e) 8 cm   (f) 12 cm

4 Work out the areas of the circles with these diameters:

(a) 20 cm   (b) 5 m

(c) 50 cm   (d) 2.5 cm

(e) 3.6 cm   (f) 8.25 cm

Exercise 26I

 Work out the area of each of the following. Give your answer to 3 s.f.

Use the 𝜋 key or
𝜋 = 3.14

1   a circle of radius 9 cm

2   a circle of diameter 9 cm

3   a circular table of diameter 90 cm

4   a circular fish pond of radius 60 cm

5   a circular paving slab of radius 15 cm

6   a circular flower bed of diameter 2.5 m

7   the end of a circular candle of diameter 1.5 cm

8   the top of a circular flower pot of diameter 6 inches

9   the end of a pencil of radius 0.3 cm

10   the end of a pen of radius 0.5 cm

Finding the radius when you know the area

Sometimes you will be given the area of a circle and asked to calculate its radius or diameter.

Example 10

A circle has an area of 2826 cm². Work out its radius.

$$\pi r^2 = A$$
$$3.14 \times r^2 = 2826$$

Dividing both sides by 3.14 gives

$$r^2 = 2826 \div 3.14$$
$$r^2 = 900$$
$$\sqrt{r^2} = \sqrt{900} \text{ cm}$$
$$r = 30 \text{ cm}$$

If you need to find the diameter then you multiply the radius by 2. The diameter is 60 cm.

Exercise 26J

 In these questions give your answers to 3 s.f.

Use the π key or
$\pi = 3.14$

1   A circle has an area of 28.26 cm². Find the diameter.

2   A circle has an area of 12.56 cm². Find the radius.

3   A circular table has an area of 3.14 m². Work out the diameter.

4   A circular fish pond has an area of 10 m². Work out the diameter.

5   A circular paving slab has an area of 90 cm². What is the radius?

6   A circular flower bed has an area of 7.5 m². What is the diameter?

7   The end of a circular candle has an area of 5 cm². Work out the radius.

8   The top of a circular flower pot has an area of 6 square inches. What is the diameter?

9   The end of a pencil has an area of 1 cm². Work out the diameter.

Area

Diameter

10   The end of a pen has an area of 2.5 cm². Work out the radius.

Answers in terms of π

On non-calculator papers you may be asked to leave your answers in terms of π.

___Example 11___

Find the area and circumference of the circle with radius 8 cm. Leave your answers in terms of π.

$\quad$ area $= \pi r^2 = \pi \times 8^2 = 64\pi$

$\quad$ circumference $= 2\pi r = 2\pi \times 8 = 16\pi$

Exercise 26K

1   Work out, in terms of π, the circumference and area of a circle with radius:

$\quad$ (a) 2 cm   (b) 5 m   (c) 9 mm (d) $3\frac{1}{2}$cm (e) 12 cm

2   Work out, in terms of π, the circumference and area of a circle with diameter:

$\quad$ (a) 6 m   (b) 8 cm   (c) 9 cm   (d) 3 m   (e) 20 cm

26.4 Parts of circles

Part of a circumference is called an **arc**.
A half circle is called a **semicircle**.

Quarter circles are called **quadrants**.

This is a **sector** of a circle.

These are **segments**.

___Example 12___

Find the perimeter of this semicircle.

First find the circumference of a
circle with diameter 10 cm.

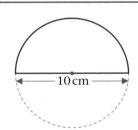

$C = \pi d$
$C = 3.14 \times 10 = 31.4$ cm

The arc length of the semicircle is *half* the circumference:

$31.4 \div 2 = 15.7$ cm

The perimeter is the curved arc length plus the straight
edge of 10 cm.
So the total length of the perimeter is

15.7 cm $+ 10$ cm $= 25.7$ cm

___Example 13___

Find the area of this quadrant.

The quadrant is one quarter of a circle.
Find the area of the circle with
radius 8 cm:

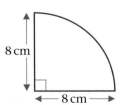

$A = \pi r^2$
$A = 3.14 \times 8 \times 8 = 200.96$ cm^2

The quadrant is one quarter of the circle, so the area of
the quadrant is

200.96 cm $\div 4 = 50.2$ cm^2 (to 3 significant figures)

Exercise 26L

In questions **1–6** give all your answers to 3 significant figures.

> Use the **π** key or
> π = 3.14

1 Find the perimeter of each of these shapes.

(a)

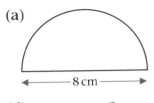

8 cm

(b)

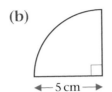

5 cm

(c)

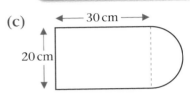

30 cm

20 cm

(d)

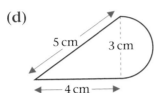

5 cm 3 cm

4 cm

(e)

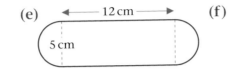

12 cm

5 cm

(f)

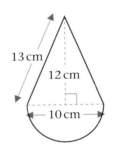

13 cm

12 cm

10 cm

2 Find the area of each of the shapes in question **1**.

3 Find the shaded area of each in these shapes:

(a)

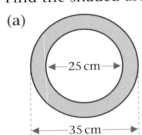

25 cm

35 cm

(b)

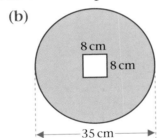

8 cm

8 cm

35 cm

(c)

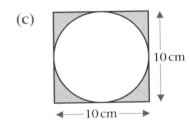

10 cm

10 cm

4 Calculate the area of a semicircular rug with diameter 90 cm.

5 An ice-cream wafer is in the shape of a quadrant of a
circle with radius 7 cm.
Work out the area of the wafer.

6 A lawn is in the shape of a rectangle
with a semicircular end.
Calculate the area of the lawn.

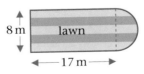

8 m lawn

17 m

7 A circular pond has diameter 3.22 m. The pond is
surrounded by a path 28 cm wide. Calculate

(a) the area of the pond

(b) the area of the path.

Give your answers in m², correct to 2 decimal places.

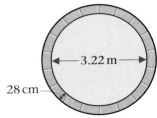

3.22 m

28 cm

26.5 Volumes and surface areas of 3-D shapes

Volume of a cuboid

You should remember from Chapter 19 that:

> The **volume** of a 3-D shape is a measure of the amount of space it occupies.
>
> $$\text{volume of a cuboid} = \text{length} \times \text{width} \times \text{height}$$
> $$= l \times w \times h$$

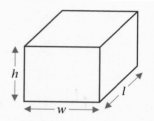

Volume of a prism

> A **prism** is a 3-D shape with the same cross-section all along its length.

A cuboid can be cut in half to make a triangular prism. For example, a 4 cm by 2 cm by 3 cm cuboid can be cut in half to make this prism.

The volume of the prism is half the volume of the cuboid so it is

$$\frac{1}{2} \times (4 \times 2 \times 3) = \frac{1}{2} \times 24 = 12 \,\text{cm}^3$$

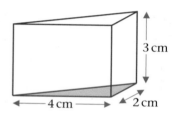

This can be thought of as

$$\frac{1}{2} \times 4 \times 2 \qquad \times \qquad 3 \qquad = 12 \,\text{cm}^3$$

or   **area of cross-section × height**.

Does this work for any prism? Try an octagonal prism:

To make an octagonal prism you could first make the shape of the octagonal base.

You would need 5 whole cubes and 4 half cubes.

The total number of cubes in the base would be $5 + 2 = 7$.

For a prism of height 3 cm you would need 21 cubes (7×3).

So the volume of the prism would be 21 cm³.

This is the **area of cross-section × height**.

If the prism is lying on its side the height is called length.

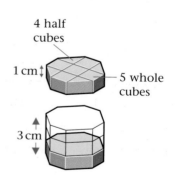

volume of a prism = area of cross-section × length

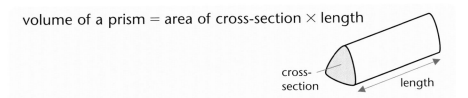

cross-section   length

Example 14

The volume of a prism is 102 cm³.
The prism has a length of 12 cm.
Find the area of the triangular cross-section.

Volume of prism = area of cross-section × length

$$102 = \text{area} \times 12$$

Divide both sides by 12

$$\text{area} = 102 \div 12 = 8.5 \text{ cm}^2$$

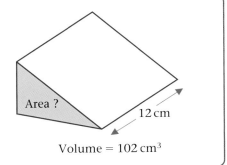

Area ?

12 cm

Volume = 102 cm³

Volume of a cylinder

A **cylinder** is a special prism where the cross-section is a circle.
The area of cross-section is πr^2, so

$$\text{area of cross-section} \times \text{height} = \pi r^2 \times h$$

volume of a cylinder = $\pi r^2 h$

Area of cross-section = πr^2

h

Surface area of a cylinder

You can work out the area of the curved surface of a cylindrical can of soup by removing the label.

Cut the label parallel to the height of the cylinder. Remove the label and open it out flat. The label should be a rectangle.

Unroll the label...

r

The length of the rectangle is the same as the circumference of an end of the cylinder.

... to give a rectangle:

The width is the same as the perpendicular height of the cylinder.

The area is the circumference of an end multiplied by the height.

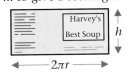

Harvey's
Best Soup

h

$2\pi r$

area of the curved surface of a cylinder = $2\pi rh$

Add two circular ends.

total surface area of a closed cylinder = $2\pi rh + 2\pi r^2$

total surface area of a cylinder open at one end = $2\pi rh + \pi r^2$

Add one circular end.

Example 15

A cylinder has a height of 10 cm and a diameter of 6 cm.
Work out **(a)** the volume **(b)** the surface area.
Use the π key on your calculator.
Give your answers correct to 3 significant figures.

As the diameter is 6 cm, the radius is 3 cm.

(a) volume of a cylinder $= \pi r^2 h$
$= \pi \times 3 \times 3 \times 10$
$= 90\pi$
$= 282.743\,338\,8$
$= 283$ cm^3 (to 3 s.f.)

> You should write out the full answer before rounding.

(b) surface area $= 2\pi r h + 2\pi r^2$
$= (2 \times \pi \times 3 \times 10) + (2 \times \pi \times 3 \times 3)$
$= 60\pi + 18\pi$
$= 78\pi$
$= 245.044\,227$
$= 245$ cm^3 (to 3 s.f.)

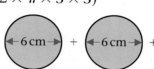

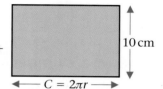

Exercise 26M

In this exercise give all your answers to 3 significant figures.

> Use the π key

1 Find the volume of each of the following solids.

(a)
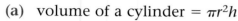

(b)
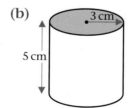

(c)
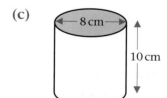

(d)
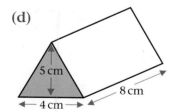

(e)

(f)
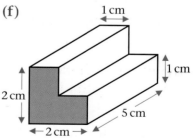

(g)
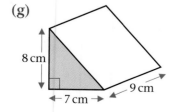

(h)
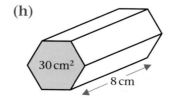

(i)
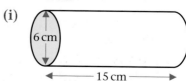

2 A box in the shape of a cuboid has a volume of $50\,cm^3$. It has a length of 8 cm and a height of 2.5 cm. What is its width?

3 A cylinder has a volume of $100\,cm^3$. Its height is 10 cm. What is the area of its circular end?

4 A cylinder has a radius of 4 mm and a volume of $230\,mm^3$. Find the height of the cylinder.

5 A triangular prism has a length of 12 cm and a volume of $60\,cm^3$. What is the area of the triangular end?

6 Calculate the volume of the wedge on the right, which is a triangular prism.

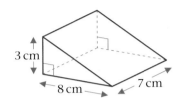

7 A closed box is a cuboid made of wood 1 cm thick. Its external measurements are 80 cm by 50 cm by 42 cm. Calculate

(a) the internal measurements of the box

(b) the inside volume of the box

(c) the total surface area of the outside of the box.

> Hint: sketch a diagram of the box to help you. Label the box with the dimensions.

8 The diagram shows a tank which is a prism with a trapezium cross-section.
Calculate the volume of the tank.

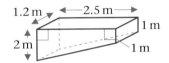

9 A gold bar is in the shape of a cylinder.
It has a diameter of 18 cm and a length of 105 cm.
The gold is to be recast into cuboids. Each cuboid is to be 30 cm long, 14 cm wide and 8 cm high.

(a) Calculate the volume of the cylinder.

(b) Calculate the volume of each cuboid.

(c) Calculate the maximum number of cuboids that can be made from the gold bar.

(d) What volume of gold is left over after the cuboids have been made?   [E]

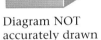

Diagram NOT
accurately drawn

10 A closed cardboard box is a cuboid with a base 63 cm by 25 cm. The box is 30 cm high. Calculate

(a) the volume of the box

(b) the total surface area of the box.

11 The cross-section of a house is shown on the right.
The house is 9 m long.
Calculate the volume of the house.

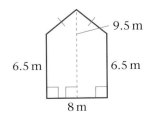

12 A flat rectangular roof measures 15 m by 20 m.
Rainwater from the roof drains into a tank which is 1.3 m
deep and has a square base of side 1.4 m.
Calculate the depth of rainfall that would just fill the tank.

13 A cuboid with a square base is 18 cm high.
The volume of the cuboid is 882 cm^3.
Calculate the length of a side of the base.

14 An open waste paper bin is a cylinder.
The diameter of the base is 22 cm and the height is 28 cm.
Calculate

(a) the volume of the bin

(b) the total outside surface area of the bin.

26.6 Accuracy of measurement

Suppose you use a ruler marked in millimetres to measure a
line as 237 mm correct to the nearest mm.

The true length could be anywhere between 236.5 mm and
237.5 mm.

We write this as 236.5 mm ≤ length < 237.5 mm, as all these
measurements will round to 237 mm correct to the nearest mm.

So the true length could be anywhere
in a range between 0.5 mm below and
0.5 mm above the recorded value:

The shortest possible length is 236.5 mm.
The longest possible length is 237.5 mm.

Example 16

The time taken to walk down some stairs is measured as
10 seconds to the nearest second.

(a) What is the shortest possible time it could be?

(b) What is the longest possible time it could be?

(a) shortest possible time is 9.5 seconds

(b) longest possible time is 10.5 seconds.

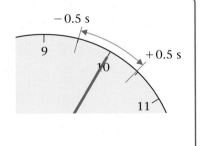

If a time is measured as 10.3 seconds to the nearest tenth of a
second, it could be anything between 10.25 and 10.35 seconds.
You can write this as

$$10.25 \text{ s} \leq \text{time} < 10.35 \text{ s}$$

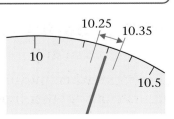

For any measurement you make:

If you make a measurement correct to a given unit the true value lies in a range that extends half a unit below and half a unit above the measurement.

Exercise 26N

1   These lengths are all measured to the nearest millimetre.
    Write down the range within which each length could lie in the form shown in the examples above.
    (a) 2.7 cm   (b) 3.9 cm   (c) 10.5 cm
    (d) 12 mm   (e) 25 mm   (f) 36 mm

2   These lengths have all been measured to the nearest centimetre.
    For each, write down
    (i) the shortest possible length
    (ii) the longest possible length.
    (a) 2.45 m   (b) 23 cm   (c) 4.00 m
    (d) 14 cm   (e) 50 cm   (f) 5.34 m

3   Iain was measuring the time it took him to run 100 m. His watch was accurate to the nearest tenth of a second and he measured the time as 12.1 seconds.
    Write down
    (a) his shortest possible time for the run
    (b) his longest possible time for the run.

4   At a race meeting these times were measured to the nearest hundredth of a second.
    For each, write down
    (i) the shortest possible time
    (ii) the longest possible time.
    (a) 22.35 s   (b) 43.67 s
    (c) 10.02 s   (d) 2 min 45.34 s
    (e) 45.00 s   (f) 50 s

26.7 Choosing an appropriate degree of accuracy

Sometimes when measurements are made they need to be very accurate but at other times a high degree of accuracy is not needed.

For example, the time for running the 100 metres in an international athletics competition needs to be measured to the nearest hundredth of a second. But the time needed to drive the 400 miles from London to Scotland for a holiday does not need that degree of accuracy. A measurement to the nearest half hour would be sufficient.

If you measure the width of this book the most sensible unit of measure would be millimetres. Using centimetres is too inaccurate and using tenths of a millimetre is too accurate.

Exercise 260

In questions **1** to **4** write down the most appropriate unit you could use to measure each quantity.

1 The time taken to
    (a) run a 200 m race   **(b)** walk to school
    (c) travel from London to Manchester by car
    (d) run 1000 m   **(e)** walk 20 miles
    (f) watch a film.

2 **(a)** the shoulder height of a zebra
    (b) the thickness of this book
    (c) the length of your class room
    (d) the lengths of your fingers
    (e) the height of a large tree
    (f) the width of a pencil

3 The area of
    (a) a leaf   **(b)** the school playing fields
    (c) the British Isles   **(d)** the school hall.

4 The volume of liquid in
    (a) a can of cola   **(b)** a car's petrol tank
    (c) a large lake.

5 Abdul and Nia are measuring the perimeter of the school field.
    (a) Write down the units they should use to measure it.
    (b) What measuring instrument should they use?
    (c) To what degree of accuracy should they give their answer?

6 Mario and Dara are carrying out an experiment with bouncing spheres. They drop spheres made from different materials from the first floor of the school building. They then measure the times the spheres take to fall and the heights to which they bounce.

   (a) Write down the units they should use to measure
      (i) the times taken
      (ii) the heights of bounce.
   (b) What measuring instruments should they use?
   (c) To what degree of accuracy should they give their answers?

26.8 Compound measures: density

Sometimes you need to work with two units at the same time. In Section 19.10 you calculated the compound measure speed. Speed is often measured in miles per hour, km per hour or metres per second.

Density is another compound measure. The density of a substance is defined as the mass per unit volume. It is worked out by the formula

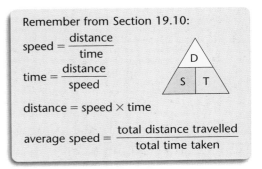

Remember from Section 19.10:

$$\text{speed} = \frac{\text{distance}}{\text{time}}$$

$$\text{time} = \frac{\text{distance}}{\text{speed}}$$

$$\text{distance} = \text{speed} \times \text{time}$$

$$\text{average speed} = \frac{\text{total distance travelled}}{\text{total time taken}}$$

$$\text{density} = \frac{\text{mass}}{\text{volume}}$$

The formula can be arranged to give

$$\text{volume} = \frac{\text{mass}}{\text{density}} \qquad \text{mass} = \text{volume} \times \text{density}$$

If the mass is measured in kilograms and the volume is measured in cubic metres the density is measured in kilograms per cubic metre. This can be abbreviated to kg/m^3 or $kg\,m^{-3}$.

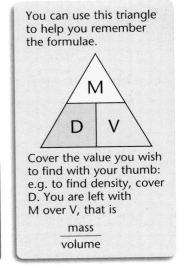

You can use this triangle to help you remember the formulae.

Cover the value you wish to find with your thumb: e.g. to find density, cover D. You are left with M over V, that is

$$\frac{\text{mass}}{\text{volume}}$$

Example 17

Calculate the density of a piece of metal that has a mass of 2000 kilograms and a volume of 0.5 cubic metres.

$$\text{density} = \frac{2000}{0.5} = 4000\,kg\,m^{-3}$$

Exercise 26P

 Calculate the densities of the following materials.

	Substance	Mass in kg	Volume in m³
1	Aluminium	5400	2
2	Copper	12 000	1.34
3	Gold	3000	0.155
4	Nickel	450	0.0506
5	Silver	2700	0.257
6	Sodium	3900	4.02
7	Tin	4000	0.547
8	Zinc	30 000	4.21
9	Lead	1	0.000 088 1
10	Uranium	10	0.000 528

Using the density formula to calculate mass or volume

If you are given the density of a material and are asked to calculate the mass or the volume then you can substitute the values into the density formula.

Example 18

Calculate the volume of a piece of oak with a density of 720 kg per m³ and a mass of 25 kg.

$$\text{density} = \frac{\text{mass}}{\text{volume}}$$

so

$$720 = \frac{25}{\text{volume}}$$

Multiply both sides by volume:

$$720 \times \text{volume} = 25$$

Divide both sides by 720:

$$\text{volume} = \frac{25}{720} = 0.035 \text{ m}^3$$

Example 19

Calculate the mass of a piece of aluminium that has a volume of 1.5 m³ and a density of 2700 kg per m³.

$$\text{density} = \frac{\text{mass}}{\text{volume}}$$

so

$$2700 = \frac{\text{mass}}{1.5}$$

Multiply both sides by 1.5:

$$\text{mass} = 2700 \times 1.5$$
$$= 4050 \text{ kg}$$

There is another way to work out the answers to Examples 18 and 19. You can substitute the values into the rearrangements of the density formula written on the previous page.

Exercise 26Q

 Copy this table and calculate the missing values.

	Substance	Mass in kg	Volume in m³	Density in kg m⁻³
1	Steel	2.5		7700
2	Douglas fir (wood)		1.5	600
3	Balsa wood		1	200
4	Common brick	50		1600
5	Breeze block	100		1400
6	Concrete		3.5	2300
7	Polypropylene		4	900
8	Iron	1000		7860
9	Magnesium	0.5		1740
10	Platinum	0.05		21450

26.9 Changing units

You need to be able to change units of speed between kilometres per hour, metres per second and miles per hour.

___Example 20___

Change 10 metres per second to kilometres per hour.

First of all you need to find how many metres are travelled in 1 hour.

So you need to multiply by $60 \times 60 = 3600$.

> There are $60 \times 60 = 3600$ seconds in 1 hour

In 1 second distance travelled = 10 m

In 1 hour distance travelled = $10 \times 3600 = 36\,000$ m

Divide by 1000 to change m to km.

In 1 hour distance travelled = $\dfrac{36\,000}{1000} = 36$ km

So the speed in kilometres per hour is 36 km per hour (or $36\,\text{km h}^{-1}$).

Example 21

Change 60 miles per hour to
(a) kilometres per hour   (b) metres per second.
(Use 5 miles = 8 km)

(a) In 1 hour distance travelled = 60 miles
$$= 60 \times \tfrac{8}{5} \text{ km} = 96 \text{ km}$$
So the speed is 96 km per hour (or 96 km h^{-1}).

(b) In 1 hour distance travelled = 96 km = 96 000 m

In 1 second distance travelled = $\dfrac{96\,000}{3600}$ m = 26.66 m

So the speed is 26.7 m/s (or 26.7 m s^{-1}) (to 3 s.f.).

Exercise 26R

1 Change 20 metres per second to metres per hour.

2 Change 30 km per hour to metres per second.

3 Change 60 miles per hour to miles per minute.

4 Change 15 metres per second to km per hour.

5 Change 20 metres per second to kilometres per hour.

6 Change 80 km per hour to metres per minute.

7 Sybil travels 80 kilometres in 4 hours.
What is her average speed in metres per second?

8 An electron travels at 600 000 metres per second.
What is this speed in km per hour?

9 A rocket must travel at 11 000 metres per second to
escape the gravitational pull of the Earth. What is this
speed in kilometres per hour?

10 The fastest land animal is the cheetah, which can travel
at 70 miles per hour.
Approximately what is this speed in metres per second?

26.10 Comparing measurements

To compare two measurements they need to have the same units.

> You have to compare like with like. To compare the speed of an electron with the speed of a rocket you need to change both speeds to the same units.

Example 22

1 tonne of coal has a volume of 0.67 m³.

80 kg of sand has a volume of 0.05 m³.

Which material has the greater density?

> 1 tonne = 1000 kg

$$\text{density} = \frac{\text{mass}}{\text{volume}}$$

$$\text{density of coal} = \frac{1000}{0.67} = 1492.537\ldots$$

$$= 1490 \text{ kg/m}^3 \text{ (to 3 s.f.)}$$

$$\text{density of sand} = \frac{80}{0.05} \text{ kg/m}^3$$

$$= 1600 \text{ kg/m}^3$$

So sand has a greater density than coal.

Exercise 26S

 Where needed use 5 miles = 8 km.

1 Which car is travelling faster, one at 40 miles per hour or one at 50 kilometres per hour?

2 The motorway speed limit in France is 130 km per hour and in England it is 70 miles per hour.
   Which is the faster speed?

3 An electron travels at 600 000 metres per second.
   What is this speed in miles per hour?

4 The fastest land animal (the cheetah) can travel at 112 km per hour.
   What is this speed in miles per hour?

5 A car is travelling on a motorway at 70 miles per hour.
   A peregrine falcon (bird of prey) can travel at 40 metres per second.
   (a) Change 70 miles per hour to metres per second.
   (b) Which is faster – the car or the bird?

6 In 1977 the land speed record was 283 metres per second and the water speed record was 330 miles per hour.

   (a) Change 283 metres per second to miles per hour.

   (b) How many times faster was the land speed record than the water speed record?

7 The speed of light in a vacuum is 300 000 000 metres per second. The speed of a neutron is 4500 miles per hour.

   (a) Change 300 000 000 metres per second to miles per hour.

   (b) How many times faster is the speed of light than the speed of a neutron?

Mixed exercise 26

1 Calculate the number of *complete* revolutions made by a cycle wheel of diameter 70 cm in travelling a distance of $\frac{1}{2}$ km. [E]

2 **(a)** Find the area of a circle of diameter 5.6 cm, giving your answer in cm² correct to two significant figures.

   (b) A fence which surrounds a rectangular field of length 300 metres and width 184 metres is taken down and is just long enough to fence in a circular paddock. Calculate the radius of the paddock. [E]

3 Light travels 300 000 kilometres in 1 second. A light year is the distance travelled by light in 1 year.
Calculate, in kilometres, how far light travels in a year of 365 days. Give your answer correct to 3 s.f.

4 Given that 1 cm³ of brass weighs 8.45 grams, calculate the weight of a solid cylinder of brass whose radius is 1.3 cm and whose height is 9.0 cm.

5 Stephanie ran 100 metres.
The distance was correct to the nearest metre.

   (a) Write down the shortest distance Stephanie could have run.

Stephanie's time for the run was 14.8 seconds.
Her time was correct to the nearest tenth of a second.

   (b) Write down
     (i) her shortest possible time for the run,
     (ii) her longest possible time for the run. [E]

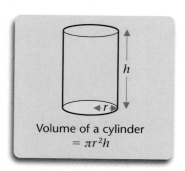

Volume of a cylinder
$= \pi r^2 h$

6 The diagram represents a swimming pool.
The pool has vertical sides.
The pool is 8 m wide.

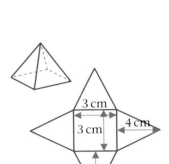

(a) Calculate the area of the shaded cross-section.

The swimming pool is completely filled with water.

(b) Calculate the volume of water in the pool.

64 m³ of water leaks out of the pool.

(c) Calculate the distance by which the water level
falls.   [E]

Diagram NOT
accurately drawn

7 The diagram represents a chocolate box in the shape of a
pyramid. The box has a square base and four triangular
faces. The net of the chocolate box is shown.

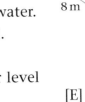

(a) Work out   (i) the area of the base
               (ii) the area of a triangular face
              (iii) the total surface area of the box.

Each net is cut from a square card of area 121 cm². Any
card not used for the box is thrown away.
n boxes are made.

(b) Write down a formula for the total area, A cm², of
card which is thrown away.

(c) Construct an accurate net for the box.   [E]

8 The diagram represents a tea packet in the shape of a
cuboid.

(a) Calculate the volume of the packet.

There are 125 grams of tea in a full packet. Jason has to
design a new packet that will contain 100 grams of tea
when full.

(b) (i) Work out the volume of the new packet.
    (ii) Express the weight of the new tea packet as a
         percentage of the weight of the packet shown.

The new packet of tea is in the shape of a cuboid.
The base of the new packet measures 7 cm by 6 cm.

(c) (i) Work out the area of the base of the new packet.
    (ii) Calculate the height of the new packet.   [E]

9 A cylindrical can has a radius of 6 centimetres.

(a) Calculate the area of the circular end of the can.
    (Use the π button on your calculator or $\pi = 3.14$.)

The capacity of the can is 2000 cm³.

(b) Calculate the height of the can.
    Give your answer correct to 1 decimal place.   [E]

10 (a) Write down a sensible **metric** unit that should be used to measure
  (i) the height of a school hall
  (ii) the weight of a pencil.
  (b) Write down a sensible **imperial** unit that should be used to measure the distance between London and Manchester.   [E]

11 Change 28 miles to kilometres.   [E]

12 Change 180 km per hour to metres per minute.

13 A circle has a radius of 3 cm.

(a) Work out the area of the circle. Give your answer correct to 3 significant figures.

Diagram NOT accurately drawn

3 cm

A semicircle has a diameter of 9 cm.

(b) Work out the perimeter of the semicircle. Give your answer correct to 3 significant figures.

Diagram NOT accurately drawn

[E]

9 cm

14 The density of gold is $19\,320\,\text{kg m}^{-3}$. Work out the mass, in grams, of $1\,\text{cm}^3$ of gold.

15 The density of oak is $720\,\text{kg m}^{-3}$. Calculate the mass of a rectangular block of oak measuring 6 m by 0.7 m by 0.12 m.

16 The density of red cedar is $380\,\text{kg m}^{-3}$. Calculate the volume in m^3 of a block of red cedar with mass 212 kg.

Summary of key points

1 area of a trapezium $= \frac{1}{2}(a + b)h$

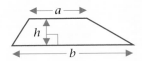

2 The perimeter of a circle is called the **circumference**:

$C = \pi d$ where C is the circumference,
or d is the diameter and
$C = 2\pi r$ r is the radius.

3 **area of a circle** $= A = \pi r^2$

4 Part of a circumference is called an **arc**.
A half circle is called a **semicircle**.

5 Quarter circles are called **quadrants**.

This is a **sector** of a circle.

These are **segments**.

6 A prism is a 3-D shape with the same cross-section all along its length.

7 volume of a prism = area of cross-section $\times$ length

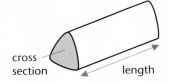

cross section   length

8 volume of a cylinder $= \pi r^2 h$

9 area of the curved surface of a cylinder $= 2\pi rh$

total surface area of a closed cylinder $= 2\pi rh + 2\pi r^2$

total surface area of a cylinder open at one end $= 2\pi rh + \pi r^2$

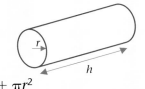

10 If you make a measurement correct to a given unit the true value lies in a range that extends half a unit below and half a unit above the measurement.

11 density $= \dfrac{\text{mass}}{\text{volume}}$ volume $= \dfrac{\text{mass}}{\text{density}}$

mass = density $\times$ volume

You can use this triangle
to help you remember
the formulae.

27 Describing transformations

Changes in the position or size of a shape are called **transformations**.

For your GCSE exam you need to know about four types of transformations: translations, reflections, rotations and enlargements.

27.1 Translations

You learned about translations in Chapter 22. You should remember that:

A **translation** is a sliding movement.

In this diagram triangle **A** is translated to **B**. All the points on **A** are moved +3 units parallel to the x-axis followed by −2 units parallel to the y-axis.

This translation is described by the **vector** $\begin{pmatrix} 3 \\ -2 \end{pmatrix}$.

To describe a translation you need to give the horizontal and vertical movements of the translation. These are written as a **vector**.

Coordinates are often used in questions involving transformations.

On the grid below, at P, $x = 3$ and $y = 1$ so the coordinates of P are (3, 1).

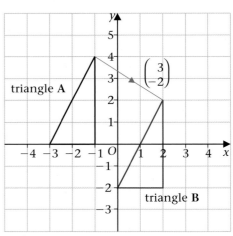

triangle A

triangle B

$\begin{pmatrix} 3 \\ -2 \end{pmatrix}$

We say that triangle **A** 'maps on to' triangle **B**.

The object and image are congruent.

Note:
Write the x value before the y value.

Note:
$R = (-1, 2)$
$S = (-2, -1)$
$Q = (2, -1)$

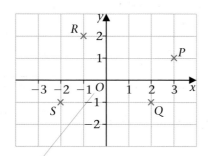

The point (0, 0) is called the **origin**.

Example 1

The shape *ABCD* is shown on the grid.

(a) Write down the coordinates of *A*, *B*, *C* and *D*.

ABCD is translated to *PQRS* so that *P*(2, −1) is the image of *A*.

(b) Plot *P* and describe fully the translation that maps *A* onto *P*.

(c) Draw the image of *ABCD*.

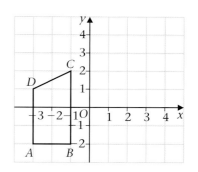

(a) *A* = (−3, −2), *B* = (−1, −2), *C* = (−1, 2) and *D* = (−3, 1).

(b) The point *A*(−3, −2) is translated to *P*(2, −1) so the *x*-coordinate is increased by 5 and the *y*-coordinate is increased by 1. This is a translation by the vector $\begin{pmatrix} 5 \\ 1 \end{pmatrix}$.

(c) All the points on *ABCD* are translated by $\begin{pmatrix} 5 \\ 1 \end{pmatrix}$.

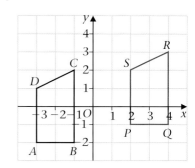

Q is the image of *B*, so the coordinates of *Q* are (−1+5, −2+1) = (4, −1).
In the same way *R* = (−1+5, 2+1) = (4, 3) and *S* = (−3+5, 1+1) = (2, 2).

Exercise 27A

You will need isometric and squared paper and a ruler.
Tracing paper could be useful.

1 Shape **A** is shown on the grid.
 A is translated using this rule:
  Move all points +4 units parallel to the *x*-axis
  followed by +2 units parallel to the *y*-axis.
 This means move them by the vector $\begin{pmatrix} 4 \\ 2 \end{pmatrix}$.

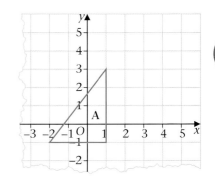

 On squared paper draw a set of coordinate axes with *x* and *y* both going from −5 to 5.

 (a) Draw the image of **A** after the translation and label it **B**.

 (b) Write down the coordinates of the vertices of shape **B**.

2 On squared paper draw a set of coordinate axes with
x and y both going from -5 to 5.
The corners of triangle ABC are $A(-1, 1)$, $B(-1, 4)$ and $C(1, 3)$.

(a) Draw triangle ABC on your grid.

Triangle ABC is translated to triangle $A'B'C'$ using this rule:
Add 3 to the x-coordinate and subtract 4 from the
y-coordinate.

(b) Work out the coordinates of A', B' and C'.

(c) Draw triangle $A'B'C'$ on your grid.

3 Describe fully the transformation which maps shape **P**
on to shape **Q**.

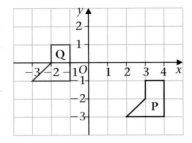

4 Make a pattern using repeated translations. You may
use one, two or more shapes.

27.2 Reflections

You learned about reflections in Chapter 22. You should
remember that:

A mathematical **reflection** has an image that is the same
distance behind the mirror line as the object is in front.

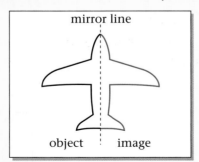

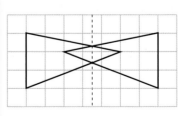

The object and image are
congruent.

Mirror lines are **two-way**. The mirror line may go through the
object, requiring reflections to go both ways.

To describe a reflection fully you need to give the equation of the line of symmetry.

Example 2

Describe fully the transformation that maps shape **A** on to **B**.

The image **B** is the same shape and size as the original shape **A**, but it is 'turned over'. So the transformation is a reflection.

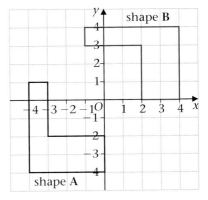

First draw the line of reflection.
Draw a line from a point on **A** to its corresponding point on **B** (shown in red on the diagram).
Find the middle point of the line. Repeat for another point on **A**. The line joining the two middle points is the mirror line (shown in black on the diagram).
The equation of the mirror line is $y = -x$. **A** maps on to **B** after a reflection in the line $y = -x$.
The transformation is a reflection in the line $y = -x$.

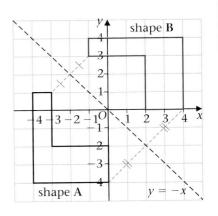

Exercise 27B

You need squared or graph paper and tracing paper.

1   Copy the grid and the shaded shape. Draw the image of the shape after a reflection in the line $y = 1$.

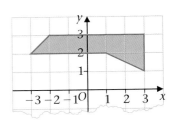

Hint: first draw the line whose equation is $y = 1$.

2 Copy triangle *ABC* and the line *TU* on squared paper. Draw the image of triangle *ABC* after it is reflected in the line *TU*. The image of the point *A* has been found for you.

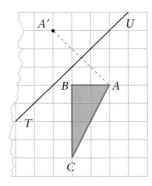

> Hint: turn the page so that *TU* is vertical.

3 Draw a grid with both *x*- and *y*-coordinate axes going from −6 to 6.

    (a) Plot the points *P*(−2, 1), *Q*(0, 1), *R*(1, 0), *S*(3, 4) and *T*(−2, 4) and join them in order to form the closed shape *PQRST*.

    (b) Draw the image of *PQRST* after a reflection in the *x*-axis.

4 Describe fully the transformation that maps shape **A** on to **B**.

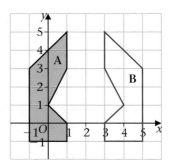

5 Use tracing paper to draw a pattern by making repeated reflections of a shape.

27.3 Rotations

You learned about rotations in Chapter 22. The minute hand of a clock **rotates** (turns) about a point near one of its ends. A blade of a pair of scissors rotates about a point part way along its length.

The clock hand and the scissor blade **turn through an angle** about a fixed point.

> A rotation turns a shape through an angle about a fixed point.

> The object and image are congruent.

Notice that the image is the same shape and size as the original shape.

Exercise 27C

You need tracing paper, a ruler and a protractor.

1 Copy the shapes. Use tracing paper to rotate each shape half a turn about the point marked with a dot.

(a)  (b)  (c)

2 Rotate each of the shapes in question **1** a quarter of a turn anticlockwise about the point marked with a dot.

3 Copy the flag shape. Draw the image after a rotation about the point R of

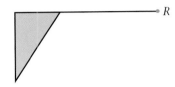

(a) a quarter of a turn anticlockwise
(b) a half turn
(c) a quarter of a turn clockwise.

4 Copy the shape. Draw the image after a rotation about the point of
(a) 120° anticlockwise
(b) 240° anticlockwise
(c) 120° clockwise

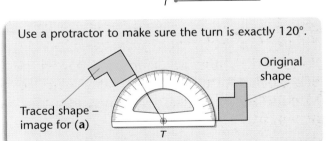

Use a protractor to make sure the turn is exactly 120°.

Original shape

Traced shape – image for (a)

When the centre of rotation is not on the object

Sometimes you need to rotate a shape about a point that is outside the shape. You can think of this as though it was the flag in question **3** of Exercise 27C without the flagpole.

Trace the shape and the dot. Then keep the dot fixed and rotate the tracing paper as before.

• R

The fixed point R is called the **centre of rotation**.

Exercise 27D

You need tracing paper.

1 Copy the shapes and the dots. Use tracing paper to rotate each shape half a turn about the point marked with a dot.

(a) 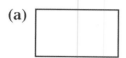   (b) 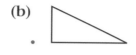   (c)

2 Rotate each shape in question **1** a quarter of a turn anticlockwise about the point marked with a dot.

3 Copy this shape and the dot.
Make a pattern by rotating the shape about the dot through these angles:
(a) clockwise: 60°, 120° and 180°
(b) anticlockwise: 60° and 120°.

Rotating shapes on a grid

You can use squared paper to help you rotate shapes.

Example 3

On squared paper draw coordinate axes with x going from 0 to 7 and y going from -3 to 7. Copy the shape $ABCDEF$ and draw its image after a quarter of a turn anticlockwise about the point $P(1, -1)$.

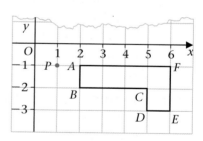

Plot image of each point on the shape and then join them to form the image.

Rotate A about P through a quarter of a turn (90°) anticlockwise and it ends up at (1, 0).

Rotate B about P through a quarter of a turn (90°) anticlockwise and it ends up at (2, 0).

F goes to (1, 4).

You could continue with the other points, but these image points are probably enough for you to complete the shape.

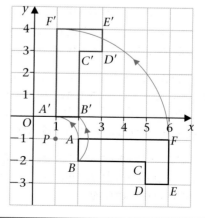

In a rotation all points in the shape rotate through the same angle. The distance of an image point from the centre of rotation is the same as the distance of the original point from the centre of rotation.

Describing rotations

To describe a rotation fully you need to give the:
- centre of rotation
- angle of turn
- direction of turn (clockwise or anticlockwise)

Example 4

Describe fully the transformation which maps shape **P** on to **Q**.

Each side of **Q** is at right angles to the corresponding side of **P** so **P** has made a quarter turn anticlockwise to get to **Q**.

To describe the rotation fully you need to say which point is the centre of rotation.

Each point on the original shape is the same distance from the centre of rotation as its image point. You might be able to see that the centre is (1, 1). So the transformation is a rotation of a quarter of a turn (90°) anticlockwise about the point (1, 1).

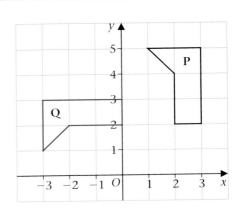

You can also find the centre of rotation geometrically. The centre is the same distance from each point and its image. So if you draw a line from any point to its image, the centre of rotation will be *somewhere* on the perpendicular bisector of the line.

To find the centre of rotation, draw lines connecting *two* points to their images. Draw the perpendicular bisectors of both lines. The bisectors are dotted lines in the diagram.

As the centre of rotation is somewhere on *both* bisectors it must be at the point (1, 1) where they cross.

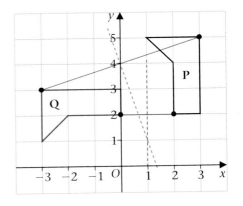

There is more about perpendicular bisectors in Section 7.7.

Exercise 27E

You will need squared or graph paper.

1 Draw coordinate axes on graph paper with x and y going from −6 to 6. Copy the shaded shape.
Draw the image of the shaded shape after

   (a) a half turn about the origin (0, 0) (label the image **A**)

   (b) a quarter turn clockwise about the origin (label it **B**)

   (c) a quarter turn anticlockwise about the origin (label it **C**).

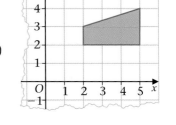

2 Draw coordinate axes on graph paper with x going from −6 to 6 and y going from −4 to 8. Copy the shaded shape.
Draw the image of the shaded shape after

   (a) a half turn about the point $P(0, 2)$ (label the image **A**)

   (b) a quarter turn clockwise about the point $P(0, 2)$ (label the image **B**)

   (c) a quarter turn anticlockwise about the point $P(0, 2)$ (label the image **C**).

3 Describe fully the transformation which maps shape **A** on to shape **B**.

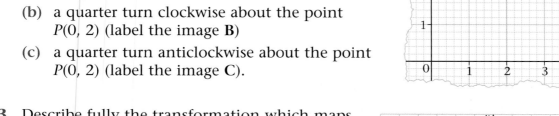

27.4 Enlargements

You learned about enlargement in Chapter 22. You should remember that:

An enlargement changes the size but not the shape of an object. The scale factor of the enlargement is the value that the lengths of the original object are multiplied by.

In an enlargement, image lines are parallel to their corresponding object lines.

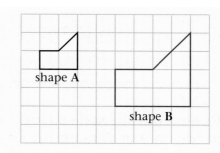

shape A

shape B

Similar shapes

In Chapter 22 you saw that

The original shape and its image after an enlargement are
similar to each other.

The centre of enlargement
determines the final position
of the enlarged image.

$CR' = 2CR$
$CP' = 2CP$
$CQ' = 2CQ$

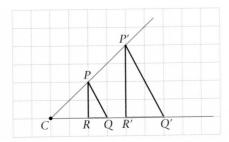

Example 5

Enlarge triangle PQR by scale factor 3 using
A as the centre of enlargement.

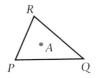

Copy triangle PQR and the point A inside the triangle.

Draw a line from A to P and continue it to P' so that AP' is
3 times AP. Mark the positions of Q' and R' in a similar way,
then join the points P', Q' and R' to form the image triangle.

The enlargement should
look like this:

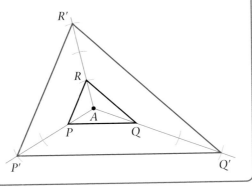

Describing enlargements

To describe an enlargement fully you need to give the scale
factor and the centre of enlargement.

To work out the scale factors, compare the lengths of
corresponding sides on the object and image.

The centre of
enlargement can be given
by the letter of the point
or by the coordinates of
the point.

Example 6

Describe fully the transformation that maps *ABCD* on to *PQRS*.

PQRS is the same shape as *ABCD*. The sides of *PQRS* are all 2 times the lengths of the corresponding sides of *ABCD*. So the transformation is an enlargement by a scale factor 2.

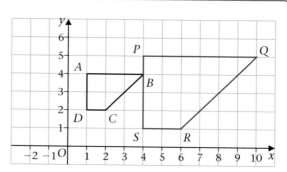

To describe the transformation fully you need to give the centre of enlargement.
To find the centre of enlargement, reverse the method used in Example 5.

> Note: you could compare the two corresponding lines as a ratio
>
> scale factor $= \dfrac{PQ}{AB} = \dfrac{6}{3} = 2$

Join *P* to *A* and continue the line.
Join *Q* to *B* and continue the line.
In the same way join *R* to *C* and *S* to *D* and continue the lines. The lines all pass through the same point $(-2, 3)$ so this is the centre of enlargement.

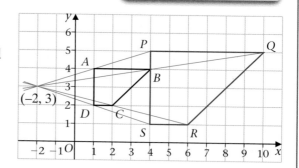

The transformation is an enlargement by scale factor 2 with centre of enlargement $(-2, 3)$.

The scale factor of an enlargement is given by the ratio of any two corresponding line segments.

Scale factor $= \dfrac{A'B'}{AB}$

 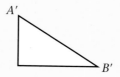

Enlargements with fractional scale factors

If you start with shape *PQRS* from Example 6 and transform it to *ABCD* the shape remains the same, but the size is changed, so the transformation is an enlargement.

The sides of *ABCD* are all $\frac{1}{2}$ the lengths of the corresponding sides of *PQRS* so the transformation that maps *PQRS* on to *ABCD* is an enlargement by the scale factor $\frac{1}{2}$ with centre $(-2, 3)$.

> An enlargement with a scale factor less than 1 means that the image will be smaller than the object.

Example 7

Draw the image of the shape *KLMN* after an
enlargement by scale factor $\frac{1}{2}$ with centre *C*.
Label the image *K′L′M′N′*.

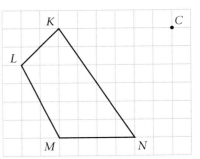

Join *CK*. *CK* = 6 units. The scale factor is $\frac{1}{2}$ so
$CK′ = \frac{1}{2} \times 6 = 3$ units.
Mark the point *K′*, 3 units from *C* along *CK*.

In the same way mark *L′* where $CL′ = \frac{1}{2} CL$,
M′ where $CM′ = \frac{1}{2} CM$ and *N′* where $CN′ = \frac{1}{2} CN$.

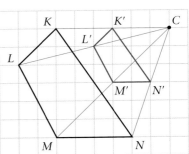

> Hint: use the squares and their diagonals
> so you can do this without a ruler.

Join *K′L′M′N′* to form the image.

Example 8

Work out the scale factor of the enlargement that takes
triangle *ABC* on to triangle *LMN*.

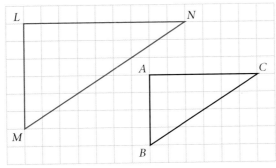

The scale factor is the ratio of any two corresponding line
segments

$$\frac{LN}{AC} = \frac{9}{6} = \frac{3}{2} = 1\frac{1}{2}$$

> Or you could use $\frac{LM}{AB} = \frac{6}{4} = \frac{3}{2} = 1\frac{1}{2}$

The scale factor is $1\frac{1}{2}$.

Exercise 27F

You will need squared or graph paper and a ruler.

1 **(a)** Copy the diagram.
Describe fully the transformation that maps shape **A** on to shape **B**.
(b) Describe fully the transformation that maps shape **B** on to shape **A**.

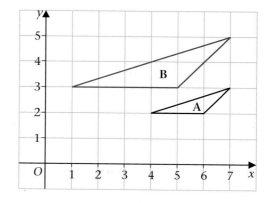

2 Copy the diagram.
With C as centre, draw the image of the shaded shape after an enlargement by
(a) scale factor $\frac{1}{4}$
(b) scale factor $\frac{3}{4}$

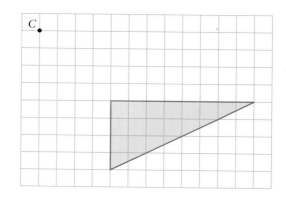

3 Copy the diagram.
With X as centre, draw the image of the shaded shape after an enlargement by
(a) scale factor $\frac{2}{3}$
(b) scale factor $1\frac{2}{3}$

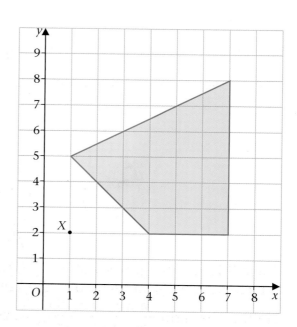

4 Describe fully the enlargement that
  (a) maps **A** on to **B**
  (b) maps **B** on to **A**.

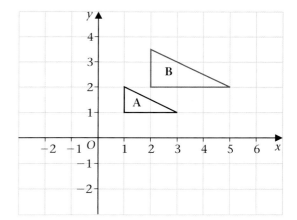

5 Describe fully the transformation that takes triangle *PQR* on to triangle *TUV*.

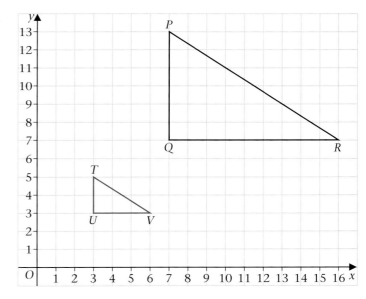

Similar circles, squares and rectangles

When two shapes are similar, one shape is an enlargement of the other.

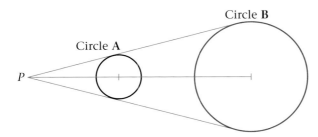

Circle B is an enlargement of circle **A** (the centre of enlargement is *P*), so the two circles are mathematically similar. The ratio $\dfrac{\text{radius of circle } \mathbf{B}}{\text{radius of circle } \mathbf{A}}$ is the same for all the radii of the two circles.

> This is true for **any** two circles **A** and **B**.

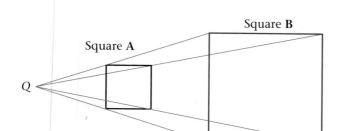

Square **A** is an enlargement of square **B** (the centre of enlargement is Q) so the two squares are mathematically similar. The ratio $\dfrac{\text{side of square } \mathbf{B}}{\text{side of square } \mathbf{A}}$ is the same for all the sides of the squares.

> This is true for **any** two squares **A** and **B**.

Look at these rectangles on the right:

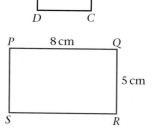

Length: PQ corresponds to AB. The ratio $\dfrac{PQ}{AB} = \dfrac{8}{4} = \dfrac{2}{1}$

Width: QR corresponds to BC. The ratio $\dfrac{QR}{BC} = \dfrac{5}{3}$

The ratios for length and width are not the same so the two rectangles are not mathematically similar.

> Any two circles and any two squares are mathematically similar but two rectangles may not be mathematically similar.

Mixed exercise 27

You need squared paper and a ruler.

1 (a) Copy the diagram.
Reflect the triangle **A** in the x-axis.
Label the reflection **B**.

(b) Reflect the triangle **B** in the line $y = x$.
Label the reflection **C**.

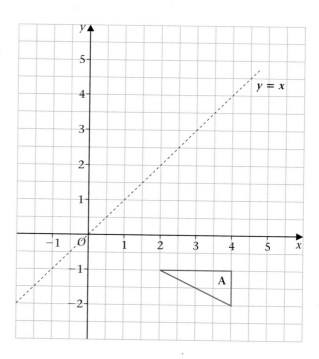

2   Copy and complete the coordinate grid so that
    x goes from -9 to 9 and y goes from -5 to 5.
    Copy the triangle **L**.
    (a) Reflect the triangle **L** in the y-axis.
         Label the reflection **M**.
    (b) Reflect the triangle **M** in the x-axis.
         Label the image **N**.

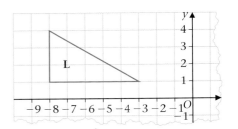

3   Write down a single transformation which is applied to
    the original tile to make each lettered part of this pattern:

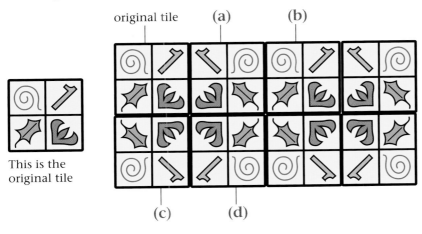

Hint: there is more than
one way of doing the
transformations for (b),
(c) and (d).

4   On squared paper draw coordinate axes so that x and y
    both go from -6 to 6.
    (a) Plot the points $(2, 2)$, $(4, 1)$, $(6, 2)$ and $(4, 5)$.
         Join them in order and label the shape **P**.
    (b) Reflect **P** in the x-axis. Label the reflection **Q**.
    (c) Rotate **P** through $180°$ about the origin $(0, 0)$.
         Label this image **R**.

5   Copy and complete this coordinate grid for
    x from -7 to 10 and y from -6 to 6.
    Copy shape **F**.
    (a) Rotate **F** through $180°$ about $(0, 0)$.
         Label the image **G**.
    (b) Rotate **G** through $180°$ about $(5, -3)$.
         Label the image **H**.

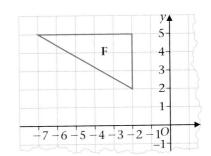

6 Copy this diagram.
   (a) Rotate triangle **A** clockwise through 90° about (0, 0). Label the image **B**.
   (b) Draw the image of **B** after a reflection in the line $y = -x$.
   Label the reflection **C**.

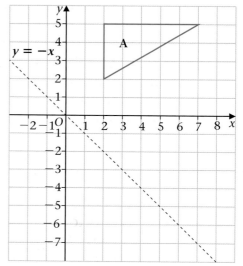

7 The triangle **Q** is an enlargement of the triangle **P**.
   (a) Write down the scale factor of the enlargement.
   (b) Work out the coordinates of the centre of enlargement.

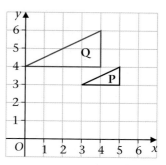

8 Draw a set of coordinate axes with x from -4 to 10 and y from 0 to 7.
   (a) Plot the points $(-2, 1)$, $(1, 3)$ and $(0, 5)$.
   Join them and label the triangle **A**.
   The triangle **A** is reflected in a line **M**. Two of the image points have coordinates $(5, 3)$ and $(6, 5)$.
   (b) Write down the coordinates of the third corner of the image.
   (c) Work out the equation of **M**, the line of reflection.

9 Rotate the triangle through 180° about centre A. On a copy of the grid draw the new position of the triangle.

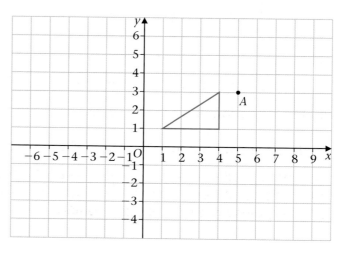

[E]

10   Draw a grid on squared paper with the *x*-axis from
     −10 to 10 and the *y*-axis from −14 to 4.
   (a) Plot the points *A*(3, 1), *B*(2, −4) and *C*(−3, 1) and
        join them to form triangle *ABC*.
   (b) Draw the enlargement of triangle *ABC* by the scale
        factor 3, using the origin (0, 0) as centre of
        enlargement.
   (c) Write down the coordinates of the vertices of the
        image triangle.

11   Copy the grid and the shaded triangle.
   (a) Draw the image of the shaded triangle after
        a rotation through an angle of 90°
        anticlockwise about the origin (0, 0).
        Label the image **S**.
   (b) Draw the image of the shaded triangle after
        a rotation through an angle of 90°
        anticlockwise about the point (2, 1).
        Label the image **T**.

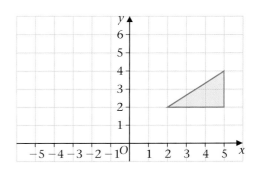

12   Draw a set of coordinate axes with *x* from −8 to 8 and
     y from −7 to 7.
   (a) Plot the points (2, 1), (6, 1) and (6, 4).
        Join them up and label the triangle **A**.
   (b) Reflect **A** in the *y*-axis. Label the reflection **B**.
   (c) Draw the line *y* = *x*.
   (d) Reflect **B** in the line *y* = *x*. Label the reflection **C**.

Summary of key points

1   Changes in the position or size of a shape are called **transformations**. Reflections,
    rotations, enlargements and translations are all types of transformations.

2   To describe a translation you need to give the horizontal and vertical movements
    of the translation. These are written as a **vector**, e.g. $\begin{pmatrix} 5 \\ -2 \end{pmatrix}$

3   To describe a reflection fully you need to give the equation of the line of symmetry.

4   In a rotation all points in the shape rotate through the same angle. The distance of
    an image point from the centre of rotation is the same as the distance of the
    original point from the centre of rotation.

5 To describe a rotation fully you need to give the:
- centre of rotation
- angle of turn
- direction of turn (clockwise or anticlockwise)

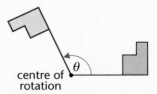

centre of
rotation

6 The original shape and its image after an enlargement are similar to each other.

7 To describe an enlargement fully you need to give the scale factor and the centre of enlargement.

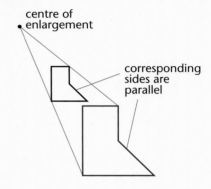

centre of
enlargement

corresponding
sides are
parallel

8 The scale factor of an enlargement is given by the ratio of any two corresponding line segments.

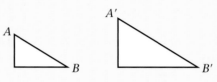

Scale factor $= \dfrac{A'B'}{AB}$

9 When two shapes are similar, one shape is an enlargement of the other.

10 Any two circles and any two squares are mathematically similar but two rectangles may not be mathematically similar.

28 Expressions, formulae, equations and graphs

This chapter shows you how to manipulate algebraic expressions, draw and interpret graphs, rearrange formulae, and solve simple quadratic and reciprocal equations.

In Chapter 3 you learned how to simplify expressions containing powers. You should remember the following key points:

To multiply powers of the same letter add the indices:

$$x^a \times x^b = x^{a+b}$$

See Section 3.11 for more explanation and examples.

To divide powers of the same letter subtract the indices:

$$x^a \div x^b = x^{a-b}$$

Any letter raised to the power 1 is equal to the letter itself:

$$x^1 = x$$

Any letter raised to the power 0 is equal to 1:

$$x^0 = 1 \text{ if } x \text{ is not zero.}$$

To simplify an expression containing different powers of the same letter multiplied or divided, write the expression as a single power of the letter.

28.1 Simplifying algebraic expressions

In Chapter 3 you learned how to simplify an algebraic expression by expanding the brackets and collecting **like terms** together. Here are some more examples:

Example 1 _____

Simplify the expression $3(3a + 2b) + 2(a - b)$.

$3(3a + 2b) + 2(a - b)$

$= 9a + 6b + 2a - 2b$ ———— First expand the brackets.

$= 9a + 2a + 6b - 2b$ ———— Change the order for adding and subtracting to put the a terms and the b terms together.

$= 11a + 4b$

Remember:
This is called collecting **like terms**.

Example 2

Simplify the expression $\dfrac{4n + 2}{2}$

$$\dfrac{4n + 2}{2} = \dfrac{1}{2}(4n + 2)$$

$$= \dfrac{1}{2} \times 4n + \dfrac{1}{2} \times 2 \quad\text{——————— Expand the brackets.}$$

$$= 2n + 1$$

Remember:
the line acts like a bracket.

Example 3

Simplify the expression $x(x + 3y) + 2x(x + y)$.

$$x(x + 3y) + 2x(x + y)$$

$$= x^2 + 3xy + 2x^2 + 2xy \quad\text{——————— Expand the brackets.}$$

$$= x^2 + 2x^2 + 3xy + 2xy \quad\text{——————— Collect like terms.}$$

$$= 3x^2 + 5xy$$

Exercise 28A

Simplify the expressions in questions 1–5.

1 (a) $2(3r + 1) + 2r$ (b) $3(4p - 2) - 10p$
   (c) $4(2x + y) + 2x - 3y$ (d) $2m - 3n + 3(m + n)$

2 (a) $4(2a + b) + 2(3a - b)$ (b) $3(p + q) + 2(p - q)$
   (c) $2(3r + s) + 4(r - s)$ (d) $3(2p - q) + 3(p + q)$

3 (a) $3(x + y) + 4(x - y)$ (b) $4(m - n) + 3(2m - n)$
   (c) $2(p - q) + 2(q - p)$ (d) $3(p - q) + 3(p + q)$

4 (a) $3(b - a) + 1(6a - 6b)$ (b) $r(r + 2) - r$
   (c) $m(n + m) + m(n - m)$ (d) $m(3 + n) + n(1 - m)$

5 (a) $3(x + 2y) + 4x$ (b) $3a + 4(5a - 6)$
   (c) $5(c - d) - 2c + 3d$ (d) $4(2p - 6q) - 3p + q$
   (e) $a(b - 2c) + 2b(a + c)$ (f) $a(b - 2) + b(a - 3)$

6 Write these expressions in a simpler form:

(a) $\dfrac{6n + 4}{2}$ (b) $\dfrac{9n - 6}{3}$ (c) $\dfrac{10n - 20}{5}$

(d) $\dfrac{6p + 10r}{2}$ (e) $\dfrac{4r - 8q}{4}$ (f) $\dfrac{6r - 3s}{3}$

Activity – Expressions

When an algebraic expression was simplified it became
$2a + b$

(a) Write down as many different expressions as you can which simplify to $2a + b$.

(b) What is the most complex expression you can think of that simplifies to $2a + b$?

(c) What is the simplest expression you can think of that simplifies to $2a + b$?

(d) Repeat this activity for some other simple expressions such as a, $\dfrac{a}{2}$, $2a - b$.

Dealing with negative numbers

The expression $-2(3a - 2)$ has a negative number before the brackets. To expand the brackets, multiply each term inside the brackets by -2:

$$-2 \times 3a = -6a$$
$$-2(3a - 2) = -6a + 4$$
$$-2 \times -2 = +4$$

Example 4

Multiply out and simplify: $4(x + 3) - 3(x + 5)$.

$$4(x + 3) - 3(x + 5)$$
$$= 4x + 12 - 3x - 15 \quad \text{Expand the brackets.}$$
$$= 4x - 3x + 12 - 15 \quad \text{Collect like terms.}$$
$$= x - 3$$

Example 5

Simplify the expression $4(2a + b) - 3(a - b)$.

$$4(2a + b) - 3(a - b)$$
$$= 8a + 4b - 3a + 3b \quad \text{Expand the brackets.}$$
$$= 8a - 3a + 4b + 3b \quad \text{Collect like terms.}$$
$$= 5a + 7b$$

Exercise 28B

Multiply out and simplify these expressions.

1 (a) $3(5x + 4) - 2(a + 3)$ (b) $8(2x + 1) - (x + 7)$
   (c) $7(a - 2) - 2(2a + 3)$ (d) $2(6q + 7) - 3(3p + 4q)$
   (e) $2(6x - y) - (x + y)$ (f) $2(4x + 3y) - 3(2x + y)$
   (g) $4(d - 2) - 3(d + 1)$ (h) $5(3c - 2) - 4(1 + 2c)$

2 (a) $3(d + 4) - 2(3 - 2d)$ (b) $2(2p + qw) - 3(p - q)$
   (c) $2(s - r) - 2(r - s)$ (d) $5(4b - 5) - (4 - 2b)$
   (e) $5(2y - 8) - 3(2 - 5y)$ (f) $3(2x + 5y) - 2(2x - y)$
   (g) $3(2n - 3) - 4(n - 2)$ (h) $5(4b - 2a) - 3(2a - 3b)$

Multiplying bracketed expressions

Sometimes you will need to multiply bracketed expressions by each other, for example $(e + f)(g + h)$.

This means $(e + f)$ multiplied by $(g + h)$ or $(e + f) \times (g + h)$

Look at the rectangles on the right.

The area of the whole rectangle is $(e + f)(g + h)$.

It is the same as the sum of the four separate areas so:

$$(e + f)(g + h) = eg + eh + fg + fh$$

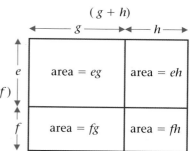

Notice that each term in the first bracket is multiplied by each term in the second bracket:

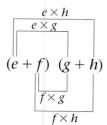

You can also think of the area of the rectangle as the sum of **two** separate parts:

$$(e + f)(g + h) = e(g + h) + f(g + h)$$

Think of multiplying each term in the first bracket by the whole of the second bracket.

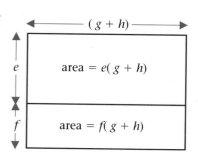

These are two ways of thinking about the same process. The end result is the same.

This is called **multiplying out** the brackets.

___ Example 6 ___

Multiply out and simplify (a) $(x + 2)(x + 3)$ (b) $(x - 4)^2$

(a) $(x + 2)(x + 3) = x(x + 3) + 2(x + 3)$
$$= x^2 + 3x + 2x + 6$$
$$= x^2 + 5x + 6$$

> Multiply each term in the first bracket by the whole of the second bracket.

(b) $(x - 4)^2 = (x - 4)(x - 4)$
$$= x(x - 4) - 4(x - 4)$$
$$= x^2 - 4x - 4x + 16$$
$$= x^2 - 8x + 16$$

___ Example 7 ___

Multiply out the brackets in the expression $(2a + 2)(3a - 4)$.

$$(2a + 2)(3a - 4) = 2a(3a - 4) + 2(3a - 4)$$
$$= 6a^2 - 8a + 6a - 8$$
$$= 6a^2 - 2a - 8$$

> $2a \times 3a = 2 \times a \times 3 \times a$
> $= 2 \times 3 \times a \times a$
> $= 6a^2$

Equations such as

$$(e + f)(g + h) = eg + eh + fg + fh$$

and $(e + f)(g + h) = e(g + h) + f(g + h)$

which are true for all values of e, f, g and h are also known as **identities**.

Exercise 28C

Multiply out and simplify these expressions.

1 (a) $(a + 4)(b + 3)$ (b) $(c + 5)(d + 4)$
  (c) $(x + 3)(y + 6)$ (d) $(a + 3)(a + 8)$
  (e) $(b + 7)(b + 4)$ (f) $(x + 6)(x + 2)$

2 (a) $(2a + 3)(a + 4)$ (b) $(3b + 2)(b + 3)$
  (c) $(4c + 3)(c + 6)$ (d) $(2a + 5)(a + 3)$
  (e) $(3b + 4)(b + 2)$ (f) $(4c + 5)(c + 2)$

3 (a) $(a - 4)(a - 3)$ (b) $(c - 5)(c - 4)$
  (c) $(x - 3)(x - 6)$ (d) $(a - 3)(a - 8)$
  (e) $(b - 7)(b + 4)$ (f) $(x - 6)(x - 2)$

4 (a) $(a - 4)(a + 3)$ (b) $(a + 5)(a - 4)$
  (c) $(x - 3)(x + 6)$ (d) $(a - 3)(a + 8)$
  (e) $(b - 7)(b + 4)$ (f) $(x + 6)(x - 2)$

5 (a) $(x + 1)(x + 2)$ (b) $(y + 5)(y - 1)$
      (c) $(d - 3)(d - 2)$ (d) $(g + 5)(g - 3)$
      (e) $(x - 6)(x + 2)$ (f) $(t - 4)(t - 2)$

6 (a) $(2a - 5)(a + 5)$ (b) $(3b + 4)(b - 6)$
      (c) $(3c - 2)(c - 3)$ (d) $(3a - 4)(a - 5)$
      (e) $(3x - 4)(x + 5)$ (f) $(2a + 3)(a - 6)$

7 (a) $(3a + 1)(a - 2)$ (b) $(3p + 2)(4p - 1)$
      (c) $(3a + 2)(a + 1)$ (d) $(4p + 2)(3p + 2)$
      (e) $(2b - 3)(b - 1)$ (f) $(4b - 1)(2b + 1)$

8 (a) $(x + 3)^2$ (b) $(y - 5)^2$
      (c) $(2x + 1)^2$ (d) $(3y - 4)^2$
      (e) $(3x + 5)^2$ (f) $(6x - 7)^2$

> Remember:
> $(x + 3)^2 = (x + 3)(x + 3)$

9 (a) $(2x - 1)(x + 4)$ (b) $(y - 10)(2y + 3)$
      (c) $(3t - 5)(2t - 3)$ (d) $(m + 5)(5m + 1)$
      (e) $(5c + 6)(5c + 4)$ (f) $(3x + 4)(2x - 7)$

10 (a) $(6 - x)(5 + 2x)$ (b) $(3 + 4x)(3x - 7)$
       (c) $(2x + 3)(2x - 3)$ (d) $(2 + 5x)(3x - 1)$
       (e $(3x - 4)(3x + 4)$ (f) $(4 - 5x)(2x + 3)$

28.2 Drawing graphs of simple quadratic functions

> $y = 2x + 3$ is called a **function**. A function is a rule which shows how one set of numbers relates to another.

A quadratic function is a function of the type
$y = ax^2 + bx + c$ in which a is not zero.
(a, b and c stand for numbers that are given.)

Here is a table of values for the quadratic function $y = x^2$:

x	-3	-2	-1	0	1	2	3
y	9	4	1	0	1	4	9

The points from the table of values are shown plotted on the graph. They do not lie on a straight line.

Exercise 28D will give you a better idea of the shape of the graph.

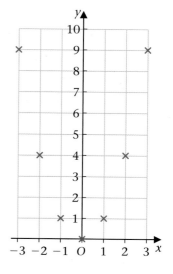

Exercise 28D

You will need 2 mm squared graph paper and tracing paper.

1 (a) Make a full-size copy of the graph of $y = x^2$ on page 528 using 2 cm for 1 unit of x and y.

(b) Copy and complete this extended table of values for $y = x^2$.

x	−2.5	−1.5	−0.8	−0.6	−0.4	−0.2	−0.1	0	0.1	0.2	0.4	0.6	0.8	1.5	2.5
y															

(c) Plot these new points on your graph.

(d) The points should appear to lie on a ∪-shaped curve. Draw a smooth curve through the points you have plotted.

> The curve should not be pointed at (0, 0).

2 On the same axes as you used for question **1**, draw the graph of $y = x^2 + 1$.

> Use the same extra values of x in your table of values as in question 1.

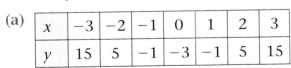

x	−3	−2.5	−2	−1.5	−1	−0.8
y	10	7.25	5	3.25	2	

3 (a) Use tracing paper to trace the axes and the graph of $y = x^2$.

(b) Slide the tracing paper up the y-axis to your graph of $y = x^2 + 1$.

> It should fit exactly.

(c) Use the tracing paper to help you draw on the same axes the graphs of $y = x^2 + 2$, $y = x^2 + 3$, $y = x^2 − 1$.

(d) Do any of the graphs have a line of symmetry?

(e) Write down anything else that you notice.

More quadratic functions

Example 8

(a) Draw a table of values for $y = 2x^2 − 3$, using values of x from −3 to 3.

(b) Draw the graph of $y = 2x^2 − 3$.

(a)

x	−3	−2	−1	0	1	2	3
y	15	5	−1	−3	−1	5	15

(b)

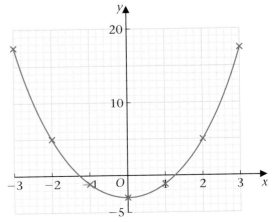

Exercise 28E

Draw a table of values and a graph for each of these quadratic functions, using values of x from -3 to 3.

1 $y = 2x^2 - 5$ **2** $y = 3x^2 - 2$ **3** $y = 5x^2 - 2$

4 $y = 5x^2 - 4$ **5** $y = 3x^2 - 4$

28.3 Drawing graphs of more complex quadratic functions

You need to be able to draw graphs of quadratic functions accurately in order to help you solve quadratic equations.

Example 9

(a) Draw the graph of $y = 2x^2 - 4x - 3$ using values of x from -2 to 4.

(b) Draw the line of symmetry and write down its equation.

(c) What is the minimum value y can have for the function $y = 2x^2 - 4x - 3$?

(d) What value of x gives the minimum value of y?

(e) Find the values of x when $y = 5$.

(a) First make a table of values.

x	-2	-1	0	1	2	3	4
y	13	3	-3	-5	-3	3	13

When $x = -2$
$$y = 2 \times (-2)^2 - 4 \times (-2) - 3$$
$$= 2 \times 4 + 8 - 3$$
$$= 8 + 8 - 3$$
$$y = 13$$

You need to draw axes with x going from -2 to 4 and y going from -5 to 13.

Plot the points then join them with a smooth curve.

> The graph should not be pointed at $(1, -5)$.

(b) The line of symmetry of the curve is the line which has the equation $x = 1$.

(c) The minimum value of y is -5.

(d) $x = 1$ gives the minimum the value of y.

(e) When $y = 5$ there are two values of x, which can be read off the graph: $x = -1.2$ and $x = 3.2$

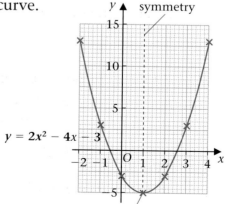

line of symmetry

$y = 2x^2 - 4x - 3$

At this point y has its minimum (smallest) value.

Exercise 28F

You need 2 mm squared graph paper.

1 (a) Draw the graph of $y = 2x^2$ on graph paper.
Use values of x from -4 to 4.

(b) Draw the line of symmetry and write down its equation.

In questions **2–7** do the same as in question **1** for the functions given.

2 $y = x^2 + 5$ **3** $y = x^2 - 2x$

4 $y = -3x^2 + 9$ **5** $y = x^2 + 2x - 1$

6 $y = -x^2 + 3x + 5$ **7** $y = 2x^2 + 3x - 5$

8 (a) Draw the graph of $y = x^2 - 7x + 10$ using values of x from 0 to 6.

(b) Write down the minimum value of y.

(c) Find the value of y when $x = 0.5$

(d) Find the values of x when $y = -2$.

9 (a) Draw the graph of $y = x^2 - 3x - 4$ using values of x from -1 to 5.

(b) Write down the minimum value of y.

(c) Find the value of y when $x = 4.4$

(d) Find the values of x when $y = -4$.

10 (a) Draw the graph of $y = x^2 - 2x - 8$ using values of x from -2 to 4.

(b) Write down the minimum value of y.

(c) Find the value of y when $x = -1.5$

(d) Find the values of x when $y = -5$.

11 (a) Draw the graph of $y = 3x^2 - 3x - 2$ using values of x from -2 to 3.

(b) Write down the minimum value of y.

(c) Find the value of y when $x = 1.8$

(d) Find the values of x when $y = 4$.

12 (a) Draw the graph of $y = 2x^2 - 5$ using values of x from -3 to 3.

(b) Write down the minimum value of y.

(c) Find the value of y when $x = 2.5$

(d) Find the values of x when $y = -3$.

28.4 Solving quadratic equations

You can use a graph to solve a quadratic equation such as

$$2x^2 + 3x + 4 = 18$$

by finding the points on the graph of $y = 2x^2 + 3x + 4$ where $y = 18$, like this:

Step 1 Draw the graph of $y = 2x^2 + 3x + 4$.

Step 2 Find the value 18 on the y-axis. Draw a line through the point (0, 18) and parallel to the x-axis to meet the curve.

Step 3 Go down to the x-axis to find the two values of x which make $2x^2 + 3x + 4$ equal to 18.

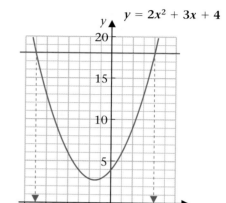

$y = 2x^2 + 3x + 4$

The **two possible solutions** to the quadratic equation $2x^2 + 3x + 4 = 18$ are $x = 2$ and $x = -3.5$.

You can check these answers using algebra.
When $x = 2$: $\qquad 2x^2 + 3x + 4 = 8 + 6 + 4 = 18$
and when $x = -3.5$: $\quad 2x^2 + 3x + 4 = 24.5 - 10.5 + 4 = 18$
So the values $x = 2$ and $x = -3.5$ satisfy the equation.

- To try to solve the equation $2x^2 + 3x + 4 = 1$ you would draw the line $y = 1$. This line does not meet the curve so this equation has **no solutions**.

- To solve the equation $2x^2 + 3x + 4 = 2.875$ you would draw the line $y = 2.875$. This curve just touches the curve at one point (where $x = -0.75$) so there is only **one solution**, $x = -0.75$.

You can solve a quadratic equation such as $ax^2 + bx + c = d$ by drawing the graph for $y = ax^2 + bx + c$ and the line $y = d$ and seeing where they intersect.

Quadratic equations can have 0, 1 or 2 solutions.

Example 10

(a) Draw the graph of $y = 2x^2 - 3x - 2$ by first making a table using values of x from -2 to $+4$.

(b) Use your graph to solve these quadratic equations:
   (i) $2x^2 - 3x - 2 = 0$
   (ii) $2x^2 - 3x - 2 = 10$

(a) Make a table of values:

x	-2	-1	0	1	2	3	4
$2x^2$	8	2	0	2	8	18	32
$-3x$	6	3	0	-3	-6	-9	-12
-2	-2	-2	-2	-2	-2	-2	-2
y	12	3	-2	-3	0	7	18

> **Remember:**
> $-2^2 = 4$, so $2 \times (-2)^2 = 8$

Draw axes with x from -2 to $+4$ and y from -4 to 18.

Plot the points and join them with a smooth curve.

(b) (i) To solve $2x^2 - 3x - 2 = 0$, look at the line $y = 0$.

At $y = 0$ on the graph, $x = 2$ or $x = -\frac{1}{2}$

> $y = 0$ is the x-axis.

> Read off the x values from the graph.

(ii) If $2x^2 - 3x - 2 = 10$, then $y = 10$.

At $y = 10$, $x = 3.25$ or $x = -1.8$

> Draw a line at $y = 10$.
> Read off the x values from the graph.

Graphs of functions of the form $y = ax^2 + bx + c$

- have a ∪-shape if a is positive
- have a ∩-shape if a is negative
- cut the y-axis at $(0, c)$.

The y-axis is only the line of symmetry when $b = 0$.

Exercise 28G

You need 2 mm squared graph paper.

1 (a) Draw the graph of $y = 2x^2 - 3x + 2$ by making a table using values of x from -3 to $+4$.

(b) Use the graph to solve the following quadratic equations:

(i) $2x^2 - 3x + 2 = 4$

(ii) $2x^2 - 3x + 2 = 11$

(iii) $2x^2 - 3x + 2 = 1$

(c) Write down the minimum value y can take in the equation $y = 2x^2 - 3x + 2$.

(d) What value of x gives the minimum value for y?

(e) Explain why the equation $2x^2 - 3x + 2 = 0.5$ does not have a solution.

2 (a) Draw the graph of $y = -x^2 + 2x - 1$. Make a table using values of x from -3 to 5.

(b) Use the graph to solve the following quadratic equations:
  (i) $-x^2 + 2x - 1 = -4$
  (ii) $-x^2 + 2x - 1 = -1$
  (iii) $-x^2 + 2x - 1 = -9$

(c) What is the maximum value y can take in the function $y = -x^2 + 2x - 1$?

(d) What value of x gives the maximum value for y?

(e) Give a value of y for which $y = -x^2 + 2x - 1$ does not have a solution.

$$\begin{aligned}
\text{When} \quad & x = -3 \\
-x^2 &= -(-3 \times -3) \\
&= -(+9) \\
&= -9 \\
\text{When} \quad & x = 2 \\
-x^2 &= -(2 \times 2) \\
&= -4
\end{aligned}$$

3 (a) Draw the graph of $y = 2x^2 + 2x - 8$ using values of x from -4 to 3.

(b) Use the graph to solve the following quadratic equations:
  (i) $2x^2 + 2x - 8 = 4$
  (ii) $2x^2 + 2x - 8 = -4$
  (iii) $2x^2 + 2x - 8 = -8$

(c) What is the minimum value y can take in the function $y = 2x^2 + 2x - 8$?

(d) What value of x gives the minimum value for y?

(e) Give a value of y for which $y = 2x^2 + 2x - 8$ does not have a solution.

4 (a) Draw the graph of $y = 2x^2 + 3$ using values of x from -3 to 3.
     Use your graph to solve these equations:
(b) $2x^2 + 3 = 4$ (c) $2x^2 + 3 = 18$

5 (a) Draw the graph of $y = x^2 - 6x + 8$ using values of x from 0 to 6.
     Use your graph to solve these equations:
(b) $x^2 - 6x + 8 = 0$ (c) $x^2 - 6x + 8 = 5$

6 (a) Draw the graph of $y = x^2 - 4x + 3$ using values of x from -1 to 5.
     Use your graph to solve these equations:
(b) $x^2 - 4x + 3 = 0$ (c) $x^2 - 4x + 3 = 2$

28.5 Graphs that describe real-life situations

You do not always need an accurately drawn graph to understand the situation that the graph represents.

In this section the axes are usually labelled, but they often have no values marked. Usually the axes meet at the point (0, 0).

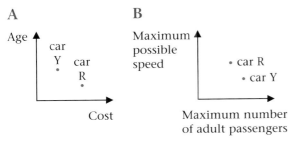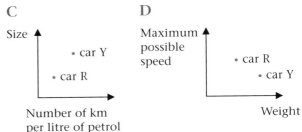

- Graph **A** shows that car Y is older than car R.
- Graph **B** shows that car R can travel faster than car Y.
- Graph **C** shows that car Y can travel further on one litre of petrol than car R.

You can use the information from graphs **A** and **B** to mark points that represent car R and car Y on this graph:

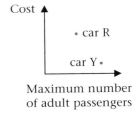

- Graph **A** shows that car R costs more than car Y so R is above Y.
- Graph **B** shows that car Y holds more adults than car R so Y is to the right of R.

You can draw **sketch graphs** to represent given information from real-life situations.

Exercise 28H

1 From graph **C** write down another statement about the cars.

2 From graph **D** write down two statements about the cars.

3 Copy each graph and mark two points to represent car R and car Y.

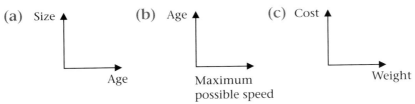

4

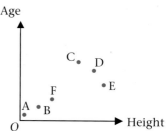

The point F on the scatter graph represents Tom.

(a) Write down the letter of each other point on the graph followed by the name of the person it represents.

(b) Use the graph to find the oldest person in the picture.

Activity – Filling containers

Collect several transparent containers like these:

A Cylindrical bowl B Measuring cylinder C Beaker D Vase

Step 1 Turn on a tap. Let the water flow into the first container at a steady rate. Watch how quickly the water level rises.

Step 2 Repeat for the other containers.

Step 3 Write down what you notice and discuss your results.

In the activity above you should find that:
- the water level rises at a steady rate in containers like **A**, **B** and **C**
- if the container is narrow the water level rises steadily but more quickly
- in a container like **D** the water level does not rise at a steady rate. It rises quickly then more slowly. The rate decreases.

Drawing graphs to show water levels

The tanks **P**, **Q**, **R** and **S** all have circular cross-sections and they contain water.

They all start off with the same depth of water. The water is pumped out of the tanks at the same steady rate.

    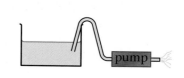

P   Q   R   S

The graph shows the relationship between the water level
in each tank and the volume of water pumped out of it.

- Tank **Q** has a bigger area of cross-section than **P**.
  When the same volume has flowed out of each tank the
  water level in **Q** remains higher than in **P**. So the graph
  for **Q** is less steep than the graph for **P**.
- The water level in tank **R** drops more quickly than in **P**,
  so the graph for **R** is steeper.
- In tank **S** the level drops more quickly and steadily at first,
  then it gradually drops more slowly. The graph is straight
  to begin with (steeper than for **R**), but then it is curved as the
  water level drops more and more slowly.

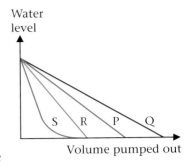

Exercise 28I

1 Here are some graphs:

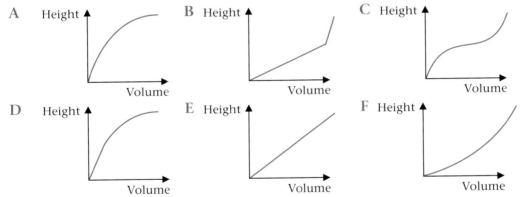

Coloured liquid is poured into each of the containers
below. For each one write down the letter of the
graph which best illustrates the relationship between the
height of the liquid and the volume in the container.

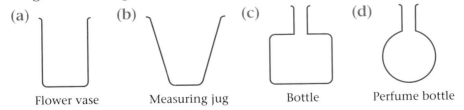

2 Water is poured into each of these containers.
Sketch a graph to show the relationship between the
water level and the volume of water in each container.

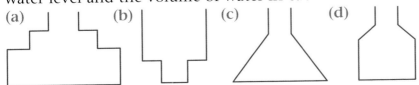

3 A DJ can control the sound level of the music he plays at a club. The sketch graph is a graph of the sound level against the time while one track was being played.

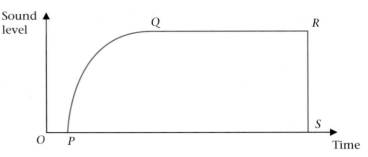

(a) Describe how the sound level changed between *P* and *Q* on the graph while the track was being played.

(b) Give one possible reason for the third part, *RS*, of the sketch graph.   [E]

4 Steve kicks a rugby ball over the goal posts. He thinks about the speed of the ball as it passes over the goal posts and tries to imagine what the graph of speed against time would look like.

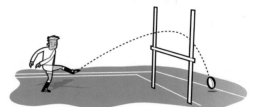

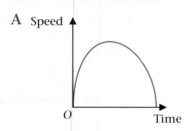 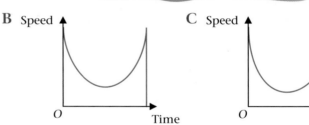

(a) Write down the letter of the graph which best illustrates the speed of the ball.

(b) Describe how the speed of the ball changes in the graph you have chosen.

5 The diagrams show the shapes of five graphs **A**, **B**, **C**, **D** and **E**. The vertical axes have not been labelled.

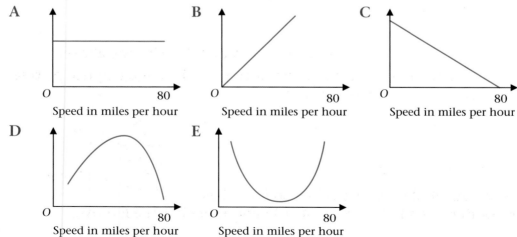

On one of the graphs, the missing label is 'Speed in km per hour'.

(a) Write down the letter of this graph.

On one of the graphs the missing label is 'Petrol consumption in miles per gallon'. It shows that the car travels furthest on 1 gallon of petrol when it is travelling at 56 miles per hour.

(b) Write down the letter of this graph.   [E]

28.6 Rearranging formulae

You can build a square picture frame using small square tiles.
Call the internal length of the picture frame l tiles long.
Call the total number of tiles used t.
t and l are connected by the formula

$$t = 4l + 4$$

Here is how the formula can be rearranged to find l for any given value of t:

This is the flowchart for the formula $t = 4l + 4$:   This is the inverse flowchart:

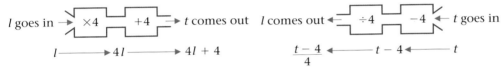

> When a number machine is used to input and output letters, not numbers, it is called a **flowchart**.

So $l = \dfrac{t - 4}{4}$

Changing the formula $t = 4l + 4$ so that it becomes $l = \dfrac{t - 4}{4}$ is called **rearranging the formula** to make l the **subject**.

The **subject** of a formula appears on its own on one side of the formula and does not appear on the other side.

Example 11

Martin uses square tiles to make square picture frames like the one above.

Work out the internal length l, as a number of tiles, of the largest square picture frame that Martin can make using 37 tiles.

Put $t = 37$ in $l = \dfrac{t - 4}{4}$

to get $l = \dfrac{37 - 4}{4} = 8.25$

But l can only take whole number values so $l = 8$ tiles.
The number of tiles used is $t = 4 \times 8 + 4 = 36$ and there is 1 tile left over.

Example 12

Rearrange the formula $a = \dfrac{b}{4} - 5$ to make b the subject.

Method 1

$a = \dfrac{b}{4} - 5$ This is the flowchart for the formula:

This is the reverse flowchart:

so $b = 4(a + 5)$

(or $b = 4a + 20$ with the brackets expanded)

$4(a + 5) \longleftarrow a + 5 \longleftarrow a$

Method 2

$a = \dfrac{b}{4} - 5$

$a + 5 = \dfrac{b}{4}$ —— Add 5 to both sides.

$4(a + 5) = b$ —— Multiply both sides by 4.

so $b = 4(a + 5)$

Method 3

$a = \dfrac{b}{4} - 5$

$4a = b - 20$ —— Multiply both sides by 4.

$4a + 20 = b$ —— Add 20 to both sides.

so $b = 4a + 20$

Example 13

Rearrange the formula $r = 2(6 - s)$ to make s the subject.

$r = 12 - 2s$ —————————————— First expand the brackets.

$r + 2s = 12$ —————————————— Add $2s$ to both sides.

$2s = 12 - r$ —————————————— Subtract r from both sides.

$s = \dfrac{12 - r}{2}$ or $6 - \dfrac{r}{2}$ —————————————— Divide both sides by 2

Exercise 28J

1   Rearrange each of these formulae to make x the subject.

(a) $m = 2x - 5$ (b) $a = 4 + 3x$ (c) $p = \dfrac{k}{x}$

(d) $q = mx$ (e) $\dfrac{w}{3} = 2x$ (f) $d = 3a + x$

(g) $p = \dfrac{3x}{2}$ (h) $y = mx + c$ (i) $a = \dfrac{x - u}{t}$

(j) $d = 3(x - 4)$ (k) $f = \dfrac{9x}{5} + 32$ (l) $k = \dfrac{px}{t}$

2   The formula to change degrees Celsius into degrees
    Fahrenheit is

    $$F = 1.8C + 32$$

    (a) Rearrange the formula to make C the subject.

    (b) What is $76\,°F$ in degrees Celsius?

3   Rearrange each of these formulae to make d the subject.
    (a) $c = 3d + 2$ (b) $c = 4d + 5$ (c) $c = 5d - 6$
    (d) $c = 7d + 8$ (e) $c = \frac{1}{2}d + 3$ (f) $c = \frac{1}{3}d - 4$

4   Simplify the right-hand side of each formula, then
    rearrange to make q the subject.
    (a) $p = 2(q + 4) + 3(q - 2)$ (b) $p = 4(q + 3) - 3(q + 2)$
    (c) $p = 5(q - 6) + 4(q + 7)$ (d) $p = 3(2q + 1) - 2q$
    (e) $p = 6(q - 7) - 5(q - 6)$ (f) $p = 4(3 - 2q) + 2(5q - 3)$

5   Rearrange each formula to make s the subject.

    See Example 13.

    (a) $r = 4(3 - s)$ (b) $r = 7(4 - s)$
    (c) $r = 2(5 - 3s)$ (d) $r = 4(3 - s) + 2(s + 1)$
    (e) $r = 6(s + 2) - 4(1 + 2s)$ (f) $r = 3(s + 2) - 4(s - 2)$

6   Make x the subject of each formula.
    (a) $y = 3x + 5$ (b) $y = 4x - 7$ (c) $y = 2(x + 3)$

    (d) $y = 3(x - 5)$ (e) $y = \dfrac{x - 4}{3}$ (f) $y = \dfrac{x + 5}{9}$

    (g) $y = \dfrac{x}{3} + 4$ (h) $y = \dfrac{x}{2} - 7$ (i) $y = \dfrac{2x - 3}{6}$

28.7 Solving simple quadratic and reciprocal equations

A **reciprocal equation** has an x term as a denominator.

$\dfrac{12}{x} = 6$ is a reciprocal equation.

Some simple quadratic and reciprocal equations can be solved
without having to draw graphs.

You need to rearrange the equation so the x term is alone.

Example 14

Solve $3 = \dfrac{12}{x}$

$3x = 12$ —— Multiply both sides by x

$x = 4$ —— Divide both sides by 3

Example 15

Solve $3x^2 + 2 = 50$

$3x^2 = 48$ —— Subtract 2 from both sides

$x^2 = 16$ —— Divide both sides by 3

$x = \pm 4$ —— Find the square root

There are two solutions to this equation as $4 \times 4 = 16$ and $-4 \times -4 = 16$.

Exercise 28K

Find any solutions to these equations.

1 $2x^2 - 8 = 10$ **2** $9 = \dfrac{27}{x}$ **3** $\dfrac{65}{x} = 13$ **4** $3x^2 - 30 = 45$

5 $8 = \dfrac{64}{x}$ **6** $4x^2 - 18 = 46$ **7** $2x^2 - 62 = 100$ **8** $\dfrac{70}{x} = 28$

9 $2x^2 - 22 = 50$ **10** $3x^2 + 53 = 200$ **11** $\dfrac{63}{x} = 7$ **12** $8 = \dfrac{100}{x}$

28.8 Solving equations by trial and improvement

An equation such as $x^3 + 2x^2 = 2$ is called a **cubic equation**.

You can solve a cubic equation (and other complex equations) by a trial and improvement method. This gives you a good approximate answer.

Example 16

Solve the equation $x^3 + 2x^2 = 2$ giving your answer correct to 2 decimal places.

Draw a table like this one:

Put x equal to a number that you think might be the answer, for example 10.

When $x = 10$, $x^3 + 2x^2$ is bigger than 2, so try x equal to a smaller number, for example 1.

Repeat this process, trying values of x that bring $x^3 + 2x^2$ closer and closer to 2.

The solution is between 0.83 and 0.84. Try putting $x = 0.835$, half way between the two.

x	x^3	$2x^2$	$x^3 + 2x^2$	Bigger or smaller than 2?
10	1000	200	1200	bigger
1	1	2	3	bigger
0	0	0	0	smaller
0.5	0.125	0.5	0.625	smaller
0.7	0.343	0.98	1.323	smaller
0.9	0.729	1.62	2.349	bigger
0.8	0.512	1.28	1.792	smaller
0.85	0.614 125	1.445	2.059 125	bigger
0.84	0.592 704	1.4112	2.003 904	bigger
0.83	0.571 787	1.3778	1.949 587	smaller
0.835	0.582 183	1.394 45	1.976 633	smaller

The solution is between 0.835 and 0.84. Any number in this range rounds to 0.84 (to 2 d.p.). So the solution of the equation $x^3 + 2x^2 = 2$ is $x = 0.84$ (correct to 2 d.p.).

You can find approximate solutions of complex equations by **trial and improvement**.

Exercise 28L

1 Solve these equations by trial and improvement. Give your answers correct to 2 decimal places.

(a) $x^3 + 2x = 4$ (b) $2x^3 = 3$ (c) $x^3 - x^2 = 3$

(d) Find a solution bigger than 0 for $x^3 - 3x = 6$

(e) Find a solution bigger than 1 for $x^2 + \dfrac{1}{x} = 5$

(f) Find a solution bigger than 0 for $2x^2 - \dfrac{1}{x} = 9$

2 Solve each of these equations.
Use a trial and improvement method, showing all your working. Give your answers to 2 decimal places.

(a) $x^3 + 1 = 11$ (b) $x^3 + x = 16$ (c) $x^3 + 3x = 28$

(d) $x^3 - x = 49$ (e) $x^3 - 4x = 100$ (f) $x^3 - 2x = 35$

(g) $x^3 + x = 31$ (h) $x^3 + 2x = 200$ (i) $x^3 + x = 9$

3 Use a trial and improvement method to find the length of the side of a cube which has a volume of 2 litres.
Give your answer correct to the nearest millimetre.

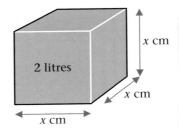

1 litre = 1000 cm³
10 mm = 1 cm
1 mm = 0.1 cm

Hint: call the length of a side of the cube x cm.

4 A cuboid has length $2x$ cm, width $3x$ cm and height x cm. The volume of the cuboid is 1100 cm³.

Use a trial and improvement method to find the lengths of the sides, correct to the nearest millimetre.

28.9 Trial and improvement on a spreadsheet

__Example 17__

The width of a rectangle is 2 cm less than the length. Use a trial and improvement method to find the length when the area of the rectangle is 30 cm².
Give your answer correct to 2 d.p.

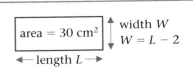

area = 30 cm²   width W $W = L - 2$
←— length L —→

Use L for the length and W for the width of the rectangle. Put the length in column A, the width in column B and the area of the rectangle in column C.

Make sure your spreadsheet has at least 12 rows and 3 columns.

Step 1 Use your spreadsheet to try values for L from 0 to 10 in steps of 1.

Step 2 For each value of L calculate a value for W using
$$W = L - 2$$

Step 3 Multiply each value of L by the corresponding value of W to find the area of each rectangle.

Step 4 Look for the two areas which are nearest to $30\,cm^2$ and record the corresponding values of L.

Step 5 Choose new values of L between the values found in Step 4. Use values of L going up in steps of 0.1 and enter them in the cells of column A.

> Notice that the values in all the other cells change automatically. You don't need to enter the formulae again.

Step 6 Repeat Steps 4 and 5 with values of L going up in steps of 0.01 and 0.001 to get an answer correct to the accuracy you need.

values of L
from 0 to 10
in steps of 1

	A	B	C
	L	W	LW
1			
2	0	−2	0
3	1	−1	−1
4	2	0	0
5	3	1	3
6	4	2	8
7	5	3	15
8	6	4	24	too small
9	7	5	35	too big
10	8	6	48
11	9	7	63
12	10	8	80

Values:
A2 = 0
Formulae:
A3 = A2 + 1
B2 = A2 − 2
C2 = A2 × B2

values of L
from 6 to 7
in steps of 0.1

	A	B	C
	L	W	LW
1			
2	6	4	24
3	6.1	4.1	25.01
4	6.2	4.2	26.04
5	6.3	4.3	27.09
6	6.4	4.4	28.16
7	6.5	4.5	29.25	too small
8	6.6	4.6	30.36	too big
9	6.7	4.7	31.49
10	6.8	4.8	32.64
11	6.9	4.9	33.81
12	7	5	35

Values:
A2 = 6
Formulae:
A3 = A2 + 0.1
B2 = A2 − 2
C2 = A2 × B2

values of L
from 6.5 to 6.6
in steps of 0.01

	A	B	C
	L	W	LW
1			
2	6.5	4.5	29.25
3	6.51	4.51	29.360
4	6.52	4.52	29.470
5	6.53	4.53	29.580
6	6.54	4.54	29.691
7	6.55	4.55	29.802
8	6.56	4.56	29.913	too small
9	6.57	4.57	30.024	too big
10	6.58	4.58	30.136
11	6.59	4.59	30.248
12	6.6	4.6	30.36

Values:
A2 = 6.5
Formulae:
A3 = A2 + 0.01
B2 = A2 − 2
C2 = A2 × B2

values of L
from 6.56 to 6.57
in steps of 0.001

	A	B	C
	L	W	LW
1			
2	6.56	4.56	29.913
3	6.561	4.561	29.924
4	6.562	4.562	29.935
5	6.563	4.563	29.946
6	6.564	4.564	29.958
7	6.565	4.565	29.969
8	6.566	4.566	29.980
9	6.567	4.567	29.991	too small
10	6.568	4.568	30.002	too big
11	6.569	4.569	30.013
12	6.57	4.57	30.024

Values:
A2 = 6.56
Formulae:
A3 = A2 + 0.001
B2 = A2 − 2
C2 = A2 × B2

You can now see that the length L lies between 6.567 cm and 6.568 cm.

So $L = 6.57$ cm correct to 2 d.p.

> This is much easier than it looks! Remember that a computer is doing all the really hard work.

Exercise 28M

1 The length of a rectangle is 3 cm more than the width. Use a trial and improvement method on a spreadsheet to find the width when the area of the rectangle is 38 cm². Give your answer correct to 2 d.p.

2 Winford, Barry and Syreeta count how much cash they each have. Barry has 45p less than Winford, and Syreeta has £1.06 more than Winford. Altogether they have £4.54. Use a spreadsheet to find how much each person has.

> Hint: let the amount that Winford has be W pence. Begin by entering values of W in steps of 10 in column A.

3 The height of a triangle is 2 cm less than the base. Use a trial and improvement method on a spreadsheet to find the base of a triangle with an area of 37 cm². Give your answer correct to 2 d.p.

Mixed exercise 28

1 Simplify
   (a) $x^4 \times x^5$ (b) $y^6 \div y^3$ (c) $12p^6 \div 4p^3$
   (d) $(3a^2)^3$ (e) $5a^2 \times 2a^3 \times 3a^4$

2 Expand and simplify $2(3x - 1) - 2(2x - 3)$.

3 Expand and simplify
   (a) $(x + 4)(x + 5)$ (b) $(a - 3)(a - 5)$
   (c) $(2b + 6)(3b - 2)$ (d) $(4 - 3x)(2x + 1)$

4 Draw a table of values and a graph of these quadratic functions, using values of x from -3 to $+3$.
   (a) $y = 2x^2 + 3$ (b) $y = -2x^2 + 7$
   (c) $y = x^2 + 3x + 2$ (d) $y = 2x^2 + 5x - 3$

5 (a) Simplify $a^5 \div a^2$.
   (b) Expand and simplify
      (i) $4(x + 5) + 3(x - 7)$ (ii) $(x + 3y)(x + 2y)$

6   **(a)** Draw the graph of $y = 2x^2 - 13x + 15$ for values of x from -2 to 7.

     (b) Use your graph to find solutions to these equations:
        (i) $2x^2 - 13x + 15 = 0$
        (ii) $2x^2 - 13x + 15 = 5$

7   Rearrange each of these formulae to make x the subject.

     (a) $y = 2x + 3$ **(b)** $y = \dfrac{ax}{2t}$ **(c)** $y = 3(2x - 5)$

8   Given $p = 3(3q - 4)$, find

     (a) q when $p = 24$ **(b)** q when $p = -30$

9   Find any solutions to

     (a) $\dfrac{72}{x} = 9$ **(b)** $3x^2 - 5 = 22$ **(c)** $12 = \dfrac{100}{x}$

10   The diagram shows a water tank. The tank is a hollow cylinder joined to a hollow hemisphere at the top. The tank has a circular base.

The empty tank is slowly filled with water.

Copy the axes and sketch a graph to show the relation between the volume, $V\,\text{cm}^3$, of water in the tank and the depth, $d\,\text{cm}$, of water in the tank.

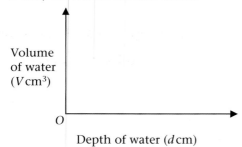

                                                      [E]

11   The equation $x^3 - 2x = 67$ has a solution between 4 and 5. Use a trial and improvement method to find this solution. Give your answer correct to one decimal place. You must show all your working.   [E]

12   The equation $x^3 + 3x = 47$ has a solution between 3 and 4. Use a trial and improvement method to find this solution. Give your answer correct to one decimal place. You must show all your working.   [E]

Summary of key points

1 To **multiply out** bracketed expressions, multiply each term in the first bracket by each term in the second bracket:

$$(e + f)(g + h) = eg + eh + fg + fh$$

You can also think of this as multiplying each term in the first bracket by the whole of the second bracket:

$$(e + f)(g + h) = e(g + h) + f(g + h)$$

2 Equations such as

$$(e + f)(g + h) = eg + eh + fg + fh$$

and $(e + f)(g + h) = e(g + h) + f(g + h)$

which are true for all values of e, f, g and h are also known as **identities**.

3 $y = 2x + 3$ is called a **function**. A function is a rule which shows how one set of numbers relates to another.

4 You can solve a quadratic equation such as $ax^2 + bx + c = d$ by drawing the graph for $y = ax^2 + bx + c$ and the line $y = d$ and seeing where they intersect.

5 Quadratic equations can have 0, 1 or 2 solutions.

6 Graphs of functions of the form $y = ax^2 + bx + c$:
   - have a $\cup$-shape if a is positive
   - have a $\cap$-shape if a is negative
   - cut the y-axis at $(0, c)$.
   The y-axis is only the line of symmetry when $b = 0$.

7 You can draw **sketch graphs** to represent given information from real-life situations.

8 The **subject** of a formula appears on its own on one side of the formula and does not appear on the other side.
   For example:

$$t = 4l + 4 \text{ can be rearranged to give } l = \frac{t - 4}{4}$$

   t is the subject l is the subject

9 A **reciprocal equation** has an x term as a denominator.
   For example, $\frac{12}{x} = 6$

10 You can find approximate solutions of complex equations by **trial and improvement**.

Examination practice paper

Non-calculator

1 Thirty-six thousand five hundred and ninety people watched United's football match last night.

    (a) Write this number in figures.

    (b) Write this number to the nearest thousand. **(2 marks)**

2 (a) Name each of these shapes. **(4 marks)**

    (i) 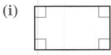   (ii)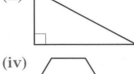

    (iii) 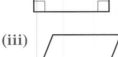   (iv)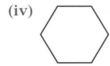

    (b) Copy the shapes that have reflection symmetry and draw in all lines of symmetry. **(4 marks)**

    (c) Write down the order of rotational symmetry for each of the shapes. **(4 marks)**

3 (a) What fraction of this shape is shaded? Write your answer in its simplest form. **(2 marks)**

    (b) What percentage of the shape is not shaded? **(2 marks)**

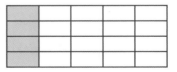

4 Choose from the numbers in the cloud and write down

    (a) two factors of 12

    (b) two multiples of 5

    (c) two square numbers

    (d) two pairs of numbers where one number is the square of the other. **(8 marks)**

5 Here is a pictogram showing the number of letters delivered at No. 23 for the last three days.

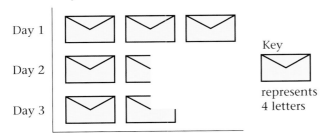

(a) How many letters were delivered on
  (i) Day 1
  (ii) Day 2
  (iii) Day 3?   (3 marks)

(b) On Day 4, 10 letters were delivered.
    Draw a pictogram for Day 4 only.   (1 mark)

6 (a) Simplify
  (i) $c + c + c + c$
  (ii) $p \times p \times p$
  (iii) $3g + 5g$
  (iv) $2r \times 5p$ (4 marks)

(b) Write an expression for the perimeter of the triangle.

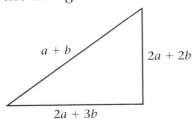

$a + b$

$2a + 2b$

$2a + 3b$ (3 marks)

7 Here is a pattern made from sticks.

Pattern 1   Pattern 2   Pattern 3

(a) Draw the diagram for Pattern 4.   (1 mark)

(b) Copy and complete the table on the right for the number of sticks used in the pattern.   (4 marks)

Pattern number	Number of sticks used
1	3
2	5
3	7
4	
10	
n	

8 (a) Convert $\frac{5}{8}$ into a decimal. **(2 marks)**

  (b) Change $\frac{4}{5}$ into a percentage. **(2 marks)**

9 Sam bought 24 coloured pens for £44.40
  (a) What was the cost of each pen? **(3 marks)**
  Sam sold all of the 24 pens for £2.05 each.
  (b) How much money did Sam collect from selling
    24 pens? **(3 marks)**

10 Lia has a box of 20 chocolates:
    5 of them are plain chocolate
    12 of them are milk chocolate
    the rest are white chocolate.
  She picks a chocolate at random from the box.
  What is the probability that she chooses
  (a) a milk chocolate
  (b) a white chocolate
  (c) a mint humbug? **(5 marks)**

11 Work out 70% of £3000. **(2 marks)**

12 Arrange these numbers in order.
  Put the smallest number first.

  $\frac{1}{2}$, 45%, $\frac{5}{11}$, 0.48, $\frac{2}{5}$ **(2 marks)**

13 (a) Write $24:6$ as a ratio in its simplest form. **(1 mark)**

  The recipe for making 12 plain buns is
    500 g flour
    200 g butter
      2 eggs
  (b) Rewrite the recipe to make 18 plain buns. **(3 marks)**

14 Solve these equations:
  (a) $y + 5 = 12$ **(1 mark)**
  (b) $2x - 3 = 9$ **(2 marks)**
  (c) $4p + 3 = 2p - 9$ **(3 marks)**
  (d) $3(2c - 5) = 4c + 5$ **(3 marks)**

15 Work out the value of the
  angle marked
  (a) r (b) t
  Write down the reasons for
  your answers.

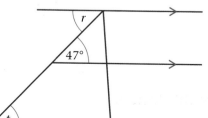

(4 marks)

16 Work out the area of this trapezium:

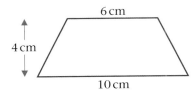

(3 marks)

17 (a) Work out the size of
each exterior angle of
a regular hexagon.

(2 marks)

(b) A different regular polygon has
an exterior angle of 40°.
How many sides has this polygon? **(2 marks)**

18 The manager at 'Fixit' records how long in minutes it
took for each repair.
Here are her results.

```
18  21  15   8  12  32  25  15  18  22
25  18  14   9  22  18  27  33  13  23
18   7  27  18  16
```

(a) Draw a stem and leaf diagram to show
these results. **(3 marks)**

(b) Use your stem and leaf diagram to work out
  (i) the median
  (ii) the range. **(2 marks)**

19 (a) Simplify
  (i) $g^4 \times g^3$
  (ii) $\dfrac{m^6}{m^2}$ **(2 marks)**

(b) Expand and simplify
  (i) $5(3p + 2) - 4(2p - 3)$
  (ii) $(x + 2)(x + 5)$ **(4 marks)**

20 The bearing of P from Q is 205°.
Work out the bearing of Q from P.

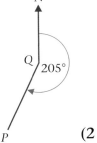

(2 marks)

21 Make t the subject of this formula:
$v = u + at$ **(2 marks)**

Examination practice paper

Calculator

1 (a) Write the number 72 305 in words.
(b) What is the value of the 3 in 72 302? **(2 marks)**

2 Write down the names of these 3-D shapes:

(a) 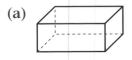   (b)   (c)

(3 marks)

3 Joe and Bethan threw a dice 30 times.
Here are their results.

5, 2, 1, 4, 3, 6, 4, 5, 3, 2, 4, 5, 2, 4, 3,
3, 2, 1, 3, 4, 2, 4, 3, 2, 1, 4, 5 6, 3, 4

(a) Design a suitable data collection table and use it to find the frequency for each score. **(3 marks)**

(b) Draw a bar chart to show their results. **(3 marks)**

(c) Use your answers to work out
(i) the mode   (ii) the median   (iii) the range.
(5 marks)

4 (a) Find the 4th and 5th numbers in this number pattern:

3, 8, 13, ..., ..., 28, ...   **(2 marks)**

(b) Write down the rule that you used to work out your answer. **(1 mark)**

(c) Work out the 20th number in the pattern.
(2 marks)

(d) Explain why 275 cannot be a number in the pattern. **(2 marks)**

(e) Write down, in terms of n, the nth term of this number pattern. **(2 marks)**

5 Work out the area of these shapes:

(a) 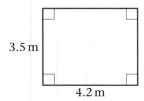   (b)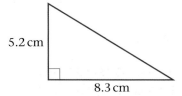

(5 marks)

6 Copy and complete these two shapes so that they have a line of symmetry.

(a)

(b)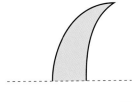

(2 marks)

7 Ella goes shopping.
She buys:

$\frac{1}{2}$ kg of apples at 72p per kg

4 bananas at 24p each

5 kg of potatoes at 25p per kg.

She pays with a £5 note.
Work out how much change she should get.　　(4 marks)

8 Work out

(a) $\sqrt{12.25}$　　　　(b) 2.4^3　　(2 marks)

9 Copy the diagram.
Show how the shape
tessellates on the grid.
You should draw at
least 5 shapes.

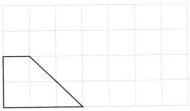

(3 marks)

10 (a) Work out the
area of this shape.

(b) Work out the
volume of this prism.

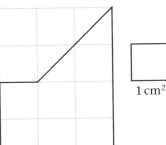

1 cm²

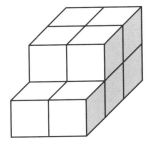

1 cm³

(2 marks)　　　　　　(2 marks)

11 Using ruler and compasses, **construct** an
equilateral triangle with side length 7 cm.
You **must** show all your construction lines.　　(2 marks)

12 The two-way table shows information about the colours of cars in a school car park on a school day and on a holiday.

	White	Blue	Red	Total
School day	10			61
Holiday		7		
Total	15	26		80

(a) Write down the total number of white cars. (**1 mark**)

(b) Copy and complete the two-way table.   (**3 marks**)

One of these 80 cars is to be picked at random.

(c) Work out the probability that this car will be blue.   (**2 marks**)

13 Katie invests £250 for 2 years at 4% simple interest. How much interest does Katie receive after 2 years?   (**3 marks**)

14 Karl invests £1000 for 2 years at 5% compound interest in a Building Society account. How much money will Karl have in his Building Society account after 2 years?   (**3 marks**)

15 The table gives the highest and lowest temperatures in some cities last year.

	London	Manchester	Exeter	Newcastle
Highest	31°C	29°C	33°C	30°C
Lowest	−12°C	−16°C	−9°C	−14°C

(a) Which city had the lowest temperature?

(b) Which city had the smallest difference between the lowest and highest temperatures?   (**3 marks**)

16 Gas bills are based on the amount of gas used. The cost of the gas used is worked out by this rule:

> cost of gas = gas used × 21p plus £11

The amount of gas used is found from meter readings. The difference in the meter readings gives the gas used. Work out the cost of gas for these readings on the right:

(**5 marks**)

First reading

`0 1 9 6 2`

Final reading

`0 2 1 5 9`

17 A shop sells storage boxes in four different colours.
The probability that a customer, choosing a box at
random, will choose a box of a particular colour is given
in the table.

Colour	Red	Green	Blue	White
Probability		0.1	0.2	0.3

What is the probability of choosing a red box? **(2 marks)**

18 Here are the results of a survey of the ways in which Year
11 students travelled to school.

Method of travel	Number of students
Walk	60
Car	
Bus	30
Bike	35
Moped	
Total	180

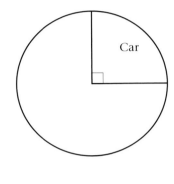

Use the information to copy and complete the table and
the pie chart. **(5 marks)**

19 (a) Find the value of C when $r = 5$ in each of these
formulae
   (i) $C = 3r$
   (ii) $C = 2r - 12$ **(4 marks)**
(b) Find the value of P when $x = 10$ and $y = 5$
in the formula

$$P = 2(x + y)$$ **(2 marks)**

(c) Find the value of x when $v = 10$ and $a = 5$
in the formula

$$v = 2 + ax$$ **(2 marks)**

20 Factorise
(a) $6a + 10$
(b) $x^2 - 5x$
(c) $5x^3 + 15xy$ **(6 marks)**

21 The cost of 12 pens is £2.88
Work out the cost of 20 identical pens. **(3 marks)**

22 In this right-angled triangle,
work out the size of the side marked h.

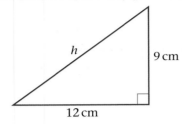

h 9 cm

12 cm **(3 marks)**

23 The equation $x^3 + x^2 = 100$ has a solution
between $x = 4$ and $x = 5$.
Use a trial and improvement method to find this
solution.
Give your answer correct to 1 decimal place.
You must show all your working. **(4 marks)**

24 Find the Highest Common Factor (HCF) of 72
and 96. **(2 marks)**

Formulae sheet

Area of trapezium $= \frac{1}{2}(a + b)h$

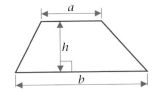

Volume of prism = area of cross section × length

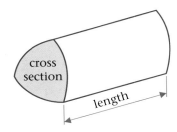

Index